SOCIAL STRATIFICATION
IN AMERICA:
A CRITICAL ANALYSIS
OF THEORY & RESEARCH

GOODYEAR SERIES IN AMERICAN SOCIETY
Jonathan H. Turner, Editor

INEQUALITY: PRIVILEGE & POVERTY IN AMERICA
Jonathan H. Turner and Charles E. Starnes

WOMEN IN AMERICA: THE OPPRESSED MAJORITY
Carol A. Whitehurst

THE URBAN CRISIS:
PROBLEMS & PROSPECTS IN AMERICA
Edgar W. Butler

SOCIAL STRATIFICATION IN AMERICA: A CRITICAL ANALYSIS
OF THEORY & RESEARCH
Leonard Beeghley

Forthcoming volumes will include perspectives on:
Crime in America
Marriage & the Family in America

SOCIAL STRATIFICATION IN AMERICA: A CRITICAL ANALYSIS OF THEORY & RESEARCH

Leonard Beeghley
University of Florida

Goodyear Publishing Company, Inc.   Santa Monica, California

Library of Congress Cataloging in Publication Data

Beeghley, Leonard.
  Social stratification in America.

  (Goodyear series in American society)
  Includes bibliographical references and indexes.
  1. Social classes—United States. I. Title.
HN90.S6B43   301.44'0973   78-1551
ISBN 0-87620-836-7

Current printing (last digit):
10 9 8 7 6 5 4 3 2 1

ISBN: 0-87620-836-7
Y-8367-8

Editing and production: Brian Williams
Cover: Michael A. Rogondino

Printed in the United States of America

For Sara

CONTENTS

PREFACE

The concept of social stratification implies, first, that unequally ranked strata or classes exist and, second, that these rankings are relatively stable over time. Thus, stratification can be defined as persisting patterns of inequality. This book is an analysis of social stratification in American society.

The social units making up any stratified society can be individuals, kinship groups (in the United States these are generally nuclear families), and large aggregates formed by some classificatory criteria. All societies have a fairly systematic way of ranking individuals and aggregates, although the basis for ranking varies greatly. Two common criteria are people's positions, such as their occupations, and the valued resources they possess, such as power, wealth, or prestige. Sometimes rankings are complicated by the possession of inherited characteristics, such as race or sex. Generally, people's positions and the valued resources they possess are correlated with one another.

Because patterns of inequality characterize all societies, stratification can be viewed as a fundamental social process. Partly because of its intrinsic importance as a social process and partly because inequality is in some ways more easily measured than other phenomena sociologists are interested in, stratification is a flourishing subfield in sociology. The journals are filled with research reports, and publishers are constantly presenting new monographs on some aspect of the topic. This book is an attempt at summarizing our knowledge about social stratification in the United States. I have tried to explicate clearly and concisely both the theoretical and the empirical literature, although unfortunately, at least for the advancement of science, the two remain rather separate entities. I have also tried to evaluate the theories and empirical findings in a relatively straightforward and nonpolemical manner.

The book is organized around three basic questions. First, what have social theorists said about the nature of social stratification? Chapters 1 through 5 are an analysis of the most important theories of social stratification as embodied in the work of six persons: Karl Marx, Max Weber, Kingsley Davis and Wilbert Moore, Ralf Dahrendorf, and Gerhard Lenski. Rather than focusing on the history of ideas (which is done too often), I have taken these men seriously as social theorists. Toward that end, each person's work is explicated in a fairly detailed manner and then criticized. Hopefully, the criticisms are not *ad hominen* in nature. The emphasis in these chapters is on problems of theory and theory construction in sociology. In chapter 6, I try to show how each theorist has contributed to our knowledge of stratification processes and present a heuristic model for the study of persisting patterns of inequality. This model provides the organizing rubric for the remainder of the book.

The second question is, how unequal is American society? Chapters 7 through 13 deal with this topic. Chapter 7 explicates and criticizes the literature on three interrelated topics: occupational prestige, class identification, and status inconsistency. These topics juxtapose the subjective and objective aspects of stratification in America. Chapters 8 through 11 portray the social characteristics of the poor, blue-collar workers, white-collar workers, and the rich in a relatively detailed yet straightforward manner. In these chapters some of the more significant biases inherent in the empirical literature are exposed. Like many people, sociologists are often guilty of letting their political biases affect their selection of topics and interpretation of data. Chapters 12 and 13 ascertain the degree of inequality in the United States in terms of caste relationships. Here the units of analysis are those large aggregates differentiated by race and sex. These chapters show that, despite a great deal of verbiage about affirmative action, it is still clearly the case that people acquire positions in American society based primarily upon their ascribed characteristics.

The third question is fundamental to any analysis of persistent patterns of inequality: how do people get into and out of positions? Chapter 14 describes the processes of status attainment and mobility in the United States. It will be seen there that people's family background and their level of achievement (especially in school) are decisive in determining occupational success in America.

One final introductory comment is necessary. No book on social stratification can avoid taking political stands. Many of the topics dealt with here—for example, poverty, racial inequality, and sexual inequality—would be considered "social problems" in other contexts, and there are inevitably political implications involved in the way data on these issues are interpreted. It is better for an author to make his or her political biases explicit so that readers can more easily see the difference between sociological and political judgments. Thus, it will be apparent that a somewhat old-fashioned liberalism pervades the empirical portions of this book. That is, it seems to me that American society would be better off if it were characterized by somewhat more equality than is generally true today.

Equality can have at least two different referents: equality of opportunity or equality of results. With a sort of knee-jerk reaction, most Americans say they believe in equality of opportunity. After that, it is every man for himself. (And that phrase, with its male orientation, immediately suggests at least one aggregate that is not granted equal opportunity.) By equal opportunity, most people mean that everyone ought to have a similar chance to succeed. Yet equal opportunity is not possible because, over the long run, those individuals who do succeed will try (often successfully) to protect their hard-won benefits and pass them on to their children. Thus, inequality of opportunity is inevitable. In practice, the only way to ensure some degree of equality of opportunity is to also ensure that some degree of equality of results exists.

Like most authors, I have had a great deal of help. Mary Anna Hovey and Jonathan H. Turner each read the entire manuscript. In addition to making many important (and sometimes face-saving) suggestions, they also helped me to write clearly. Several other people also read and commented upon various chapters, among them Wilber Bock, Nicole Cauvin, Henri Cauvin, Judy Corder-Bolz, Benjamin Gorman, Joan Huber, Gerald R. Leslie, Angela O'Rand, Ellen Van Velsor, and Joseph Vandiver. Even though I did not heed all their suggestions, I am most grateful. For two summers, Ron Ferrall graciously provided office space and secretarial help at the State University of New York, Albany.

A final note: many authors acknowledge the indirect contributions made by their spouses and children, and I must do the same, for my wife and daughter have been supportive throughout. At the same time, however, they have often impeded completion of this project. Their hindrance has made me more contented.

Gainesville, Florida   L. B.

1
KARL MARX. INEQUALITY, CLASS, AND CONFLICT

Karl Marx was both a revolutionary and a social scientist. His goal was to provide a theoretical justification for revolutionary conflict. As a result he authored a political creed as well as a theoretical analysis of society. While Marx's writings span several academic disciplines, this chapter is an attempt at suggesting his contributions to the study of social stratification. Toward that objective, the following issues are dealt with: (1) the relation between revolution and theory in Marx's work; (2) the assumptions underlying his theory; (3) his method for studying social inequality; (4) his model of the process of stratification; (5) his theory of stratification; and, finally, (6) some brief critical comments.

REVOLUTION AND THEORY IN MARX'S WORK
Marx was a revolutionary who engaged in a life-long struggle to overthrow capitalism. He was a participant, organizer, and often a leader of radical groups during the nineteenth century (see Fernbach, 1974a; 1974b; 1974c; Berlin, 1963). Much of Marx's written work is explicitly revolutionary in intent, and the remainder is designed to be the scientific underpinning for such political activity. As a literary genre, revolutionary writings are nearly always polemical and argumentative, since they are designed to provoke action. Such works also tend to deal with historically unique events in a jargon-laden manner (Friedland, 1973). These traits make understanding

difficult for modern readers, who are often unfamiliar with the historical situation in which revolutionaries worked.

Marx saw the great inequality that existed in early industrial societies. He saw that the masses of people lived in great misery, and he wished to stimulate people's attempts to reorganize their social arrangements so that the needs of all could be met. In this regard, no better example of revolutionary literature exists than the *Communist Manifesto*. Like all such literature, the *Manifesto* is a call to arms. In this case, it is an appeal to the proletariat of nineteenth-century Europe to usher in a new society. As Isiah Berlin (1963:164) has observed, no other political movement has produced a document of such power and eloquence.

It is a document of prodigious dramatic force; in form it is an edifice of bold and arresting historical generalizations, mounting to a denunciation of the existing order in the name of the avenging forces of the future, much of it written in prose which has the lyrical quality of a great revolutionary hymn whose effect, powerful even now, was probably greater at the time.

Berlin (1963:159–79) continues by noting that the *Manifesto* helped to spark the revolution of 1848 in Europe.[1] It is as a revolutionary pamphlet that the *Manifesto* is most often remembered, especially in the popular mind.

However, the *Manifesto* is also a theoretical document of great importance. Unfortunately, the theory of class and class conflict which it contains has often been too dogmatically interpreted, even by sympathetic commentators (for instance, Dahrendorf, 1959). The problem is that Marx's more strictly theoretical analysis must be extrapolated from a highly polemical context (see Marx, 1974a; 1974b; 1974c). For example, among his most famous statements in the *Manifesto* are "the history of all hitherto existing societies is the history of class struggle" and "society as a whole is more and more splitting up into two great hostile camps, into two great classes directly facing each other: bourgeoisie and proletariat."[2] These two arguments are much more complex than they first appear, for Marx knew well that no society actually divides into only two classes.[3] The *Manifesto* contains two sorts of theoretical contributions. First, it is an example of Marx's use of a model of the stratification process (as in the two statements quoted above). Second, it contains a theory of class formation that is still useful today. The remaining sections of this chapter are an explication of these two points.

ASSUMPTIONS UNDERLYING MARX'S SOCIAL THEORY

The assumptions upon which Marx based his theory of social inequality in particular and his analysis of society in general are straightforward. They are conclusions extracted from his study of history.[4] The first conclusion is that social theory must be empirically based and grounded in "the existence of living human individuals." Thus, all social analysis should begin by examining actual people in the real world who face the practical problem of surviving. Marx's second conclusion is that, unlike other animals, only people manipulate and alter their environment. "They begin to *produce* their means of subsistence, a step which is conditioned by their physical organization." In so doing, he said, people are "conscious"; that is, they are self-reflective and rational. This last point has important implications, for individuals who can reflect on themselves and their situation are capable of assessing their positions in society and acting in terms of their own interests. Marx argues that one effect of such abilities has been the growth and maintenance of inequality throughout history.

Having arrived at these conclusions, Marx then realized that the major task in any actual analysis is to discover how people have organized themselves throughout history, both socially and in relation to their physical environment. The empirical basis of such organization lies in three social facts that are common to all societies.[5] Marx clearly states that he is not referring to successive historical stages of development. Rather, he argues that all these facts "have existed simultaneously since the dawn of history and the first men, and they still assert themselves in history today."

The first social fact common to all societies is that people must produce sustenance from their physical environment in order to live and thereby "make history." As Marx observes, human "life involves before anything else eating and drinking, a habitation, clothing, and many other [material] things." All he is suggesting here is that the satisfaction of such basic physical needs as food, clothing, and shelter must occur or no society can survive and hence no history can exist. Need satisfaction is only possible through production, that is, interaction with the environment in some socially organized manner. By focusing on the production of material goods, Marx makes work the center of human life, since people cannot survive without it. At the same time, by focusing on work, he also reflects general tendencies in Western thought—including beliefs in the efficacy of social action, in people's ability to master both nature and society, and (most fundamentally) in progress (see Diggins, 1972; Nisbet, 1969).

The second social fact underlying Marx's analysis of stratification processes is that people are always creating new needs. The reason is that production or work always involves the use of tools or instruments of various sorts, which are constantly being improved upon so as to provide a better material life (food, clothing, shelter, and so on). Thus, production and consumption structure each other in a cumulative fashion, and as one set of needs is satisfied, new ones appear.[6] Because people constantly acquire new instruments, these new needs are also satisfied. This process continues in a generally escalating fashion, and people are able to satisfy not only their purely biological needs, but also their socially created ones. As Dupre (1966:148) has pointed out, Marx argues that it is in the production of "luxury" that people become human, which is to say civilized. "Because there is no limit to the needs he can create, or to the means of satisfying them, man continually transcends himself." Production thus serves a dual purpose: (1) to satisfy physical needs and (2) to express people's humanity—in Marx's terms, their "species being." Marx (1964:113) argues that other animals produce only to satisfy an "immediate physical need, whilst man produces even when he is free from physical need and only truly produces in freedom therefrom." He amplifies this point in the *Economic and Philosophic Manuscripts of 1844* (1964:113).

Indeed, labor, life-activity, productive life itself, appears in the first place merely as a means of satisfying a need —the need to maintain physical existence. Yet the productive life is the life of the species. It is life-engendering life. The whole character of a species—its species character—is contained in the character of its life activity; and free, conscious activity is man's species character. Life itself appears only as a means to life.

Throughout history, people have been producing material goods, satisfying their physical needs, and creating new socially defined needs. Thus, what people produce and the way they produce (that is, how the work process is organized) is an indicator of their historically developed human characteristics. An important implication is that human nature is not something eternally fixed but varies with the social environment.

The two social forces noted above—the necessity to produce and the creation of needs—are both structured by a third, which cannot be separated from the others: people form groups and propagate the species. The generation of tools and their use in production involves at least some cooperation among people. "By social," Marx says, "we understand the cooperation of several individuals, no matter under what conditions, in what manner and to what end." When people organize and cooperate together in groups, they also tend to propagate. As a result of the combination of all three facts, human population can expand. The proliferation of people is both stimulus for and a result of the concomitant creation of new needs, new instruments, and the latter's application in the productive process. This process occurs within groups where people cooperate with one another and propagate. The modes of cooperation are simple at first, as befitting the available instruments. They only become more complex with the passage of time. Humans cooperate first within the family and then, later, outside of it. Marx suggests that "the family which to begin with is the only social relationship, becomes later, when increased needs create new needs, a subordinate one."

As should be clear, Marx's analysis of these three social facts is explicitly circular and historical. Like all his essential ideas, each implies all the others, and when taken together they also imply additional phenomena of importance.[7] Humans are inherently social animals (Marx, 1970b:189) who live and make history in terms of the social structure into which they are born. This is why it is important to emphasize that social theory must be empirically based and to remember that only human beings produce their sustenance by manipulating and altering their environment.

Today these seem like simple and not very controversial ideas. But during the nineteenth century they were quite radical, for Marx was writing in opposition to the then dominant philosophic discourse and at a time before the legitimacy of social scientific research had been established. At that time, the task of systematically studying the real world was precisely what many philosophers were avoiding, especially those whom Marx called the German Ideologists.[8] He saw that in their purely philosophic writings "struggles" occurred, "revolutions" were launched, and "victories" won, but only in terms of abstract ideas. Marx believed that the German Ideologists dealt only "with the shadows of reality," for they did not inquire "into the connection of German philosophy with German reality, [or] the relation of their criticism to their own material surroundings." For this reason, Marx argued that much nineteenth-century philosophic debate was empty and meaningless. It had no basis in the real world where people were living quite miserably.

Marx asserted that when the practical problems of living people who organize, cooperate, produce, and try to survive are made the cornerstone of analysis, then "philosophy as an independent branch of activity loses its medium of existence" and science begins. This position constitutes a fundamental epistemological break with much previous philosophy (especially German philosophy), for Marx in effect "stood Hegel on his head" by giving philosophy an empirical basis.

Basing philosophy on the activities of living individuals does more than make it relevant by converting it into a social science. Marx saw problems of social life in very practical terms. Philosophic discourse that proceeded without reference to living and dying people served to justify and maintain the status quo by failing to identify the actual social conditions and needs of the masses. Contrary to much popular belief, Marx knew that ideas do have an impact on the world, since it is in ideological terms that people become conscious of their positions and their interests. In any society, those persons who originate and distribute the predominant ideas (in this case, philosophers) tend to do so in terms of their own interests. According to Marx, this is why German "philosophers have only *interpreted* the world differently, [when] the point is to change it." By basing science in the real world, Marx had the theoretical and, by extension, the political tools to do just that.

MARX'S METHOD FOR STUDYING SOCIAL INEQUALITY

Like the theoretical assumptions underlying his work, Marx's method for studying social inequality is also straightforward. It is clearly stated in his most important methodological text, the "Introduction" to the *Critique of Political Economy* (Marx, 1970b:188–217). The method consists of a series of four steps. First, one always begins analysis of the social by examining the concrete existence of people in the real world. As he notes, "the subject, society, [is] the precondition of comprehension."[9] Second, the observer constructs an abstract model comprised of those social facts that (1) are intrinsic to the study of inequality and (2) seem to appear in all societies.

The third step in Marx's method is to systematically compare the abstract model with the real world. The purpose of this step is very clear. He observes that while "the most modern period and the most ancient period will have [certain] categories in common, it is precisely their divergence from these general and common features which constitutes their development." Again, Marx is most interested in events in the real world—the empirical "divergence" from an abstract model. This is why Marx studied history. Such analyses provided data from which to make abstract generalizations, as well as the means for evaluating a society at a particular stage of development. As Engels observed, "our conception [that is, theory] of history is above all a guide to study, not a lever for construction after the manner of the Hegelian. All history must be studied afresh."[10]

The final step in Marx's analysis is to evaluate a society at its particular stage in history. This task is vital because social relationships are a product of specific historical conditions, and the models used to elucidate them "are nothing but abstract conceptions which do not define any of the actual historical stages of production."

The theoretical strategy outlined here can be summarized as follows. Marx constructs an abstract logical model based upon events in the real world and then uses it as the baseline from which to compare the intricate relationships that have developed in that world. As such, this strategy is nothing more than the venerable ideal-type method. It is commonly thought that ideal types as a mode of theory construction originated with the German sociologist Max Weber (see Chapter 2). However, as Lopreato and Alston (1970) point out, it has a long history in all the sciences. But Marx adds a unique wrinkle, which is seen in his last step. He not only attempts to compare his model with the real world, but also tries to assess the "historical stages of production" displayed by each society and projects their development into the future. Marx believed he had discovered the laws of historical development and that, at some point, all societies pass through certain developmental stages. He tried to suggest that general direction of history by asserting "the country that is more developed industrially only shows, to the less developed, the image of its own future" (Marx, 1967:8–9).

MARX'S MODEL OF THE STRATIFICATION PROCESS

The theoretical focus of Marx's study of systems of inequality is the concept of class. His model of stratification is designed both to expose the empirical existence of classes and lead to a theory of their formation and consequences. His point is to show that the existence of inequality implies both class formation and revolutionary class conflict. This section is divided into three parts. (1) Marx uses the concept of class in such a cavalier way that much misunderstanding has resulted. Thus, a brief note on some of the problems connected with his use of class is a necessary introduction to his model of the stratification process. That model has two elements, which make up the second and third parts of this section. (2) The model identifies the key variables in the study of class. (3) It forms the basis for Marx's dialectical interpretation of the stages of human history in terms of classes.

The Problem of Class[11]

The problem with Marx's use of class is simply that he uses the term promiscuously. As Ollman (1968) suggests, Marx identifies varying numbers of classes as existing in the same society, at the same time, often in the same text. He also changes the operational criteria that are used to define classes and, again, often in the same text. For example, in *Capital*, Marx says there are only two great classes—the capitalists (also called the bourgeoisie) and proletarians. This usage conforms to the division suggested in the *Manifesto*. However, in *Capital*, Marx also refers to the existence of three great classes— capitalists, proletarians, and landowners. Furthermore, in the same text he refers to the peasants as a class, to the existence of "ideological classes," and to a specific occupation (bankers) as a class. His other writings are also dotted with inconsistent usage. After dividing society into two parts in the *Manifesto*, Marx then refers to the "lower middle class" and also describes the lowest layer of society as the *lumpenproletariat*—the "dangerous class."

Marx obviously uses the concept "class" very loosely. At least three general tendencies can be identified in his work.

First, often Marx simply wishes to label a group, faction, or layer in society that is of particular interest. For example, in the *Class*

Struggles in France, he uses the terms "ruling class" and "ruling faction" interchangeably (Ollman, 1968). When using class as a labeling device, Marx is mainly interested in analyzing people's positions, their relations to others, and to the whole society.

Second, sometimes Marx tries to sketch the actual relations among the various strata. The complexity of such analyses is only suggested in the *Manifesto:*

In the earlier epochs of history we find almost everywhere a complicated arrangement of society into various orders, a manifold gradation of social rank. In ancient Rome we have patricians, knights, plebeians, slaves; in the Middle Ages, feudal lords, vassals, guild masters, journeymen, apprentices, serfs; in almost all these classes, again, subordinate gradations.

Thus, when doing actual historical analyses, Marx said, the real relations among specific classes had to be taken into account. As Engels (1959:400) noted, "when it came to presenting a section of history, that is, to making a practical application, it was a different matter and there no error was permissible."

Marx's third way of using class is more abstract in that he tried to extrapolate beyond the welter of specific relations and get at those which were most important. He often used either the tripartite division or the dichotomic division in this fashion. These two types are not necessarily inconsistent if it is remembered that Marx recognized old ways of life, such as that of the landed aristocracy, often maintained themselves even within the context of new modes of production. As Ossowsky (1963:83) concludes, "the dichotomic scheme is intended to characterize capitalist society with regard to its dominant and peculiar form of relations of production, while the multidivisional scheme reflects the actual social structure."

Key Variables in the Study of Class

Crucial to Marx's methodology is constructing a model of the process of stratification by abstracting out those social facts that are common to all societies. He begins with the three variables identified above. (1) In all societies, conscious and rational people produce their basic sustenance in order to survive. (2) Historically, they increase productivity levels in order to satisfy increasing needs. (3) The population increases and modes of cooperation change (generally in the direction of increasing complexity). These three variables constantly interact with one another over time, and together they imply a division of labor. While the division of labor remains a mushy concept even today (see Gibbs and Poston, 1975), it basically refers to the fact that in a society various people perform different but interdependent tasks. For example, Marx notes the importance of economic factors, since people must produce in order to survive. In all societies, some persons must gather resources from the environment (for instance, by hunting game or gathering roots), while some persons must translate resources into usable goods (for instance, by curing meat or grinding corn). Thus, a division of labor can occur simply within the economy. But there are also other institutional spheres in which activity usually takes place. For example, some persons must placate the gods (religion), some must bear and raise children (family), some must decide where and how the group will obtain food (polity). The extent of the division of labor will vary from one society to another, and it is precisely this variation that is most interesting to Marx.

The existence of a division of labor, no matter how limited, implies inequality—that is, classes. And, as will be shown, the existence of classes implies conflict between them. Marx observes that with the division of labor "is given simultaneously . . . the unequal distribution (both quantitative and qualitative) of labor and its products, hence property: the nucleus, the first form of which lies in the family where wife and children are the slaves of the husband." That is, the division of labor embodies, as part of its definition, Marx would say, the unequal distribution of work in the population as well as unequal control over the products of work, especially private property. This inequality in a population is relatively systematic and can be described in terms of classes. Here lies one of the keys to Marx's use of class. Regardless of the specific aggregate he chooses to so label, it is necessary to ask only two questions (Ollman, 1968). (1) Who is the enemy? (2) Why are they the enemy? Marx argues that a person's position in the social structure implies both certain interests and certain experiences, and he always answers the two questions in these terms.

For example, if a person's position in society is such that starvation is a constant problem, if it prevents the expression of one's human creativity, then such an individual is clearly in a subordinate position compared to others and has an interest in changing the status quo. On the other hand, if a person's position in society is such that one's needs are satisfied (or perhaps even satiated), and if it ensures both control over one's own activities and the expression of one's human creativity, then such an individual is clearly in a superordinate position and has an interest in preserving the status quo.

In his study of history, Marx saw that the division of labor and the inequality accompanying it was generally, although not perfectly, associated with the private ownership of property. And private control of property—whether people, land, or capital—is control over the means of production. Those who own property generally assume superordinate positions and have an interest in preserving the status quo, while those who do not own property generally assume subordinate positions and have an interest in changing the status quo.

Karl Marx: Inequality, Class, and Conflict **9**

Within such a context, it is clear that those who control property have power. By threat, force, or fraud, they can usually maintain their positions. (As an aside, it can be seen that this point of view underlies Marx's fondness for dichotomies in describing class divisions in society.)

At the same time, people can know reality only from a certain vantage point in society. Their experiences are always framed by their class position, which is why Marx (1970a) argues that "it is not the consciousness of men that determines their existence, but their social existence determines their consciousness." This would seem to mean that members of different classes would, or at least could, become aware of their interests. But such is usually not the case. As Birnbaum (1953) has argued, Marx was well aware of the fact of consensus in all societies. In most cases, societies display relative agreement on basic values and people generally "want to do what they have to do, and voluntarily, even eagerly, perform their social roles." While class position indicates people's interests, and while class interests often result in social action, for most people the relationship is mediated by an ideology. Marx clearly says that ideological beliefs often restrain or prevent change. In the *Manifesto,* he argues that "the ruling ideas of each age have ever been the ideas of its ruling class." Regardless of class position, people see the world, including their own experiences, through an ideological prism imposed upon them by the class that controls the means of production. Members of subordinate classes are therefore often unaware of their true interests. An important question, then, involves the conditions under which subordinates will become aware of their true interests.

In summary, these key variables hang together and form a schema useful in the analysis of any society at a particular point in time, for they indicate the key social facts to look for and suggest some of the ways they might be interrelated. Observers should assess (1) the way people produce their sustenance, (2) the nature and extent of their needs, and (3) the mode of cooperation that exists. Such an assessment will establish the basis and extent of inequality. The class divisions in a society can then be identified in terms of people's diverse interests and experiences. Although it has not yet been shown, Marx argues that these class divisions imply revolutionary conflicts. This schema is presented in diagrammatic form in Figure 1.

The Stages of History and the Development of Classes

The schema elaborated in the previous section allowed Marx to examine the class structure of any specific society. In each case, he could (1) analyze people's concrete existence, what they produced and how they produced; (2) construct abstract categories that appear to be common to all societies; (3) compare his abstractions with the

Figure 1
Marx's model of the process of stratification. Double-headed arrows mean that each variable implies all the others.

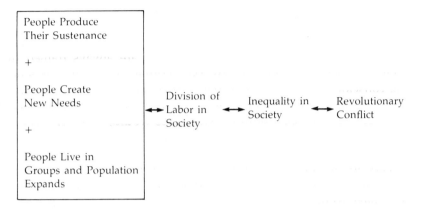

society under study; and (4) use them to study other societies as well. But Marx's goal was more grandiose, for he hoped to understand the nature and direction of historical change. As noted above, Marx believes this is the final step necessary for a complete analysis of social stratification. His goal was "to explain why structures giving advantages to one group are destroyed and replaced by structures giving advantages to other groups" (Stinchcombe, 1968:93). Political economy as it then existed was incapable of this task and so, as a result of his philosophical training, Marx turned to what is called the Hegelian dialectic and applied it to the study of history. In order to explain what the dialectic is, it is necessary to understand Marx's criticisms of the economic analyses of the time.

Marx saw two major problems in the analysis of capitalism by then contemporary political economists, both of which are ideological in nature. First, they attempted to pass off bourgeois social relations, and the tremendous inequality typical of them, as the "irrefutable natural laws of society" (Marx, 1970b:192). But Marx knew these relations were historically unique and believed that while they might be historically necessary, they were certainly not immutable. By taking the existence of wage-labor, private property, and all the other characteristics of capitalism for granted, the political economists tried, in effect, to justify and support the bourgeoisie. Marx judged this attempt to be immoral, for it ignored the fact that under nineteenth-century capitalism the masses of people lived in wretched misery, while only a few obtained all the benefits. For Marx, the most important question, the very reason for doing social science, was to assess the extent to which social arrangements allowed the satisfaction of all people's needs and to stimulate change if they did not. However, because political economists had a stake in the status quo, they justified as eternal the existence of a mode of social organization which was really historically transient.

The second problem Marx saw was that the methods employed by political economists were defective. Such analysts developed an ideologically suitable methodology that treated each part of society as separated from other parts. For example, all the social relations involved in the process of production, exchange, distribution, and consumption were analyzed as though each were discrete phenomena. Actually, all of them are interrelated in very complex ways and all of them imply a plethora of additional relationships (familial, legal, political, and so on). By examining each discretely, political economists failed to see the intimate connection between wage-labor and capital. He believed that acknowledgement of this connection implies the recognition that classes exist.

Marx's application of the Hegelian dialectic alleviated both problems. As was noted above, by grounding theory in the real world where people must satisfy their material needs, Marx had "stood Hegel on his head." Having done so, however, Marx continued to apply the Hegelian mode of analysis to this different subject matter. Use of the dialectic is the most important source of continuity between the two (Hook, 1962:60–76). Thus, the phrase "dialectical materialism," which is the most famous description of Marxism, aptly describes both the continuity and the difference between Hegel and Marx.

In Marx and Engel's hands, dialectical materialism has four overarching characteristics.[12] First, as Smelser (1973) has suggested, Marx was a systems theorist. He saw the social in terms of interrelated parts that together form an integrated whole. Marx and Engels convey this point by arguing that even though the parts of the social "appear opposite and distinct [they] are in reality joined by internal relations; they are not logically independent of one another" (Ollman, 1971:55). When viewing a social system, then, the angle of the observer is all important. In tracing through all the connections among social units, it can be seen that from one angle a specific label can be applied (for example, bourgeoisie), while from another angle an opposing label will apply (for example, proletariat). But there is an inherent connection between the two, which is why Marx argues in the *Manifesto* that it is tautologous to speak of wage-labor without capital.

Second, change is imminent within all social systems. Marx avoids causal analyses, preferring to see change as inherent in the essence of things. For example, he believed that just as a flower is inherent in the nature of a certain kind of seed, so more complex forms of social organization are the inevitable result of less complex forms. The example points to the third aspect of the dialectic. That is, within social systems, change has both direction and continuity. In this respect, the dialectic is illustrative of the metaphor of growth and progress which has pervaded Western thought for centuries (see Nisbet, 1969:157–88; Pachter, 1974). For according to Marx (1970b:208), social development, or history, generally proceeds from less complex to more complex forms. "The procedure of abstract reasoning which advances from the simplest to more complex concepts," he writes, ". . . conforms to actual historical development." Greater social complexity, as indicated by the division of labor, is a sign of progress because it shows an increasing productive capacity and therefore the potential for all people to satisfy their needs and express their humanity. However, Marx very clearly states that history does not proceed in linear fashion, and his historical studies bear out his recognition of this fact. Rather he suggests a spiral format, which makes clear that progress is not uniform, since there are retarding factors, but it is inevitable and can be studied in a systematic way.

4) The fourth aspect of the dialectic is that the historical mechanism stimulating change and progress within a social system is contradiction among the parts of the social system. The process is as follows. Within a society (a social system) a way of producing things exists, both in terms of what is produced and the social organization of production.[13] Marx called this aspect of the mode of production the "productive forces." In a society, the productive forces are established and maintained in terms of property relations, and all the interests and experiences that correspond to them. Those who have power by means of their private control over property attempt to maintain it. At each stage of history, Marx says, "there is found a material result: a sum of productive forces, that is a historically created relation of individuals to nature and to one another" (Marx and Engels, 1947:29).

However, over time, new ways of producing things are devised, whether based on advances in technology, changes in the way production is organized, or both. Such new forces of production better satisfy old needs and also stimulate new ones. They exist in contradiction to (in opposition to) existing property relations, which Marx called the "relations of production." Marx (1970a) writes: "at a certain stage of their development, the material forces of production come into conflict with the existing relations of production, or— what is but a legal expression for the same thing—with the property relations within which they had been at work."

As the new forces of production are adopted, the relations of production must alter. These changes are cumulative and inevitable. After a certain point, it becomes possible to say that a society has transformed itself into something entirely new. Marx and Engels call this process the law of "transformation of quantity to quality." Historically, the transformation from one mode of production to another is inherently conflictful, often violently so, and has a revolutionary result. In this regard, it should be remembered that when Marx refers to revolution, he does not have any common change of government or even form of government in mind, but nothing less than the establishment of a new world order.

In sum, in reaction to bourgeois political economists, Marx applied the Hegelian dialectic to the study of history. Dialectical materialism involves four elements: (1) the society displays systemic qualities; (2) change is imminent within all social systems; (3) social change has both direction and continuity; and (4) the historical mechanism stimulating change is contradiction among the parts of the society. Dialectical materialism is Marx's way of understanding how class structures are established and how they give way to new class structures.

In applying the dialectic to the study of Western history, Marx saw three broad revolutionary epochs—the ancient, the feudal, and the bourgeoisie—each of which was characterized by successively different modes of production and hence different class structures.[14] In all three cases, the key to understanding the class structure is to examine the division of labor, which is to say property relations.[15] The ancient mode of production was based on slavery. The feudal mode of production was based upon estate property, land with serfs tied to it, and craft labor. The bourgeois mode of production was based upon wage-labor and the development of capital, that is, in the most simplified sense, property that is convertible to money. In each case, it is not difficult to figure out who benefits, and it is not the slaves, serfs, or wage-laborers, but those who privately control property. In each case, Marx tried to show how class structures giving advantages to one group were destroyed and replaced by class structures giving advantages to another group.

Marx argues that capitalism emerged from the inherent development of the feudal social system.[16] "From the serfs of the Middle Ages sprang the chartered burghers of the earliest towns. From these burgesses the first elements of the bourgeoisie were developed." He says that these changes were not historical accidents but the inevitable results of people acting in terms of their own interests. The feudal nobility had exhausted itself by constant warfare. Further, its wasteful and spendthrift way of life had become consumptively oriented as it was increasingly exposed to other cultures. These two emphases gave rise to a wealthy merchant class that, at first, was created to serve the nobility. However, over time, money rather than land became the key to power in Western Europe, for only in this way could the nobility obtain the commodities necessary to satisfy their consumptive needs. Because of their need for money, the lords drove the serfs from the land and eventually, Marx says, "left remaining no other nexus between man and man than naked self-interest, than callous 'cash payment.'"

This process had three consequences. (1) It produced an army of landless proletarians who had to sell their labor in order to survive. (2) It produced a new market, for these people were no longer self-sufficient because they were no longer producing goods at home for their own consumption. (3) A new class developed as former artisans, petty burghers, and even proletarians managed to become entrepreneurs and eventually wealthy. The *Manifesto* summarized the results in the following way.

The feudal system of industry, under which industrial production was monopolized by closed guilds, now no longer sufficed for the growing wants of the new markets. The manufacturing system took its place; the guild masters were pushed on one side by the manufacturing middle class; division of labor between the different corporate guilds vanished in the face of division of labor in each single workshop.

Meantime, the markets kept ever growing, the demand ever rising. Even manufacture no longer sufficed. Thereupon steam and machinery revolutionized industrial production. The place of manufacture was taken by the giant, modern industry, the place of the industrial middle class by industrial millionaires, the leaders of whole industrial armies, the modern bourgeois. . .

We see then: the means of production and of exchange, on whose foundation the bourgeoisie built itself up, were generated in feudal society. At a certain stage in the development of these means of production and of exchange, the conditions under which feudal society produced and exchanged, the feudal organizations of agriculture and manufacturing industry, in one word, the feudal relations of property, became no longer compatible with the already developed productive forces; they became so many fetters. They had to be burst asunder, they were burst asunder.

In a similar manner, Marx tried to show the demise of capitalism as equally inevitable. He observed that the "bourgeoisie, during its rule of scarce one hundred years, has created more massive and more colossal productive forces than have all proceeding generations together" and suggested some of the many technological changes that had occurred during that period. As a result, the organization of production was no longer capable of operating efficiently as a competitive system in which people tried to maximize their individual profits. Marx argued that "the productive forces at the disposal of society no longer tend to further the development of the conditions of bourgeois property; on the contrary they have become too powerful for these conditions, . . . they bring disorder into the whole of bourgeois society, [and] endanger the existence of private property."

One reason for this state of affairs is that capitalism brings with it, for the first time in human history, "an absurdity—the epidemic of overproduction." Commercial crises are gotten through mainly by

distribute } ← *concentrated*

a more thorough exploitation of old markets and the continual conquest of new ones. But this is ultimately a losing battle. Bourgeois
society "has conjured up such gigantic means of production and of
exchange, [that it] is like the sorcerer who is no longer able to control the powers of the nether world whom he has called up by
his spells."

NEW CLASS ARISES   The second reason productive forces contradict bourgeois relations
of production is the concomitant development of a new class—the
proletarians. "Not only has the bourgeoisie forged the weapons that
bring death to itself," Marx writes; "it has also called into existence
the men who are to wield those weapons—the modern working
class—the proletarians." There are two aspects to his argument
here. The first involves the relationship between industrialization
and inequality. Marx saw that with the advance of industrialization
in the nineteenth century the ranks of the proletariat swelled as formerly middle-class people sank into it because they could not compete with modern industry. As a result, "in proportion as the repul-
siveness of the work increases, the wage decreases" and everyone's
wages are equalized at the same low level. Thus, people become
poorer and poorer. The second way in which the bourgeoisie helps
create the proletariat is by providing the conditions that stimulate
their transition from a class "in itself"—that is, a mere statistical
aggregate to a solidary and cohesive class "for itself." Such a transformation requires social arrangements that could occur only in an
industrialized society. Marx summarizes them in the *Eighteenth
Brumaire* (1963:124).

*Insofar as millions of families live under economic conditions that separate
their mode of life, their interests, and their culture from those of other
classes and put them in hostile opposition to the latter, they form a class. Insofar as there is merely a local interconnection among these small-holding
peasants and the identity of their interests begets no community, no national bond, and no political organization among them, they do not form a
class.*

Marx believed that "the proletariat alone is a really revolutionary
class" and that it would emerge from the inexorable operation of the
capitalist system. He also believed the proletariat would promulgate
a revolution that would destroy the old relations of production (private property) in favor of arrangements "in which the free development of each is the condition for the free development of all." It is
important to understand that he perceived these developments as
inevitable. While Marx clearly states that events in each society will
be modified by their peculiar circumstances, he also emphasizes that
the "theoretical conclusions of the Communists are in no way based
on ideas or principles that have been invented, or discovered, by

this or that would-be universal reformer. They merely express, in general terms, actual relations springing from an existing class struggle, from a historical movement going on under our very eyes."

The dialectical analysis of the stages of human history completes Marx's model of the stratification process. With it he not only conceptualizes the key variables in the process of stratification and their relationships within a society, he can also predict where such a system is going. This last step is fateful and is open to much criticism, as will be seen in the concluding section.

MARX'S THEORY OF SOCIAL STRATIFICATION

Marx's Theory

In the *Manifesto*, Marx enunciates a theory of social stratification which can be extrapolated from its polemical context and phrased in a testable fashion. The variables and their interrelationships in Marx's theory can be summarized in the following manner. Increases in the productive capacity of a society (in the quantity and variety of material goods desired by the populace) and in population sizes are associated with an increasing division of labor. The increasing complexity of the division of labor is associated with the rise of industrialization. Marx clearly suggests that the greater the industrialization, the greater the inequality.

In addition to inequality, Marx says that industrialization is also associated with formation of a solidary and cohesive subordinate class and with a greater rate of conflict between dominant and subordinate classes. The conditions under which a solidary and cohesive subordinate class will form are clearly stated by Marx, and may well constitute his most enduring (which is to say unrefuted) contribution. First, the greater the communication among subordinates, the greater their class solidarity and cohesion. Communication, in turn, requires that subordinates have opportunities for education, common life experiences, and live in urban areas. Second, the more subordinates become aware of their common interests, the greater their class solidarity and cohesion. Becoming aware of their common interests requires widespread feelings of alienation among subordinates, a greater range of inequality, the disruption of stable subordinate relationships, low skill and wage levels, and high rates of downward social mobility. The third condition stimulating the development of a subordinate class is that its members possess a unifying ideology. The latter requires the recruitment of ideological leaders, and an inability of dominants to regulate socialization practices or communication networks among subordinates. When all these conditions are met, Marx hypothesizes that subordinates will form a solidary and cohesive class.

Further, the more both dominants and subordinates form classes, the more polarized they will be. And the greater the polarization in a society, the more likely is conflict to be violent. Marx's final proposition brings all these variables together in a single summary statement.[17] The greater the inequality in a society, the more subordinates form a solidary and cohesive class, and the greater the polarization in society, *then* the greater the rate of conflict and the more likely is revolution to occur. Marx's theory and the definitions of the key variables comprising it are presented in tables 1 and 2.

Some Comments on This Presentation of Marx's Theory

The propositions contained in Table 1 are simple bivariate statements, with the exception of the final one. As such, they can be arranged in a deductive format for ease of presentation. It should be emphasized, however, that the real world is not bivariate and (assuming for the moment that the propositions are not false) the actual relationships among them are quite complex. A complete analysis would have to show the mutuality of influence among these variables.

Many of Marx's concepts are not useful today because they are spatially and temporally bound, as well as being ideologically loaded. For example, such concepts as "proletariat" and "bourgeoisie" have highly concrete referents and would be difficult to define in a manner both relevant to the American class system and politically neutral. Many Americans will identify themselves as members of the working class, but few would call themselves proletarians. Thus, in tables 1 and 2, some of the concepts have been altered so as to get at Marx's subject matter in a reasonably neutral way.

The propositions contained in Table 1 are organized in terms of Marx's concern with social inequality. Their arrangement in this manner is somewhat arbitrary for two reasons. First, if one were interested in other aspects of Marx's thought, similar propositions might be presented in a different format—for example, by changing their order or reversing the independent and dependent variables. Turner (1975), for example, extrapolated similar propositions from the *Manifesto* in the context of an examination of the foundations of "conflict theory." Ollman (1971) interprets Marx's thought in terms of a theory of alienation, and many formal propositions could be extrapolated from this work. However, like most Marxists, Ollman does not perform this task, since he is tied to a dialectical mode of presentation which precludes the statement of discrete propositions.

Second, any attempt at extracting statements of covariance (no matter how complex) from discursive writing involves subjective judgments about what is important and how important things are interrelated. Marx's work is rich and suggestive, and there is bound

Table 1 Marx's Theory of Social Stratification

1. The greater the industrialization in a society, the greater the inequality.
   a. The greater the division of labor in society, the greater the industrialization.
      i. The greater the productive capacity in a society, the greater the division of labor.
      ii. The greater the quantity and variety of material goods desired by the populace, the greater the division of labor.
      iii. The larger the population, the greater the division of labor.
2. The greater the industrialization, the more subordinates will form a solidary and cohesive class.
3. The more subordinates form a solidary and cohesive class, the greater the rate of conflict between dominant and subordinate classes.
   a. The greater the communication among subordinates, the greater their class solidarity and cohesion.
      i. The more educational opportunities among subordinates, the greater the communication.
      ii. The more urbanized are subordinates, the greater their communication.
      iii. The more subordinates have common life experiences, the greater their communication.
   b. The more subordinates become aware of their common interests, the greater their class solidarity and cohesion.
      i. The more widespread are feelings of alienation among subordinates, the more they are aware of their common interests.
      ii. The greater the inequality in a society, the more subordinates are aware of their common interests.
      iii. The more actions by dominant classes disrupt stable relations among subordinates, the more the latter are aware of their common interests.
      iv. The more skills and wages are equalized at a very low level, the more subordinates are aware of their common interests.
      v. The greater the rate of downward mobility in a society the more subordinates are aware of their common interests.
   c. The more subordinates develop a unifying ideology, the greater their class solidarity and cohesion.
      i. The more subordinates recruit or generate ideological leaders, the greater their ideological unification.
      ii. The less dominant classes are able to regulate socialization practices among subordinates, the greater the ideological unification of the latter.
      iii. The less dominant classes are able to regulate communication networks among subordinates, the greater the ideological unification among the latter.
4. The more polarized are dominants and subordinates, the more likely is conflict to be violent.
   a. The more subordinates form a solidary and cohesive class, the more polarized are dominants and subordinates.
   b. The more dominants form a solidary and cohesive class, the more polarized are dominants and subordinates.
5. The greater the inequality in a society, the more subordinates form a solidary and cohesive group, and the greater the polarization in society, *then* the greater the rate of conflict and the more likely is revolutionary conflict to occur.

Table 2 Definitions of Key Variables in Marx's Theory of Social Stratification

Variable	Definition
Alienation	A person's diffuse sense of powerlessness or lack of control over one's life.
Class	An aggregate of people whose members perceive their common cultural heritage and their mutual interdependence, display a resistance to division, and are ready to act together.
Communication	Interaction in which persons exchange information or knowledge.
Conflict	Any form of antagonistic interaction.
Division of Labor	The different but interrelated tasks performed by people in a society.
Dominants	Those persons higher in rank who have power or authority over others.
Education	Literary skills and general knowledge of social conditions.
Ideology	A set of ideas serving to explain aspects of life and justify social action.
Ideological Leaders	Persons who can explain the meaning of people's experiences to them in terms that stimulate awareness of their common interests and the need to pursue them in a united way.
Industrialization	Refers first to technological development—that is, the increasing use of complex machines powered by more efficient types of energy (other than animal or muscle power). Also refers to the social organization of production—that is, the increasing division of labor in factories.
Inequality	The range of disparities in a population in terms of wealth, income, and power.
Interest	Anything that is valued by people.
Material Goods	Usable commodities.
Mobility	Upward or downward change of position in society.
Polarization	Patterns of division in a population.
Productive Capacity	The ability to produce a certain variety and quantity of material goods.
Revolution	A complete and fundamental change in social organization.
Socialization	The manner in which people learn to act according to common norms.
Subordinates	Those persons lower in rank and subject to the power or authority of others.
Urbanization	Decreased spatial distance among persons.

to be some disagreement about his contribution (as the disputes within the discipline suggest). Yet it is often less important where ideas come from—for example, the study of Marx—than that they are testable. Sociological theory advances when statements are phrased in a way that allows their refutation. As a discipline, sociology tends to study old, dead Europeans—which is fine if the only goal is to stay in touch with the key issues that motivated the founders of the field, especially the problem of the causes and consequences of modernization. However, if one's goal is the development of sociological theory, then it seems better to selectively incorporate the contributions of our sociological forebears (Coser, 1967). The best way to do that, and to compare them with one another, is to state their work in propositional form.

CONCLUSION: AN EVALUATION
OF MARX'S CONTRIBUTION

The crux of Marx's contribution lies in the model and theory presented above. The theoretical yield from his work is greater than many commentators on social stratification, especially American, have been willing to admit. However, Marx can be criticized on a number of important issues, five of which are briefly dealt with here. They are (1) his use of the dialectic (2) the proposed relation between industrialization and inequality, (3) his theory of class formation, (4) his conception of the dimensions and bases of inequality, and (5) his idea of human nature.

The Dialectic

FLAW IN DIALECTIC

Marx's use of the dialectic is ill-founded because it is not possible to predict the future in scientific terms (Popper, 1964). More technically, no scientific predictor, whether it be a human being, a computer, or a method of analysis, can possibly predict its own future results scientifically (Magee, 1973:97). Marxists often argue that the dialectic is not designed to make predictions at all, that it is merely part of a model that is a useful guide to reality. They further point to Marx and Engels's many assertions about the importance of studying actual history. Nonetheless, the attempt to show the inherently antagonistic character of capitalist society and to link that contradiction to an interpretation of the stages of human progress leads inexorably to the prediction that capitalism will be destroyed. Of course, such destruction has not occurred. In actuality, communism appears to be a prelude to industrialization in many societies, rather than an inherent result (Bendix, 1974). Rather than taking these facts as refutation, some Marxists simply assert that the full working out of all the contradictions in capitalism has not yet occurred. But this is a never-ending process of justifying what has become an essentially political doctrine, not a scientific theory. At some point, theories must be subjected to what Popper calls a critical test; that is, a situation must be devised which is capable of refuting the theory. The dialectic cannot be so tested in principle and therefore cannot be scientific (although it may still be the foundation for political action).

Change does not result from contradiction in the manner suggested by the dialectic.[18] Nor are there identifiable and inherent stages to human history. As an aside, it should be noted that Marx is not alone in his attempt to understand the direction of history. All the giants of the discipline were preoccupied with the historical transition from so-called "traditional" to "modern" societies, and developed typologies such as *gemeinschaft* vs. *gesellschaft* and mechanical vs. organic solidarity to understand it. However, as Bendix (1969) has noted, all these efforts are of limited applicability to the study of development, since they often presuppose what it has come to mean in the already developed West (especially the United States and England).

Industrialization and Inequality

Unlike the dialectic, the propositions contained in Table 1 are testable. It has long been known that the first proposition, the major one in Marx's work, is not true (see Chapter 6). While Marx's major proposition has been falsified, this is not the case for the proposed relation between the division of labor and industrialization. Gibbs and Martin (1962) have shown these two variables to be highly associated. In addition, they also show that the degree of urbanization is related to the division of labor in society. As suggested above, all the variables Marx deals with are interrelated in complex ways.

Marx's Theory of Class Formation

The degree of class formation can be conceptualized in terms of the following stages. (1) Members of an identifiable aggregate are individually aware of their common situation. (2) Members of an aggregate are aware of themselves as a group or class—they are "class conscious." (3) Members of a class are able and willing to engage in conflict with other classes. (4) Members of a class are able and willing to engage in revolutionary conflict with a dominant class.

In Marx, a fully developed class appears at stage 3 above. In his phrasing, a class "in itself" becomes a class "for itself" when its members perceive their common cultural heritage and their mutual interdependence, display resistance to division, and are ready to act together. Marx's propositions suggest an intuitively satisfying set of conditions under which this state of affairs might come about, and they are clearly testable. However, it is one thing for an aggregate to recognize its own interests and be willing to act upon them in the political arena (stage 3), it is quite another to desire the overthrow of an entire political system (stage 4). In any ongoing political system, classes may be opposed to each other to varying degrees. But they are also tied to one another in a variety of ways—structurally and culturally. As Bendix (1974) argues, citizenship, nationalism, religion, ethnicity, language, and many other things bind people together despite any class divisions that may occur. Further, to the extent a subordinate class participates effectively in a political system, as when it obtains some class-related goals—it acquires an interest in maintaining that system. Most mass movements composed of politically disenfranchised persons appear to want to get into the system rather than to overthrow it. In the United States, the labor movement, various racial and ethnic movements, and the feminist movement are all examples of this tendency. So it is important to know the conditions under which the social bonds tying people together will be broken and result in revolutionary conflict.[19] Marx has not specified them.

The Concept of Inequality

Marx's analysis of the relation between class conflict and revolutionary conflict is weak partly because he did not adequately analyze the various dimensions of stratification. In Marx, inequality refers to the degree of power and the amount of wealth or income an individual or group possesses. An underlying hypothesis, not contained in Table 1, is that the two are highly correlated. This allows Marx to plausibly argue that people's "class situation" (defined in economic and political terms) more or less automatically produces a "class organization." What this says about Marx's vision of human nature will be suggested below. Here, it is important to note that there is a third dimension to stratification. People can also be unequal in terms of prestige, status, or what Max Weber called "social honor." Prestige in this sense involves subjective assessments of communal identity. Such assessments are at least as enduring a basis of class formation as the more objective dimensions of power and wealth. As will be shown in Chapter 2, Weber (1968:302–7; 926–40) argued that much social behavior cannot be understood unless it is recognized that people often prefer prestige to economic advantage. Bendix (1974:153) summarizes this tendency: "classes arise out of common economic interests," while "status groups are rooted in family experience." Some of the implications of this point of view will be explored in the next chapter.

Human Nature in Marx's Work

In Marx's work, people's "social existence determines their consciousness." One's position in society, and the accompanying interests and experiences implied by it, determine a person's ideas and values. The connection between one's position and ideas or values is automatic. But it is important to explain the mechanism by which class position produces a class ideology so that how and why proposed social processes occur can be understood. Such an explanation requires a recognition of the importance of people's decision-making and interpretive capacities, such as developed by Parsons (1951). Unfortunately, in Marx's writings there is no notion of a unique personality structure through which individual experiences are filtered

(Ollman, 1971). Rather, somewhat surprisingly, in Marx's work most people are "oversocialized," pushed and pulled around by the social relations in which they are entangled.

In summary, Marx made a grandiose attempt at interpreting the stages and direction of human history, showing the linkage between social and theory and political behavior, and suggesting the proper strategy for theory construction in sociology. He failed in all these efforts. Nonetheless, his work constitutes a significant contribution to sociological theory in general and stratification theory in particular in three ways. First, even though his overall strategy is not useful, by emphasizing that social thought must be empirically based and that the parts of society are interconnected, Marx stimulated the development of the discipline of sociology and fundamentally influenced the work of the "classical" social theorists, such as Max Weber, Emile Durkheim, George Simmel, and many others. Second, as will be shown in Chapter 6, Marx identified many of the key variables in the study of social stratification, factors that must be incorporated in any model of persistent patterns of inequality. Third, the propositions making up Marx's theory constitute a clear contribution, even if they are all refuted. This last point is not a play on words, for a science advances only via conjecture and refutation (Popper, 1963).

NOTES

1. In addition to Berlin (1963), which is an excellent intellectual biography, see the analyses of Marx's impact on the revolution of 1848 by Aron (1968:303–40) and Fernbach (1974a).

2. All quotations from the *Manifesto* are from the Moore translation. It is reprinted in Marx and Engels (1959) and in Marx (1974a). Marx and Engels were close collaborators for more than forty years. A good bibliography of both their individual and joint works can be found in Marx (1974a:346–49). However, in general in this text I shall follow the usual practice of simply referring to Marx when works by both men are being discussed.

3. Intrinsic to Marx's many historical analyses is an examination of the complex structure of classes extant in various societies. Two of the most famous are *The Class Struggles in France (1848–50)* (1934) and *The Eighteenth Brumaire of Louis Bonaparte* (1963). Smelser (1973), among others, has recently suggested that these writings are Marx's most valuable sociological work. I believe this judgment is too hasty.

4. Unless otherwise noted, the quotations below are from the *German Ideology* (Marx and Engels, 1947:1–9) and from the "Theses on Feuerbauch," which is reprinted in the *German Ideology*, pp. 197–99.

5. Unless otherwise noted, the quotations in the text below are from the *German Ideology* (Marx and Engels, 1947:16–21). The reader should compare the analysis offered here with that by Bendix and Lipset (1966), which is based on the same section of the *German Ideology*. I am using Durkheim's term, "social facts," to refer to those social phenomena that exist separately from individuals and can thus be studied empirically as "things." In the *German Ideology*, Marx uses the philosophic term "moment" to refer to "a determining active factor" in history (see page 18 for the context, and footnote 17 for the explanation). Thus, the three variables identified in the text

are all "moments" in Marx's terminology. Marx and Durkheim probably had similar intentions, and I have used the latter's more familiar concept to add clarity.

6. Because production and consumption are so closely interrelated, Marx says that each is "simultaneously" the other, in that it is impossible to talk about one without the other. See Marx's analysis in the "Introduction" to his *Critique of Political Economy* (1970b:195–99). The idea that one thing can be "simultaneously" another is simply Marx's way of suggesting that society is a system, albeit a dialectical one.

7. Marx's conceptual tactics are peculiar, and he never fully explains them. Since society is a system with interconnected parts, each one implies every other. To the extent, then, that concepts are isomorphic to reality, each one implies every other. This logic allows Marx to take great linguistic license. Since each concept implies all others, each can be substituted for any other with no loss of meaning. This is why he so often suggests that X is "identical" to Y or X is "simultaneously" Y. It is also why Marx is so inordinately difficult to read, for he analyzes social relations first from one angle (for example, the division of labor) and then from another (for example, private property). But the two are clearly stated to be "identical" (Marx and Engels, 1947:21–22), and he often simply substitutes one term for the other—without telling the reader, who must divine Marx's point. The clearest explanation of this whole problem is in part I of Bertell Ollman's excellent book, *Alienation: Marx's Conception of Man in Capitalist Society* (1971:1–71).

8. The German Ideologists were the intellectual descendants of Hegel. Marx, of course, shared in this philosophical heritage. Sidney Hook's *From Hegel to Marx* (1962) is a good analysis of Marx's development vis-à-vis Hegel and the Young Hegelians. A brief description can also be found in Fernbach (1974a). The argument interpreting Marx's "epistemological break" with Hegel, reported later in the text, can be found in Althusser (1970).

9. Unless otherwise noted, all quotations in this section are from the "Introduction" to the *Critique of Political Economy* (Marx, 1970b:188–217). In regard to this first step, it is interesting to observe the continuity in Marx's thought. As noted in the text, Marx emphasized the importance of basing analysis on events in the real world in the *German Ideology*, originally written in 1845–46. He reasserts it in the "Introduction," written in 1857 (see 1970b:217). Those who argue that there are great differences between the "young Marx" and the "mature Marx" are wrong. This example is only one of many possibilities.

10. The quotation is from Engel's (1959:396) letter to Conrad Schmidt. These "letters on historical materialism" provide valuable insight into Marx's methodology.

11. This paragraph is based upon Ollman's (1968) provocative discussion of "Marx's Use of 'Class.'" All the examples in it are culled from this piece. They were chosen so as to show the continuity in Marx's thought—for example, between the *Manifesto* and *Capital*.

12. The following account is influenced by Nisbet (1969:159–88) and Ollman (1971:52–69). The original source is Engel's (1954) enunciation of the dialectic. Ollman argues persuasively that Marx fully participated in and approved of Engels summary of their thought. As Ollman observes, Engels claims to have "read the whole of *Anti-Duhring*, which contains the fullest treatment of the dialectic, to Marx before he published it—not sent it but *read* it to him."

13. Marx and Engels (1947:18) write: "a certain mode of production, or industrial stage, is always combined with a certain mode of cooperation, or social stage, and this mode of cooperation is itself a 'productive force.'" Marx was not the naïve economic determinist that has so often been caricatured.

14. In the "Preface" to a *Critique of Political Economy*, Marx (1970a) identifies a fourth, a non-Western, mode of production, the Asiatic. As Aron (1968:159–60) has argued, the existence of this regime opens the possibility for alternative lines of development. Furthermore, he notes, since it is defined in terms of the workers' subor-

dination to the state, it is possible to argue that capitalism can give way to an Asiatic mode of production rather than communism

15. Marx and Engels (1947:9) write: "the various stages in the division of labor are just so many different forms of ownership; i.e., the existing stage in the division of labor determines also the relations of individuals with reference to the material, instrument, and product of labor."

16 Unless otherwise noted, the quotations in the remainder of this section are from the *Communist Manifesto*.

17. In phrasing multivariate propositions, it is best for one to adopt some convention that distinguishes between the independent and dependent variables. In all such statements contained in this book, the independent variables precede the word "then," while the dependent variables follow it.

18. In the *Manifesto*, Marx asserts only that the unrestrained competition characteristic of capitalism inevitably generates contradictions within the social and, ultimately, a communist revolution. The theoretical explanation for these relations did not occur until *Capital* (1967), published some years later. As many commentators have shown, this explanation is flawed (see Aron, 1968).

19. One might hypothesize such variables as the degree of legitimacy enjoyed by government, the degree of historical stability, and the extent to which a subordinate class comes to accept communist principles all affect the likelihood of revolutionary conflict.

2
MAX WEBER: CLASS, STATUS, AND PARTY

Max Weber was a German sociologist whose major writings were completed more than a half century after Marx's.[1] Unlike Marx, Weber worked in an academic environment and, as will be shown, his work reflects a different perspective as a result. Weber's massive scholarly output can be arranged into four partially overlapping categories (Aron, 1970:219). The first consists of studies in theoretical methodology and philosophy (see Weber, 1949). The second comprises strictly historical works, many of which are still untranslated from the German (but see Weber, 1950). The third category is made up of his studies of the sociology of religion, the most famous of which is *The Protestant Ethic and the Spirit of Capitalism* (1958). Finally, and standing alone, is Weber's massive effort at interpretative sociology, *Economy and Society*.

His two short sketches on social stratification appear in this last work (1968, I:302–307; 1968, II:926–39).[2] Their brevity is not indicative of their importance, for together these two essays provide the basis for a modern theory of social stratification. In essence, Weber's study of social stratification builds upon Marx's work by showing the complex nature of persisting patterns of inequality and the way in which such patterns are systematically related to the development of social institutions in industrial societies. In order to explain how Weber performs these tasks, this chapter is organized into three sections: (1) the differences between Marx and Weber; (2) Weber's distinction among class, status, and party; and (3) the empirical relationship among these three concepts.

DIFFERENCES BETWEEN MARX AND WEBER

Weber's intellectual world was in large part shaped by Marx, with whom he carried on a "silent dialogue."[3] Weber disagreed with Marx in three fundamental areas: (1) historical inevitability, (2) science and revolution, and (3) economic determinism.

MARX – WEBER DISAGREEMENTS

Historical Inevitability

Marx was searching for historical laws of development, while Weber was not. As suggested in Chapter 1, Marx saw capitalism as an inevitable outgrowth of feudalism. Furthermore, he believed that communism would inevitably triumph over capitalism. Weber, on the other hand, saw no such historical progression. He argued that while political, economic, religious, and other social phenomena combine to shape social action, they do so in probabilistic terms.

This idea simply means that some actions become more likely than others. For example, in *The Protestant Ethic*, Weber tried to discover "*to what extent* the historical development of modern culture can be attributed to those religious forces [such as Calvinism] and to what extent to others" (1958:192; emphasis added). By phrasing the issue in this way Weber avoided interpreting either the rise of modern capitalism or its proposed relation to Calvinism as being inevitable. He saw the Marxian "materialist" interpretation of Western history as too one-sided and specifically avoided substituting an equally one-sided "spiritualistic" (or religious-oriented) interpretation.

Weber believed that both capitalism and Protestantism arose in the West through a series of historical accidents. In this connection, it should be emphasized that, unlike Marx, Weber saw the course of history as being decisively shaped by individual decision-making capacities. From this point of view, society is perpetually balanced between opposing forces and, as a result, the historical "difference made by a war, a political movement, or even the influence of a single man may be of very far-reaching consequences" (Parsons, 1942:169). Weber's essays on social stratification illustrate the consequences of individual decision making. As will be shown below, while the structure of classes and status groups in a society is important, Weber emphasizes that it is the on-going calculation of interest and evaluation of prestige by individuals which sustains any system of social stratification. In sum, Weber argues that historical laws of development do not and cannot exist because of the variable impact of human decisions. In this way, he removed the illusion of inevitability from history.

Science and Revolution

Marx combined science and revolution, while Weber saw science as the search for knowledge. Weber was an academician and partly as a result he sharply distinguished between the search for verifiable knowledge, which is the scientific task, and action based on that knowledge, which is a political task. He believed that the combination of revolution and science has two deficiencies.

First, it leads to forms of historical determinism that undermine any ethical motives one might have, since "what is" and "what ought to be" become confused. Marxists were (and are) motivated by moral outrage at the conditions under which most people have to live. But Weber believed that moral judgments, which every person must make, cannot be justified by scientific knowledge. Rather, science has verifiable knowledge as its fundamental value. As such, scientific knowledge cannot tell people how to live, how to organize themselves, or how to deal with scientific findings. In this light, it can be seen that one reason Weber's essays on social stratification are written in a dry and unemotional tone is that, in his role as sociologist, he is less interested in judging societies or historical epochs than in describing them.[4]

According to Weber, the second reason Marx's combination of revolution and science is deficient is that it led him to misunderstand the most fundamental and far-reaching implication of capitalism. Weber argued that the most important characteristic of capitalism is not who owns the means of production but rather its bureaucratic organization. According to Weber, the need for a rational organization of production would persist regardless of who owns the means of production: the state (as in most communist societies), the proletarians, or capitalists. Weber (1946:155) described the consequences of bureaucratization in poignant terms. "The fate of our times is characterized by rationalization and, above all, by the 'disenchantment of the world.' Precisely the ultimate and most sublime values have retreated from public life either into the transcendental realm of mystic life or into the brotherliness of direct and personal human relations."

MARX—WEBER DISAGREEMENTS

Economic Determinism

Weber opposed Marxist economic determinism. By the turn of the century, Marxists were arguing that economic arrangements, especially the ownership of property, inevitably caused specific political and other social arrangements. This argument is a distortion of Marx's position, for by 1900 a crude and vulgar form of Marxism, or "historical materialism," had arisen in European intellectual and academic circles. In the Marxist literature of the time, the "dialectic posture" had given way to a crude form of economic determinism, and it was this congealed version of Marx with which Weber sometimes dealt.

In opposing the idea of economic determinism, Weber suggested that it would be more accurate to recognize that the causal linkages among the parts of social structures are highly variable. To illustrate this point, Weber referred to Marx's oft-quoted dictum that the hand-mill results in feudalism and the steam-mill in capitalism. According to Weber, this statement is (a) confused because "it is a technological, not an economic construction," and (b) is demonstrably false anyway. The statement is confused because it implies a form of technological causation by suggesting that the form of energy used in the productive process—muscle or steam power—determines the mode of social organization. This point is pedantic and, at least partially, a misinterpretation of what Marx meant. However, more generally, Weber's *Economy and Society* is a demonstration that the hand-mill, or muscle power, has been associated with all sorts of economic and political "superstructures," not just feudalism. At the same time, "the steam-mill fits without difficulty into a state-socialist [or a capitalist] economy" (Weber, 1968).

Similarly, while Weber realized that economic factors shaped stratification systems (for example, income allows certain lifestyles and prevents others), his point was to emphasize the importance of noneconomic sources of stratification: prestige, religion, ethnicity, family background. To summarize: in replying to Marxists of the time, Weber argued that no "one factor, be it technology or economy, can be the 'ultimate' or 'true' cause of another. If we look at the causal lines [connecting the parts of a social structure], we see them run, at one time, from technical to economic and political matters, at another from political to religious and economic ones, etc." (quoted in Roth, 1971a:242).

CLASS, STATUS, AND PARTY

The full title of one of Weber's essays on social stratification suggests his intent: "The Distribution of Power Within the Political Community: Class, Status, and Party." In his analysis, Weber tries to explore the consequences of the use of power in various contexts. His conceptual tools in this task are the three concepts alluded to in the title: class, status, and party. They are ideal types, intended as a guide to the various dimensions of social stratification in modern industrial societies. Such societies form the background for his analysis. Weber argues that these entities are "political communities" and that each has the following four characteristics: (1) a bounded territory, (2) "the availability of physical force for its domination," (3) legal regulation of social interaction within the territory, and (4) a system of laws perceived as legitimate by the inhabitants (1968, II:901-904).

Within such a normative context, which Weber called a rational-legal system of domination, people attempt to obtain power for a variety of ends. Power is "the chance of a man or a number of men to realize their own will in a social action even against the resistance of others who are participating in the action" (1968, II:926). Power, then, involves coercive ability. It can exist in a variety of contexts. Weber argues that "'classes,' 'status groups,' and 'parties' are phenomena of the distribution of power within a community" (1968, II:927). Classes are associated with the economic order, status groups with the social order, and parties with the political (or legal) order. As will be shown, they are interrelated in complex ways.

Class

In Weber's work, a class consists of those persons who have a similar ability to procure goods for themselves, obtain positions in society, and enjoy them via an appropriate lifestyle (1968, I:302). Weber's analysis of class and class relations is an aspect of his more general exposition of the economic characteristics of the market in modern society (Giddens, 1971:163). Economic action is oriented toward obtaining the goods and services that are available in a society (1968, I:63). As such, economic action is an example of what Weber called "instrumentally rational" action—that is, action based on a calculation of appropriate means and ends.

As a type of economic action, class-oriented action is individualistic. It is not oriented toward a group to which the person belongs. For example, the investor trying to make money at the stock exchange and the chess player contemplating the best move are each engaged in instrumentally rational action. In their modern form, classes (aggregates of people with similar ability to obtain goods or positions) can exist only in the context of a money market, where income and profit are the desired goals. In such a context, then, a person's class can be determined very objectively, based upon one's power to "dispose of goods or skills for the sake of income" (1946:181). Income, of course, can be exchanged for goods or services, or for education that can qualify a person for some position. This is why Weber says that one's "class situation is, in this sense, ultimately [a] market situation (1968, II:928). Two of the most important characteristics of a money market are that, in its logically pure form, it is impersonal and objective. For example, a person's ethnicity, religion, or family background are irrelevant to the purchase of stock. All that matters is one's cash and credit rating.

In Weber's work, these same characteristics describe one's class situation. In summary, according to Weber the existence of classes implies an objectively determined system of stratification in which those persons who control comparable goods and services belong to the same class. Classes also imply the dominance of "instrumental rationality," as people attempt to calculate their interests and act upon them. As noted above, Weber stresses the importance of individual decision making in shaping social situations, in this case, stratification arrangements. By ranking people in terms of their common economic (or, in Marxian terms, material) interests, Weber can identify aggregates of people who have common life-chances.

A key problem, of course is this: on what basis are people to be identified as having common interests and placed together in classes? Giddens (1973:78) has charged that the Weberian analysis allows for the possibility of an infinite number of classes. His argument is based on the idea that since no two people will have exactly the same possessions or skills, they presumably cannot have common economic interests. But he is incorrect. Weber is quite aware that since people are never exactly alike, it is necessary to delineate the class structure in some way that is both useful to observers and meaningful to the participants. He therefore provides observers with some still useful guidelines.

Class Like Marx, Weber begins by distinguishing between those who have property and those who do not. The possession or nonpossession of capital-producing property allows fundamentally different lifestyles—and, as will be shown, here is one way social class and social status are interrelated. But in Weber's hands, the dichotomy between the propertied and nonpropertied leads to a more complex analysis of class relations than Marx's. Considering first those who own capital-producing property, Weber argues that they are differentiated according to the use to which their possessions are put. "The propertied, for instance, may belong to the class of rentiers or to the class of entrepreneurs" (1968, II:928). Rentiers are those who receive a fixed income from investments—whether in slaves, land, or capital goods. The German Junkers of Weber's time were rentiers. These old, aristocratic families controlled much of the land and received their incomes from peasants or tenant farmers, who actually farmed it. The Junkers, meanwhile, led a less acquisitive lifestyle. Entrepreneurs are those persons who own and operate businesses, such as merchants, shipowners, and bankers. Weber calls them a commercial class because they actually work their property for economic gain.

This distinction between the uses to which capital-producing property is put allows Weber to identify those who work as an avocation and those who work because they must. For example, a person may pursue affairs of state in order to make a contribution to the society—in the United States, by becoming governor of New York or ambassador to the Soviet Union. Alternatively, owners of commerical property work to make more money for themselves. In most societies, there exist status groups, such as rentiers, which "consider almost any kind of overt participation in economic acquisition as absolutely stigmatizing," despite its potential economic advantages (1968, II:937). As will be emphasized below, there are noneconomic elements intrinsic to all stratification systems.

Despite these differences, the possession of capital-producing property by both rentiers and entrepreneurs provides them with great advantages and sharply distinguishes them from those who do not own such property.[5] Both rentiers and entrepreneurs are able to monopolize the purchase of expensive consumer items—such as homes, automobiles, appliances, and many other less practical but highly desired items. Both can pursue monopolistic sales and pricing policies, whether legally or not, and thereby ensure a continued source of wealth for themselves. To some extent, both can control opportunities for others to acquire wealth and property. This restriction can occur by the establishment of monopolies, setting occupational standards, controlling the use of loan capital, and controlling access to executive positions in business. Finally, both rentiers and entrepreneurs can monopolize costly status privileges, such as education, which provide young people with future contacts and skills. In these terms, there is little difference between rentiers and entrepreneurs. The distribution of property, in short, tends to prevent nonowners from competing for highly valued goods and perpetuates the system of stratification from one generation to another.

Weber next considers those who do not own property and, again unlike Marx, he sees that such people are not uniformly without economic resources. They are also meaningfully differentiated into a number of classes, this time in terms of the worth of their services and their level of skills. Both factors are important indicators of a person's ability to obtain an income. In Weber's work, the "middle classes" are composed of those individuals who today would be called white-collar workers: public officials, such as politicians and administrators; managers of businesses; the professions, such as doctors and lawyers; teachers and intellectuals; and specialists of various sorts, such as technicians, low-level white-collar employees, and civil servants (1968, I:304). The skills these people sell generally do not involve manual labor. According to Weber, the less privileged propertyless classes are composed of people who today would be called blue-collar workers. Weber says they can be classified into three skill levels: skilled, semiskilled, and unskilled workers (1968, I:304).

In summary, Weber describes a complex class structure in which the key factors distinguishing one class from another are the uses to which property are put by those who own it and the worth of the skills and services offered by those who do not own it. These factors combine in the marketplace to produce identifiable aggregates, each of which has common class interests. As an aside, it is interesting to note that Weber's sketchy classification of propertyless people is used today, although in somewhat modified form, by the United States Bureau of the Census (see below, Chapters 8–10).

The final topic of importance in Weber's analysis of social class is the possibility of group formation and action based on class membership. Weber argues that "the rise of societal or even communal action from a common class situation is by no means a universal phenomenon" (1946:183).[6] It will be recalled that Weber does not see historical relationships as inevitable. By itself, the fact of similar economic interests says nothing about group formation and action. Rather, such behavior is dependent upon people's decisions in specific situations. In most cases, communal action based on a common class situation is doubtful because most people simply fail to recognize their similar interests. As a result, action resulting from a common class situation is often restricted to inchoate mass reactions.

Nonetheless, throughout history differences in life-chances have periodically led to class struggles. In most cases, however, they have focused on purely economic issues, such as wages or prices (1968, I:930–31). While Weber only briefly alludes to the conditions under which the members of classes organize for conflict, he identifies some of the same variables as does Marx. (1) Large numbers of persons must be in the same class situation. (2) They must be ecologically concentrated, as in urban areas. (3) Clearly understood goals must be articulated by an intelligentsia. In this third case, Weber suggests people must be shown that the causes and consequences of their class situation result from either the given distribution of property or the structure of the economic order. (4) The opponents must be clearly identified (1968, I:305; 1968, II:931).

The reason for the last criterion is that, historically, the most bitter class struggles occurred between the direct antagonists. "It is not the rentier, the share holder, and the banker who suffer the ill-will of the worker, but almost exclusively the manufacturer and the business executive who are the direct opponents of workers in wage conflicts" (1968, II:931). This is true despite the fact that rentiers often profit the most. For this reason, class situation often plays an important role in the formation of political parties, as threatened classes or status groups seek allies.

In summary, according to Weber, group action is not an inevitable result of common class situation. Empirically, it rarely occurs. But when it does, group action is usually narrow in focus and often displaced on the wrong people.

Status

In Weber's work, social status refers to the evaluations people make of one another. A status group, then, is comprised of individuals who share, "a specific, positive or negative, social estimation of honor" (1968, II:932). The concepts of status and status groups are Weber's means of distinguishing between the spheres of monetary calculation and prestige evaluation. His point is to show that the actions of people cannot be understood in economic terms alone. In principle, classes, the sphere of monetary calculation, can be objectively determined, whereas status groups, the sphere of prestige evaluation, are subjectively determined.

The composition of status groups is illustrative of what Weber calls "value-rational" action—that is, action based on some value or values held for their own sake. Rather than acting in terms of one's economic interests, status oriented action is that "taken by an individual acting as a member of a particular community [or group] with which he shares a specific 'style of life' as well as a given quantum of 'social honor' " (Hechter, 1976). For example, corporate executives dining together rather than with their blue-collar employees are engaged in value-rational action. They are acting rationally in terms of their values or ideas of honor and they are expressing their common lifestyle.

In principle, prestige or honor can be based on virtually any quality that is both valued and shared by an aggregate of people. Status groups exist at all levels and their differences have both positive and invidious aspects. For example, the German farm workers Weber studied were as much a status group as the *Junkers* or rentiers. Despite their positions as tenant farmers, their "resistance to personal subservience had become as ineradicable an element of their whole outlook as the patriarchal manner had become part and parcel of the *Junker's* way of life" (Bendix, 1962:85–86). The quotation points to the defining quality of status groups: prestige or social honor results from a specific style of life that is expected of all those who belong to the group.

Weber notes that individuals appropriate lifestyles as a result of parental upbringing, formal education, and occupational experience (1968, I:306).[7] On such bases, people at all levels tend to associate with others who have roughly similar lifestyles, and they frequently try to prevent the entry of outsiders into the group. Use of the word "group" in this section is deliberate, for the members of status groups are both aware of their situation and active in maintaining their distinctive lifestyle. The mechanism by which this is accomplished is subjective but consciously used and powerful in its consequences: social discrimination. Bendix (1974:153) has noted the significance Weber sees in this mechanism.

Status groups are rooted in family experience. Before the individual reaches maturity, he has participated in his family's claim to social prestige, its occupational subculture and educational level. Even in the absence of concerted action, families share a style of life and similar attitudes. Classes without organization achieve nothing. But families in the same status situation need not communicate and organize in order to discriminate against people they consider inferior.

At all levels, Weber says, people express and protect their lifestyles by (1) restricting potential marriage partners to social equals, (2) extending hospitality only to social equals, (3) monopolizing "privileged modes of acquisition," and (4) practicing social conventions and traditions of various kinds (1968, I:306). Thus, he writes, status honor "always rests on distance and exclusiveness" (1968, II:935). In the United States, members of status groups practice all four of these tactics (see below, chapters 8–11).

In its extreme form, the segregation of status groups can evolve into closed castes in which status is guaranteed by legal and religious sanctions as well as by economic power. But Weber argues that caste differences usually develop only when based on underlying ethnic differences, as has occurred in the United States. However, Weber notes also that ethnic segregation does not inevitably, or even normally, produce caste relations. Rather, its occurrence is always dependent on specific historical events (1968, II:933).

In summary, status groups are based upon the level of prestige attributed to their members. Such prestige is subjectively determined based on people's style of life. Members of status groups protect their lifestyles by discriminating against others in various ways.

Party

In Weber's work, parties are free associations of people who attempt to acquire power for their "leaders in order to attain ideal or material advantages for [their] active members" (1968, I:284). Weber is most concerned with understanding how parties operate in the framework of modern societies that have a rational legal system of authority (1968, II:938). The system of law in such societies has, at least in its logically pure form, the following three characteristics (1968, I:217–20). (1) An abstract body of law exists which has specified jurisdiction. For example, there are specific laws applicable to the conduct of federal officials. (2) These laws apply to all those who occupy an office and pertain only to their conduct while in office. For example, the Congress enacts such laws; the Justice Department and the courts interpret and enforce them. (3) The administrative "sphere of office" is explicitly separated from that of "private affairs." This last criterion is important, for in a rational legal system people do not simply appropriate administrative offices for themselves nor do they pass such offices on to their children. Furthermore, the members of an administrative staff do not own the means of production, although they often regulate them. Finally, there is a spatial as well as legal separation of the "office" from the "living quarters" of the staff members.

Within this context, Weber says that "the business of politics is the pursuit of interests" (1968, I:285). A particular political party may represent either class or status interests, or both. Similarly, it may recruit members from either classes or status groups, or both. A party's internal structure.and its political goals will vary depending upon the extent to which it is dominated by classes or status groups. Within a rational legal context, parties are the forms in which classes and status groups struggle for control. Ideally, the point of the struggle is always to influence the administrative staff but in a legitimate way. That is, parties obtain offices for their members or influence those who occupy offices while adhering to the rules of the political community within which they struggle. Thus, a rational legal system of authority provides the context and political parties the means by which class and status interests struggle.

In summary, unlike Marx's, Weber's analysis is explicitly multidimensional. He suggests the various social contexts in which people exercise power. He thus rounds out Marx's analysis by conceptualizing classes, status groups, and parties as ideal types. They are conceived in their logically pure form in order to show the complex nature of social stratification in modern societies. However, and Weber was well aware of this fact, in the real world, classes, status groups, and parties are not empirically distinct.

˅THE EMPIRICAL RELATIONSHIP AMONG CLASSES, STATUS GROUPS, AND PARTIES

Classes, status groups, and parties are described above as analytically distinct phenomena. But in reality they are not. Ideal types are conceptual artifacts designed to provide a guide to reality. They do not exist in their logically pure form. Thus, "in practice economic interest and the quest for prestige tend to reinforce each other" (Bendix, 1974:154). Classes and status groups tend to coalesce such that, on the one hand, class situation is often an important determinant of status situation. This relationship occurs because appropriate lifestyles are frequently made possible by income (regardless of its source). As Weber observes, the possession of capital-producing "property as such is not always recognized as a status qualification, but in the long run it is, and with extraordinary regularity" (1968, II:932). Among the propertyless, one's personal possessions or occupation can serve to confirm one's place in the group. On the other hand, classes and status groups tend to coalesce such that status situation is an important determinant of class situation.

Thus, one of the motives in the quest for status (although rarely the only one) is the "monopolization of ideal goods and material interests" (1968, II:935).

This last point has important implications, for Weber emphasizes that the existence of status groups generally hinders the development of the free market. In fact, the market never operates in the pure manner described above. For example, positively privileged status groups may withhold goods, such as property, from the market. By maintaining their monopoly over property, such persons preserve their economic and social power. Similarly, social and economic opportunities of all kinds can be appropriated and monopolized by status groups (see 1968, I:341–43).

At all levels, people in common status situations try to close off social and economic opportunities to outsiders in order to protect their occupational investments.[8] Particular sorts of skills or expertise (for example, in medicine or carpentry) acquired over time limit the possibility for acquiring other skills. They "represent cumulative and increasingly irreversible commitments to an occupational way of life with its rewards and liabilities" (Bendix, 1974:154). The desire to protect one's way of life is one of the most important reasons why classes and status groups coalesce and persist. It is also why Marx's prediction that workers will engage in revolutionary conflict proved false (Bendix, 1974). Rather than becoming revolutionaries, competing individuals "become interested in curbing competition." They join together and, in spite of their continued competition against one another, attempt to close off opportunities for outsiders. Such attempts at occupational closure are ever-recurring at all levels. They are "the source of property in land as well as of all guild monopolies" (1968, I:342–43).

One final point ought to be made in this context. By defining class and status as analytically distinct categories, Weber could more easily assess the degree to which economic or familial considerations dominate individual decisions in any particular society. He was also able to formulate a preliminary theory of social change which mirrors the tension between class and status. That is, when the economic and technological bases on which goods are acquired and distributed are stable, then a society will tend to be dominated by status considerations. However, technological or economic changes will tend to make class considerations more predominant and stratification arrangements will become more fluid. Those societies (such as the United States) in which class is important also tend to undergo technological and economic transformations. They also have relatively high rates of social mobility. Alternatively, Weber says, a slowing of technological and economic changes tends to produce the growth of status structures (1968, II:938).

In summary, classes and status groups reinforce each other be- *IMPORTANT* cause, over time, classes try to appropriate and protect their particular lifestyles while status groups try to monopolize economic opportunities. As an aside, Weber's work has had important research implications. In modern terms, people who are status-consistent belong to classes and status groups that are at the same or similar levels, whereas those who are status-inconsistent belong to classes and status groups at different levels. The causes and consequences of status consistency and inconsistency have become key research questions in stratification research.

In addition to its usefulness as a guide to reality, Weber's distinction among class, status, and party is related to his concern with the development of social institutions in industrial societies. By describing people's motivation in terms of their economic interests or their membership in groups, Weber suggests some of the changes that have occurred with industrialization. It will be recalled that Weber sees society as being perpetually balanced among opposing forces. His analysis of stratification is an application of that point of view. He argues that modern societies display a continuous tension between instrumental rationality and value rationality or, in this case, between social class and social status.

Weber's interpretation is as follows. In those relatively nonindustrial societies where the household was the unit of both production and consumption, the distinction between class and status is merely analytical because in that context people only acted in terms of their (family's) membership in groups. But Weber has a different historical situation in mind when he points out: "with some oversimplification, one might thus say that classes are stratified according to their relations to the production and acquisition of goods; whereas status groups are stratified according to their *consumption* of goods as represented by special styles of life" (1968, II:937). He is suggesting that in industrial societies the distinction between class and status has empirical significance. The difference, and tension, between action based on economic interests and that based on values becomes important. The economy and the family become distinguishable social institutions. The basis for this assertion is that, in industrial societies, the household is no longer both the productive and consumptive center of people's lives. Rather, one's productive activity in the work place is legally and spatially separate from the family household (1968, I:375–81; see also Bendix, 1974: 156–58). In such a situation it makes sense to refer to closely related but separable dimensions of social stratification.

Similarly, Weber's concept of "party" also has institutional significance in industrial societies. It represents an early attempt at distinguishing between society and the state—that is, between social

WEBER'S DISTINCTION OF STATUS + CLASS

or economic position and public office (Bendix, 1974:156). In those more traditional societies where public office is simply a function of social rank and wealth, there is little difference between society and the state and little need for political parties. But in industrial societies, at least those of the democratic sort, the distinction becomes useful. On the one hand, it is often necessary to identify and analyze "those privileged people who, without exercising actual political functions, influence those who govern and those who obey, either because of the moral authority they hold, or because of the economic or financial power they possess" (Aron, 1966:204). On the other hand, those who lack social or financial resources are not necessarily excluded from political participation in such societies, although it is obviously more difficult. Thus, according to Weber, the appearance of parties in the context of a rational legal system of authority means that while the state and society are closely related, they are "separable complexes of organized, collective action" (Bendix, 1974:156).

CONCLUSION

Weber's analysis provides the basis for a great deal of current work in social stratification. His description of class structure is still useful today and, in part, is used in the second section of this book. His analysis of the way status groups are formed—based on parental upbringing, formal education, and occupational experience—provides the backdrop for nearly all research on social mobility and status attainment. Further, his emphasis on the importance ethnicity and other inherited factors play in the origin and maintenance of status groups is confirmed when strata and castes in the United States are analyzed. Finally, the distinction among class, status, and party has opened up an important area of stratification research—the causes and consequences of status inconsistency.

As noted throughout this chapter, Weber's work in social stratification is also related to his more general concern with the impact of industrialization on society. This concern is one he shared with several other classical social theorists, among them Durkheim and Tonnies. The distinction between class and status, or between instrumental and value rationality, parallels other famous dichotomies used to describe the changes that occurred with the rise of industrial societies: mechanical versus organic solidarity (Durkheim) and gemeinschaft versus gesellschaft (Tonnies). This parallel is perhaps the reason why Parsons (1967) has labeled Weber an evolutionary thinker. However, this point is controversial and has not been completely resolved at the present time.

Finally, Weber's analysis of the interrelationship between class and status leads to an important insight. It will be recalled that social stratification has been defined as persistent patterns of inequality.

Weber argues that classes and status groups tend to coalesce as their members try to appropriate lifestyles and protect their economic interests. The more general insight contained in this analysis is that rewards, regardless of their origin, can often be used as resources to obtain additional benefits. This factor is an important element in the origin and maintenance of persistent patterns of inequality (see Chapter 6).

NOTES

1. Among the best recent studies of Weber's work are those by Aron (1970) and Bendix (1962). Bendix (1974), Birnbaum (1953), Roth (1971a), and Giddens (1971) all compare Marx and Weber with some felicity. On Weber's use of ideal types, see Roth (1971b).

2. These two essays are also available separately in paperback excerpts of Weber's work (see 1946:180–95; 1947:424–29). There are some differences of opinion as to how Weber's complex German prose ought to be translated. I shall generally use the 1968 edition, prepared by Roth and Wittich.

3. Weber never formally analyzed Marx's work, and refers to him only in passing. For example, Marx is not cited at all in *The Protestant Ethic* (1958), and only twice in *Economy and Society* (1968:112 and 305). The first reference simply asserts that Marx was an evolutionary thinker and a socialist. The second suggests that the unfinished last chapter of *Capital* "apparently was intended to deal with the issue of class unity in the face of skill differentials"—one of Weber's own concerns. The material in this section on Marx and Weber deals with a number of methodological issues raised by Weber. Giddens (1971) and Aron (1970) provide good methodological critiques of Weber.

4. See Weber's famous essays "Politics as a Vocation" and "Science as a Vocation" (1946:77–158). He argues that academic prophecy dressed in the garb of science "will create only fanatical sects but never a genuine community."

5. This paragraph is extrapolated from Weber's discussion (1968, I:303).

6. The more evocative Gerth and Mills translation has been used here. Societal action is based upon a "relationally motivated adjustment of interests" among people. Communal action is based upon "the feeling of the actors that they belong together" (1946:183). This distinction was eliminated in the Roth and Wittich translation (see footnote 13, 1968, II:940).

7. See below, Chapter 14. With some prescience, Weber identified three of the variables that are still important in the status attainment literature.

8. It is often the case that ethnic background is a crucial factor determining a person's memberships in status groups. Weber writes that "usually one group of competitors take some externally identifiable characteristic of another group of (actual or potential) competitors—race, language, religion, local or social origin, descent, residence, etc.—as a pretext for attempting their exclusion" (1968, I:342). See Hechter (1974; 1976) for discussions of the importance of ethnicity in Weber's work.

3
KINGSLEY DAVIS AND WILBERT MOORE: THE FUNCTIONALIST VIEW

There are three main lines of theory in social stratification. The first is represented by Marx's work. He attempts to provide a theoretical justification for revolutionary activity by suggesting how systems of inequality emerge, how they are maintained over time, and how they are changed. Marx does this by focusing on a number of key variables: people's rationality, their alienation, the calculation of interest, the division of labor (and its inherent inequality), and the evolution of history.

Weber's work represents the second line of theory. He refines Marx's analysis by emphasizing the importance of noneconomic factors as motives in human behavior, by showing how institutional and stratification arrangements are intertwined in modern societies, and by suggesting that there can be no scientific laws of history. But, like Marx, Weber sees the key theoretical questions as involving the emergence, persistence, and change of stratification systems.

Representing the third line are Kingsley Davis and Wilbert Moore. Rather than trying to assess how stratification systems work, Davis and Moore ask: why does stratification exist in all societies? Their answer is contained in an article entitled "Some Principles of Stratification." Originally published in 1945, this short essay sparked a thirty-year debate in the sociology literature and raised important methodological as well as substantive issues.[1] Their essay is being used here as an example of the functionalist analysis of social stratification. The Davis-Moore essay is shorter and more concise than that of their colleague and mentor, Talcott Parsons (1954b), but their analysis parallels his in many important respects. Furthermore, the Davis-Moore thesis is by far the most famous and controversial functionalist analysis of stratification.

The chapter is organized into three sections. The first is a summary of the Davis-Moore thesis. The second traces the debate that followed and identifies the key issues and problems connected to the thesis. The final section attempts to draw some general conclusions about the importance of asking the right questions and the usefulness of functionalist interpretations of stratification. A final note on Parsons's analysis will be appended.

THE DAVIS-MOORE ARGUMENT

Davis and Moore begin from an empirical generalization: all societies display some form of inequality. In their terminology, this is the same as stratification. For Davis and Moore, the concept of stratification simply refers to the unequal rewards that are attached to positions. They argue that in all societies varying levels and kinds of rewards are in some (unspecified) way "built into" positions. These rewards are the duties ("rights") associated with a position and its privileges ("perquisites"). For example, in American society, sanitation workers are obliged to pick up garbage while college professors must write lectures. These are some of their duties. At the same time, sanitation workers have to work outside, are restricted to a thirty-minute lunch break, and receive wages for their performance. College professors, on the other hand, work in air-conditioned offices, select the time and length of their lunch break, and usually receive considerably higher wages than do sanitation workers. These are some of the privileges that go along with their respective jobs.

Such inequalities occur in all societies. As Davis and Moore say, "if the rights and perquisites of different positions in a society must be unequal, then the society must be stratified, because that is precisely what stratification means."[2] This is a strangely limiting definition, since it precludes the possibility of examining the process of stratifying—that is, how inequality arises and is maintained over time. But it is entirely consistent with their clearly stated purpose. "It is one thing to ask why different positions carry different degrees of prestige, and quite another to ask how certain individuals get into those positions." While the two issues are related, Davis and Moore assert that the "why" question logically precedes the "how" question. Toward that end, they seek "to explain, in functional terms, the universal necessity which calls forth stratification in any social system." This is a fateful step. For they are asserting that an empirical-universal, inequality, must have some purpose, must fulfill some need of society. Furthermore, they attempt to explain this need using functional imagery. As will be shown, both tactics are open to question.   *WHY WE HAVE STRATIFICATION*

The <u>functional necessity of stratification</u> is "explained" by Davis and Moore in the following way? *First*, <u>all societies have a division of labor</u>, a set of interdependent positions that have to be filled. These positions can be seen as clustered in four functionally necessary areas: <u>religious</u>, <u>political</u>, <u>technological</u>, and <u>economic</u>. The last is given some priority because in modern societies there is an economic aspect to all positions.

2) *Second*, <u>people must be motivated to fill positions and enact roles</u>. For example, people must desire to become sanitation workers as well as college professors. Further, they must actually pick up garbage and write lectures. According to Davis and Moore, the function of inequality is to motivate people. They state, "the main functional necessity explaining the existence of stratification is precisely the requirement faced by any society of placing and motivating individuals in the social structure."

3) *Third*, <u>societies systematically use the existence of unequal rewards as the means of motivating people</u>. "Inevitably, then," Davis and Moore say, "a society must have, first, some kind of rewards that it can use as inducements, and second, some way of distributing those rewards differentially according to positions." As noted above, reward differentials are somehow "built into" positions and are a part of the social system. Davis and Moore note that there are several kinds of rewards—for example, those that produce sustenance and comfort, humor and diversion, self-respect and ego expansion. More prosaically, rewards are things like prestige, power, or money. The latter is especially important, for it "becomes convenient for the society to use unequal economic returns as a principle means of controlling the entrance of persons into positions and stimulating the performance of their duties."

4) *Fourth*, <u>some positions have more important functions than others</u>. In each of the four areas identified above—<u>religious</u>, <u>political</u>, <u>technological</u>, and <u>economic</u>—Davis and Moore argue that some positions have more serious consequences for the survival of society than do others. For example, one religious status is that of worshipper. Another, perhaps more important, religious status is that of priest. Davis and Moore admit that functional importance is difficult to establish, but they offer "two independent clues" that can serve as criteria. The first clue is "the degree to which a position is functionally unique," such that no other position can perform the same function. For example, there are often many worshippers, but only one priest. The second clue is "the degree to which other positions are dependent on the one in question," in terms of expertise, direction, or financing. For example, worshippers often do not know the holy scriptures, how to interpret them, or the desires of the gods.

Only priests are presumed to have such knowledge. For these reasons, Davis and Moore claim that positions have varying degrees of importance and that "functional importance is . . . . a necessary but not a sufficient cause of high rank being assigned a position."

5) Fifth, some positions are more difficult to fill than others because they require scarce talent, extensive training, or both. According to Davis and Moore, the other cause of high rank being assigned to some positions rather than others is the differential scarcity of personnel available to fill them. As they see it, the development of talent and the training of people to fill positions inevitably involves sacrifices—financial, temporal, physical. Their example is from modern medicine. They assert that while most people have the capacity to become physicians, medical education is so burdensome and costly that virtually no one would be motivated to obtain an M.D. if the position did not carry rewards commensurate with the sacrifice.

6) Sixth, and here is the crux of their argument, in every society those positions that are _both_ functionally important and require extensive training are provided with scarce and desired rewards adequate to ensure they are competently filled. For example, the position of sanitation worker is clearly important, since uncollected refuse is a health hazard. But the talent and training required for the position are minimal, so it is usually not very highly rewarded. On the other hand, college professors are more important to the society, since they have a hand in the dissemination of ideas, the expansion of knowledge, and the transformation of society. Because their training is both difficult and costly, they are usually more highly rewarded than sanitation workers. In this regard, however, Davis and Moore note that "a society does not need to reward positions in proportion to their functional importance. It merely needs to give sufficient rewards to ensure that they will be filled competently."

The Davis-Moore answer to the question of why inequality exists can now be clearly seen: social inequality is necessary in order to motivate people to fill functionally important positions and enact roles. In their now famous phrase, "social inequality is thus an unconsciously evolved device by which societies insure that the most important positions are conscientiously filled by the most qualified persons."

The above description of the functions of inequality implies a purely competitive society in which those with the greatest talent and training obtain the most highly rewarded positions. While some societies resemble this situation, no society is completely competitive. Alternatively, in some castelike societies, many people obtain positions based on their birth rather than on talent or training. Again, while some societies may resemble this situation, no society is completely ascriptive. In order to deal with this problem, Davis

(1948:369–70) modified the original thesis by simply arguing that the functional necessity calling forth inequality does not operate independently of other functions. Thus, he notes, the functional necessity of the family "for the reproduction and socialization of children requires that stratification be somehow accommodated to this organization. Such accommodation takes the form of status ascription." That is, families attempt to pass on the benefits of their positions to their children, in the form of skills, training, money, and the like. It is in this context, then, that "the functional necessity behind stratification seems to be operative at all times, despite the concurrent operation of other functions" (Davis, 1948:370).

THE DEBATE OVER THE DAVIS-MOORE THESIS
In order to get at the significant issues surrounding the Davis-Moore debate, it is necessary to cut away some of the intellectual underbrush that has accumulated over the past thirty years. Reactions to and criticisms of the thesis can be grouped into three general categories: (1) criticisms irrelevant to the argument because their authors misunderstood the limited nature of Davis and Moore's intent, (2) criticisms relevant and highly damaging to the argument, (3) reactions that attempt to explore the empirical implications of the Davis-Moore thesis. This last category is a more recent and useful development.

Irrelevant Criticisms
Tumin (1953; 1955; 1963) and Schwartz (1955) have argued that social inequality is not inevitable. They can imagine ways of motivating people to fill important and difficult positions without inequality. Davis and Moore, however, have correctly replied that what might be, or what is possible, is irrelevant to the argument. Rather, the Davis-Moore thesis deals with a simple fact, the existence of social inequality in virtually all societies, and tries to "explain" this fact in terms of its function for society (see Davis, 1953).

Wesolowski (1966) and Tumin have argued that there are other rewards that can be used to motivate people besides money and prestige, the two Davis and Moore focus upon. This is clearly true, but Davis and Moore assert only that a society must use *some* kind of rewards in order to motivate people to fill functionally important and difficult positions. The existence of alternative kinds of rewards does no harm to the Davis-Moore argument.

A third criticism, also by Tumin, is that inequality is dysfunctional for society because much talent goes undiscovered and untrained. Further, inequality inhibits motivation to succeed on the part of those less fortunate, breeds hostility, and generally undermines social solidarity. Moore (1963) argues that Tumin and other critics are wedded to an ideological stance dictating that inequality is bad for society and equality is good. He notes that while talent is wasted in all societies, it is not clear that a more egalitarian system would optimize its use. Further, Moore asserts, it must be remembered that fairness is not the same as equality, and Americans value fairness far more than equality.

The final irrelevant criticism is by Simpson (1956), who argues that some positions receive greater rewards than necessary. For example, some entertainers receive greater rewards than seems necessary for the survival of society. But Davis and Moore do not argue that every position must be important. Nor do they argue that all positions receiving high rewards are both functionally important and difficult to fill. All they state is that, among those positions which are important and difficult, rewards must be sufficient to motivate people to obtain and fill them. That some reward levels are perceived as being excessive by observers is irrelevant. None of the criticisms above get at the most serious problems inherent in the Davis-Moore thesis, despite their repetition in the secondary literature.

Relevant Criticisms
The problematic core of the Davis-Moore argument involves two issues: the imputed functional importance of positions and the attempt at explaining the functional necessity of inequality. In sociology, the function of a social fact usually refers to its consequences, typically for the survival of a society. Like many other sociologists, Davis and Moore construct a list of functional prerequisities. That is, they analyze the division of labor in terms of those tasks (or functions) they think must be performed if a society is to survive.

As noted above, Davis and Moore believe that the positions in a society can be organized in terms of four functionally necessary areas—economic, political, technological, and religious. Positions in each area are defined as functional prerequisites because Davis and Moore believe they contribute to the survival of society. For example, every society must adapt to its environment by obtaining raw materials, transforming them into usable goods, and distributing them. The positions involved in this effort are called economic. In each of the four spheres, some positions are more important than others. According to Davis and Moore, then, those positions that are objectively more important (functionally important for the survival of society) must be rewarded adequately enough to ensure that they will be competently filled. This is an evolutionary argument suggesting that those societies survive that use unequal rewards with the greatest facility (Moore, 1963a).

There are two interconnected problems here. The first is that the use of functional prerequisites is merely a useful heuristic device. That is, it serves as a convenient way of organizing and classifying positions in a society. One could pick other organizing rubrics, and many have (see Goode, 1973). But though functional prerequisites are a useful heuristic device, it is a leap of faith to jump from them to the assertion that actual positions in a specific society are of greater functional importance than others. Davis (1953) seems to recognize this problem when he argues that the Davis-Moore thesis deals only with inequality "as a general property of social systems." As such, he asserts, the argument is so abstract that it is impossible to move from it to more descriptive propositions about real societies.

Yet, and this is the second problem, that is precisely what they do. For example, Davis and Moore stress "that a position does not bring power and prestige *because* it draws a high income. Rather, it draws a high income because it is functionally important and the available personnel is for one reason or another scarce" (emphasis in original). This statement ignores the fact that rewards—and income is only one kind of reward—can be either consumed or used as resources to obtain additional rewards (see Eisenstadt, 1968; Wrong, 1959). It is also hard to avoid the implication that the current structure of inequality in any society is justified, since the society is surviving. But the most important point is that the idea of functional importance is in reality an empirical assertion, one for which criteria must be established.

As noted above, Davis and Moore provide two "independent clues" as to functional importance. But they are not helpful. Many functionally unique positions exist, such as personal servant or associate dean of a college, which are hardly necessary for the survival of society.[3] Further, as Grandjean (1975) has suggested, it is just as plausible that great pressure would exist to develop and maintain functional alternatives for important tasks. If this occurs, then the unique positions would generally be the less important ones. Finally, those positions on which others are dependent are usually superordinate ones, requiring great training. But, as has been shown, the importance of training is emphasized in other portions of the argument. Its appearance here is redundant.

Thus, the two Davis-Moore "clues" are not adequate criteria by which to infer functional importance. In fact, no independent or objective criteria exist for determining the functional importance of positions. Sociologist who impute functional importance to some positions rather than others cannot do so without reference to "value-laden criteria" that they arbitrarily impose (Tumin, 1953). Alternatively, the concept can refer only to what positions the public thinks are important (Simpson, 1956). Davis (1953) seems to recognize this latter point when he suggests that governments and corporations must in practice decide which positions are most important. But such perceived importance is often a result of political or public relations necessity, which often has little to do with the survival of society. Positions that are perceived as important by citizens or politicians may not be objectively important. In sum, then, the concept of functional importance is either so abstract that it can serve only as a convenient heuristic device or it can refer only to the perceived importance of positions. In neither case does it have anything to do with the survival of any real society.

As emphasized at the beginning of this chapter, the thrust of the Davis-Moore thesis is an attempt at explaining the functional necessity of inequality. The initial problem with this effort is semantic, and of lesser importance. Davis and Moore titled their essay "Some Principles of Stratification." But this is misleading, since for most sociologists the term stratification refers to patterns of inequality that persist over time—as individuals obtain positions, maintain them, and pass them on to their children. To avoid confusion, their essay probably should have been titled "The Functional Necessity of Inequality," since that is their explicit concern.[4]

The more serious problem lies in Davis and Moore's assertion that inequality is necessary because it is the way society motivates people. This argument is an illegitimate teleology. A teleological statement is one that imputes inherent ends or final causes to some phenomenon. Teleological assertions involve the search for evidence of design or purpose in nature. It can be plausibly argued, for example, that a machine such as an automobile is designed and constructed with a specific task in mind. This is teleological in that the task is inherent in the design and construction of the machine. But the application of such an argument to human behavior is problematic. Individuals often have goals—for example, to arrive home on time or to receive a passing grade in school. Particular societies often have goals as well—for example, to put a person on the moon or provide adequate housing for people. But it cannot be reasonably suggested that such tasks are inherent in the design and construction of people or societies in general.

Davis and Moore assert that inequality, a social fact that seems to appear in all societies, arises because of the inherent needs of society, which the fact fulfills. But societies were not designed with that purpose in mind. Such an argument is thus an illegitimate teleology. Davis and Moore have taken an empirical universal and arbitrarily transformed it into a functional necessity. After a thirty-year debate, it is unfortunate that sociologists know little more than they knew in the beginning: inequality exists in all societies. Why inequality exists simply cannot be ascertained in functional terms.

Empirical Implications

Sociologists have been slow to explore the empirical implications of the Davis-Moore thesis.[5] For example, Davis (1953) and Tumin (1953) have argued over the significance of students' collegiate experiences. Davis has suggested that college really involves sacrifices and training for which greater subsequent rewards are necessary, whereas Tumin has argued that time in college is really a period of leisure which has its own intrinsic rewards. Neither notes that the issue might be testable. By preferring to keep the debate on a polemical level, they resemble the German Ideologists whom Marx vilified.

Clearly, the degree to which college students see themselves as sacrificing now in order to obtain greater rewards later is, in itself, a fairly significant empirical question. But is it, or should it be, related to functionally important positions? Recall that, according to Davis and Moore, those positions that are functionally important and require training (such as four years of college) are provided with adequate rewards by society. Several recent studies have focused upon the concept of perceived functional importance as the only viable means of subjecting the Davis-Moore thesis to empirical test. They have shown that the concept is not clearly perceived by the public (Land, 1970), that it is only weakly associated with other variables in the theory (Grandjean and Bean, 1975), or both (Lopreato and Lewis, 1963).

In the three studies above, sample respondents were simply asked to rate the importance of various occupations. Abrahamson (1973) tries to assess functional importance in a different way. Following a suggestion by Stinchcombe (1963), Abrahamson proposes that "during times of war the rewards of positions with direct bearing on the war effort will rise relative to the rewards of positions that are not directly related to the war effort." The assumption, of course, is that war-related positions are more important and, hence, more highly rewarded during times of war than during times of peace. Here again, the data are inconsistent (see also Leavy, 1974; Abrahamson, 1974). But even if the data were unambiguous, all we would know is that when those persons who govern a nation decide to make war, they increase military rewards because they believe military positions are important (Vanfossen and Rhodes, 1974). Thus, the data still refer to perceived functional importance, since objective functional importance cannot be determined. The problem is that war, or any other national policy, may not contribute to the survival of society. In summary, while the Davis-Moore argument deals with a number of significant empirical issues, these issues are inevitably linked to the problems of functional importance or the functional necessity of stratification. The result is usually ambiguous or, at best, not useful.

CONCLUSION
Davis and Moore have asked the wrong question and, as a result, their argument is not a theory of either inequality or stratification. First, they explicitly avoid several important questions. How do people get into positions, maintain themselves in them, and move

out of them? How and to what extent do patterns of inequality emerge, persist over time, and change? These are important questions that are not and cannot be dealt with in terms of the functions of inequality. Although Davis and Moore assert that the latter issue is "logically prior," they fail to show it—either in logic or analytically.

Second, despite their focus upon positional arrangements, Davis and Moore have still neither "explained" nor "accounted for" the existence of inequality. As was shown, neither objective functional importance nor the functional necessity of stratification can be determined. In fact, it is precisely because the argument is cast in functional terms that it is not a theory. Theories ask refutable questions, usually by phrasing statements of covariance. Functional terminology prevents this task. As Goode (1973) has observed, the concept of function is a way of suggesting a relationship among variables without specifying the causal nexus adequately. The Davis-Moore debate is an excellent example of the way in which the concept impedes both theoretical and empirical investigation.

As noted in the introduction, the Davis-Moore thesis is similar to other functionalist analyses of stratification, especially Talcott Parsons's. Parsons argues that the fundamental reference point in studying stratification must be the values dominant in a society (1954a). These values reflect functional importance in that one societal subsystem (such as the economy) is seen as making the greatest contribution to valued ends in the society (1954b). Furthermore, within each subsystem, role differentiation occurs, with the result that prestige and power go to those positions functionally important to the subsystem (1954b). For example, because Americans value achievement, the economy is the most important subsystem. The economy is differentiated into a variety of occupational roles and income levels. In effect, those with high occupational prestige and income fill the functionally most important positions in the functionally most important subsystem (Tausky, 1965).

The parallel between Parsons's and Davis and Moore's analyses should be evident. As a result, the criticisms of the use of function can be applied to Parsons's work as well. However, one important qualification must be added. Unlike Davis and Moore, who try to explain the fundamental "principles of stratification," Parsons emphasizes that there is a great deal of discrepancy between his conceptual analysis and the real world where power and stratification are inevitably linked. Power can be seen in the fact that (1) people come to have special interests because of the positions they occupy, (2) some people are permitted to engage in deviant behavior even though it is not positively sanctioned, and (3) some people have and keep control of more or better possessions (1954b:391). So for Parsons, the relationship between his functional model of society and "the empirical state of affairs" is a major area of investigation. As will be seen in the next chapter, not all the commentators have fully appreciated this aspect of Parsons's work.

NOTES

1. The single best review of the Davis-Moore debate is by Huaco (1970). Abrahamson (1973) notes some limitations to Huaco's analysis.

2. Unless otherwise noted, the quotations in this chapter are from Davis and Moore (1945:242–49).

3. The example of personal servant is taken from Simpson (1956), although it is used here in a somewhat different context.

4. On the definitional issue, see the acrimonious exchange between Buckley (1958) and Davis (1959). See also, Moore's comment (1963a).

5. Two exceptions are studies by Rosenfeld (1951) and Schwartz (1955). Both of these efforts explore the possibility of alternative reward systems using the Israeli kibbutz as a data base. But, as indicated in the text, the possible existence of alternative rewards and, hence, alternative systems of inequality is perfectly consonant with the Davis-Moore argument.

4
RALF DAHRENDORF: THE MODERN CONFLICT VIEW

Rather than following Davis and Moore's lead, Ralf Dahrendorf elaborates a theory of social stratification that emphasizes the importance of conflict and coercion in shaping patterns of inequality. For this reason, his writing represents a continuation of Marx's and, to some degree, Weber's emphases.

Dahrendorf's work exploded on the American sociological scene during the late 1950s and stimulated considerable reorientation of thought and theory. His writings were effective partly because he writes very well (a skill most sociologists are notably lacking). More importantly, however, Dahrendorf set himself in opposition to Talcott Parsons, the dominant American theorist of this century. He chose Parsons as a polemical foil in order to debunk functionalist thought as a whole, and apparently the time was right for such an effort. During the 1950s and 1960s, increasing numbers of sociologists became dissatisfied with social theory as enunciated by Parsons, Davis and Moore, and functionalists generally. Dahrendorf, C. Wright Mills (1959), and a few others tried to reorient social theory by stressing the importance of conflict and coercion (Friedrichs, 1970). These factors had not been recognized largely because American sociology lacks a vibrant Marxian tradition.

Dahrendorf tries to debunk Parsonian theory for two reasons. First, he believes it is politically conservative. According to Dahrendorf, a functionalist "approach" cannot "contribute to bringing about a society in which men may be free" (1968a:ix). Rather, he believes that Parsons's theory implicitly reinforces the status quo in society because it does not recognize the importance of power and conflict in social life. Second, according to Dahrendorf, functionalism is theoretically inadequate, again because it fails to take into account the effect of power and conflict. In opposition to Parson's position, Dahrendorf makes some extraordinary claims about the theoretical benefits of his own work.

The constraint approach is superior to the equilibrium approach. There is no problem that can be described in equilibrium terms that cannot be described at least as well in constraint terms. . . . The constraint approach, being more general, more plausible, and generally more informative about the problems of social and political life, should for these reasons replace the approach now so surprisingly in vogue in social science (1968b:150).

This chapter is an evaluation of Dahrendorf's theory. It is divided into two parts. The first is a straightforward explication of his theory of social stratification. The second part is a critical evaluation of that theory.

DAHRENDORF'S THEORY OF SOCIAL STRATIFICATION

As noted above, Dahrendorf's (1968c:165) work is an "attempt to formulate a theory of social stratification that is theoretically and, above all, empirically fruitful" because it emphasizes the importance of such factors as conflict, power, and constraint in shaping social relationships. For Dahrendorf, social stratification refers to a rank order of positions which can be thought of independently of those individuals who occupy them (1968c:168). Although this point of view seems similar to Davis and Moore's definition, Dahrendorf is less concerned with the mere existence of ranked positions than with the more important question of how people move into and out of them.

Dahrendorf constructs his theory of social stratification in three steps.[1] First, he elaborates a series of assumptions about the inherent nature of society.[2] Second, he transforms these assumptions into a causal model of society, which, as will be shown, has both testable and nontestable components.[3] Third, he formulates a set of testable propositions that are (presumably) based on or derived from the model.

Dahrendorf's Theoretical Assumptions

As noted above, Dahrendorf elaborates his assumptions in the context of criticizing Parsons's work, especially *The Social System* (1951). Based upon his reading of Parsons, Dahrendorf (1959:161–62) juxtaposes two "alternative images of society": one held by those he labels "Utopians" and the other held by "Rationalists."

The Utopian (another name for a Parsonian theorist) assumes society is a persisting, stable, and well-integrated structure of elements. The elements here can be individuals, groups, or aggregates of various sorts. In such a society, each element has its unique function and each element shares a consensus of values with others. Dahrendorf (1958a) argues that such assumptions are absurd; they could only characterize a utopian or nonexistent society.

As a Rationalist (or conflict theorist), Dahrendorf argues that "we shall have to revise our assumptions radically" and move away from the utopian image of society embodied in Parsonian functionalism.[2] He thus makes a set of alternative assumptions: society is based upon the coercion of some elements by others; it is continuously subjected to disintegration, conflict, and change. He has reiterated these assumptions in a number of places (for example, 1958a; 1958b; 1967). He argues that they present a more realistic picture of what societies are really like. Dahrendorf believes that societies are not stable, but in continuous flux. He also believes that there is not consensus over values but rather coercion, conflict, and change. Such assumptions, it is argued, are useful for scientific analyses generally, and for understanding stratification processes in particular (1959: 161).

Dahrendorf's Model of the Process of Social Stratification

According to Dahrendorf, the second step in constructing a theory of social stratification is to build a model of the process by which people move into and out of ranked positions. Before proceeding with the substantive analysis, a word about model building is in order here.

There are two distinct ways of using models in sociology (see Lopreato and Alston, 1970). First, a model can be conceived causally. In this form, it is a concise means of summarizing patterns of social relations by indicating the ways in which several variables influence each other. Second, a model can also be conceived as a heuristic device. In this form, the elaboration of a set of concepts sensitizes researchers as to what is important and stimulates the development of testable propositions. Dahrendorf's model is used in both ways. This section is an explication of his mode of causal analysis.

Dahrendorf transforms his assumptions about the nature of society into a causal model in which important aspects of the process of stratification are linked by nontestable definitions and assumptions. This point is clearly stated in several places. He writes, for example, "I shall try to show how, on the assumption of the coercive nature of social structure, relations of authority become productive of clashes of role interest which under certain conditions lead to the formation of organized antagonistic groups within limited social organizations as well as within total societies" (1959:165).

This statement conveys in condensed form all the elements of Dahrendorf's model of coercion, conflict, and stratification. This process is a constantly recurring one that can be summarized in the following way (1959:157–240; 1968c). All societies are comprised of differentiated roles, by which Dahrendorf means sets of positions and the behaviors associated with them. This idea implies, as he admits (1968c), that all societies constitute a "moral community" in that they have norms that are enforced by positive and negative sanctions (see Weingart, 1969). Thus, Dahrendorf says, the origin of social stratification lies in the fact that in every society someone, or some group, must enforce sanctions. The ability to enforce sanctions, either positive or negative, implies that power relationships exist. For Dahrendorf, "the system of inequality we call social stratification is only a secondary consequence of the social structure of power" (1968c:174). Patterns of inequality, then, reflect power relationships. Following Weber, Dahrendorf calls the pattern of organized and coercive relationships that exist in every society "imperatively coordinated associations." An important consequence of the existence of power is that it operates in the context of a moral community and is transformed into authority such that some roles (not persons) embody the legitimate right to dominate or coerce those who occupy subordinate roles. The point to remember in this analysis is that all these relationships are assumed. According to Dahrendorf, it is not necessary to empirically assess the degree to which members of a society share common norms. Further, he does not believe it is necessary to ascertain either the conditions under which power is transformed into authority or the extent and nature of coercion. Rather, "I have assumed . . . that authority is a characteristic of social organizations as general as society itself" (1959:168).

Dahrendorf continues by assuming that authority causes social conflict because it is the most basic scarce resource over which contending groups fight. As he notes, authority "pervades the structure of all industrial societies and provides both the determinant and substance of most conflicts." Further, "group conflicts . . . come forth wherever authority is exercised" (1959:71 and 166). The reason for this postulated relationship is that Dahrendorf also assumes that differing positions (roles) within society have absolutely differing interests (1959:174). In this context authority is defined, again following Weber, as "the probability that a command with a given specific content will be obeyed" (1959:237). However, neither authority nor interests is conceived as a variable phenomenon, for "no attempt will be made in this study to develop a typology of authority" (1959:169). Rather, Dahrendorf believes that testable propositions are unnecessary in a causal model that summarizes the "constraint approach" to society. All that is necessary is a dichotomous division of society based upon the possession or nonpossession of authority.

These dichotomous aggregates, then, have absolutely conflicting interests: dominants in preserving the status quo and surbordinates in changing it. As a result, authority is always precarious, since those individuals who have identical interests form what Dahrendorf calls "quasi-groups." That is, they are groupings of people which have the potential for becoming organized conflict groups because their members share common roles and interests, even though they may be unaware of them.

After enumerating all these assumptions, Dahrendorf then includes three true theoretical questions as part of his model (1959:183). (1) "Under [what] conditions do interest groups come to be formed?" (1959:183). (2) "What forms can the struggle among such conflicting groups take?" (3) "How does conflict among such groups effect a change in social structure?" This last question is mainly concerned with assessing the degree and rate of change. Dahrendorf argues that under specifiable conditions, members of quasi-groups will become aware of their interests and engage in various forms of conflict. The result of such conflict is structural change. This process generates new authority relationships, which inevitably produce new quasi-groups, setting the conflict process into motion again. Given the transformation of a quasi-group into a conflict group, Dahrendorf argues that conflict continuously recurs in a systematic way based on "the assumption that those who are less favorably placed in society will strive to impose a system of norms that promises them better rank" (1968c:177).

Dahrendorf's model of the process of stratification and conflict is summarized in capsule form in Figure 1. He argues that in order to develop "a sociological theory of conflict, little needs to be added to what has been stated here" (1959:172). Empirically, he assumes, group conflict is always "conflict about the legitimacy of relations of authority," the possession or nonpossession of which determines the existence of quasi-groups whose members have common latent interests. Only the conditions of group formation, the forms of conflict, and the resulting change can be hypothesized and tested. These issues form the basis for the theory presented in the next section.

Dahrendorf's Theory of Social Stratification
According to Dahrendorf, the third step in constructing a theory of social stratification is to derive a set of testable propositions from the assumptions and model. This section describes his theory of social stratification and conflict. This theory and the definitions of its key variables are shown in tables 1 and 2. As can be seen from the

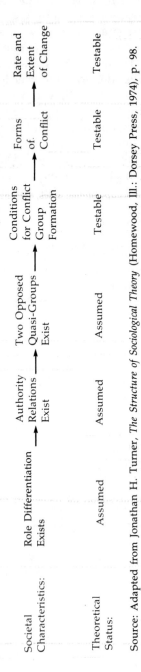

Societal Characteristics:	Role Differentiation Exists	→	Authority Relations Exist	→	Two Opposed Quasi-Groups Exist	→	Conditions for Conflict Group Formation	→	Forms of Conflict	→	Rate and Extent of Change
Theoretical Status:	Assumed		Assumed		Assumed		Testable		Testable		Testable

Source: Adapted from Jonathan H. Turner, *The Structure of Sociological Theory* (Homewood, Ill.: Dorsey Press, 1974), p. 98.

Figure 1 Dahrendorf's model of the process of social stratification

Table 1 Dahrendorf's Theory of Social Stratification and Conflict

Conditions of Group Formation

1. The more organized a subordinate group, the more likely it is to conflict with a dominant group (1959:184–85).
   a. The more a leadership cadre develops within a quasi-group, the more organized the group will become (1959:185).
   b. The more a consistent ideology is available to the members of a quasi-group, the more organized the group will become (1959:185).
   c. The more a dominant group allows members of subordinate quasi-groups to become aware of their own objective interests, the more organized the group will become (1959:185).
   d. The greater the communication among members of quasi-groups, the more organized the group will become (1959:187).
   e. The greater the ecological concentration of members of a quasi-group, the more organized the group will become (1959:187).
   f. The more subordinates occupy similar roles, the more organized the group will become (1959:187).
   g. The more members of quasi-groups internalize their role interests, the more organized the group will become (1959:187).
   h. The greater the rate of social mobility, the less organized the group will become (1959:191).

Intensity of Conflict

2. The more organized are conflicting groups, the more intense the conflict among them (1959:212–13).
3. The more disparate conflicts overlap with one another, the more intense they are (1959:215).
4. The more the distribution of authority and other rewards and facilities overlap one another, the more intense the conflict (1959:215–17).
5. The lower the rate of mobility between superordinate and subordinate groups, the more intense the conflict between them (1959:212–22).

Violence of Conflict

6. The more organized are conflicting groups, the less violent the conflict (1959:213).
7. The greater the regulation of conflict, the less violent it is (1959:225–31).
   a. The more each group recognizes the objective interests of the other, the more conflict is regulated (1959:225).
   b. The greater the organization of the conflicting groups, the more conflict is regulated (1959:226).
   c. The more established norms supply the framework for conflict processes, the greater their regulation (1959:226).
8. The greater the inequality within a group, the more violent is conflict between dominants and subordinates (1959:217–18).[a]

Consequences of Conflict

9. The more intense the conflict, the greater the degree of structural change that will occur (1959:235).
10. The more violent the conflict, the greater the rate of structural change (1959:240).

[a]The definition of inequality and its use in proposition 8 is a reformulation of what Dahrendorf calls "relative deprivation"; see his *Class and Conflict in Industrial Society* (Stanford, Calif: Stanford University Press, 1959), pp. 219 and 239. The latter is defined as "the situation in which those subjected to authority are at the same time relatively worse placed in terms of socioeconomic status." He appears to be referring to inequality. In American sociology, relative deprivation usually refers to perceptions of injustice by individuals who compare their lot with others; see, for example, L. A. Coser, "Violence and the Social Structure," in L. A. Coser (ed.), *Continuities in the Study of Social Conflict* (New York: Free Press, 1967), pp. 53–72.

Table 2 Definitions of Key Concepts in Dahrendorf's Theory of Social Stratification and Conflict

Variable	Definition[a]
Communication	A social process whereby information is conveyed from one person to another.
Conflict	Any antagonistic relationship between organized collectivities that is not random (1959:238).
Dominants	Those persons higher in rank who have power or authority over others.
Ecological Concentration	Decreased spatial distance among people (1959:187).
Ideology	A set of ideas "capable of serving as a program or charter of groups" (1959:186).
Inequality	Disparities of wealth, prestige, or power and authority (1959:61).
Intensity of Conflict	The emotional involvement of the conflicting parties (1959:211).
Interests	Anything that is valued by people.
Internalization	The process by which people's role interests penetrate their personalities (1959:190–91).
Leadership Cadre	Persons who attempt to organize a group (1959:185).
Organized Group	An aggregate whose members are in regular contact and possess a recognizable structure in that action is regulated by norms, members are identified, and the purpose of the aggregate is known to them (1959: 179–80 and 184–85).
Regulation of Conflict	Any form of conflict control (1959:225).
Roles	The positions people occupy in a society (1959:120).
Social Mobility	A social process whereby individuals change from one role to another (1959:191).
Structural Change	"The entire structural arrangement of . . . forms of society can change" (1959:121), or "changes involving the personnel of positions in imperatively coordinated associations" (1959:231).
Subordinates	Those persons lower in rank and subject to the power and authority of others.
Violence of Conflict	The destructiveness of conflict, whether in lives or property (1959:211).

[a]All definitions that do not have a reference appended have been supplied here.

citations, both are taken from Dahrendorf's major study, *Class and Class Conflict in Industrial Society*.

By stating the theory formally and providing definitions for the key concepts, Dahrendorf tries to perform two important but, as he emphasizes, often neglected tasks in sociology (1959:182–240; but see pp. 236–40 for his summary table). Such explicitness is generally useful because it allows other researchers to know exactly what is being conjectured. Unfortunately, it has proven necessary to reformulate and reorganize Dahrendorf's propositions for presentation here in order to present them in the best possible light.

As noted in Table 1, Dahrendorf's first concern is with the conditions under which a subordinate group will arise and engage in conflict. In his text, Dahrendorf describes these conditions in terms of a proposition "involving the following partly analytical, partly hypothetical steps" (1959:239).

In any imperatively coordinated association, two, and only two, aggregates of positions may be distinguished, i.e., positions of domination and . . . subjection. Each of these aggregates is characterized by common latent interests; the collectivities of individuals corresponding to them constitute quasi-groups. Latent interests are articulated into manifest interests; and quasi-groups become organized interest groups . . . [The] articulation of manifest interests and [the] organization of interest groups can be prevented by the intervention of empirically variable conditions of organization.

This sort of discursive phrasing of propositions is why it is more efficient and precise to reformulate them into formal statements of covariance, as in Table 1. It is then possible to see explicitly how all the variables are interrelated.

The propositions are reorganized because, in the case of those subsumed under the "conditions of group formation" in Table 1, Dahrendorf's own arrangement is unclear. In arranging this first set of propositions (1a through 1h in the table), Dahrendorf calls them "empirically variable conditions of organization" and classifies them under three rubrics: the "technical," "political," and "social conditions of organization." According to Dahrendorf, "technical" conditions refer to an ideological "charter," the development of norms, and a membership. They appear to be common social variables, and it is unclear why they were differentiated from "social" conditions. The latter refer to processes of communication and ecological concentration. It is not clear why these are the only social conditions influencing group organization. "Political" conditions refer to the suppression of freedom of coalition by dominants. Again, it is not clear why such conditions are not social. The relationship among these factors is unclear because they are defined by example, which is always a poor tactic. Since this mode of classifying propositions is unclear, it has been eliminated in the present discussion.[3]

Turning now to Dahrendorf's theory, as presented in Table 1, his first concern is with the conditions under which a subordinate group will organize into a conflict group. Like Marx, Dahrendorf argues that the more organized a subordinate group is, the more likely it is to conflict with a dominant group. He then identifies a set of factors contributing to the degree of group organization: the existence of a leadership cadre, a consistent ideology, group awareness, communication, ecological concentration, role similarity, and common interests. As is apparent, virtually all these variables are obtained from the *Communist Manifesto*. (Compare Dahrendorf's propositions with Marx's—see Table 1 in Chapter 1.)

Dahrendorf's second concern is with the intensity and violence of conflict. This follows, he argues, since after "assuming the ubiquity of conflict and change, we have to try to discover some of the factors that influence its course" (1959:210). As shown in Table 1, he suggests that the more organized conflicting groups are, the more their disparate conflicts overlap, the greater their polarization, and the lower the rate of mobility, *then* the more intense the conflict. Further, the more organized the groups and the more regulated the conflict, *then* the less violent it is. All Dahrendorf's arguments about the intensity and violence of conflict are drawn directly from Coser's (1956) and Simmel's (1955) work, and indirectly from some of the other secondary literature on conflict then available (for example, Mack and Snyder, 1957; Dubin, 1957).

Dahrendorf's final interest is with social change. As shown in Table 1, he formulates two hypotheses. The first is the more intense the conflict, the greater the degree of structural change. The second is the more violent the conflict, the greater the rate of structural change. These conjectures are not elaborated upon. They are, however, again drawn from Coser's and Simmel's work.

In summary, Dahrendorf constructs a theory of social stratification in three stages. First, he assumes that society is based upon coercion and that it is continuously ridden with disintegration, conflict, and change. Second, he builds a model of the process of stratification and conflict which assumes that all societies display role differentiation that requires authority relations to exist. According to Dahrendorf, authority relations inevitably produce two opposed "quasi-groups" that have contradictory interests. Their differing interests lead to testable hypotheses, which comprise the final three parts of his model: (1) the conditions of group formation, (2) the forms conflict can take (its intensity and violence), and (3) the rate and degree of structural change. Finally, as shown above, Dahrendorf's theory of social stratification deals with these three issues, although it has been reorganized and reformulated here in a more precise and efficient format.

In conclusion, Dahrendorf suggests that in order to develop "a sociological theory of conflict, little needs to be added to what has been stated here" (1959:172). Despite this rather impolitic statement, Dahrendorf's work is not without its problems. His analysis is evaluated in the next section.

A CRITICAL EVALUATION OF DAHRENDORF'S WORK

Dahrendorf's analysis is an intuitively satisfying way of approaching the study of stratification and conflict. After all, it seems only reasonable that conflict and coercion have something to do with stratification. Further, his work has helped stimulate a reorientation of sociological theory (Friedrichs, 1970). Nonetheless, a number of conceptual problems permeate his analysis, which make it considerably less useful than it might otherwise be. Each stage of his thought will be dealt with in turn.

Dahrendorf's Theoretical Assumptions

As noted above, Dahrendorf believes that his assumptions about the importance of coercion, disintegration, conflict, and change are useful in all social-scientific analyses, and especially for understanding social stratification. But, in fact, they are not. Rather, his assumptions prevent an understanding of the process of social stratification as well as the pursuit of a science of society. There are two reasons for this assertion. First, he arbitrarily assumes precisely those characteristics of social structure that can and must be studied. Second, he confuses the scientific problem of order with the political problem of order. Each of these issues is considered in turn.

(1) All sciences make assumptions. For example, it is usually necessary to proceed as if the real world exists—a basic, if crudely stated, ontological assumption. It is also usually necessary to proceed as if the real world is knowable or perceivable by humans—a general epistemological assumption. Finally, it is often useful to search for causal relationships among variables even though, strictly speaking, such relationships cannot be proven.[4] Although assumptions such as these are often necessary and useful, no science can proceed by assuming the relationships among those phenomena it is supposed to be studying. Just as biologists cannot make assumptions about the functions or relationships among bodily organs and bones, neither can sociologists make assumptions about the nature of society or how its parts are interrelated. It is useless to assume that society is based upon coercion. Rather, the scientific task is to test for the extent and nature of coercion, disintegration, conflict, and change under a variety of conditions. By the testing of propositions, it will be possible to ascertain the degree to which and the conditions under which coercion or conflict exists, and how it affects stratification processes. Because he avoids these tasks, it is impossible to know how realistic Dahrendorf's description of society is. In conclusion, then, a theoretical strategy that makes assumptions about the social rather than attempting to discover its characteristics can never aid in the development of a theory of stratification, or any other social process.

(2) Dahrendorf (incorrectly) interprets Parsons as assuming that the need for order is a fundamental characteristic of all societies. As a result, he argues, Parsons assumes society is more consensual and integrated than it really is. Regardless of the merit of his analysis of Parson's work, Dahrendorf reacts to it by adopting a set of alternative assumptions designed to expose "the ugly face of society": coercion, disintegration, conflict, and change. By doing so he focuses on

the political problem of order rather than the scientific problem of order. But the two are quite different. The political problem is that of control. That is, how can one maintain control or prevent control over a population? This problem focuses directly upon the issues of coercion, power, and authority, and it has a long history as a topic in social theory (Janowitz, 1975). The scientific problem of order is altogether different. It is the search for patterns. In this sense, the basis of all human knowledge is the search for order, whether in the physical or social world.

The scientific problem can be simply stated. Although nothing ever recurs in exact detail, social phenomena appear to be reasonably patterned, repetitive, and causally interrelated. That is, such phenomena have structure (or patterns) to them. Unlike lay persons, scientists choose not to make generalizations about unique events or the unique aspects of events but only about those aspects that have structure. In sociology, then, one asks two interrelated questions. (1) How is it that a degree of orderliness, or structure, is possible in social relations? (2) What is the extent and nature of this orderliness? Thus, just as the structure of atoms and other physical phenomena have been identified, so the structure of small groups, formal organizations, societies, and other social phenomena have been identified (at least tentatively). Clearly, the patterns of behavior that are summarized by the concept of social structure can be cooperative, conflictful, or (more likely) some combination that must be proposed for particular types of situations.

In conclusion, then, Dahrendorf cannot lay the groundwork for a theory of social stratification by assuming that society has certain characteristics. This is because he has assumed what must be tested and has misconstrued the problem of order. Nonetheless, it is still possible that Dahrendorf's work can be useful. By ignoring his untenable assumptions, perhaps one could extract from Dahrendorf's work a viable theory of social stratification. This possibility is explored below.

Dahrendorf's Model of the Process of Social Stratification

As noted above, Dahrendorf assumes that societies are composed of differentiated roles which inevitably involve the need for one group to impose sanctions on another group, based upon its possession of authority. Empirically, he assumes, group conflict is always over "the legitimacy of relations of authority," the possession or nonpossession of which determines the existence of quasi-groups whose members have common latent interests. It will be recalled that in Dahrendorf's model only the conditions of group formation, the forms of conflict, and the resulting change can be hypothesized and tested.

Criticisms of Dahrendorf's model of the stratification process can be lumped into two categories: its empirical implications and its causal problems. Once again, each of these issues is examined in turn. (1) Dahrendorf's arbitrary and unnecessary assumptions about the nature and relationships among variables renders his model empirically useless. He explicitly limits the empirical relevance of his analysis of stratification and conflict to the three questions noted above. These are exciting and important questions, but it is not clear why a plethora of arbitrary assumptions is needed in order to deal with them. For example, it is simply not clear why one must assume "the ubiquity of conflict and change" in order to "discover some of the factors that influence its course." Furthermore, by making these assumptions, Dahrendorf ensures that his model does not resemble actual authority relations and class conflicts that occur in the real world. Rather, his assumptions lead into a number of rather silly arguments. For example, "from the point of view of a theory of conflict there can be no such entity as a middle class." While acknowledging that some persons occupy middle positions in terms of income and prestige, "in a situation of conflict . . . this kind of intermediate position just does not exist" (1959:52–53). It cannot exist because Dahrendorf assumes the social structure is divided into those who have authority and those who do not and their respective interests are absolutely opposed. As noted above, he argues that such a situation of inequality leads inexorably to conflict.

For Dahrendorf, the important theoretical issue is not the way in which inequality causes social conflict but merely the conditions under which quasi-groups become organized. As a result, he solves empirical problems by conceptual fiat. For example, Lopreato (1968) has found that within industrial enterprises (which are one kind of imperative association) conflicts between individuals who have varying amounts of authority are more salient than conflicts between those who have some and those who have none. He also found significant differences between upper- and lower-echelon authority wielders in their view of authority as legitimate and their willingness to acquiesce in its use. These are predictable and reasonable findings—if authority is seen as a variable—and they cast into doubt Dahrendorf's assumption that quasi-groups can be meaningfully divided "just above the zero-point of the authority gradient" and that they have absolutely opposed interests.

(2) Even more serious than its empirical implications are the causal problems that appear inherent in the model. Other observers have been highly critical of Dahrendorf on this point (Weingart, 1969; Atkinson, 1972; Zeitlin, 1973; Turner, 1974). In varying ways, they have wondered how it is that conflict arises from legitimate roles—as in a parliamentary election, a civil suit, or a basketball game. But

to ask, as Turner (1974) does, why the same structure of roles can generate both integration and conflict is to forget that it is often conflict that ensures integration. Thus, conflict does not always produce change and—by allowing political participation, emotional satisfaction, and the like—it may prevent change (Cohen, 1968:183–91). Clearly, any ongoing society or group displays conflictful processes, many of which have little to do with authority. But there is a more far-reaching question inherent in Dahrendorf's model. That is, how is it that conflict arises from legitimate role relations to produce change? Most of the causal problems in the model occur because the notion of change is confused and contradictory, and as a result the model becomes either sociologically insignificant or tautologous.

In any analysis of social change, the key theoretical questions involve what changes and how much (Moore, 1963). Dahrendorf explains change in two different ways. First, in his elaboration of propositions based on the model, "structural change" refers to role changes that occur as organized subordinates supplant dominants in positions of authority (1959:231–33).[5] By focusing upon actors who change roles (or social mobility), Dahrendorf ensures that his model is irrelevant to the study of social change. Such social movement implies *structural* continuity, since change only occurs when the available roles themselves are reorganized, invented, or eliminated, and it is a relatively rare phenomenon (Nisbet, 1969). Dahrendorf explicitly recognizes this second definition of change at one point (1959:120–21). But if change is defined in this way then his model is tautologous, for it does not suggest how the legitimate use of authority produces alterations in social structure. Actually, as Zeitlin (1973:109–22) points out, it is often abuses of authority—that is, its nonlegitimate use—that produce change.

While there is no exclusively proper way to build a theory of social stratification or to use models, Dahrendorf has some obligation to show the theoretical (as opposed to polemical) benefits of his particular strategy. That is, it must be demonstrated that his tactics provide "more general, more plausible, and . . . more informative" theories than alternative ones. Unfortunately, the model does none of these things. First, too much is assumed. Second, it is either irrelevant to the study of change or tautologous. Despite his claim that "there are some tautologies worth stating" (1959:173), Dahrendorf's mode of causal analysis is clearly not useful.

Dahrendorf's Theory of Social Stratification
It was noted above that Dahrendorf intends his model to be used in two distinct ways: causally and as a heuristic device. Its lack of usefulness in causal terms was noted in the previous section. Unfortu-

nately, the same conclusion also applies to its utility as a heuristic device. Dahrendorf's model simply does not stimulate the development of an adequate theory of social stratification, despite his grandiose claims to the contrary. His theory is distinguished by three characteristics: (1) its paucity, (2) its dependence on secondary sources without reference to the model, and (3) its restricted nature because of the conceptual blinders imposed by the model.

Dahrendorf's theory is remarkably limited in number and in scope. Even when spread out in simple bivariate statements, it comprises only 21 statements about four issues. Many questions go unanswered. For example, while it is important to know the conditions under which subordinates (or any group) will organize, how did such persons become subordinate in the first place? This question cannot be answered with an assumption. The limited nature of Dahrendorf's theory can be seen best, perhaps, by a look at his analysis of change. Ignoring the confusion over the nature of change noted above, the two propositions in Table 1 only begin to identify, as Dahrendorf puts it, the "specific conditions [under which] particular modes of structure change must be expected." If one were to review then extant work by Coser, Mack and Snyder, Marx and Simmel, all of whom Dahrendorf cites in this section, it would not be difficult to come up with additional propositions of greater specificity than he has here. And even within the constraints of the questions he raises it is easy to see a number of additional relationships. Under what conditions does emotional involvement get translated into "more far-reaching demands"? Empirically, do "far-reaching demands" refer only to changes in authority relations? Under what conditions are demands actually translated into change? An adequate heuristic device should lead Dahrendorf to these and other questions. Instead, it appears to preclude them.

Actually, in formulating specific propositions, Dahrendorf was totally dependent upon the then available secondary literature, from Marx to Coser. In no case is it clear why Dahrendorf's assumptions must precede the (important) empirical questions he wishes to address. In fact, he simply juxtaposes issues previously raised in the secondary literature with his model, without specifying how or why the two are related. Consider, for example, proposition 3 in Table 1. It reads: the more disparate conflicts overlap with one another, the more intense they are. In Dahrendorf's own words the proposition is phrased as follows: "there is a close positive correlation between the degree of superimposition of conflicts and their intensity." This proposition is taken directly from Coser's (1956:77) essay on conflict, albeit with some inelegant changes in phrasing. Coser notes that if "one conflict cuts through a group, dividing the members into two hostile camps . . . the single cleavage will very probably put into question the basic consensual agreement, thus endangering the continued existence of the group." Coser is, by the way, a functionalist and is cited several times in this section of Dahrendorf's book.

In addition to its paucity and dependence upon secondary sources without reference to the model, Dahrendorf's theory suffers because the model he is using appears to impose conceptual blinders. This point can be illustrated by examining proposition 4 in Table 1. He is suggesting the relation between conflict intensity and "the distribution of authority and other rewards and facilities" (1959:215–17). Those "other rewards" are important stratification variables. They refer to such things as property relations, economic position, and prestige, all of which Dahrendorf admits "do belong to the factors influencing the empirical course of clashes of interest between conflict groups." If this is true, and it seems reasonable, then it is not clear why these important variables are not part of his model of social stratification or explicitly used in the propositions presumably resulting from it. Instead of stimulating propositions that could add to the theory and refine it, the model precludes such questions because authority relations are assumed to cause social conflict.[6]

CONCLUSION

Dahrendorf's argument that "the constraint approach [is] more general, more plausible, and generally more informative about the problems of social and political life" is clearly false. Although he has focused upon several exciting and crucial factors in the stratification process—power, authority, conflict, and change—he has done little to advance understanding of how such variables are interrelated. His work suggests that the formulation of "theoretical approaches" is a useless activity for two reasons. First, such efforts often involve the elaboration of assumptions about the nature of society. In Dahrendorf's work, neither his assumptions nor their arbitrary transformation into a causal model are an adequate conceptual representation of the stratification process. Given this finding, the question remains: how should sociologists go about building a theory of social stratification? At the risk of seeming mundane, it is clear that theory building should involve as few assumptions as possible. Those that attribute social characteristics to the social phenomena under investigation are especially suspect. Further, it is probably less useful to ask "whose model best fits?" than to scavenge both the classical and modern literature in search of the important variables and the crucial conceptual distinctions that can become part of a useful model of the stratification process.

Second, the theory of stratification and conflict which presumably results from Dahrendorf's "theoretical approach" is limited in scope and applicability, and could have been arrived at without recourse to such an "approach." It is unfortunate that in most of his work

Dahrendorf has chosen to reiterate the need for conceptually vacuous alternative approaches rather than concentrating on the more important and more difficult task of testing propositions. For in the long run, attempts at substituting one nontestable "approach" for another are self-defeating and cannot result in theoretical advancement.

NOTES

1. Dahrendorf (1959:ix) argues that sociology must become "an exact social science with precisely formulated postulates, theoretical models, and testable laws." As shown in the text, theory construction (at least for Dahrendorf) involves the three steps suggested in the quotation. While the most systematic exposition is in *Class and Class Conflict in Industrial Society* (1959), see his other essays also (1958a; 1958b; 1967; 1968a; 1968b).

2. Dahrendorf's interpretation is a misreading of Parsons (see Weingart, 1969; Turner and Beeghley, 1974). However, even if his assessment was correct, his solution is not. The argument here deals only with Dahrendorf and can proceed without regard to Parsons's work.

3. Turner (1974:100) includes Dahrendorf's rubrics and even uses them in statements of covariance. However, in that context they become tautologous.

4. In the nineteenth century, Hume showed that causation is not demonstrable. Scientists, however, have generally ignored this philosophical point. They have come to agree that in order to infer that change in one phenomenon causes change in another, the following criteria must be met. (1) *Association*. A change in variable X must be associated with a change in variable Y. (2) *Temporality*. The change in variable X must occur prior in time to the change in variable Y. (3) *Non-spuriousness*. The relation between variables X and Y must occur even when the influence of additional variables is eliminated. (4) *Rationale*. There must be an explanation as to why this relation exists.

5. Despite his confusion over the problem of order, Dahrendorf (1959:120–21) has a clear notion of social structure as referring to recurrent patterns of interaction. It is thus unclear why he would later label movement by individuals among roles (that is, social mobility) as "structure change."

6. Actually, Dahrendorf deals with this problem by using his model to make *ad hoc* explanations. In trying to explain "the inverse relation between authority and prestige," he notes that "probably, the theory of class conflict with its assumption of opposing role interest would account for this phenomenon" (1959:217). But Dahrendorf cannot "account" for any empirical phenomena by such an assumption. The model is used in this way in several different places.

5
GERHARD LENSKI: THE ATTEMPT AT SYNTHESIS

Gerhard Lenski's book, *Power and Privilege* (1966), is a product of the continuing controversy between functionalist and conflict interpretations of inequality and stratification. By means of an exhaustive survey of the world's known societies, Lenski tries to place them in evolutionary sequence and, on that basis, synthesize the conflict and functionalist perspectives. As noted earlier, those who hold each perspective tend to have divergent interpretations of both the nature of stratification and the appropriate questions to ask about it. Lenski tries to bridge this gap by using a highly simplified version of the "Hegelian dialectic" as a framework within which to set his analysis.

In order to use the dialectic, he sets up a conceptual straw man. He argues that the basic controversy in all writing about social inequality, from that of the ancient Greeks to that of modern sociologists, is between two competing schools of thought. He calls the competing schools the "thesis" and "antithesis." According to Lenski's artificial dichotomy, the "thesis" school consists of "conservatives" (or functionalists), who generally approve of social stratification, while the "antithesis" school consists of "radicals" (or conflict theorists), who generally disapprove. But Lenski believes that "theories as contradictory as those of Marx and Mosca, or of Dahrendorf and Parsons, can be understood within a single unified framework."[1] This new framework is Lenski's synthesis.

Lenski states that the first step in achieving such a synthesis is to reformulate the problem of social stratification in scientific terms. "Whereas both thesis and antithesis are essentially normative theories of inequality, i.e., primarily concerned with moral evolution and the question of justice, the synthesis is essentially analytical, i.e., concerned with empirical relationships and their causes" (p. 17). In short, Lenski proposes to apply "the scientific method" to the study of social stratification. He argues (p. 21) that there are three general questions in every field of study. (1) "What is the nature of the phenomenon in question?" (2) "What are the causes of its uniformities and variations?" (3) "What are the consequences of its existence or action?" His own analysis is confined to the first two questions; that is, he wishes to assess the characteristics of stratification systems and their causes. In this way, Lenski hopes to achieve two goals: a theoretical rapprochement between functionalists and conflict theorists, and a useful evolutionary framework within which future analyses can be couched.

The first section of this chapter is a straightforward explication of the research and theory contained in *Power and Privilege*. The second section is a critical evaluation of his work. The third section is a brief attempt at placing the book in perspective.

LENSKI'S THEORY OF SOCIAL STRATIFICATION

Who Gets What and Why?

Lenski begins by defining social stratification as "the distributive process in human societies—the process by which scarce values are distributed" (p. x).[2] This definition leads him to a fundamental question, one Lenski believes underlies all analyses of social stratification—namely, "Who get what and why?" In order to answer this question in evolutionary terms, Lenski seeks, first, to identify the principles by which goods and services are distributed in all societies, and, second, to document how systematic variation in stratification systems occurs from one society to another.

Lenski deals with the first problem by formulating "two laws of distribution" (p. 44). The first law is that people "will share the product of their labor to the extent required to insure the survival and continued productivity of those others whose actions are necessary or beneficial to themselves." The reason people act out of self-interest in this manner is that in those societies where productivity is low and there is little or no surplus, the survival of the society is predicated on some sort of communal arrangement. However, in those societies where productivity is high enough to result in a surplus, the situation is quite different. This difference leads to the second law: "power will determine the distribution of nearly all of the surplus possessed by a society." Lenski believes that in most societies privilege and prestige (or high social status) flow from the distribution of power. Power here is defined in Weberian terms as the ability to obtain one's goals even over the opposition of others.

The most important factor producing variation in stratification systems is the level of technology.[3] By combining the varying impact of technology with the "laws of distribution" above, Lenski comes up with two major propositions.[4] The first is: the greater the level of technology, *then* the greater the productivity in a society. Lenski asserts that this relationship occurs because, for most of human history, increases in knowledge about the environment have been applied to the practical tasks of obtaining sustenance. The second proposition is: the greater the productivity in a society, *then* the greater the inequality. The reason increases in productivity lead to greater inequality is that, according to the second law of distribution, when there is a surplus of goods and services available those who have power will determine how it is divided up. Since they are not likely to give things away, inequality will increase as power holders acquire most of the surplus for themselves.

This is not, however, a single-causal theory, for Lenski is quite aware that other factors may also have an impact on stratification systems. He points to three variables in particular, while leaving open the possibility that other unknown factors may also be significant. The first variable, which is of minor importance, is that the lower the level of technology, *then* the greater the impact of environmental variation on productivity and, hence, on inequality. Lenski argues that among those societies that have access only to low levels of technology, environmental factors, such as climatic conditions, will have a profound effect on productivity. The second variable, also of minor importance, is that, given comparable levels of technology, the greater the proportion of adult males used in military operations, *then* the less inequality in a society. The reason for this proposal is that when military needs are satisfied by a small group of specialists, they are likely to acquire power and privilege for themselves. This process is less likely to occur when the military is large (p. 49).

The third variable is the greater the legitimacy of the state, the less inequality exists. In Lenski's views, the power of the state becomes increasingly important as evolutionary advancement takes place. Thus, the nature of the polity is an important intervening variable throughout the analysis. "It is clear," Lenski writes, "that at certain levels of technological development, a considerable degree of variation in political development becomes possible. This has significant political consequences for the distributive process because the level of political development is clearly a major determinant of the character of distributive systems" (p. 436). As will be shown below, Lenski believes that democratic governments in the Western style represent an evolutionary advance over other forms of government largely because they stimulate a reduction in inequality. Unfortunately, he is wrong.

The Characteristics of Distributive Systems

Despite the admitted impact of these additional variables, it must be emphasized that Lenski considers technology to be the primary factor influencing stratification systems. "This theory predicts that variations in technology will be the most important single determinant of variations in distributive systems" (p. 90; see also p. 435). Accordingly, he develops a typology by which to classify all the world's societies, past as well as present. This typology, he says, "is predicated on the assumption that there is an underlying continuum, in terms of which all societies can be ranked. This continuum is a measure of a society's overall technological efficiency, i.e., the value of a society's gross product in international markets divided by the human energy expended in its production" (p. 93). On this basis, Lenski organizes his material in terms of five basic types of society, each of which represents an evolutionary advance over previous ones: (1) hunting and gathering, (2) simple horticulture, (3) advanced horticulture, (4) agrarian, and (5) industrial. While there are some variations of each of these types (for example, maritime societies are often at about the same level of technolgoical development as agrarian), Lenski argues that the five he has chosen are of "crucial importance in human history" and "they cover the total range of variation in technological efficiency" (p. 93).

In his analysis of each of the five types of society, Lenski selects four interrelated indicators of the application of technology: the size of the population, the level of productivity, the extent of the division of labor, and the degree to which force is concentrated in the hands of a few. He argues that in each case access to different levels of technology implies different common societal characteristics, which can be called the determinants of distributive systems. For each type of society, Lenski then notes the characteristics of the polity and the manner in which it influences the stratification system. Finally, for every societal type, Lenski uses two main indicators of the characteristics of distributive systems: (1) the degree of inequality, and (2) the rate of vertical mobility.[5] These two factors clearly focus on the key issues in the study of stratification: who benefits and to what extent benefits are passed on to children. Lenski suggests a hypothesis about each. The first follows from the propositions above. "The degree of inequality in distributive systems will vary with the size of a society's surplus" (p. 85). The second is that the rate of vertical mobility in a society will "vary directly with the rate of technological and social change" (p. 86).

The following paragraphs are a brief summary of Lenski's description of the five basic types of society noted above. Three qualifications should be noted. First, the summary is couched primarily in terms of the variables identified above. Lenski's own analysis is so richly laden with ethnographic and historical materials that a brief sketch could never do justice to it. Second, Lenski classifies highly disparate societies in terms of their "technological efficiency." Thus, he is comparing societies at different places and times which happen, for one reason or another, to display the same level of technology. For example, he classifies both the pygmies of the Congo and the Siriono of eastern Bolivia as hunting and gathering societies. Similarly, the Yoruba of Nigeria and the Incas of South America are both classified as advanced horticultural societies. Finally, agrarian societies range from ancient Rome to Spain during Columbus' time to various Indian and Chinese empires. As will be suggested below, there are major pitfalls to this type of analysis. Third, it should be noted that despite the effort to classify literally hundreds of societies along a single evolutionary dimension, Lenski emphasizes that there is a great deal of variation within each type.

Hunting and Gathering Societies

Hunters and gatherers, Lenski says, are "the most primitive of all human societies with respect to technology." Because they lack the capacity to manipulate resources in the environment, such people always live close to subsistence levels. For example, some hunters and gatherers have not even mastered techniques for making fire. More generally, Lenski observes that their "primitive techniques of food production hamper the development of tools and weapons by making occupational specialization impossible, while the primitive character of tools and weapons makes advances in methods of food production difficult" (p. 97). Thus, although there is some variation, hunting and gathering societies can be typified in the following manner. They are small, numbering generally from 50 to 100 people, and nomadic or seminomadic in lifestyle. There is little division of labor. Everyone must perform the same basic economic tasks— hunting and gathering foodstuffs. Religious or political tasks can only be part time in nature. As a result, distributive systems are characterized by a relatively low level of inequality due to the lack of any surplus. Lenski argues that what differences in privilege, and prestige as do exist are "largely a function of personal skills and ability" (p. 109). As a result, inheritance of privilege is low and both intra- and intergenerational mobility is high (although both the number of potential positions and the hierarchical "distance" one can move are limited). Hunting and gathering societies are achievement oriented and classless. They have to be to survive, since the central fact of life is the lack of an economic surplus.

Simple Horticulture Societies

These societies are built on "the foundation of a garden economy," using primitive digging sticks. They do not use plows, practice irrigation or terracing, use fertilizers, or know the use of metallurgy. But under comparable conditions, simple horticultural societies are larger (averaging 100 to 200 persons) and more productive than hunters and gatherers. The increase in productivity can be seen by the fact that they produce various "nonessential" goods—for example, better and stronger housing—than do hunters and gatherers. Further, members of simple horticulture societies have "leisure time" available for such things as ceremonial activities and warfare. The level of force concentration remains relatively low, since the only weapons are those immediately available in the natural environment. The division of labor is a bit more complex than in hunting and gathering societies, as "numerous organizations" other than family and kin arise. Further, political offices are often full-time positions and invested with special prerogatives, such as the right to wear special costumes, exemption from manual labor, the receipt taxes or their equivalent, and ability to make public policies. As a result, Lenski says, "not only are the inequalities greater [than in hunting and gathering societies], they are also more institutionalized" (p. 131).

Inequalities of power, privilege, and prestige all occur as a complex function of both personal attributes and office. "The development of offices in society represents an important early step in the direction of stabilizing, solidifying, and institutionalizing systems of social inequality" (p. 132). Thus, there is less inter- and intragenerational mobility than there is among hunters and gatherers but considerably more than in more technologically advanced societies.

Advanced Horticultural Societies

While advanced horticultural societies are also based upon gardening economies, they have access to important technological advances, especially the use of metal hoes and other tools. This advantage means that productivity increases, and greater quantities and varieties of crops and other resources are available. As a result, these societies have a greater surplus, they are larger (ranging from a few thousand persons to several hundred thousand) and more urban, and they display an extensive division of labor.

One of the most significant characteristics of some of these societies is the appearance of a complex political organization, the state. Some advanced horticultural societies constituted the first empires, as technologically advanced people possessing more deadly metal weapons conquered those who were less advanced. Lenski argues that there is a strong reciprocal relationship between technological development and political development. Further, and as a result, "variations in the level of political development are the chief proximate causes of variations in the level of inequality in advanced horticultural societies" (p. 163). In such societies, a person's relation to the state (or those in charge of it) and to racial or ethnic collectivities become important bases of inequality. Inter- and intragenerational mobility decrease, compared to that in less technologically and politically advanced societies, because of the "substantial growth in both the number and value of transferable assets or resources" (p. 181).

Agrarian Societies
Agrarian societies typically have access to new sources of energy (animal power, wind and water power), as well as have relatively advanced knowledge of metallurgy, engineering, and other specialized forms of knowledge. As a result, their productivity is much higher than that of advanced horticultural societies. Their population often comes to several million people spread over vast areas. As in societies with less well developed technologies, most people in agrarian societies are rural. But nearly all agrarian societies are dominated by urban centers, which occasionally have populations of a million or more. Such urbanity, along with vastly increased productivity, is associated with a much more complex division of labor than exists in any of the less technologically developed societies. The great agrarian states are also warfare states. Having made important advances in military technology (such as developing chariots, cavalry, fortifications, and protective armor), many of these societies make territorial conquest a way of life. Lenski argues that, in addition to military success, these advances "created an important social cleavage. No longer was it possible for every man to make himself weapons as good as every other man" (p. 194). Thus, force becomes concentrated in the hands of those who control weaponry.

In agrarian societies "the institutions of government are the primary source of social inequality" (p. 210). Essentially, Lenski argues, as the available surplus increases and military technology expands, the power of the state increases and those who act in the name of the state ensure a very high level of inequality as they strive to obtain as much power, privilege, and prestige as possible. The result is a fairly complex and rigid class structure. Most agrarian societies have had a governing class composed of less than 2 percent of the population, who controlled the majority of wealth and other aspects of power and privilege. Below this small class, according to Lenski, there is a variegated status hierarchy: retainers (who serve the political elite), merchants, priests, peasants (by far the largest class), artisans, and expendables (or degraded classes). In this hierarchy, mobility rates are quite low, although movement is not impossible either intra- or intergenerationally. In agrarian societies, Lenski asserts, downward mobility is far more common than upward mobility because elites produce more children than there are positions to be filled.

Industrial Societies

Industrial societies display far greater technological advances, of course, than any of the other types considered. These advances make for drastic changes in the economy. Because they have access to new sources of energy, such as fossil fuels and nuclear power, industrial societies are the most productive in history. The quantity and variety of goods and services available to people is unsurpassed. Evidence for this assertion can be seen, Lenski says, in the fact of larger markets, the increased importance of money and other financial service, improvements in transportation and communication, and most importantly, in the vastly increased occupational specialization that occurs. No other societies have such a complex division of labor. Demographic changes also occur with industrialization. The population grows exponentially and becomes urbanized. As a result, few people are economically self-sufficient. Lenski also believes that the concentration of force is lower in industrial societies than in agrarian, despite the greater magnitude of military power. He observes that there have been no military coups in industrial societies and takes this fact as an indicator of less military influence on the stratification system.[6]

The drastic changes in the economy that are indicative of an industrialized society also produce two changes in the polity. First, compared to agrarian societies, industrialization carries with it an "increase in the functions of the state" (p. 304). Second, Lenski believes such societies are also more likely to be democratic. Political democracy arises in industrial societies for three reasons, Lenski says: (1) the spread of literacy to the majority of the population, (2) the modern pattern of warfare involving entire populations, and (3) the rise of a "new democratic ideology" which asserts that the state should serve all the people rather than only a few (p. 317).[7] According to Lenski, such societies are characterized by relative political equality because now "the many can combine against the few." As a result, while the propertied classes are still the dominant force, "in the majority of the more advanced industrial societies all, or nearly all, segments of the population are permitted to organize and act

politically, even for the purpose of opposing the policies and programs of those currently in power" (p. 318). Lenski believes that the
ability to organize has meant the diffusion of political power and the
emergence of mass political parties in some industrialized societies.

As a result of these massive changes in the economy and polity,
Lenski argues, "the appearance of mature industrial societies marks
the first significant reversal in the age-old evolutionary trend toward
ever increasing inequality" (p. 308). That is, based on his survey of
the characteristics of distributive systems in industrial societies,
Lenski concludes that their level of inequality decreases and, at the
same time, their rate of vertical mobility increases.[8] For the moment,
however, the first finding is of greatest importance. By inequality
Lenski is referring mainly to the distribution of income and wealth.
He notes that since this form of inequality decreases somewhat in
industrial societies, his original hypothesis (that a greater level of
productivity is associated with or causes a greater level of inequality)
will have to be modified.

Lenski says there are two main factors responsible for the "surprising" reversal of the historical relationships between productivity
and inequality, and they have to do with changes in the economy
and polity, respectively.[9] First, technology has expanded so much
that those in authority can neither know nor control the productive
apparatus, and they must delegate authority along with its perquisites: power and privilege. As a result, for most people in industrial
societies, one's occupation is "the chief determinant of power,
privilege, and prestige."[10] Second, the rapidity and magnitude of
the increase in productivity means that elites can make economic
concessions and still gain in absolute terms, because in industrial
societies elites have a larger amount of absolute wealth than do elites
in agrarian societies, but a smaller proportion of the total wealth.[11] It
is not any misplaced altruism that has led elites to make the sort of
concessions described by Lenski. Rather, according to the second
law of distribution—that power determines the distribution of
surplus in a society—other factors can be used to account for elite
behavior. While Lenski does not make the connection explicit, it is
clear from his analysis that the diffusion of political power (especially in the form of democratic governments) is a major factor in
reducing the proportion of wealth held by elites in industrial
societies. An important factor underlying the diffusion of political
power, which Lenski also fails to state explicitly, is a set of values
held to varying degrees by both elites and nonelites: the "new democratic ideology."

In summary, Lenski argues that advances in technology cause industrialization. Industrialization in turn, causes the development of

political democracy. And political democracy results in greater equality in the distribution of income. These proposed relationships are linear in nature (see his diagram, p. 436).

Lenski's description of the determinants and characteristics of distributive systems in each type of society is summarized in capsule form in Table 1.[12] As can be seen in the table, at each evolutionary stage the level of productivity, the division of labor, and population size continually increase. The degree to which force is concentrated in society is more erratic, remaining low, then increasing, and finally decreasing with industrialization. Lenski's rationale for this variation was noted above. The point to be remembered, however, is that all four factors are to a large extent reflections of the technological differences characteristic of each type of society. The power of the state serves as an important intervening variable, according to Lenski. As shown in the table, for most types of societies its existence and power appear to have little independent effect (independent, that is, of technology). In industrial societies, however, the state is an important factor in changing historical patterns of inequality, largely (by the way) because it is buttressed by a new set of values.

Finally, then, Table 1 shows Lenski's description of the stratification system characteristic of each type of society. Here is his answer to the question posed above. That is, "who gets what and why?" Regardless of the level of technology, in most societies only a few people obtain most of the power and privilege and, except in hunting and gathering societies, they often succeed in passing their benefits on to at least some of their children. Thus, under the impact of technology and according to the "laws of distribution," Lenski says that inequality increases steadily while mobility rates decrease. As noted, he argues that a great reversal of this trend has occurred with industrialization.

Conflict and Functionalist Theories of Social Stratification

Based upon the analysis above, Lenski concludes that the general theory he has proposed is plausible. This theory is comprised mainly of the two "laws of distribution" and the modified propositions relating technology, productivity, and inequality. As a result, Lenski believes, it is possible to confront the key issues dividing functionalist and conflict theorists from one another and arrive at a synthesis. He argues that there are eight such issues dividing the members of each camp, and he provides a solution, or synthesis, for each of them (pp. 441–43).

The issues, Lenski's interpretation of each camp's position on them, and his synthesis are presented in Table 2. Only his own position on each of the issues is summarized here. (1) Human nature is primarily self-seeking. (2) Societies are imperfect systems that are

Table 1 Determinants and Characteristics of Distributive Systems in Five Types of Society, According to Lenski

	Type of Society				
	Hunting and Gathering	Simple Horticulture	Advanced Horticulture	Agrarian	Industrial
Determinants					
Level of Productivity	Low	Increasing	Increasing	Increasing	Increasing
Division of Labor	Low	Increasing	Increasing	Increasing	Increasing
Degree of Force Concentration	Low	Low	Increasing	High	Decreasing
Population Size	Small	Increasing	Increasing	Increasing	Increasing
Intervening Variable					
Power of State	None	None	Low	High	High
Characteristics					
Degree of Inequality	Low	Increasing	Increasing	High	Decreasing
Rate of Vertical Mobility	High	Decreasing	Decreasing	Low	Increasing

mainly the setting within which struggles over power take place. (3) Within societies, inequality is maintained by means of coercion wherever there is a surplus available. (4) Although he admits to having little direct evidence, Lenski suspects that inequality generates conflict in most societies. (5) However, the importance of overt force in the acquisition of rights and privileges is highly variable from one society to another. (6) Nonetheless, some inequality is inevitable in every society, Lenski believes, although the amount is highly variable. (7) The state and law are sometimes instruments of oppression and exploitation and at other times they contribute to the common good. (8) Finally, classes are generally aggregates of people who have similar characteristics and, except under very special conditions, they are not organized interest groups. Lenski clearly intends these statements to be empirical generalizations based upon his study of stratification systems. Along with the theory elaborated in the main portion of the book, these eight statements are designed to provide a basis for further theoretical advancement.

SOME CRITICAL COMMENTS ON LENSKI'S WORK

Lenski's book is an ambitious attempt at constructing a theory of social stratification applicable to all societies, regardless of time or place. Like many ambitious books, it does not totally succeed. There are problems with (1) the attempted synthesis, (2) the theory itself, and (3) the empirical analysis. Each of these areas will be considered in turn.

The Attempt at Synthesis

There are two comments here, the first one minor. Lenski's use of the "Hegelian dialectic" is misleading. As suggested in Chapter 1, the dialectic is a fairly complex methodological tool. Lenski has taken one aspect of it, the idea that change occurs as a result of contradiction, and used it as a heuristic device. This is not necessarily wrong, but it is not Hegelian or Marxian either.

More generally, the problem of conflict and functionalist interpretations of social stratification is not one that can be solved in the manner Lenski has chosen. He clearly intends his "synthesis" to be a set of empirical generalizations about each of the issues presumably dividing the two camps. But not much is learned from his assertion that people have self-seeking natures. Nor is much learned from his assertion that the state and law are sometimes repressive and sometimes useful for the society as a whole. Substantively, then, Lenski's synthesis is a set of safe but trivial statements with which few people would disagree. Methodologically, however, the synthesis is a renewed attempt at stating universals, a task that can never succeed. The entire debate, including the attempt at synthesis,

Table 2 Lenski's Synthesis of Conflict and Functionalist Theory

Issue	Conflict Perspective	Functionalist Perspective	Lenski's Synthesis
1. Human Nature	Humans are good; social institutions are alienating	Humans are not good and need the restraint of social institutions	Humans have a self-seeking nature
2. Nature of Society	Society is setting for struggles over scarce resources	Society is a system of interrelated parts generally serving useful purposes	Societies are imperfect systems characterized by struggle
3. Is Inequality Maintained by Coercion?	Yes	No; inequality results from innate differences and is based on consensus	Functionalists correct when surplus low; conflict theorists correct when surplus high
4. Does Inequality Produce Conflict?	Yes	No	Yes (tentatively)
5. How Are Rights and Privileges Acquired?	Inheritance, force, and fraud	Innate ability and hard work	Both factors operate
6. Is Inequality Inevitable?	No	Yes	Given human nature, yes; but the amount is highly variable
7. Nature of State and Law	Instruments of repression and exploitation	Used by and for society as a whole	Both factors operate
8. Nature of Class	Aggregates with common interests	Aggregates with similar characteristics	Generally, aggregates with similar characteristics

is futile. In fact, Lenski's theory of social stratification does not require an artificial synthesis of conflict and functionalist perspectives.[13] It can stand or fall on its own merits.

Lenski's Theory

As shown above, Lenski's theory has two parts: the laws of distribution are supposed to account for the common features of stratification systems in all societies, while the major propositions are designed to explain why these features vary in a systematic way. Both are inadequate. The laws of distribution posit need and power as the two principles governing the distribution of goods and services in society. Need is seen as important in less technologically advanced societies and power is important in those more advanced. But, as Allardt (1968) has suggested, "in technologically very primitive societies some have the privilege of staying alive while others will die because their needs are not met. It seems hard to explain these differences otherwise than on the basis of differential power." Thus, it might be more useful to hypothesize that the amount of surplus and the amount of power vary independently of each other (Allardt, 1968).

Furthermore, the example above is suggestive of the tautology inherent in *Power and Privilege*. That is, Lenski asserts that "privilege is largely a function of power" and to explain "the distribution of privilege in a society, we have but to determine the distribution of power" (p. 45). But privilege is not a passive phenomenon. In most cases, rewards—whether economic, political, or social (in the sense of prestige)—can also be used as resources. In Lenski's terminology, most privileges involve the privilege of exercising some sort of power. He fails to recognize this crucial point.

In his major propositions, Lenski argues that productivity varies with technology and, until mature industrial societies appear, inequality varies with productivity. Fallers (1966) labels this argument as utilitarian and "conceptually primitive as a result." These propositions, and the principles on which they are based, fail to recognize (at least explicitly) the importance of values in human behavior. For Lenski, the only value is the calculation of self-interest or relative advantage. In effect, in Lenski's analysis the goals of action, such as power and privilege, are objectively given and universal in all societies. Yet, as Parsons (1937) has argued, the founders of sociology abandoned the utilitarian view long ago. Lenski fails to recognize, explicitly at least, that people's goals are often culturally defined. For example, he argues that the high correlation between income and education with occupational prestige shows that such prestige is a "reflection of occupational power and privilege." But as Fallers (1966) observes, it is just as plausible to argue that such correlations suggest the "high value Americans give to occupational achievement and especially to achievement in materially productive occupations." Furthermore, pervading the entire analysis of "who gets what and why" is a recognition that those who benefit from the distributive system always have to justify their claims. In effect, like some of the classical social theorists, Lenski smuggles values into the analysis through a conceptual back door. This is clearly revealed when he suddenly observes that democratic values may well have preceded industrialization rather than resulted from it (p. 317).[14]

The reason Lenski (1975) regards the impact of values as negligible is because he is committed to an evolutionary interpretation of history in which the key causal variable is the level of technology. This mode of analysis has both strengths and weaknesses. As shown above, it does provide an intuitively satisfying way of classifying societies and of showing what clearly is a historical trend. It seems reasonable, at least at this point in history, to suggest that societies having access to higher levels of technology are, in that sense at least, more "advanced." Further, allowing for some variation, in the long run technologically more advanced societies have tended to dominate those that are less advanced. But this evolutionary interpretation of history is not a theory of social change (Nisbet, 1969). Lenski's analysis is essentially static. He does not show how the distributive system in one society "develops" or "evolves" into a different distributive in the same society. That is, for example, at no point does Lenski show how a particular hunting and gathering society changed into a simple horticultural society. Rather, all that is shown is that societies which have existed at different times and places can be classified together in terms of their level of technology. Although this procedure is useful for certain purposes, it reveals nothing about change.

Lenski's Empirical Analysis

Nearly all the questions surrounding Lenski's empirical analysis have to do with his description of industrial societies. Cutright (1967a; 1967b) provided some initial support for Lenski's interpretation of the relationship among technology, industrialization, political democracy, and decreasing inequality. However, more recent work by Paukert (1973) and Jackman (1974; 1975) has cast aspects of Lenski's analysis into serious doubt.

The relationship between industrialization and inequality will be considered first, followed by an assessment of the importance of political democracy as an intervening variable.[15] While Paukert's (1973: 120–21) analysis supports Lenski's view that "there is a clear long-term trend toward equality," it shows the relationship as curvilinear rather than linear. That is, "with economic development income inequality tends to increase, then become stable and then decrease." More recently, however, Jackman (1974:41; 1975) has reported quite the opposite finding. His data suggest a curvilinear relationship in which "industrialization results in greater social equality in the earlier phases of economic development, [but] a threshold is reached in later phases of this process where the effects of industrialization on social equality become progressively weaker." These contradictory propositions are presented in diagrammatic form in Figure 1, along with those by Marx and Lenski. Two conclusions can be drawn from the figure. The first is that, as Treiman (1970:229) notes, "we actually know very little about the relation between industrialization and stratification." Lenski's data are impressionistic, at best. While Paukert's and Jackman's data are considerably better, many societies (including the United States) still either do not collect appropriate data or do so incompetently, making the resulting analyses very tenuous. Nonetheless, a second conclusion is also possible. That is, Lenski's hypothesis of a linear relationship between industrialization and inequality is probably incorrect. Both Paukert and Jackman's findings suggest that the relationship is probably more complex than Lenski believes.

It will be recalled that Lenski believes political democracy is an important intervening variable between industrialization and inequality. But there is virtually no support for either aspect of this argument. That is, first, industrialization is related only to the emergence of democracy in Western Europe and the United States. In the modern world, some form of totalitarian or dictatorial form of government often seems to precede industrialization. Such governments do not subsequently fade away. Second, when forms of inequality other than political are focused upon, it is clear that on the whole democratic societies are not any more egalitarian than nondemocratic ones. Thus, Jackman (1974:38) concludes that "when democratic performance is specified as an intervening variable . . . it does not interpret or add to the basic relationship between economic development and social and economic equality." It should be noted that Jackman's data (and Paukert's as well) are for noncommunist nations. If data on the communist countries were available, they would probably also show that Lenski's hypothesis is incorrect.[16]

CONCLUSION

The key problem in Lenski's analysis is that he chose to answer the question in evolutionary terms. As noted above, this evolutionary emphasis led him to hypothesize the fundamental principle by which goods are distributed in all societies and the factor that produces variation from one society to another. Now it is perfectly reasonable to assert that power or, in altered form, authority helps determine the stratification system in all societies (with or without a surplus). But by positing that power is the only, or even the single most important, factor shaping stratification Lenski ignores the

Figure 1 Diagram of four propositions relating industrialization and inequality

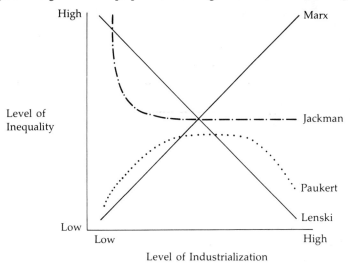

Marx: The greater the industrialization in a society, the greater the inequality.

Lenski: The greater the industrialization in a society, the less the inequality.

Jackman: There is a curvilinear relation between industrialization and inequality such that: as industrialization increases inequality decreases, but past a certain level industrialization is not associated with a reduction in inequality.

Paukert: There is a curvilinear relation between industrialization and inequality such that: as industrialization increases inequality increases, then it becomes stable for a time, and then inequality decreases.

whole of Max Weber's contribution. Indeed, Weber is cited only once in the entire text.

Further, while Lenski is forced to recognize the influence of values on social stratification, in the form of a "new democratic ideology," he fails to recognize that most people in most societies at all levels of the stratification heirarchy believe in and actively support the social status quo. As Marx recognized, convincing people of the need for change is often a difficult political task. Similarly, it is reasonable to assert that technology makes possible certain variations in stratification systems. But, as argued above, technology does not exist in a vacuum. Surprisingly, Lenski, an American sociologist, posits a form of technological determinism of which Marx was so often, but incorrectly, accused. In fact, simply because societies can be classified in terms of their technological level does not mean that their stratification system can be predicted. Lenski conveniently ignores this fact by excluding from his analysis the many "herding," "fishing," "maritime," and other hybrid societies that his own research reveals exist at all levels of technology (see his diagram p. 92).

Nonetheless, the great strength of *Power and Privilege* is its historical and comparative emphasis. It is worth reading for this reason alone. Further, unlike Davis and Moore, Lenski clearly addresses the right issue. Whether in studies of one society or many, an answer to the question "who gets what and why?" will provide insight into the nature of social stratification. That Lenski's own answer is less satisfactory than one might hope suggests the awesome nature of the task he attempted.

NOTES

1. Unless otherwise specified, all unattributed references are to Lenski (1966). Italicized phrases permeate Lenski's book, including some of the quotations below. I generally prefer to avoid the use of italics and have eliminated them from all quotes.

2. This definition is less different than it might seem. As will be noted below, Lenski is interested in the same phenomena as most other stratification theorists: the causes of inequality, the extent of inequality, and the degree to which people pass on their benefits to their children. In what follows, I shall use "distributive systems" and "stratification systems" interchangeably.

3. Technology is poorly defined by Lenski. At one point (p. 436) he refers to it as "the cultural means by which a society relates to its environment." But this is unclear. A definition that seems to catch his intent is: technology is verified knowledge about the environment (see Turner, 1972:19). By the way, Turner's analysis of social institutions parallels Lenski's analysis of stratification systems.

4. The wording of these propositions is mine, not Lenski's. I have tried to catch the central thrust of his work with these two statements (see also Fallers, 1966).

5. Lenski also refers to a third indicator, the degree of class hostility, but he makes only intermittent use of this variable and it has been omitted here.

6. This is a controversial point. Mills (1956) and many others would disagree with Lenski.

7. Significantly, Lenski points out that "there appears to be as much justification for the thesis that this new ideology contributed to the emergence of industrial societies as for the converse" (p. 317).

8. Lenski argues that all industrial societies have relatively high and stable rates of vertical mobility and in most cases display "a gradual rise in upward mobility" (p. 415). As will be shown below, in Chapter 14, the first assertion is correct but the second is probably incorrect.

9. Lenski also mentions two other factors as helping to cause the reversal: the spread of effective methods of birth control and the rapid expansion of knowledge that equips more people with salable skills.

10. Women are clearly an exception here, as Lenski notes. He argues that while "women still do not enjoy complete equality," it is unlikely that further reductions of inequality will occur (p. 402–6).

11. For example, Lenski calculates that, in agrarian societies, 1 to 2 percent of the population controls at least 50 percent of the income, while in industrial societies, the top 2 percent receives about 10 percent of the income. But in absolute terms, the top 2 percent in industrial societies have a greater income than their compatriots in agrarian societies (p. 309).

12. My friend Eldon Wegner of the University of Hawaii suggested putting this material in tabular form.

13. This argument ignores the political conditions in the discipline at the time Lenski was writing.

14. Despite this inconsistency, Lenski (1975:51) has recently reaffirmed his position that technology is the key variable in explaining the evolution of human societies. "Not much of the basic variance in social systems seems to require the invocation of cultural values." Some problems with this evolutionary point of view are noted below.

15. There is now a long literature on the relation between industrialization and inequality. The focus of these analyses is nearly always on the distribution of income and wealth as the most important elements of inequality. See the references in Trieman (1970), Paukert (1973), and Jackman (1975).

16. On this point, see Inkeles (1969).

6
A HEURISTIC MODEL FOR THE STUDY OF SOCIAL STRATIFICATION

Reinhard Bendix (1974:149) argues that sociologists still "do not have a theory of social structure and inequality." He is clearly correct, especially if theory is taken to mean a deductive set of propositions. Nonetheless, the six theorists dealt with here have all contributed to the development of a theory of social stratification. The study of these men reveals a rich legacy of prescient observations and provocative hypotheses. Like the other classical social theorists, Marx fundamentally reoriented social thought. Because of his emphasis on identifying people's place in the social structure and testing hypotheses about their behavior in a concrete historical context, Marx remains the Copernican hero of stratification theory.[1] At the same time, however, Weber's work is a more enduring theoretical contribution to the study of stratification, largely because he was able to see the consequences of industrialization in more precise analytical terms than Marx. The modern scholars considered here are disappointing in comparison to Marx and Weber, although it is a bit unfair to compare anyone to such geniuses. The theories of Davis and Moore, Dahrendorf, and Lenski all have fundamental problems that make them essentially untenable for the purpose of a theory of social stratification. Nonetheless, much can be learned from their work, if often from their mistakes.

This chapter is a brief attempt at building on the theorists discussed above by speculating about the major elements that make up stratification systems and providing an analytical framework for the study of social strata in the United States. The analysis in this chapter is not a theory, for it cannot be tested. Rather, it is conceived as a heuristic model that can sensitize observers to the common social processes that seem to characterize all stratification systems. In that way, it can perhaps provide a useful guide to the study of the persistent patterns of inequality existing in any particular society but especially in the United States.

Two qualifying comments are necessary. First, the model developed here is directed toward the analysis of stratification in societies. While persistent patterns of inequality in collectivities, small groups, and other social structures are also of inherent interest, and even though some of the comments below are probably applicable to other levels of analysis, the concern here is with societies in general, and American society in particular.

Second, to some degree, all societies are social systems. That is, they can be conceived as being composed of parts that are interrelated with one another and as being boundary-maintaining entities. As will be seen, these parts can be divided in a number of convenient ways. There is no absolutely correct way to dissect a social system. However, as social systems, societies are neither teleological nor impermeable. It will be recalled that a teleological assertion imputes inherent purpose to some object. There is very little about a society, or any social system, that is teleological. The problem of permeability has to do with what gets into and out of a society; that is, with its relationship to the environment, both physical and social. Most societies are open systems (or permeable) such that a great deal of interaction with the environment occurs. In this context, it is important to emphasize that the particular structural arrangements characterizing a society and its relation to the environment are always matters for empirical analysis. They should never be assumed.

THE GENERAL CHARACTERISTICS OF STRATIFICATION SYSTEMS

It is not possible to ascertain in any definitive way how stratification systems emerge. Nonetheless, based in part on a reading of the theorists discussed above, it is possible for us to suggest the main social facts characterizing existing stratification systems. Briefly, there appear to be three key elements: (1) the division of labor, (2) inequality (as indicated by differences in rewards and evaluations), and (3) restrictions on people's access to positions. These elements occur together. As Marx would say, the division of labor, inequality, and restrictions on access to positions are social facts that exist in all societies. However, following Weber, it should be emphasized that the precise configuration among these factors is quite variable, both from one society to another and in the same society over time. There is no fixed or historically inevitable relationship among them.

The Division of Labor

All the theorists dealt with here emphasize that the extent of the division of labor is one of the keys to understanding stratification in a society. For Marx, the division of labor indicated people's interests and, by extrapolation, their class affiliation. Weber suggested that with increasing division of labor in industrial society, distinct social institutions emerge, each of which displays inequality. Davis and Moore speculated that some minimal division of labor among familial, economic, political, religious, and other institutional spheres is essential for the survival of society. While they cannot prove this point, their reasoning is based on the insight that the basic tasks in each sphere generally must be performed and, except in the smallest and least complex societies, each person cannot perform them all. Finally, Lenski used the division of labor as an important indicator of the extent of industrialization and its evolutionary relationship to inequality.

Despite their great differences, each of these scholars is fascinated by the fact that all societies display both a division of labor and inequality. For such a division of tasks implies that the many positions people fill are to some degree both interdependent and unequal. While the precise relationship between the division of labor and inequality is quite variable, the two factors are nearly always associated with each other. It can be speculated (and only speculated, for it is not known for certain) that the relationship results from the interaction of two related social facts that have been subsumed under the rubric inequality: unequal rewards and unequal evaluations.

Inequality

The first reason the division of labor appears to be associated with inequality is that the various statuses in society are unequally rewarded. All the theorists dealt with here emphasize this point. "It is probably a universal fact of social life that in all groups and societies different positions receive differential rewards" (Eisenstadt, 1968:68). These rewards, as Davis and Moore observe, are such things as prestige, property, deference, and power.

Weber argued that the most important characteristic of rewards is that they can be used in two different ways. First, they may be consumed. For example, consumption of rewards occurs as people use income to purchase homes, food, and services. Rewards may also be consumed symbolically, as people engage in valued activities that reflect their positions in society. For example, the rich and well-born may send their children to exclusive prep schools from which others are excluded. Second, and more importantly, rewards can also be used as resources in order to obtain even greater rewards in the future. For example, in sufficient quantity, income can be used to purchase property, which can produce even greater income in the future. As Davis and Moore emphasize, the ability to obtain rewards and use them as a resource provides many people with an interest in and the capacity to maintain the *status quo* in society.

Although all societies seem to display inequality of rewards, it is unclear how much of this disparity is either necessary or beneficial to them (Tumin, 1967). Nonetheless, it is possible to rank the positions in a society according to the kind and level of rewards the people who fill them receive. This ranking can be done in terms of highly specific indicators, such as level of wealth or income, occupational prestige, or education. These are the main indicators used in the sociological literature today. Often the multiple dimensions upon which people are ranked will coalesce so that it becomes meaningful to speak of their oveall ranking and to identify the various social strata existing in a society (see Landecker, 1960). However, it is also the case that individuals or groups may have different rankings on several dimensions of stratification. This possibility was first raised by Weber, although it is now called status inconsistency. It will be dealt with in greater detail below.

The division of labor and inequality are also related because, as both Weber and Davis-Moore argue, the various positions that are divided among the members of a society are unequally evaluated. Some of the positions people occupy are seen as more worthy, more important, more popular, or more preferable than others (Tumin, 1967). Thus, in industrialized societies, the position of teacher is generally more highly regarded and more preferred than that of ditch digger. As Tumin also indicates, the scope of evaluation can vary greatly. Often it is role-specific and not generalized. Sometimes, however, it can refer to one's overall social standing. In the United States, one's occupation is the best single index of a person's social standing (Kahl and Davis, 1955; Gordon, 1963). But regardless of scope, the fact of differential evaluation implies standards, which are a result of common values. As both Dahrendorf and Parsons suggest, all societies are moral communities (at least to some degree). This means that the division of labor and its accompanying level of inequality—as indicated by unequal rewards and evaluations—are, to varying degrees, accepted by most members of the society. In most cases, people share common values. These common values provide the basis for receiving and interpreting rewards, and evaluating people's social standing.

The existence of differences in rewards and evaluations both imply that people have differing interests because of their unequal relationship to one another. However, Marx is wrong and Dahrendorf is silly in their respective extrapolations from this point. As Weber emphasized, most of the time people are not concerned with overthrowing the entire social order. Nor are they generally concerned with changing authority relationships. Rather, Weber argued, most people merely wish to enhance or protect their particular niche within a society. People's perceptions of their interests are influenced, but not determined, by their position in society, their experiences, and their values. In order to understand any ongoing system of social stratification, then, it is important to ascertain people's interests and their perceptions of their interests. From this point of view, it is clear that some degree of conflict characterizes all systems of stratification (and all forms of social organization). Furthermore, as Marx emphasized, the nature and level of class consciousness are important factors in any analysis of social stratification.

Restrictions on Access to Positions

The final, and most important, element intrinsic to stratification systems involves restrictions on people's access to positions. Marx, Weber, Dahrendorf, and Lenski all emphasize that people's rewards and evaluations produce interests, leading them to attempt to restrict the chance of others to obtain statuses similar to their own. Such restrictions are the key to establishing and maintaining a system of stratification, for there is no inherent reason why inequality must persist over time. One can acquire positions in a society in a variety of ways: through achievement, ascription, maturation, or the creation of new statuses (Tumin, 1967). For the moment, however, concern focuses on the first two.

Achievement refers to the attainment of a status after meeting some requirement that is more or less equally applied to all persons who attempt to obtain it. Such a requirement usually involves performance criteria, as when certain levels of education are expected of applicants for a particular job. An emphasis on achievement in status attainment is a characteristic of most modern societies.

Ascription is the process of assigning people to positions on a basis other than performance, such as according to their sex, race, or family background. Nearly all societies, including industrialized ones, display some level of ascription. Thus, even in societies such as the United States (where achieved social statuses are emphasized) people act to ensure that they, their descendants, and often even their neighbors have or acquire advantages over other members of the society. These efforts are not confined to upper strata people. For example, members of country clubs and labor unions alike have always engaged in exclusionary practices.

When such efforts at discrimination succeed, and they often do, a stratified society results. However, as with inequality, restrictions on people's access to positions usually are (and must be) justified in terms of prevailing values or norms. For example, it is seen as right and proper that parents provide their children with as many economic and educational advantages as possible. It is also seen as right and proper that a teacher or a physician be certified by attaining a certain kind and level of education. Yet such a situation is inevitably stratifying because the children of teachers and doctors are often better prepared, have more "appropriate" experiences, and have adequate monetary subsidies to ensure that they, too, will obtain professional occupations. Children of parents who have less prestigious occupations have more disadvantages and are, to some degree, restricted from attaining the more preferred positions. Occasionally, when the divisions in a society come to be seen as either too rigid or unfair (or both), massive social movements may appear, such as the civil rights or feminist movements, which attempt to force social change.

The argument in this section is summarized in Figure 1. As noted above, the starting point in this analysis of social stratification in societies is the division of labor. The manner in which tasks are divided is related to the extent of inequality in societies, as indicated by differences in rewards and evaluations. Regardless of its extent or the spheres in which it occurs, inequality usually must be justified in terms of dominant values. Finally, levels of inequality provide people with interests which they often try to protect in various ways. This effort leads to restrictions on others' access to positions. Usually, such restrictions also must be justified valuatively. The result is a stratified society.

Figure 1 The characteristics of stratification systems. Double-headed arrows show the relationships are reciprocal and not causal.

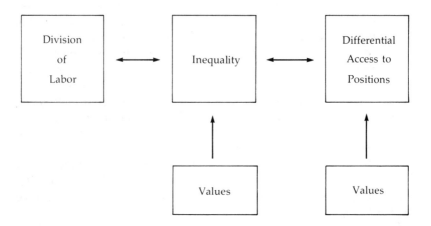

While it must be emphasized that the analysis here is speculative, thinking about social stratification in this way has important implications for the analysis of change. For example, it is entirely possible to alter the level of inequality (of wealth, say) without changing the extent to which positions are restricted at all. In such a situation, while the distance between the most and least wealthy might be altered, the ability of the rich to pass their economic rewards on to their descendants would be unimpaired. Or, alternatively, it is possible to change the extent to which positions are restricted without altering the level of inequality. Using the above example, enactment of stiff inheritance laws (which are quite lax in the United States) would decisively affect the ability of the rich to pass on their wealth to their descendants. This simple change, but one that is very hard to achieve, would decisively alter the system of stratification in this country.

SOCIAL STRATIFICATION IN AMERICA

In order to study the characteristics of a stratification system, it is necessary to have a preliminary conceptual model of society which shows its parts and how they fit together. Once again, such a model is designed to be a heuristic device, an analytical framework for studying reality. It is not a theory and cannot be tested. The model used in this book is best explained using a geometric analogy.

Imagine, for example, that American society was encapsulated within a block. Such a block has, of course, both vertical and horizontal dimensions. Observers can examine the block from either angle and gain important insights. By looking down on the top of the block, observers can examine the division of labor by grouping the various tasks that are usually performed in the society into conceptual units called social institutions. Social institutions are patterns of social interaction related to important goal-oriented activities in the society. They are a useful way of classifying and studying the interrelated economic, political, legal, religious, familial, and educational tasks that are usually performed in a society. In a sense, then, the top of the block (or the United States) can be conceived as being divided into six parts, one for each element of the division of labor.

Figure 2 displays such a six-sided block. From this angle of vision it is possible to examine the complex manner in which the "parts" of the block are interrelated. The analysis of social institutions is very common in sociology (see Turner, 1972; Smelser, 1973a:191–492) and can be pursued without reference to social stratification.

Observers can also, of course, examine the vertical dimension of such a block by looking at its sides. In the analysis of society, an examination from this angle of vision involves the study of social stratification. Like social institutions, the various levels of inequality,

Figure 2 Social institutions in American society

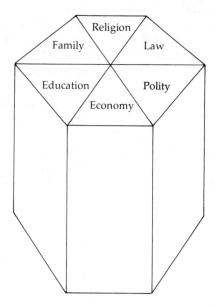

called either strata or classes, can be conceptualized and fitted together in a preliminary manner. In this way, the extent of inequality,
its correlates, and the amount of social mobility can be studied in
a systematic way. In studying the extent of inequality, most sociologists begin by examining the distribution of socioeconomic
status (SES). The concept of socioeconomic status is used in the
sociological literature as a proxy for such specific variables as income, occupation, education, or an index that combines them in
some fashion. These variables are the main indicators of the distribution of rewards and evaluations in the United States. As will be
noted in the following chapters, the correlates of inequality, or SES,
can be studied by examining the economic, political, legal, religious,
familial, and educational characteristics of people. Social mobility
can be studied by examining the overall rates of intra- and intergenerational mobility on the part of the population and various segments of it. Related to the issue of social mobility is the study of
status attainment; that is, how individuals come to occupy various
statuses, regardless of their mobility.

In this book, four social strata are examined: the rich, white-collar
people, blue-collar people, and the poor. While there is no generally
accepted way of identifying social strata in industrial countries
(Broom and Jones, 1977), these four strata are distinguishable hierarchical divisions in American society. The rich are set off from the
other three strata because they possess capital-producing property

in enormous quantity. Further, a clear distinction exists between blue- and white-collar people in American society, both in terms of occupational prestige and mobility rates (see Vanneman, 1977; Blau and Duncan, 1967). Finally, the poor are viewed with such opprobrium by the nonpoor that they can also be conceived as comprising a separate social stratum. The characteristics of each stratum will be elaborated in considerable detail in the chapters to come. It should be emphasized, however, that these strata are statistical constructs and are not to be used too rigidly. In practice, their boundaries are extremely permeable.

By analogy, it can be suggested that, just as the vertical and horizontal dimensions of a block are interrelated, so are social institutions and social strata. This interrelationship is diagrammed in Figure 3, which again displays a six-sided block. The use of this extended analogy is not an attempt to suggest that American society is block-like. Rather, by means of a three-dimensional image, it is possible to visually display how the parts of American society can be divided up so that social stratification can be studied in a relatively systematic manner. Thus, the top, or horizontal, portion of the figure again depicts the various social institutions that can be identified in a society, although it should be noted that not every society will display all these institutions. The side, or vertical, portion of the figure depicts the social strata that can be identified in the United States. It should also be noted that the number of strata can vary from one society to another. By looking at society in this way, it is possible to show the multidimensional nature of social stratification in the United States. In Figure 3, the four stratified layers are shown as cutting across the six social institutions, each of which constitutes a discreet ranking system. Although the real world does not display the neat divisions shown in Figure 3, these divisions suggest a preliminary analytical framework that can be useful for studying social stratification in the United States.

Chapters 7 through 14 of this book focus on the extent and dimensions of inequality in the United States. Figure 3 provides a systematic means of visualizing what must be studied. Chapter 7 introduces the empirical literature on social stratification by dealing with three issues: occupational prestige, class identification, and status inconsistency. These issues all focus on the relationship between objective and subjective aspects of social stratification. For example, while sociologists may assert that there are objective differences between blue- and white-collar workers, these people's subjective perceptions need not be the same.

Chapters 8 through 11 describe each social stratum, beginning with its economic situation and proceeding to its other social characteristics. In a sense, then, the analysis in each of these chapters sim-

Figure 3 Social institutions and social strata in American society

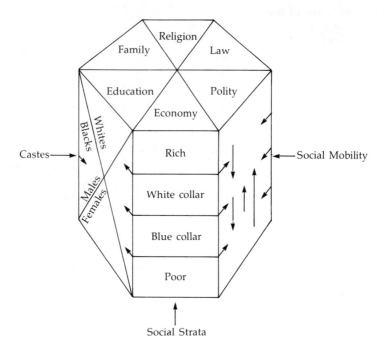

The labels in the figure: Religion, Family, Law, Education, Polity, Economy, Whites, Blacks, Males, Females, Castes, Rich, White collar, Blue collar, Poor, Social Mobility, Social Strata

ply revolves around the analogical block shown in Figure 3. The description always begins with a consideration of each stratum's economic characteristics because, in the United States as in most other industrial societies, people's occupations provide them with resources that decisively influence their other social characteristics.

However, the analysis of the four social strata does not exhaust the important elements of stratification in America. Chapters 12 and 13 describe two fundamental caste divisions in this country: race and sex. A caste can be defined as a relatively fixed hierarchical division in a society in which membership is hereditary and relatively permanent (Berreman, 1960). In terms of the block analogy being used here, imagine two criss-crossing lines demarcating the racial and sexual divisions in each institutional sphere. For illustrative purposes, these divisions are shown only in the educational sphere in Figure 3. In chapters 12 and 13, the analysis will once again start with the economic situation of each caste and proceed to its other social characteristics.

The final chapter of this book deals with how people get into and out of positions. This issue is analyzed in terms of the interrelated processes of status attainment and mobility. It is important to know both the factors influencing people's occupational attainment and their rates of mobility among various jobs. For illustrative purposes, the importance of these factors is shown by the vertical arrows in the political sphere in Figure 3.

NOTE

1. The phrase is Bernard Barber's (1968:289).

7
OCCUPATIONAL PRESTIGE, CLASS IDENTIFICATION, AND STATUS INCONSISTENCY

The most important characteristic of any modern stratification system is its extreme complexity. People view persistent patterns of inequality in different ways at different times, depending upon their experiences and the questions asked (Bott, 1972). The three issues discussed in this chapter are similar to one another in that they all focus upon the relationship between objective indicators of socioeconomic status and subjective perceptions or consequences of stratification in the United States. The first topic is the study of occupational prestige; it deals with people's evaluations of the rankings of various occupations. The second topic is class identification; it is an attempt to discover the extent to which people identify with a specific social class or stratum. It will be argued that these two issues imply quite different models of the stratification system. The third topic is status inconsistency; it focuses upon the extent and consequences of holding positions that are differentially evaluated.

OCCUPATIONAL PRESTIGE
Occupations provide the central focus for people's lives, both psychologically and materially. Along with such related factors as education and income, people's jobs provide relatively objective indicators of their socioeconomic status. However, a key problem involves how people subjectively perceive their social status, the relationship between subjective perceptions and various objective factors, and

the consequences of this relationship for people's attitudes and behavior. More generally, how do people conceive of themselves and their milieu, and to what extent are their actions influenced by these perceptions?

The study of occupational prestige is an attempt at dealing with these issues by assessing the social standing of the jobs people have in the United States. The hierarchy of occupational prestige is one of the most studied aspects of stratification systems. There have been at least one hundred attempts at identifying such a hierarchy, both in the United States and in many other societies.[1] Occupational prestige generally refers to those jobs people consider to be the most desirable. For example, in a classic study by the National Opinion Research Corporation (1947), the major research question was "What are the best jobs?" Similarly, in other typical studies, occupational prestige has been taken to mean such things as the "general social standing" of occupations, their "overall prestige," their "social status," the "honor or importance" accorded them, the extent to which they "are looked up to," and the like.

The most common research technique has been to assess the most desirable jobs by giving respondents a card or several cards and asking them to rate the occupations listed therein according to whether they are of excellent standing, good standing, average standing, somewhat below average standing, or poor standing in the society or community. The individual ratings for each job are averaged to obtain a prestige score, and all the occupations used in the study are then placed in rank order. These are the general procedures followed in the NORC study. It forms the benchmark against which all subsequent efforts have been compared.

The sociological literature reveals two major findings that are often described as being among the "great empirical invariants" in sociology (Marsh, 1971). The first finding is that hierarchies of occupational prestige are similar over time within the same society (Hodge et al., 1966a). This assertion appears to be especially true for the United States, but data do exist that point to the same temporal stability in other societies as well (see Hodge et al., 1966b). In the United States, the product-moment correlation between the 1947 NORC study of occupational prestige and the 1963 replication carried out by Hodge and his associates (1966a) is .99. This correlation means that the two sets of scores are very close to being identical. Neither the scores nor the rankings of the 90 occupations used in the two studies changed very much over a 20-year period.

The occupational prestige of a sample of the 90 jobs used in the two studies is shown in Table 1. It can be seen in the table that such occupations as U.S. Supreme Court Justice, physician, scientist, state governor, and college professor are among the highest rated (that is, they are seen as being among the most desirable) jobs in the

Table 1 Occupational Prestige in the United States, 1947 and 1963

Occupation	1947 Prestige Score	1947 Rank	1963 Prestige Score	1963 Rank
U.S. Supreme Court Justice	96	1	94	1
Physician	93	2.5	93	2
Scientist	89	8	92	3.5
State Governor	93	2.5	91	5.5
College Professor	89	8	90	8
Lawyer	86	18	89	11
Dentist	86	18	88	14
County Judge	87	13	88	14
Minister	87	13	87	17.5
Member of Corporate Board of Directors	86	18	87	17.5
Airline Pilot	83	24.5	86	21.5
Public School Instructor	79	34	82	27.5
Accountant for Large Business	81	29	81	29.5
Factory Owner	82	26.5	80	31.5
Artist	83	24.5	78	34.5
Novelist	80	31.5	78	34.5
Labor Union Official	75	40.5	77	37
Electrician	73	45	76	39
Trained Machinist	73	45	75	41.5
Farm Owner	76	39	74	44
Welfare Worker	73	45	74	44
Police Officer	67	55	72	47
Bookkeeper	68	51.5	70	49.5
Carpenter	65	58	68	53
Mail Carrier	66	57	66	57
Railroad Conductor	67	55	66	57
Plumber	63	59.5	65	59
Barber	59	66	63	62.5
Garage Mechanic	62	62	62	65.5
Truck Driver	54	71	59	67
Store Clerk	58	68	56	70
Restaurant Cook	54	71	55	72.5
Dockworker	47	81.5	50	77.5
Coal Miner	49	77.5	50	77.5
Janitor	44	85.5	48	83
Sharecropper	40	87	42	87
Garbage Collector	35	88	39	88
Street Sweeper	34	89	36	89
Shoe Shiner	33	90	34	90

Source: Adapted from R. W. Hodge, P. M. Siegel, and P. H. Rossi, "Occupational Prestige in the United States, 1925–63," in R. Bendix and S. M. Lipset (eds.), *Class, Status, and Power* (New York: Free Press, 1966), pp. 324–25.

United States. On the other hand, shoe shiner, garbage collector, sharecropper, and janitorial occupations are among the least desirable. It should be noted that, except at the extremes, neither Table 1 nor the full list of 90 occupations shown in the Hodge replication (1966b:324–25) displays a clear-cut distinction between blue and white-collar jobs.[2] The middle rankings in the table show a mixture of the two types of occupations, with some blue-collar jobs rating above some white-collar ones. For example, in both years, electrician and machinist occupations outranked welfare worker and book-keeper. The reason for this lack of a blue collar–white collar distinction will be shown in the section on class identification below.

Because all the studies conducted since 1925 show essentially the same findings, Hodge et al. (1966b:329) conclude that "there is evidence that the overall structure of prestige is invariant under quite drastic changes in [measurement] technique." Furthermore, they argue, "all segments of the population share essentially the same view of the prestige hierarchy and rate occupations in much the same way." Thus, there are few variations by region of the country, size of town in which the respondents reside, age, sex, or economic level. There are, however, slight variations in the ratings by educational level. Those respondents with lower levels of education tend to give a slightly greater proportion of excellent ratings. In addition, respondents who are evaluating occupations that are close to or resemble their own jobs tend to give those occupations somewhat higher rankings. This tendency, however, is cancelled out in the overall rankings.

The second major finding in the sociological literature on occupational prestige is that hierarchies of prestige are quite similar among different societies, regardless of their level of industrialization (Hodge et al., 1966b; Inkeles and Rossi, 1956). The average coefficient of determination between the 1963 study of occupational prestige in the U.S. and 24 other countries that have also been examined is .83 (Marsh, 1971). This correlation means that in those countries where occupational prestige hierarchies have been assessed, the scores and rankings of jobs are very similar to those shown in Table 1. Across societies, there appears to be substantial agreement as to which occupations are the most and least desirable. Those countries displaying similarities in occupational prestige hierarchies are listed in Table 2. As can be seen in the table, they are a mixture of Western and non-Western societies. All of these nations have been studied since World War II.

An important problem involves how these two findings are to be understood. This issue is important because, as Hodge and his associates observe (1966a:309), occupations are "the major roles through which rewards are distributed and power exercised" in a society. As such, occupational prestige is a key issue in the study of social stratification. Taking the two findings above at face value, the best predictors of occupational prestige appear to be the amount of education required to perform or engage in an occupation and the extent of responsibility exercised while performing it (Simpson and Simpson, 1960; Marsh, 1971). A good indicator of people's level of responsibility in a job is the number of subordinates they must

Table 2 Countries Displaying Similarities in Occupational Prestige Hierarchies

Australia	Netherlands
Brazil	New Zealand
Canada	Norway
Denmark	Philippines
Germany	Poland
Ghana	Sweden
Great Britain	Taiwan
Guam	Turkey
India	U.S.S.R.
Indonesia	United States
Japan	Zaire (Belgian Congo)
	Zambia (Northern Rhodesia)

Sources: For Taiwan data, see R. M. Marsh, "The Explanation of Occupational Prestige Hierarchies," *Social Forces* 50 (December 1971): 214–22. All other studies are compiled in R. W. Hodge, P. M. Siegel, and P. H. Rossi, "Occupational Prestige in the United States, 1925–63," in R. Bendix and S. M. Lipset (eds.), *Class, Status, and Power* (New York: Free Press, 1966), pp. 324–25.

supervise. Marsh concludes that "both education and number of subordinates exert a separate, significant, and strong influence upon [occupational] prestige."[3] Furthermore, he argues, the relationship among the two independent variables is compensatory in that when a person's education is high, then the number of subordinates becomes less important in determining prestige; but when the number subordinates is high, then education becomes less important. The reason education and responsibility influence occupational prestige is apparently that people reward, in a symbolic sense, those who have ability and strive for occupational success (Villemez, 1974). Those occupations that require both, as indicated by educational accomplishment and supervisory responsibility, are provided with occupational prestige.

This line of reasoning suggests, as Hodge et al. observe, that occupational prestige is based upon a fairly uniform set of subjective meanings or values. Occupational prestige can be seen as "a particular form of social advantage and power" granted and acknowledged by all segments of the population in the United States and in other nations as well. As such, the hierarchy of occupational prestige embodies patterns of superordination and subordination in a society (see Goldthorpe and Hope, 1972; Lauman, 1966). People defer to their supervisors, as indicated by their respective occupations. They accept as equals those with roughly similar jobs. Such persons comprise the eligible population whom one can entertain, court, marry, and engage in other forms of intimate social interaction (Lauman, 1966; Jackman and Jackman, 1973). Finally, people derogate their inferiors by making them acknowledge, in some way, their own inferiority and by avoiding intimate social relationships with them (Sennett and Cobb, 1973). These patterns of interaction occur because having prestige has important symbolic consequences. It is no accident that one of the first questions strangers ask each other is, "What do you do?" The answer provides an immediate, if stereotypic, guide to appropriate behavior. As a concluding note, the finding that there is a similarity in occupational prestige hierarchies over time within the same society is not very surprising. Most people live orderly lives and develop a set of relatively enduring attitudes toward themselves and others. For these reasons, social stability is much more characteristic of societies, including the United States, than change (Nisbet, 1969). The study of occupational prestige provides some evidence for this tendency.

Nonetheless, there are troubling questions that can be raised about both of the findings reported above. First, and less serious, it is often not clear what respondents are really saying when they judge occupations as being of high or low social standing (see Reiss, 1961). For example, in the original NORC study, it was concluded that people judged the desirability of occupations according to their own unique experiences, ambitions, and needs. Further, Gusfield and Schwartz (1963) argue that prestige scales may confuse several dimensions of occupational prestige because of the various (and unmeasured) points of view the respondents may take. That is, respondents may (1) provide their personal opinions as to which occupations are the most desirable, (2) act as natural sociologists and provide their assessment of how jobs are viewed by other members of the society, (3) assess those jobs that carry the most honor and respect in society, or (4) evaluate the distribution of prestige in terms of its justness or fairness. The suspicion that respondents use differing criteria in judging the social standing of occupations is strengthened by Villemez's (1974) finding that various segments of the American population differentially evaluate the ability and effort they perceive as intrinsic to occupations.

The second problem is far more serious and has to do with the finding of cross-societal similarities in occupational prestige hierarchies. There are significant sampling problems inherent in all these studies, as Hodge et al. (1966a) point out. These sampling problems involve both the characteristics of the respondents and the occupations compared. Sixteen of the 23 studies cited by Hodge and his associates use students, mostly university and high school, as the sample population. Five other studies are confined to urban or suburban residents of large cities. Only three studies (in the United States, Denmark, and the Netherlands) use some sort of nationwide sample. Armer (1968) has suggested that the high intersocietal correlations obtained in the study of occupational prestige may result from oversampling in those subpopulations of both industrialized and relatively nonindustrialized nations that are most heavily influenced by Western (especially American) values.[4] Villemez (1974) points out that "such oversampling would be equivalent to comparing findings in one country to findings in structurally similar regions" of other countries. At least one study provides some support for this criticism. In Czechoslovakia (which is not included in the countries listed in Table 2), the occupational prestige hierarchy appears to be different from that found in all other nations (Penn, 1975). Penn argues that such a finding should not be unexpected because the Czechs have generally accepted the values of socialism and, as a result, place much higher value on blue-collar work than is typical in nonsocialist societies. The problem of biased samples is compounded by the problem of assessing comparable occupations. The average number of comparisons between the United States and other countries in the studies cited by Hodge is 30 occupations, with a low of only 13 and a high of 75. Further, there are often real problems in formulating comparable job titles (Marsh, 1971). For these reasons, then, whether occupational prestige is a cross-societal invariant remains an open, and important, question.

CLASS IDENTIFICATION
The study of class identification is an attempt at assessing the extent to which people see themselves as belonging to various strata or classes. Unfortunately, while the literature on class identification is quite long, the findings are not nearly so uniform as those dealing with occupational prestige. In order to sort out this literature, five topics are dealt with in this section. First, there is an initial problem in that two terms, class identification and class consciousness, are often used interchangeably, even though they mean different things. Second, beginning with Centers's (1949) classic study, postwar trends in class identification are shown. Third, some of the attitudinal and behavioral consequences of class identification are indicated. Fourth, the extent of class identification among working women (an important omission in the literature) is briefly explored. Finally, the relationship between class identification and occupational prestige is noted. Each literature implies a different model of social stratification in America.

Class Identification and Class Consciousness
Sociological concern with class consciousness stems, of course, from Marx's work. It will be recalled that Marx was concerned with the general problem of the conditions under which exploited groups would rebel against their oppressors. His answer can be summarized under the general rubric of class consciousness (Portes, 1971). That is, when people come to recognize the structural source of their oppression, when they correctly identify the oppressing class, and when they act in the political arena to eradicate their oppression, then they can be said to be class conscious. This process involves the transition of an aggregate from a "class in itself" (a

Class in itself — Class for itself
Class conscious

mere statistical aggregate) to a "class for itself." In the United States, sociologists have generally not dealt with Marx's hypothesis. The reasons are partly ideological and partly because radical political behavior of the sort Marx was interested in is not an important element in American life. Instead, most studies focus upon a related topic, the extent of class identification in the United States. This phenomenon is usually measured by some variant of Centers's (1949:233) original question. "If you were to use one of these four names for your social class, which would you say you belonged in: the middle class, lower class, working class, or upper class?" Thus, the intent of this type of question is merely to assess the class or stratum with which people identify.

The relationship between class identification and consciousness can be seen by means of a simple model (Morris and Murphy, 1969): (1) People may perceive no status differences among themselves and, hence, have no subjective feelings of inequality. (2) People may perceive a continuous range of inequality and even be able to place themselves and others along that range, but they may not see discrete ranked categories. Studies of occupational prestige imply this level of consciousness. (3) People may perceive discrete social strata, or classes, and be able to place themselves and others in them. This is the level of class identification. (4) People may identify with and have commitment to stratum interests and ideology. This level marks the beginning of class consciousness, in Marx's sense. (5) People may act on behalf of their perceived interests and ideology in the economic and political arena. Such joint behavior may, but need not necessarily, involve radical or leftist political action. While this last criterion is clearly a turn away from Marx's concern, it can still be referred to as class consciousness. In this context, then, most sociological studies of class identification which use a variation of Centers's question are simply measures of the ability of people to place themselves into a set of categories (level 3, above). Sociologists have then gone on to assess some of the correlates of this ability.

The Extent of Class Identification Over Time

Table 3 shows trends in the subjective class identification of employed white males in the United States between 1945 and 1975. Three different questions were used to elicit class identification. The first is that by Centers, noted above. He examined employed white males, and nearly all subsequent studies have been made comparable to his data. The second, by the Survey Research Center, merely distinguishes between the working and middle classes, with no allusion to upper or lower classes.[5] In 1975, the National Opinion Research Corporation asked a variation of the Centers question which again identifies all four possible classes.[6]

The conclusions from Table 3 are fairly clear. Periodic studies indi-

Table 3 Class Identification in the United States, Employed White Males, 1945–75[a]

Class Identification	1945	1952	1956[b]	1960	1964	1968[b]	1975
Upper	3%	1%	—%	—%	—%	—%	3%*
Middle	43	35	39	33	43	45	49
Working	51	61	58	65	53	52	46
Lower	1	2	—	—	—	—	2
Rejects Classes	1	1	2	2	1	1	—
Don't Know	1	—	1	—	2	2	—
	100%	100%	100%	100%	100%	100%	100%

Sources: The year 1945 is from Richard Centers, *The Psychology of Social Classes* (Princeton, N.J.: Princeton University Press, 1949), p. 77. The years 1952–1968 are from Survey Research Center, University of Michigan, reprinted from E. M. Schreiber and G. T. Nygreen, "Subjective Social Class in America: 1945–68," *Social Forces* 48 (March 1970): 348–56; copyright © The University of North Carolina Press. The year 1975 is from National Opinion Research Corporation, "General Social Survey, 1975," unpublished data.

[a]All these data are for adults, over age 21. For the year 1975, patterns of class identification among employed women were as follows: upper, 3%; middle, 41%; working, 55%; lower, 1%.

[b]Combines respondents who identified themselves as upper middle class with middle, and upper working class with working.

cate that, at least among employed white males, most people have little difficulty in placing themselves into one of two classes: the middle or working. The proportion of men who reject the existence of these categories is always quite small. However, there is a fairly clear trend in regard to working-class identification. The proportion identifying themselves as working class appears to have risen until about 1960 and has been dropping fairly consistently ever since (see Schreiber and Nygreen, 1970).

Variations in class identification are generally seen as the result of socioeconomic status, especially one's occupation (Hodge and Treiman, 1968; Jackman and Jackman, 1973). However, the most recent findings by Vanneman and Pampel (1977) go even further.[7] They show clearly that class identification does not vary along a continuum of socioeconomic status. Rather, blue- and white-collar workers have quite different patterns of class identification. (1) White male blue-collar workers in those occupations with the lowest occupational prestige scores nearly all identify themselves as working-class people. (2) White male white-collar workers in jobs with the highest prestige scores nearly all identify themselves as being middle class. (3) Among whites, blue- and white-collar men whose jobs have overlapping prestige scores show much different patterns of class identification. That is, given identical levels of prestige, blue-collar males are substantially more likely to see themselves as being working class than white-collar males, and vice versa.

These findings remain after controlling for education and income. They imply the existence of discrete and identifiable strata in the

United States, not just as statistical constructs but as subjectively relevant categories in people's minds. Vanneman and Pampel (1977) conclude that "the effect of the manual–nonmanual dichotomy is equivalent to about 47 points on the [occupational] prestige scale." Furthermore, they argue, "working class and middle class labels reflect the content of the class division [in the United States], i.e., manual and nonmanual labor, and are not merely prestige judgments." Like most studies since Centers's, Vanneman and Pampel focus upon white males. These findings are not necessarily generalizable to other populations. Thus, Jackman and Jackman (1973) found that the class identification process is much different among blacks and whites. Race, in short, constitutes such an overriding cleavage in the United States that there are essentially two different subjective class hierarchies. Furthermore, blacks appear to be more class conscious than are whites (Legget, 1969).

The Consequences of Class Identification

Class identification has been related to political attitudes (or ideology), and voting behavior (Converse, 1958; Guest, 1974; Vanneman and Pampel, 1977). However, the findings are tentative ones. Those who identify themselves as working-class people tend more readily to agree that government intervention is necessary to solve social problems, such as guaranteeing employment opportunities and providing adequate medical care. However, these class-related differences diminish when other government programs, such as aid to education, are considered (Guest, 1974).

In general, whether political behavior is class related seems to depend upon the circumstances. Vanneman and Pampel (1977), for example, argue that while the 1964 and 1968 presidential elections were fought along class lines, the 1972 election was not—since no clear manual–nonmanual dichotomy in voting behavior can be found. Thus, at least in American society, it is not possible to argue that political behavior is strictly class oriented. Whether class lines form is a result of the issues being considered.

A Note on Class Identification Among Employed Women[*]

As shown above, the literature on class identification generally focuses upon men. Schreiber and Nygreen (1970), for example, use data for employed white males only, yet they generalize to the entire population. As is usual in the stratification literature, analyses of class identification assume that the family is the proper unit of analysis, that women (even if they are employed) obtain or "borrow" their objective status from their husband, and that there are no important differences between married men's and married women's subjective perceptions of their social status.

[*]This section was written in collaboration with Ellen Van Velsor.

The theoretical underpinning for these assumptions stems from the functionalist assertion that the family is the proper unit of analysis in stratification research (Parsons, 1954b; 1954c; 1954d; Barber, 1957). Parsons argues that the family is a unit of diffuse solidarity in which all members share essentially the same social status, that derived from the husband's occupation. Barth and Watson (1964) call this the postulate of equivalent evaluation. Parsons argues further that in American society wives are not expected to work. He claims that when women do work it is because of economic necessity and is clearly not the culturally preferred pattern. When it is not possible for wives to remain at home, Parsons argues that they do not "compete" for social status with their husbands. Thus, Parsons sees the marital couple as having an asymmetrical relationship to the occupational structure. That is, regardless of the woman's educational or occupational background and regardless of her employment status while married, the woman's social status is "conferred" by her husband.[8] This argument assumes that a married woman has no significant social characteristics other than her marital status.

However, whether employed wives "borrow" their status from their husbands is clearly a testable question. It need not be assumed. There have been three recent studies of class identification among women. Using 1972 NORC data, Felson and Knoke (1974) examined the process of class identification among four groups of people: working wives, nonworking wives, working husbands, and nonworking husbands. They found that both husbands and wives determine their subjective social status mainly in light of the husband's objective status (his job). Thus, for wives, even when employed, a "status-borrowing" model best fits their data. However, the Felson and Knoke finding may be affected by the inclusion of nonworking spouses in the sample. Using the Survey Research Center's election studies from 1960 to 1970, Ritter and Hargens (1975:938) compare only working husband and wives. They report quite different results. "A working wife's occupational status has roughly the same effect upon her class identification as does the occupational status of her husband." Thus, in this study, the objective statuses of both spouses influence the subjective status of working wives. Finally, using 1975 NORC data, Van Velsor and Beeghley (1977) also found that an employed woman uses both her own and her husband's socioeconomic characteristics as points of reference in determining her class identification.[9]

While the findings in these two studies are by no means definitive, they do suggest that the assumptions above ought to be modified. Most importantly in this context, sociologists should either use individuals as their unit of analysis or develop family indexes of socioeconomic status which take both spouses into account. More generally, the pervasive practice of using the attitudes and behavior of the "male head of household" as a proxy for family units ought to be reexamined. The conditions under which wives and husbands will display similarities and differences are not altogether clear and should not be assumed.

Class Identification and Occupational Prestige

The study of class identification also has broader conceptual implications, for it implies that respondents have a much different perception of the stratification system than that revealed by the study of occupational prestige. Indeed, an old controversy in sociology involves the question of whether American society can best be described in continuum or categorical terms.[10] Phrased differently, does the American system of inequality display a relatively continuous hierarchical order, with no sharp breaks in the distribution of income, power, prestige, or is it divided into discrete social strata within which people share common lifestyles?

Studies of occupational prestige, as well some studies of the perceptions of social status in small towns, have shown that Americans see a continuous hierarchy of inequality rather than distinct social strata (Warner, 1949; Lenski, 1952; Hodge et al., 1966b). It will be recalled, for example, that Table 1 does not reveal a clear split between blue- and white-collar occupational prestige. Such findings have led some sociologists to argue that a continuum model best describes social stratification in the United States.

However, Vanneman (1977) has recently shown that, in terms of patterns of interaction, there is a real class division in American society between blue- and white-collar workers. Evidence for this division can be clearly seen based upon residential homogeneity and mobility barriers. Further, to the extent that Americans perceive themselves and act in terms of membership in discrete and bounded social groups, such as strata or castes, then a model utilizing these categories could be interpreted as the best one for describing social stratification in the United States (Vanneman and Pampel, 1977). Of course, which model is used is dependent upon one's purpose. For it is evidently the case that people can distribute occupations (and other stratification phenomena) into an evaluatively ranked continuous hierarchy. And such distributions are stable over time. However, it is also the case that people can clearly and decisively identify themselves and others as belonging to specific social strata.

STATUS INCONSISTENCY

Like occupational prestige and class identification, the concept of status inconsistency refers to the relationship between objective indicators and subjective perceptions of social status. It is also one of the most intuitively compelling concepts in sociology, with a research tradition that is both long and highly controversial. Status inconsistency refers to the effects of occupying statuses that are unequally evaluated.[11] For example, a person might be highly educated but earn a relatively low income. Or a person might come from a subordinate (or "low") ethnic group but have high occupational prestige, such as a black physician.

The idea that inconsistent statuses might have important empirical consequences originates in Weber's work (Benoit-Smullyan, 1944). But Lenski's (1954) now classic article first explored the conceptual and empirical implications of status inconsistency. He proposed to examine a "nonvertical dimension" of social status that "would be capable of accounting for some of the variance in political behavior which is left unexplained by traditional methods of stratification analysis."

Research has subsequently focused upon the relation between status inconsistency and a wide variety of factors: political behavior, voluntary association membership, psychosomatic stress, suicide, and many more. The theoretical rationale underlying the literature on status inconsistency is as follows. Most people are expected to have consistent statuses; that is, their rankings on a variety of vertical dimensions—say, income, occupation, education, and ethnicity—are expected to be balanced. However, in any complex stratification system, some people will have inconsistent, or unbalanced, statuses—for example, a combination of high occupation, low ethnic background, high education, and low income. It is argued that for people having such discrepant statuses, rewards are highly variable, interaction is unpredictable, and great psychological stress results. Presumably, such persons will act to reduce their stress in ways that are different from those who occupy a balanced set of statuses.

Unfortunately, Lenski's expectation that the concept of status inconsistency would enhance sociologists' ability to explain human behavior has not been realized. Despite the intuitive plausibility of the "theory sketch" above, the literature on status inconsistency generally produces "findings which show no effects, ambiguous effects, or effects which are disappointingly small in magnitude" (Meyer and Hammond, 1971:92). These findings are briefly reviewed below.[12] Following that review, the major methodological and theoretical criticisms of the status inconsistency literature are noted. As will be shown, these criticisms are so serious as to put the usefulness of the entire research tradition into question.

Inconsistency among the various achieved statuses (education, occupation, and income) appears to have no effect on anything (Treiman, 1966). But inconsistency between achieved and ascribed statuses has been found to have moderate effects, depending upon the methods of measurement used. The ascribed status that is most often significant is race or ethnicity. Being black is equated with low ascribed status because blacks occupy a subordinate position in American society, while being white is equated with high ascribed status. There are no studies that use sex as an ascribed factor.

It has been found that low-ascribed and high-achieved social status is associated with a desire for political change (Lenski, 1954; 1967; Olsen and Tully, 1972; Segal, 1969). However, in these and other studies, desire for political change really means such innocuous things as "liberal attitudes" or voting for the Democratic party.[13] Further, Olsen and Tully (1972) show that while status inconsistency is related to liberal political activities, they emphasize that it explains only 1½ percent of the variance in such behavior. When the pattern of inconsistency is reversed, low levels of achievement and high ascribed status have been associated with psychological stress of various sorts (Jackson, 1962; Jackson and Burke, 1965; House and Harkins, 1975), with withdrawal from certain forms of social interaction, such as voluntary association membership (Geschwender, 1968), and with right-wing political activity (Eitzen, 1970).

However, in all these cases, and others not cited, the findings are of such low magnitude that their usefulness can be questioned. Further, there are many studies that have found that no form of status inconsistency affects political attitudes or behavior, again depending upon the methods of measurement (Kenkel, 1956; Kelly and Chambliss, 1966; Brandmeyer, 1965). In other areas, inconsistency has been shown to be unrelated to prejudice (Treiman, 1966) and religiosity (Demarath, 1965).

As noted above, the reason for these contradictory findings appears to lie in a variety of methodological and theoretical problems inherent in status inconsistency research. The major methodological problem has been exposed by Blalock in a series of publications.[14] Basically, it is extremely difficult methodologically to separate the effects of status inconsistency from the effects of the various independent variables making up the inconsistency scale. For example, Lenski (1954) found that being black and of high socioeconomic status (a low ascribed–high achieved pattern) is associated with a desire for political change. But an equally plausible interpretation of his results is that in Detroit (the location of the study) ethnicity is a more powerful predictor of political attitudes than is socioeconomic status (Treiman, 1966). In general, the amount of methodological manipulation necessary to find any inconsistency effect and the tenuous nature of the findings both suggest that the effort simply is not worth the result.[15]

This conclusion is reinforced by the fact that even when status inconsistency has been shown to have an effect on attitudes or behavior, the findings are based upon a number of quite dubious theoretical assumptions, among them the three following. First, most studies assume that a single common status system exists that people are aware of and find significant (Hope, 1975; Hartman, 1974). Stated differently, any attempt at comparing positions on disparate ranking systems implies that there is a single common status system that can be used as a reference point. Yet the existence of such an overall status system is doubtful. Rather, as shown in the analysis of occupational prestige and class identification, people use different ranking systems for different purposes in different contexts.

Second, in order to measure status inconsistency, comparable scales must be used (Hartman, 1974). That is, they must be of the same level of generality and importance to the respondents. Further, one scale should not be a subset of another. Yet the literature is filled with a weird variety of measures of status, both ascribed and achieved, such that comparisons among studies are quite difficult. It is simply not clear whether the many studies of status inconsistency are measuring the same thing, regardless of their results.

Third, assessment of the effects of status inconsistency assumes that holding different ranks on various scales is significant to people, thus causing them stress that must be reduced. But this assumption is virtually never tested (Box and Ford, 1969; Hartman, 1974). Like the methodological problems noted above, these unfortunate assumptions cast the findings in the literature on status inconsistency into considerable question.

These methodological and theoretical problems are so serious that it is doubtful whether research into this area is any longer useful. This unhappy conclusion is warranted because, after nearly a quarter century of research, both the theoretical and empirical payoff from the concept of status inconsistency remain dubious. Olsen and Tully (1972) argue that while they did confirm Lenski's original hypothesis "in a strictly technical sense," the proposition that status inconsistency affects political attitudes and behavior (or anything else) is "relatively worthless" because so small a proportion of the variance is explained. Political behavior is far better explained by more direct measures of such things as demographic factors (age, race, sex), experience or perception of power, economic security, or the nature of the political system. Olsen and Tully conclude that the concept of status inconsistency probably ought to be filed under the heading "valid but trivial information."

SUMMARY

The study of occupational prestige, class identification, and status inconsistency all show the extreme complexity of social stratification in the United States. The literature on occupational prestige reveals two major findings: (1) hierarchies of occupational prestige are similar over time in the same society, and (2) prestige hierarchies are similar among different societies regardless of their level of industrialization. This second finding may be a methodological artifact. The main reason for the stability of hierarchies of occupational prestige appears to be that people provide a symbolic reward to those individuals who hold jobs requiring both education and responsibility.

The literature on class identification shows that, among men, the proportion identifying themselves as working class rose steadily between World War II and 1960 and has been falling since that time. Nonetheless, among blue- and white-collar men there are quite different patterns of class identification. Not as much is known about patterns of class identification among women, but preliminary findings suggest that working women use both their own and their husbands socioeconomic characteristics in assessing their subjective social status. The study of occupational prestige and class identification reveals that people use different, and complementary, models of social stratification.

Finally, the literature on status inconsistency shows that differences in people's objective social statuses have few consequences for their attitudes or behaviors.

NOTES

1. See the citations under "occupational prestige" in Glenn et al. (1970) and Goldthorpe and Hope (1974).

2. Blue-collar jobs are those involving manual labor. White-collar jobs are those that do not involve manual labor. For a more extensive description and examples, see chapters 10 and 11.

3. In the United States, the level of income associated with an occupation is highly correlated with its occupational prestige (Hodge et al., 1966a). However, this finding does not appear to occur cross-societally (Marsh, 1971).

4. It should be noted that Armer failed to find support for his hypothesis. On the issue of sampling problems, see also Haller and Lewis (1966).

5. The Survey Research Center asked the following question: "There's quite a bit of talk these days about different social classes. Most people say they belong either to the middle class or to the working class. Do you ever think of yourself as being in one of these classes?" If yes: "Which one?" If no: "Well, if you had to make a choice, would you call yourself middle class or working class?" See Schreiber and Nygreen (1970:349).

6. In 1975, the National Opinion Research Corporation asked the following question: "If you were asked to use one of four names for your social class, which would you say you belonged in: the lower class, the working class, the middle class, the upper class?"

7. I thank Reeve Vanneman for sharing this manuscript with me prior to its publication.

8. In fairness, it should be noted that Parsons' current views are unknown. His analysis was probably appropriate on an impressionistic basis during the 1940s.

9. More precisely, Van Velsor and Beeghley (1977) found that neither the husbands' nor the wives' socioeconomic characteristics significantly affect her class identification *net of its counterpart*. However, each makes a statistically significant contribution to the variation in wives' class identification.

10. On this controversy, see the collection of readings in Roach et al. (1969:74–148).

11. The terms "status congruence" and "status crystallization" also have been used to refer to the effects of occupying statuses that are equally or unequally evaluated.

12. The citations below are not exhaustive of the voluminous literature on status inconsistency. For a more complete list, see Glenn et al. (1970) and Lebowitz (1974).

13. As an example of a less innocuous desire for political change, Portes (1972) found no relationship between status inconsistency and leftist radicalism in Chile.

14. See Blalock (1966; 1967a; 1967b) and Mitchell (1964).

15. Hope (1975) has recently argued that the concept of status inconsistency is neither confused nor worthless. Rather, the methods used "for testing it are not quite strong enough for their purpose." However, he has yet to show that application of new methodological techniques will produce significant results.

8
THE POOR

The poor are socially isolated and invisible to most Americans. There are at least five reasons for such ignorance (Harrington, 1971). First, the poor are concentrated in areas one never sees and sometimes consciously avoids. They are not shown on weekly television and cannot be observed from the highway. Indeed, it is possible to cross any city without seeing skid row, the black or brown ghetto, or the roominghouses of the poor, the aged, and the sick. It is possible to cross the continent without seeing rural poverty associated with Appalachia, the deep South, Indian reservations, or migrant-labor camps. One of the latent consequences of the interstate highway system has been to increase this possibility. In general, most people live, work, shop, and go to school without contact with the poor.

The second reason poor people are invisible is that clothes and other products of mass society make them difficult to identify. Harrington argues that America has the best dressed poor people in the world and he contends it is much easier to be decently clothed in the U.S. than decently housed, fed, or doctored. Third, many of the poor are unseen simply because of age. The old are often sick or infirm, without relatives, and without mobility. The young tend to stay exclusively in their own neighborhoods. As a result, both groups are invisible to the rest of America.

Fourth, the poor are politically impotent. Despite the mandate of "maximum feasible participation" during the "war on poverty," the poor do not generally influence legislative or administrative decisions because they do not participate in the political arena. Finally, a variety of conflicting attitudes toward American society and the poor serves to insulate most individuals from recognizing the fact that poverty exists. Some people believe there is little poverty in the United States and that Americans are becoming more equal all the time. Many also believe America is a land of equal opportunity and those who wish to achieve success only need to work hard. One result of these views is that when poor people are considered at all, it is largely in terms of pejorative stereotypes.

The purpose of this chapter is to make the poor more visible. The first section discusses the nature and extent of poverty in the United States. The second section identifies those aggregates of the population that are more likely than others to be poor. The third section contrasts some stereotypes of poverty and poor people, especially welfare recipients, with reality. The fourth section deals with the causes and consequences of poverty. The final section attempts to sum up the most important social characteristics of the poor.

THE NATURE AND EXTENT OF POVERTY

Definition of Poverty

Above all else, poverty refers to people's lack of money or other assets. It also signifies social and political exclusion from the American way of life. Income and occupation are two of the most important indicators of prestige in America. Income is important because it is a proxy for consumptive habits in general. Occupation is the major source of income and prestige for most individuals. However, poor people often do not work, work intermittently, or work in occupations that are economically and socially marginal.

The most practical way of analyzing poverty is to begin by seeing it in terms of income deficiency. There are three basic ways of doing this (Miller and Roby, 1970:21–51). The first is to define poverty in terms of the cost of living by establishing a budget based on a poverty threshold. The second defines as poor those people who earn less than some proportion (usually half) of the median income. The third definition refers to the share of total national income going to the bottom 10 or 20 percent of the population.

The Poverty Line

The official poverty line adopted by the United States government is that developed by Orshansky (1965; 1969) for the Social Security Administration. It is an admittedly subjective attempt at defining the poverty threshold in terms of the minimum income that could support families of various characteristics and circumstances. The poverty line "is based on the amount needed by families of different size and type to purchase a nutritionally adequate diet on the assumption that no more than a third of the family income is used for food" (Orshansky, 1969:38). The results can be seen in the official poverty levels for 1975. As shown in Table 1, the poverty line for a family of four in the United States in 1975 was $5,469. This is the single figure that is most often used to denote those who are poor. But taken alone it provides only a rough approximation of poverty (Williamson and Hyer, 1975).

Table 1 Official Poverty Levels, by Selected Characteristics, 1975

Size of Family Unit	Poverty Level
1 Person	$2,717
14–64 Years	2,791
65 Years and Over	2,572
2 Persons	3,485
Head, 14–64 Years	3,599
Head, 65 Years and Over	3,232
3 Persons	4,269
4 Persons	5,469
5 Persons	6,463
6 Persons	7,272
7 Persons or More	8,939

Residence and Sex of Head for a Four-Person Family	Poverty Level
Nonfarm Family	$5,500
Male Head	5,502
Female Head	5,473
Farm Family	4,695
Male Head	4,697
Female Head	4,616

Source: U.S. Bureau of the Census, "Money Income and Poverty Status of Families and Persons in the United States: 1975 and 1974 Revisions," *Current Population Reports*, Series P-60, no. 103, table 16.

As the table shows, the poverty line also varies by several other important social and demographic characteristics. The larger the family, the higher the poverty line, since it costs more to feed a large family than a small one. Similarly, because it costs less to live in a rural environment than an urban one, the poverty level is somewhat lower for rural families than urban ones. (Although not shown in the table, these figures are also calibrated by family size.) Age and martial status combine in complex ways. It costs less for an older single person to live than a younger one and for an older couple than a younger one, so the poverty line varies by age. Finally, female-headed families, both rural and urban, presumably need less to live on than male-headed families. The logic is apparently that a male-headed family of four includes a female adult. However, it is assumed that a female-headed family of the same size does not include a male adult.

In order to get an idea of the reality behind these figures, let us examine the poverty level for an urban family of four with a male head of household. As shown in Table 1, such a family at the poverty level earns $5,502 per year. Assuming the family spends a third of its income on food, it has $1.27 per person per day for the entire year for food.[1] In order to survive on this amount of money, a family would have to prepare all meals at home while buying only the most nutritious food at the cheapest possible prices. Such behavior, however, requires a degree of psychological strength and marketing sophistication that few persons in our society possess. It further assumes people have adequate time, transportation, and awareness of the need to shop wisely. Many poor people possess none of these attributes. Finally, the poverty budget for an urban, male-headed family of four leaves $306 per month for all expenses other than food, such as housing, utilities, clothing, and medical care. But, of course, it is often the case that the amount needed for these items exceeds $306, with the result that some necessities such as heat, light, or medicine are not acquired, or the rent is not paid.

It should be remembered that the figures being used in this example are for a family living at the poverty line. The average poor family's income is well below this level. So in order to see what the average poverty-stricken family actually has to live on, these figures would have to be lowered significantly. As is clear, the official poverty levels are set quite low, and neither the poor nor those who are near the poverty line live well in our society.

While any measure of poverty is subjective, when thresholds are set in the manner and at the levels indicated above, it can be safely asserted that everyone falling at or under them is indeed poor. The establishment of the official poverty lines at these levels is useful, then, partly because they are politically realistic and partly because they indicate the extent of poverty and the social characteristics of the poor.[2] Trends in the extent of poverty in the United States are presented in Table 2. Two aspects of the table are important. First, according to these official figures, the percentage of poor people fell rather steadily between 1959 and 1968, although part of the decrease was due to data manipualtion. However, since 1969, the percentage of poor people seems to have stabilized between 11 and 13 percent. Second, although the absolute number of poor people has generally declined, according to official figures there remain at least 25.9 million poverty-stricken persons in the United States. An excessive preoccupation with declining percentages often leads observers to forget that a population more than three times the size of New York City remains officially poor in our affluent society.

Table 2 Persons Below Poverty Level, 1959–75

Year	Number (in millions)	Percentage of Total Population
1959	39.4	22.4
1960	39.9	22.2
1964	36.1	19.0
1965	33.2	17.3
1966	28.5	14.7
1967	27.8	14.2
1968	25.4	12.8
1969	24.1	12.1
1970	25.4	12.6
1971	25.6	12.5
1972	24.5	11.9
1973	23.0	11.1
1974	23.4	11.2
1975	25.9	12.3

Source: U.S. Bureau of the Census, "Money Income and Poverty Status of Families and Persons in the United States: 1975 and 1974 Revisions," *Current Population Reports*, Series P-60, no. 103, table 17.

WEAKNESS OF CHART

Despite its utility, the poverty index has a number of serious shortcomings. First, the assumption that families spend a third of their income on food is based on information obtained in 1955 by the United States Department of Agriculture. Whether such an assumption is tenable nearly 25 years later is clearly doubtful (Miller, 1971a:120). If it were found, for example, that families now spend only 25 percent of their income on food, then the total food-based budget would have to be multiplied by four, with the result that poverty levels would be set considerably higher. Second, no allowance is made for regional variations in the cost of living, other than rural-urban. And the rural-urban ratio that is used (85 percent) is quite arbitrary. Third, the figures used in calculating the poverty line are based upon the "economy food budget" developed by the Department of Agriculture. This budget is explicitly designed for emergency use only and is not presumed capable of providing an adequate diet over the long run. It has been estimated that only one-tenth of those families who actually spend the allocated amounts for food do in fact have a nutritionally adequate diet (Orshansky, 1969:38).

However, the two most serious shortcomings of the poverty index are that it is a fixed standard that fails to take into account changes in the standard of living, and that "needs" are socially defined relative to what others enjoy (Miller, 1971a). A fixed standard assumes it makes no difference that the poor maintain the same level of living while that of the rest of society is rising. As Miller and Roby (1970:24) put it, "an income level that permits a family to survive is one thing; an income level that brings families closer to prevailing norms is quite another; and an income level that provides a stimulus for social mobility . . . is probably still another." But the political advantage of adopting a fixed standard is that it is possible to eliminate or at least drastically reduce poverty in statistical terms.

However, the reduction in poverty that has seemingly occurred since 1959 is a statistical, and political, charade. This fact can be seen in Table 3, which displays the way in which the poverty line has been manipulated in relationship to the median income. As can be seen in the table, in 1959 the median income for a four-person family was $6,070, while the poverty line was $2,973. Thus, the poverty line was 49 percent, or nearly half, of the median income. By 1970, the median income for a four-person family was $11,167, while the poverty line had risen only to $4,137, or 36 percent of the median income. By 1974, the last year for which this sort of data are available, the poverty line had fallen to 34 percent of the median income. In other words, the poverty line has been set further from the median income with each advancing year. By employing a fixed standard it is possible to make it appear as though the extent of poverty in the United States has decreased. But in reality it has not. This fact can be seen as soon as variable standards are used to measure poverty.

Table 3 Median Income and the Poverty Line[a]

Year	Median Income for Four-person Family	Poverty Line for Four-person Family	Poverty Line as a Percentage of Median Income
1959	$ 6,070	$2,973	49
1965	7,800	3,223	41
1970	11,167	3,968	36
1971	11,626	4,137	36
1972	12,808	4,275	33
1973	13,710	4,540	33
1974	14,747	5,038	34

Source: *The Measure of Poverty* (Washington, D.C.: U.S. Department of Health, Education, and Welfare, 1976), table 7, p. 72.

[a]The median incomes shown here are for four-person families. They are not overall median incomes for the years indicated.

Variable Standards in the Measurement of Poverty

The second way of measuring poverty has already been alluded to. By defining as poor all those who earn less than 50 percent of the median income it is clear that there has been very little reduction in poverty in America. If the data are calibrated in terms of a "typical" family of four, in 1974 about 20 percent of the population lived in families that earned less than half the median income. This percentage has remained virtually unchanged since 1965. In other words, despite the figures in Table 2 (above), there are about 41 million poor people in the United States (see U.S. Department of Health, Education, and Welfare, 1976:113–26).

The third way of defining poverty is also in relative rather than fixed terms. It involves examining the share of total income received by each fifth of the population. If poverty has really been reduced, as the official indicators suggest, then it seems reasonable to expect that some income redistribution has occurred. Table 4 shows that during the period between 1950 and 1975 very little income redistribution occurred in the United States. The percentage of total income money going to each fifth of the population has remained remarkably stable during this time. Among all families, the percentage of total money income going to the bottom fifth has been about 5 percent between 1950 and 1975. As a caveat, lest one think that all those at the higher levels are wealthy aristocrats, a family fell into the top fifth if it had an aggregate income of $22,037 in 1975. It fell into the top 5 percent of all families if it had an aggregate income of $34,144 in 1975. As Miller and Roby (1970:37) observe, the much touted "income revolution" of the 1950s has fizzled. Inequality has not given way to the beneficent forces of economic growth. In industrialized societies, there is no inherent relationship between economic growth and patterns of inequality, regardless of what official figures on the extent of poverty may lead one to believe.

Table 4 Percent of Aggregate Income Received by Each Fifth and Highest 5 Percent of Families and Individuals, by Year

	1950	1960	1970	1975
Families				
Lowest Fifth	5%	5%	5%	5%
Second Fifth	12	12	12	12
Middle Fifth	17	18	18	18
Fourth Fifth	24	24	24	24
Highest Fifth	43	41	41	41
	101%[a]	100%	100%	100%
Highest 5%	17%	16%	16%	15%
Unrelated Individuals				
Lowest Fifth	3%	2%	3%	4%
Second Fifth	7	7	8	9
Middle Fifth	13	14	14	15
Fourth Fifth	27	26	24	24
Highest Fifth	50	51	51	48
	100%	100%	100%	100%
Highest 5%	17%	20%	21%	19%

Source: U.S. Bureau of the Census, *Statistical Abstract of the United States, 1977* (Washington, D.C.: U.S. Government Printing Office, 1976), table 651.

[a]Does not add to 100% because of rounding.

Up to this point, concern has focused on the definition, measurement, and examination of the overall extent of poverty in the United States. The following section identifies those segments of the population that are more likely to be poor. Despite the limitations of the poverty-line approach, the most complete and readily accessible data often are available only in its terms. Thus, the analysis below occasionally is skewed toward those individuals who are really poor. This will not affect identification of aggregates and locations where poverty is more likely to occur. It does mean that official figures would be much lower than if a relative standard were adopted.

WHO ARE THE POOR AND WHERE DO THEY LIVE?

Regardless of which indicator is used, poverty is more likely to characterize the young and old, members of ethnic minorities, women, (especially when they are heads of households), and people who can be called social outsiders: the working poor, the illiterate and unemployable, and people with physical or psychological disabilities. Poverty is also more likely to occur in certain areas of the United States, especially in rural areas (such as Appalachia), and the South. It should be emphasized that none of these characteristics are absolute. That is, not all old people or blacks or female heads of households are poor, of course. Similarly, not all Southerners or rural residents are poverty stricken. It does mean that disproportionate numbers of people in these categories are poor. These findings are summarized in tables 5 and 6 and in the text below.

The data in Table 5 refer to families having incomes below the official poverty thresholds. The table does not include unrelated individuals. Since the data are official figures, they underestimate the proportions of people who are poor. The percentages in Table 5 refer only to families in each category. For example, among those families whose head is 14 to 24 years of age, 21 percent are poor. This figure, however, varies by race: among white families whose head is 14 to 24 years old, 17 percent are poor, while among similar black families, 46 percent are poor. As another example, among those families headed by a female, 33 percent are poor. This last figure varies by race in the same pattern as above.

Race

The most significant social divisions in American society are by race and sex. In 1975, 8 percent of the 49.8 million white families were officially poor, while 27 percent of the 5.6 million black families suffered this fate.[4] In absolute numbers there are, of course, many more poor whites than blacks. But a far greater proportion of blacks are poor than whites. As shown in Table 5, this finding is true for every important social characteristic, without exception. Regardless of the size of the family, the age, education, work experience, occu-

Table 5 Selected Characteristics of Families, by Poverty Status, 1975

	Percentage Below Low-Income Level		
	All Races	White	Black
Age of Head			
14–24 Years	21%	17%	46%
25–44 Years	10	8	28
45–64 Years	7	6	19
65+ Years	9	7	29
Size of Family			
2 Persons	8%	7%	23%
4 Persons	8	6	28
6 Persons	15	11	40
7+ Persons	26	19	44
Education of Head			
8 Years or Less	18%	15%	31%
High School or Less	9	7	26
College	3	3	7
Work Experience of Head			
Worked 50 Weeks or More	3%	3%	8%
Worked 1–49 Weeks	16	13	32
Did Not Work Last Year	25	20	56
Occupation of Longest Job Held by Head			
Professional and Managerial	2%	2%	7%
Clerical and Sales	5	4	12
Craft	4	4	9
Operatives (including transportation workers)	7	6	12
Service (including private household)	16	12	27
Nonfarm Laborers	11	10	14
Farmers and Farm Laborers	22	20	48
Sex of Family Head			
Male	6%	6%	14%
Female	33	26	50

Source: U.S. Bureau of the Census, "Money Income and Poverty Status of Families and Persons in the United States: 1975 and 1974 Revisions," *Current Population Reports,* Series P-60, no. 103, table 19.

pation, or sex of the head of the household, far greater proportions of black families than white families are poor. This has been true over time, as well. In 1970, 8 percent of all white families were officially poor, compared to 30 percent of all black families. Similarly, in 1966, 9 percent of all white families were poor compared to 36 percent of all black families. If unrelated individuals were included in these figures, the proportions would increase for both races, though the black increase would be greater (see footnote 4).

Some solace can be taken from the fact that the proportion of black poor has been decreasing at a greater rate than among whites, but it is not clear whether this tendency will continue in subsequent years. Cause for pessimism can be found in Friedlander's (1972) finding that job discrimination against minorities increased during the 1960s (see Chapter 12). As a final note, the disproportionate number of black poor also occurs if other indicators of poverty are used, except the gap is even wider. In 1975, 18 percent of all white and 41 percent of all black families earned less than $7,000, which is about half the median income. Clearly, the civil rights revolution has had little impact on the relative proportion of poor black people in America.

Sex

As shown in Table 5, families headed by women are far more likely to be officially poor than families headed by men. Although not shown in the table, this is also true regardless of the size of the family, ages of the various family members, education, work experience, occupation, or race of the head (see U.S. Civil Rights Commission, 1974). As above, in absolute numbers there are more poor families headed by males (3 million) than females (2.4 million). But a far greater proportion of female- than male-headed families are poor. This has been true over time, as well. In 1970, 7 percent of all male-headed families were officially poor, compared to 33 percent of all female-headed families. Similarly, in 1965, 11 percent of male and 38 percent of all female-headed families were poor. As above, if unrelated individuals are included in these data, the proportions increase for both sexes.[5] (For a more complete analysis of the position of women in American society, see Chapter 13.)

Age

One's stage in the life cycle is significantly related to poverty status, regardless of what measure is used. Families headed by a relatively youthful person (14 to 24 years old) are more likely to be officially poor than families headed by a person of any other age. This likelihood is far greater if the young family head is black, female, or both. Families headed by older people (65 years of more) are more likely to be poor than those headed by a person in the middle stages of the life cycle. However, casting the analysis in terms of families does not reveal the true incidence of poverty among aged people. Of the 3.3 million aged persons who are officially poor, 2.1 million are unrelated individuals living alone, and most of them (1.7 million) are women. Of all aged people, 15 percent were poor in 1975. Like other official data, the proportion of aged poor has appeared to drop steadily since 1959.[6] Yet 82 percent of all aged persons earned less than $7,000 in 1975.

Plainly, being old is not a pleasant time for many Americans. The relatively high incidence of poverty among older people results from lower proportions of them working and greater reliance on social security payments for their main source of income (Grad, 1973; Thompson, 1974). The aged would constitute a far greater proportion of the poor if many of them did not benefit from assets obtained at younger ages and from the support of other family members (Streib, 1976).

Outsiders

Lower levels of education and skill are significantly associated with poverty status and, as above, this relationship is true regardless of the measure of poverty used. As shown in Table 5, the poor comprise 18 percent of all those families in which the head has an eighth-grade education or less. More significantly, many families are officially poor despite the fact that the head worked full time during 1975. Among those employed in low-skill blue-collar occupations, most of whom were in the labor force full time, poverty levels range from 11 to 22 percent.[7] These percentages refer to 1.3 million families, or (as a crude estimate) 5.2 million people. Disregarding occupation, among those who worked full time in 1974, 3 percent were officially poor. Among those who worked part time (usually involuntarily, or as a result of seasonal employment), 16 percent were poor. Most of the poverty of the working poor can be accounted for by differing wage structures in various industries and regions rather than lack of effort or personal instability (Bluestone, 1974).

When variable measures of poverty are employed, the number of working poor increases dramatically. Among all households (families plus unrelated individuals), 29 percent earned less than $7,000 in 1975.[8] For the most part, these are people who are social and cultural outsiders (Harrington, 1971). Because they have physical or psychological disabilities, or because they lack education, job skills, interpersonal skills, and self-confidence, it is often difficult for them to locate job opportunities, obtain jobs, or keep them (Goodwin, 1972a). The President's Commission on Income Maintenance Programs (1969:701) has summarized the problems such persons face.

The effect of limited education is pervasive. For many of the undereducated, the most routine job-seeking activities may be difficult. People who are embarrassed by their inability to speak correctly, or to understand questions and the reasons behind them, or to fill out detailed forms quickly, or to grasp instructions, are particularly disadvantaged in securing a job. When a job opportunity is extended some of the undereducated do not take it because of their conviction that they cannot compete effectively.

Residence

Table 6 shows the residence location of persons (not families) who are poor according to governmental criteria. It can be seen that most people in America, including most of the poor, do not live on farms.

Table 6 Residence Location of Persons, by Poverty Status and Race, 1975

	Whites Below Poverty Level		
	Total Whites (millions)	Number (millions)	Percentage of Total
Nonfarm	175.6	16.7	10%
Farm	7.5	1.1	14
North and West	128.5	11.5	9%
South	54.7	6.2	11
Inside Metropolitan Areas	121.6	10.0	8%
Inside Central Cities	45.2	4.9	11
Outside Central Cities	76.4	5.1	7
Outside Metropolitan Areas	61.5	7.8	13

	Blacks Below Poverty Level		
	Total Blacks (millions)	Number (millions)	Percentage of Total
Nonfarm	23.6	7.3	31%
Farm	.4	.2	51
North and West	11.2	2.8	25%
South	12.9	4.7	37
Inside Metropolitan Areas	18.0	5.0	29%
Inside Central Cities	13.9	4.0	30
Outside Central Cities	4.1	.9	23
Outside Metropolitan Areas	6.1	2.6	42

Source: U.S. Bureau of the Census, "Money Income and Poverty Status of Families and Persons in the United States: 1975 and 1974 Revisions," *Current Population Reports*, Series P-60, no. 103, table 20.

This is true for both blacks and whites. But a greater proportion of rural than urban people are poor. In this regard, blacks are far worse off than whites. Similarly, a greater proportion of southern residents are poor than those who live in the North and West. Again, the situation is far worse for blacks than whites. It should be remembered that the South remains the least industrialized region of the country, although this situation appears to be changing. These findings parallel the one for metropolitan versus nonmetropolitan residents. People living in nonmetropolitan areas are more likely to be poor than are those who live within metropolitan areas. Again, this is true for both blacks and whites.

Finally, the proportion of poor people is greater within central cities than outside of them. However, despite stereotypes to the contrary, it is interesting to note that the vast majority of the residents of central cities are not poor (at least by official standards). This is true for both races. When variable measures of poverty are used, the relation between residential location and poverty remains. Among households, 29 percent of those who did not live on farms earned less than $7,000 in 1975. The comparable figure for those living on farms was 36 percent.

The rural poor are often those who have been left behind by social and technological change and by migration. Many of them lack the education and skills to compete in modern industrial life. Further, the population distribution in many rural areas reveals greater proportions of older people than is characteristic of urban environments. Finally, rural poor people are often tied into kinship and friendship networks that prevent them from taking advantage of opportunities that arise.

ATTITUDES TOWARD THE POOR AND THE CONSEQUENCES OF POVERTY

Perceptions and Reality of Poverty

As noted above, the poor are relatively invisible Americans. This invisibility occurs partly because the poor are socially isolated and partly because many of them work full or part time. As a result, despite the fact that they often have inadequate resources on which to live, their misery and deprivation go publicly unnoticed. When poor people or families go on welfare, however, then everyone has opinions about them. While these opinions are usually both inaccurate and pejorative, they serve to set the poor apart as a unique social stratum.[9] In this section, five pervasive beliefs about welfare recipients are contrasted with the reality of poverty and welfare status in America. In this way, some of the consequences of poverty can be identified.

(1) "There are too many people receiving welfare money who should be working." In one nationwide sample, 84 percent of the respondents agreed with this generalization (Feagin, 1975). But this belief contrasts sharply with the facts. First, most of those who receive welfare money cannot really be expected to work. The U.S. Department of Health, Education, and Welfare (HEW) has found (1972) that welfare recipients are disabled (11.7 percent), aged (14.9 percent), mothers (16.7 percent), or children (55.8 percent). Only 0.9 percent of all recipients are able-bodied unemployed males.[10] Yet most Americans greatly overestimate the percentage of able-bodied males receiving welfare (Williamson, 1974a). The public levels strong criticism at mothers and families who are receiving Aid to Families with Dependent Children, called simply AFDC (Williamson, 1974b). Yet most children (68 percent) are on the rolls less than three years (U.S. Department of HEW, 1972).

Second, it is generally the case that some member of most welfare families is in the labor force. This is true before, during, and after they receive AFDC or other forms of welfare support (Schiller, 1973).

But being in the labor force often does little good for three reasons (Schiller, 1973). (a) These people lack vocational skills or education. (b) There are not enough jobs for all the unemployed, even if they qualify. And (c) those jobs that are available generally do not pay enough or last long enough to alleviate their poverty, regardless of the criteria used.

Such problems are compounded by the fact that government vocational and educational programs generally do not provide participants with marketable skills (Wellman, 1974). As a result, studies show that male graduates of one work-incentive program (called, somewhat incongruously, WIN) earn slightly less than $2.50 per hour, while female graduates earn about $2.00 per hour. This adds up to less than $5,200 per year for males, which will not get most families out of poverty. In addition, most of the jobs WIN graduates obtain last less than one year (Schiller, 1973). Clearly, the vast majority of those people who receive welfare either cannot work or do work but with little success.

(2) "Most people on welfare who can work do not try to find jobs so they can support themselves." This is the work-incentive issue, and most Americans (54 percent in Feagin's study) believe that the poor are lazy, shiftless, and do not try to find jobs. In addition, the spurious assumption that welfare recipients need some type of extra incentive to work underlies both public debate and political action directed toward welfare "reform." But the idea that the poor will not work or that they have no aspirations does not square with the facts.

First, in terms of actual work behavior, studies show that poor people work even when there is little chance that their jobs will provide economic security. They work even though welfare programs often provide both more income and security (see Schiller, 1973, for a review of this extensive literature). Second, in terms of attitudes and aspirations, all the evidence suggests that the poor, the near-poor, and welfare recipients not only desire to work, but want to get out of poverty and be occupationally and economically successful (see Davidson and Gaitz, 1974; Van Til, 1974; Kaplan and Tausky, 1972; Goodwin, 1972b). As Goodwin (1972a) concludes, despite the fact that middle-class people "draw sharp distinctions between themselves and the welfare poor," the two groups display little difference in work attitudes. This finding is clearly supported by poor people's response to realistic job or income opportunities (see Wellman, 1974; Schiller, 1973; Wright, 1975). In her study of the New Jersey negative income tax experiment, Wright (1975:561) found that work activity increased for most participants. She concludes that:

. . . the labor force participation of the poor has been shown, here as elsewhere, to be determined by factors over which they generally have little *or no control: occupational and racial discrimination, inadequate training, poor health, restrictive and regressive welfare programs which penalize recipients for work, and so on. In the context of such external inhibitions, the particular attitudinal traits of the poor seem largely inconsequential.*

Despite beliefs to the contrary, welfare recipients do work and want to work.

(3) "Many people getting welfare money are not honest about their need." In Feagin's study, nearly three-quarters of the respondents agreed with this statement. Strong feelings against "welfare cheaters" are pervasive in the United States (Williamson, 1974a; Alston and Dean, 1972). But such beliefs are factually wrong. Fraud is established in less than 0.4 percent of all welfare cases (U.S. Department of HEW, 1972). Only about 5.6 percent of all families receiving welfare are ineligible. Only 14.6 percent of all families received overpayments of varying amounts, while 9.7 percent received underpayments. The Department of Health, Education, and Welfare has found that most of these errors are made by state and local welfare agencies. It does not appear that welfare recipients are any more dishonest than the rest of the population.

(4) "Many women getting welfare money are having illegitimate babies to increase the amount of money they get." Fully 61 percent of Feagin's respondents agreed with this assertion, which has been described as the "brood sow myth." The argument is that the existence and level of welfare payments causes illegitimate childbearing. Placek and Hendershot (1974) suggest that the public, policy makers, and even some social work professionals all accept this argument. Yet it is not true.

As Feagin (1975:109) notes, most illegitimate children do not receive public assistance and most children on welfare are legitimate. While illegitimacy rates are higher among poor people than among other segments of the population, there is no relationship between these rates and welfare status (Cutright, 1973; Placek and Hendershot, 1974, Presser and Salsberg, 1975). Furthermore, these same studies show that participation in AFDC programs is related to greater access to family planning information and greater use of various forms of contraception. Illegitimacy rates are related to ignorance and the nonavailability of birth-control methods, not welfare status.

Apart from beliefs about illegitimacy, Americans also believe that poor families have large numbers of children. Williamson (1974a) asked his Boston sample, "How many children are there in the average AFDC family?" The average response was 4.8 children. In reality, HEW statistics show that the average AFDC family has only 2.6 children, and 54 percent have two or less. Further, while 44 percent of Williamson's respondents believed that the AFDC birth rate is increasing, in reality it has been decreasing steadily since 1967. Finally, the typical AFDC increase for each additional child is $35 per month, a figure that does not cover the expenses incurred by having more children, and many states have ceilings on the number of children for which a mother may receive money. It seems clear that welfare recipients' "family building decisions (or nondecisions), like those of other Americans, rich and poor, are influenced by a complex of motives, not simply cost benefit considerations" (Placek and Hendershot, 1974:669).

(5) "A lot of people are moving to this state from other states just to get welfare money here." In Feagin's study, 41 percent of the respondents agreed with this assertion. The public believes that differences in welfare payment levels motivates people to migrate to large cities (Long, 1974). But this belief has little basis in fact, especially when directed toward blacks.

While states with higher median income levels tend to have higher welfare support levels, it is not clear whether people move for one or the other. Most people say they moved because of jobs (Tilly, 1973), and the evidence seems to bear out many such assertions. Using 1970 census data, Long (1974) compared poverty and welfare status among migrants and nonmigrants in six large northern cities. Among black family heads, those born in other states were less likely to be on welfare or below the official poverty line than nonmigrants. The same pattern occurred when southern-born black family heads were compared to nonmigrants. For whites, the situation is somewhat different. That is, among white family heads, there were no differences in welfare status between those born in other states and nonmigrants. But white family heads born in other states were more likely to be officially poor than nonmigrants. Similarly, southern-born white heads of families were more likely to be both poor and on welfare than were nonmigrants.

Long concludes that, in terms of poverty or welfare status, being born in one of the six cities is a far greater handicap than is southern birth for blacks. For whites, the situation is partially reversed. While the reasons behind these findings remain unclear (see Van Til, 1974; Long, 1974:54–55), it can be safely argued that welfare rates do not cause migration, and Americans' beliefs to the contrary are incorrect.

The Consequences of Poverty

Despite the inaccurate nature of Americans' stereotypes about welfare recipients, such opinions have social consequences which ensure that the poor comprise a distinct social stratum. Two of those consequences are examined here. First, by blaming poverty on poor people, it is possible for other Americans to use them as a negative point of reference in order to justify dominant values relating to work and the importance of occupational achievement.[11] Americans generally believe that success or failure in this world is the result of personal characteristics and motives. Accordingly, when asked, "Why are there poor people in this country?" most respondents place responsibility on the poor themselves. They attribute failure to such personal qualities as laziness, lack of desire to work, dishonesty, loose morals, and the like (Feagin, 1975; Huber and Form, 1973; Williamson, 1974b; Goodwin, 1972b).

Thus, to be poor in America is to be stigmatized. As Williamson (1974b:213) puts it, "those who are stigmatized have attributes, either alleged or real, that detract from their character and reputation, making it difficult for others to relate to them in a normal way." The stigma associated with poverty is one reason why public opinion is especially aroused against welfare recipients. Following Simmel's lead, Coser (1965) has argued that a person is socially defined as poor by seeking and obtaining public assistance.[12] In an important sense, then, poverty is not only lack of occupation or income; it is also a public status of dependency. In a society that stresses the importance of individual achievement and hard work, being dependent upon public aid is stigmatizing. The degradation of welfare recipients is one reason why many poor persons do not try to obtain the benefits to which they are entitled (Piven and Cloward, 1971:165–75).

Second, blaming poverty on poor people makes it easier to justify the economic and political exploitation of the poor and also tends to isolate them as a unique social stratum. Such exploitation benefits the majority of Americans in a variety of ways, although most people do not recognize this fact. Many see that welfare rates have risen dramatically in recent years and conclude that the poor are unjustifiably living on the dole. Data presented above clearly show such a conclusion to be unwarranted. Nonetheless, it is true that total public expenditures for welfare programs doubled between 1965 and 1970, and doubled again by 1975.[13]

Most people fail to see that this money represents (1) a means of politically coopting the poor and (2) positive economic control over them. Piven and Cloward (1971) have shown that welfare policies function to regulate and exploit the poor. During periods of public disorder, which are often accompanied by mass unemployment, welfare programs are initiated and expanded so as to absorb and control labor and restore public order. This happened during the Great Depression and again during the urban explosions of the 1960s. On the other hand, during periods of relative political stability, low-wage work is enforced by restricting welfare rolls and forcing people out into the labor market.[14]

Such exploitation occurs because most Americans benefit from the existence of poverty. As Gans (1972) points out, "the positive functions of poverty" are numerous. There are millions of temporary, menial, dangerous, and dirty jobs that must be performed in any industrial society. The existence of poverty ensures that there are people who can and will perform such tasks. Further, because these jobs often pay very low wages, the poor, in effect, subsidize both consumption and investment activities for the majority of Americans. Furthermore, because the poor pay a far greater proportion of their income in taxes (because of regressive taxes, as on sales), they disproportionately subsidize governmental activities.

It is not often recognized that the existence of poverty also creates jobs for many middle-class people who "serve" the poor, from penologists and police officers to ministers, social workers, wine and liquor dealers, and pawn-shop operators. (To this list one must also add social scientists who "study" the poor.) Thus, many occupations have a stake in the existence (and defenselessness) of poor people. Who would social workers "help" if there were no poverty?

Further, the poor subsidize the economy (creating jobs and profit in the process) by purchasing goods and services that others, the more affluent, do not want. For example, they buy day-old food, second-hand clothes, and deteriorating merchandise. They patronize badly trained or incompetent professionals—doctors and lawyers—who are shunned by the affluent. Finally, the poor are made to absorb the economic and political costs of change and growth in American society because they are powerless. In conclusion, then, while poverty is stigmatizing for those who endure it, its existence is both economically and politically advantageous to large segments of the more affluent American public.

THE CHARACTERISTICS OF THE POOR: A BRIEF OVERVIEW

The previous section described poor people as belonging to a social stratum that is perceived by most Americans, including the poor themselves (Horan and Austin, 1974), as stigmatized and distinct from other strata. And, in fact, the poor are different from others, at least to some degree. But the important questions involve how much different and in what areas. Accordingly, this section is a brief review of the most important characteristics of poor people in America.

Three qualifications are necessary, however. First, while most of the propositions below can be taken as empirical generalizations (that is, there exists some empirical support for them), they are nearly always based on samples that have limitations of various sorts (Blum and Rossi, 1969). Second, the propositions offered below are not exhaustive. They are merely designed to highlight some of the characteristics of the poor. Third, it is often the case that the definition and measurement of poverty, the "near-poor," and other classes or strata vary radically from study to study. This means that their findings are not as comparable to each other as one might wish (Williamson and Hyer, 1975). So although it is certainly possible to make some generalizations about the characteristics of the poor, it must be remembered that many of them are tentative. This is true of most social scientific knowledge.

Culture and Poverty

Any attempt at summarizing the characteristics of poor people must begin with the relationship between cultural values and poverty status. This is a controversial topic that has important implications for public policy. There are two main views about this relationship. The first sees poverty as resulting from the possession and transmission of values that are inappropriate for occupational achievement in America. The second point of view reverses the causal arrow by arguing that the possession of traits or values that prevent achievement are the result of the poverty experience.

The first argument is called the "culture of poverty" thesis. It has been elaborated mainly by Oscar Lewis (1969), although others such as Banfield (1975) have also tried to support it. Lewis argues that the poor comprise a distinct subculture in American society, which he labels the culture of poverty. This culture, or subculture, has two major components (see the summary by Della Fave, 1974).

First, it is hypothesized that, like other subcultures, the poor have a different "way of life" based on values that originally developed as a reaction to their impoverished environment. Sometimes it is suggested that these values are formed in opposition to those held by most Americans, and at other times it is merely asserted that they are different. In either case, the culture of poverty presumably represents an effort on the part of poor persons to cope with feelings of marginality and hopelessness by the development of a set of alternative values and a lifestyle that reflects those values. For example proponents of the culture of poverty thesis argue that the poor do not desire to be upwardly mobile, lack work commitment, and are present-time oriented (and therefore cannot plan for the future or delay gratification). In addition, they also assert that the poor value consensual unions (rather than marriage), and that they approve of sexual promiscuity and violence. Indeed, much space has been devoted to the presumed sexuality and physical expressiveness of the poor (see Lewis, 1965).

The second, and even more important, aspect of the culture of poverty thesis is that, once such a culture has arisen, it becomes an ongoing "way of life that is passed down from generation to generation along family lines" (Lewis, 1969). In other words, Lewis argues that a poor family is likely to have children who will also be poor when they become adults because they have internalized the culture of poverty. According to this thesis, then, those people who are poor (and this applies especially to the very poor) constitute a different and self-perpertuating subculture in American society.

The idea that there is a culture of poverty has important implications for public policy. For example, to take only one characteristic, it is possible that the poor are, in fact, more present-time oriented and do have more trouble planning for the future than other Americans (O'Rand and Ellis, 1974). The culture of poverty thesis implies that possession of such characteristics causes people to be poor. The importance of this relationship is that if being present-time oriented is seen as causing poverty, then public policies designed to provide opportunities, incentives, or skills to poor persons will probably not do very much good. This is because those poor people who participate in the culture of poverty are presumed to have values that preclude their taking advantage of such situations. It is then possible, as Banfield (1975) has done, to justify the elimination of many programs designed to help the poor.   CRiteisns oF Hypo

The culture of poverty thesis has been widely criticized. First, studies of the values held by the poor indicate that they are similar to those held by other Americans (Goodwin, 1972a; Valentine, 1968). In addition, studies of poor people in terms of the specific values Lewis attributes to them show little support for this aspect of the culture of poverty thesis (Coward et al., 1974). Second, as Willie (1969) concludes, although there is some intergenerational transmission of poverty, there is not nearly so much as is generally assumed. Rather, data show that intergenerational upward mobility is by far the most common experience among the children of poor parents. The same people are not poor from one year to the next, or one decade to the next. Willie believes that when poverty is passed from one generation to another it is the result of a peculiar combination of familial and personal circumstances along with structural factors, such as patterns of unemployment and racial discrimination.[15]

The second hypothesis about the relationship between poverty and cultural values is the "situational interpretation" of poverty, and it has been elaborated by Valentine (1968), Liebow (1967), and several others. The situational interpretation stems from a recognition that no matter how it is defined or measured, poverty is a social condition that embodies human suffering, both material and psychological. Above all else, the personal experience of poverty involves the constant exposure to one's own powerlessness and failure. From this point of view, then, it would be surprising indeed if poor people did not become in some ways different from others. In a now classic study, Liebow (1967:222) argues that neither the street-corner men with whom he dealt nor the poor in general are carriers of an independent cultural tradition. He suggests that the poor person's "behavior appears not so much as a way of realizing the distinctive goals and values of his own subculture, or of conforming to its models, but rather as his way of trying to achieve many of the goals and values of the larger society, of failing to do this, and of concealing his failure from others and from himself as best he can." So the situational interpretation argues that many of the differences in values or behavior manifested by poor people result from their experience of being poor.

Summary

This point of view also has important policy implications. If it is true, then public policies designed to alleviate poverty may be useful in helping many people escape from it. Returning to the example used above, a poor person's present-time orientation may be a realistic reaction to one's own powerlessness and failure. In order to value planning for the future, a person not only needs access to resources during the present, but also the assurance of continued steady access in the future. The person trying to feed a family on $1.27 per day has neither.[16] There are very few areas in which poor people can realistically believe they have control over their own lives. Rather, most believe that their lives are determined by external forces over which they have no control (Gurin and Gurin, 1970). Thus, it can be argued that becoming present-time oriented is merely the result of being poor.

Criticisms of Hyp.

While the situational interpretation of the relationship between poverty and culture is intuitively attractive, it is probably too exaggerated and needs to be modified. That is, although it is reasonable to assert that many of the characteristics and values held by poor people are a result of their poverty, it is also reasonable to suggest that some poor persons will not abandon them easily. All people tend to use their past experience as a prism through which their present situation and future possibilities can be filtered and understood. So the situational interpretation of poverty must be modified by taking the socializing effect of people's own experiences into account.

Rodman (1963:209; 1974) has attempted to do this by arguing that the basic values of American society are common to all social strata, including the poor. As noted above, there is some evidence to support this position. At the same time, however, he asserts that poor people develop "a wider range of values" so "they need not be continually frustrated by their failure." Rodman calls this process the "lower-class value stretch." As a result, he argues, poor people often "come to tolerate and eventually to evaluate favorably certain deviations from middle-class values." Given their economic situation, perhaps the poor have no other choice.

This point of view suggests that the poor become, in effect, bicultural. As a result, they move awkwardly between two contradictory worlds. Once this dilemma is recognized, it becomes plausible to assert that poor people, like everyone else, develop emotional ties and commitments to their family and friends, to their place of residence, to the pattern of their lives. For these reasons, it is reasonable to expect that poor persons will strive for success as much as (or more than) most people. But is also likely that even when they achieve some economic success and stability, such persons will often continue to display patterns of behavior and values characteristic of poor people in general. Furthermore, it is also reasonable to expect that, when presented with legitimate opportunity, some individuals will not be able to take advantage of it. These are precisely the findings in one study of job creation for the so-called "hard-core unemployed." While no single study can be considered definitive, Padfield and Williams (1973) show clearly the social, legal, and familial complications that result when chronically unemployed persons try (as they must) to commute between two worlds. Yet, because they strived harder for occupational success than many middle-class people, most of the men in this study "made it."

The argument presented here has important implications for both public policy and sociological research. In policy terms, programs that provide realistic opportunity for poor persons will probably be useful to many of them. However, it is not reasonable to expect all poor people to react alike or to succeed. Further, it is not reasonable to expect that "they" will become just like "us" after achieving some occupational success. Sociologically, the process by which people learn to cope with their marginality, failure, and powerlessness is not altogether clear. Similarly, the process by which people who have learned to cope without work or with intermittent work become integrated into the mainstream is much more complex than most sociologists have realized.[17] There is much work yet to be done in this area.

Economic and Occupational Status[18]

The economic and occupational status of poor people has already been described in this chapter. In brief, the poor tend to be those who occupy marginal economic and occupational positions. They are generally the least skilled persons in our society, whether measured in terms of literacy, educational attainment, or actual job proficiency. As a result, when they are employed, poor persons are likely to work at domestic-service or menial-service jobs, as unskilled labor, or at farm labor. These are not occupations that generally produce economic security or comfort. Nor are they jobs that carry a great deal of prestige in our society. As a result, the lives of poor people are often characterized by intermittent employment, long periods of unemployment, and the periodic necessity of relying on public assistance for income (Blum and Rossi, 1969:351).

Political Participation

The role of the poor in the political process can be summed up with a single proposition: the lower the socioeconomic status, the lower the rate of political participation.[19] Measures of political participation found to have this relationship to socioeconomic status are awareness of national issues, identification of leaders or candidates, membership in political parties, membership in interest groups that might stimulate or direct political activity and voting behavior (Verba and Nie, 1972). This finding is stable over time and true in other countries as well. The data indicate that "rising levels of socioeconomic status—in particular increased education, but also higher income and higher status occupations—are accompanied by increased civic orientations such as interest and involvement in politics, sense of efficacy, and norms that one ought to participate. This leads to participation" (Verba, Nie, and Kim, 1971:55).

This finding can be illustrated by examining voter participation in the 1972 presidential election. Of those persons with an elementary school education, only 47 percent voted. This compares with fully 61 percent of the high school educated, and 79 percent of the college educated who voted. Looking at employment status, only 50 percent of the unemployed voted, compared to 66 percent of the employed. By occupation, 49 percent of all laborers voted in the 1972 election. This compares with 61 percent of all crafts workers (the most skilled blue-collar workers) and 76 percent of all white-collar workers.[20] Because the poor do not participate in the political process by voting or in other ways, their needs are neither represented nor taken into account in the formation of public policy.

There are at least three possible reasons why the poor participate in the political process at such low rates. First, a variety of bureaucratic procedures must be followed in order to participate, and the poor are often ignorant of them. For example, in order to vote, one must register by finding the office and completing some forms. Even given awareness of the need to register, this process remains difficult for those who lack transportation or education. Second, participation often requires social and verbal skills that the poor do not possess. Such skills are necessary in order to lobby representatives and to organize interest groups. Third, and perhaps most important, participation in the political process implies a sense of personal efficacy; that is, the feeling that people have control over their own lives and over what others do to them or for them. Poor people tend to lack this sense of personal control over what happens to them.

Religious Affiliation and Belief

The relationship between socioeconomic status and religious affiliation is much more complex than traditional analyses have suggested
(Stark, 1972).[21] The idea that religion provides a spiritual or psychological haven for the poor is too simple. Perhaps surprisingly,
Stark's findings (1972:500) clearly show that "in the population at
large religious involvement is positively related to social class no
matter what kind of commitment is specified." In particular, for
white non-Southerners, Stark says "the economically deprived are
those for whom religious options are least likely to be relevant."
Stark's data show that organized religion is dominated by middle-
and upper-strata persons. For example, in his study, fully 70 percent
of the church members were white-collar workers. The poor generally do not participate in organized religion. This finding is true
"even in the fundamental sects, traditionally thought to be special
havens for the poor, [where] the vast majority are comfortably middle class" (Stark, 1972:487).

However, when only church members are considered, rather than
the entire population, then it can be seen that the poor have a different kind of religious commitment than do the nonpoor. In the case
of those white non-Southern poor who are church members, Stark
(1972:495) finds that the "religion as haven" interpretation fits his
data. Among such church members, he says, "the poor show
greater religiousness in those aspects of faith which can serve as
mechanisms for relieving their suffering: the comforts of a promised
redress in the hereafter when the last shall be first and the moral
support through religious experience, the catharsis of prayer, and
the comforts of human relations." Stark concludes that "although
the church may be relatively unable to enlist the poor, it seems able
to provide traditional transvaluational and emotional comforts for
those poor it does enlist."

The Legal System and the Poor

Crime is best understood as a violation of law (Turner, 1972a). On
this basis, criminal behavior is pervasive in the United States. There
are so many laws, covering such a wide range of activity, that it is
hard not to violate them. This supposition is lent some credence by a
nationwide study done for the President's Commission on Law Enforcement and the Administration of Justice (1967:v). In that study,
fully 91 percent of all adults "admitted that they had committed acts
for which they might have received jail or prison sentences." Regardless of socioeconomic status, all adults commit crimes. There is
no evidence that disproportionate amounts of criminal behavior
occur at one status level or another (Hirschi, 1972). However, individuals at various socioeconomic levels commit different kinds of

crimes and are differentially labeled as criminal by law-enforcement agencies.

Here the concern is with those crimes committed by poor people and their relationship to the criminal-justice system. The first issue can be summarized by the following proposition: the lower the socioeconomic status, the greater the arrest rate for crime against property and violent crimes. Despite the fact that these are not the most serious crimes, either economically or politically (Clark, 1970), these two sorts of illegal behavior are the focus of the criminal-justice system. This paradox exists because the public perceives violent crimes and crimes against property as being both the most serious and the most threatening. No one wants to be mugged. As a result, both law-enforcement agencies and the courts are almost exclusively oriented toward those crimes committed by poor people. This orientation produces official crime rates that make it appear that only poor people are criminals. Chambliss (1969:86) has summarized the relationship between the poor and the criminal-justice system in graphic terms.

The lower-class person is (1) more likely to be scrutinized and therefore be observed in any violation of the law, (2) more likely to be arrested if discovered under suspicious circumstances, (3) more likely to spend the time between arrest and trial in jail, (4) more likely to come to trial, (5) more likely to be found guilty, (6) if found guilty, more likely to receive harsh punishment than his middle- or upper-class counterpart.

The consequences of this orientation are clearly revealed when the characteristics of prisoners are examined. In a study of the nation's nearly 4,000 local jails, the Law Enforcement Assistance Administration (1972) found that most inmates are young, male, and poor and that they are disproportionately black. Fully 59 percent were less than 30 years of age, and 95 percent were male. At the same time, 55 percent of all prisoners in local jails earned less than $3,000 in the year prior to their arrest. (This figure is one-third the median income for that year.) Finally, 42 percent of all jail prisoners were black, despite the fact that blacks made up only 11 percent of the total population.

Most crimes are economically motivated—"their main purpose is to obtain money or property" (Clark, 1970:38). This is as true of crimes committed by poor people as it is of crimes by corporations, white-collar workers, or racketeers. The difference, as Clark puts it, is that the nonpoor have "an easier, less offensive, less visible way of doing wrong." As a result, they are often neither treated nor labeled as criminals. On the other hand, when the poor engage in criminal activity, they often must threaten or commit violent acts in order to obtain their goals (Gordon, 1971). This argument has important implications. If one's goal is to eliminate or reduce the incidence of certain kinds of crime, for example "crime in the streets," then specific policies are clearly appropriate. As the President's Crime Commission (1967:15) concludes, "the most significant action that can be taken against [such] crime is action designed to eliminate slums and ghettos, to improve education, to provide jobs, to make sure every American is given the opportunities that will enable him to assume his responsibilities." All other options simply reinforce the status quo.

Poverty and Family Life
Rainwater (1974) has recently summarized the relationship between poverty and family life. The discussion of these two factors can be conveniently divided into two general areas: mating behavior and family relations. PovERly + FAMiLY LiFE

Mating behavior will be considered first. The lower the socioeconomic status, the younger the age of marriage, although, as Rainwater observes, the differences are not as great as they were two generations ago. Further, the lower the socioeconomic status, the more often marraiges are forced by pregnancy (Coombs et al., 1970).[22] Finally, the lower the socioeconomic status, the higher the rate of illegitimate children. As noted above, although illegitimacy rates are relatively low for all social strata, they are higher among poor people. These mating patterns have important social consequences. Poor families often begin at younger ages than families among other strata, and the parents, or sometimes a single mother, often have not acquired the training and skills necessary to attain economic security. The presence of children frequently ensures that these young adults will never acquire such training or skills.

As to family relations, within the marriage, the lower the socioeconomic status, the greater the number of children and the more rapidly they arrive. Although family size differences by socioeconomic status, are declining, it is still the case that poorer families are often larger ones. It is clear, however, that large families are not desired by the poor (Presser and Salsberg, 1975). Thus, as Ryder and Westoff (1971) have argued, the main barrier to family planning among the poor is lack of available information and contraceptive devices. This has important policy implications in terms of the relationship between family size and poverty status. For example, in 1974, a family composed of two adults and five children which had an income of $6,000 fell well below the official poverty line. If that same family had only two children, it would be above the poverty line and, at least officially, not poor. Fewer children means everyone can live better, and poor people are quite aware of this. Cutright (1971a:171–72) has calculated that if poor people had only the number of children they desired, then the official rate of poverty would be cut in half.

As suggested above, poor people tend to have more children and at a faster rate than do the nonpoor. At the same time, however, the lower the socioeconomic status, the higher the rate of marital instability, as evidenced by separation, desertion, or divorce rates (Cutright, 1971b). Being poor often means greater tension between mates and greater dissatisfaction in the marriage. This is partly because poor people often have or desire to have a fairly traditional and rigid division of labor within the family (Rainwater, 1974). Put simply, this means men provide income and status while women keep house and raise children. Such poor families are often caught in a vicious circle: wives complain that their husbands do not provide enough, while husbands complain that their wives do not "make do" enough. Such marriages are not happy.

One final generalization about family relations must be mentioned. The lower the socioeconomic status, the greater the emphasis on strictness and obedience in child rearing (Rainwater, 1974). Poor parents generally focus on their children's overt behavior: what was done rather than why it was done. They believe that children must learn to obey rules, laws, and the like. And they generally do not (often because they are unable to) explain why children must follow rules (see Kerckhoff, 1972). As Rainwater notes, a strategy oriented toward using power to control a child can only work in a communal environment. It is vitiated as soon as the child enters school, where peers begin to influence behavior (Kerckhoff, 1972). Further, such strategies are associated with the development of negative self-concepts.

Poverty and Education

As was shown in Table 5, the lower the level of education, the greater the rate of poverty. Indeed, the now voluminous studies on the process of status attainment show that education is one of the crucial factors influencing adult occupational status (see Chapter 14). Education is related to being in the labor force, unemployment rates, occupational status, and lifetime earnings. The reason for these relationships is that schools are credentialing agencies. By using achievement and intelligence tests, tracking (or "ability" grouping), and awarding degrees, schools effectively sort and allocate people into the adult world (Beeghley and Butler, 1974). Many of those individuals who, for a variety of reasons, cannot or do not perform in school end up being poor. This process is perpetuated in part because, as Berg (1970) argues, academic credentials are often important only for getting jobs, not doing or keeping them.

SUMMARY AND CONCLUSION

This chapter has described the social position of poor people in America. Above all else, the poor are those individuals who lack money and other assets, and as a result they are excluded from the American way of life. The most common indicator of those who are poor is the poverty line adopted by the Social Security Administration (see Table 1). This line is set so low that there is little doubt that those persons who fall below it are indeed poor. However, the official poverty level has been manipulated in such a way that a steadily decreasing number of people have been classified as poor (see tables 2, 3, and 4). By using other indicators, it can be shown that the incidence of poverty probably has not declined much in recent years. Regardless of the definition that is used, it is clear that some segments of the population are disproportionately poor: the young and old, ethnic minorites, women, persons who lack skills (see Table 5). Poverty is also more likely to occur in rural areas and in the South (see Table 6). Although, as noted above, the fact that poverty occurs for disproportionate numbers of certain types of people or among those who live in certain areas, it does not mean that all (or even a majority) of such persons are poor.

Those Americans who are not poor have very uncharitable attitudes toward those who are. These attitudes are directed primarily at welfare recipients, who serve as an ideological proxy for poor people in general. As was shown above, none of the stereotypes held by the nonpoor are correct. Yet most Americans believe that poverty is the fault of poor people, and poor persons are socially stigmatized, economically exploited, and politically impotent as a result. That such factors may have a hand in keeping people poor is not often recognized. In valuative terms, the poor appear to be much like most other Americans. At the same time, poor people clearly adapt their desires and goals to the reality of their situation. That situation can best be characterized as a high degree of economic, political, religious, legal, and educational exclusion from American society. What is particularly sad is that, despite the rhetoric of the recent past, very little has changed. Neither the real percentage nor the characteristics of the poor has changed since 1959. As will be shown throughout this book, the American system of stratification is relatively stable over time.

NOTES

1. The calculations are as follows: $5,502 ÷ 12 = $458.50 per month. $458.50 ÷ 3 = $152.83 for food per month, leaving $305.67 for housing, clothes, utilities, and all other expenses. $152.83 ÷ 4 equals $38.21 for food for each person per month. And $38.21 ÷ 30 = $1.27 for food for each person per day.

2. It is not often recognized that Orshansky (1969) and her associates in the Social Security Administration developed two measures of poverty. The Office of Economic

Opportunity and the Council of Economic Advisers adopted the lower of the two measures as the poverty line for political reasons.

3. The logic behind this statement is as follows: If a poor family spends $100 per month on food and that is one-third of its income, then the poverty level would be $300. But if the family spends $100 per month on food and that is one-fourth of its income, then the poverty level would be $400.

4. The data here and in Table 5 refer to families. If unrelated individuals were included, the proportion of poor people in both races would go up, although the increase would be greater for blacks than whites. In 1975, 10 percent of all whites were poor (including unrelated individuals), while the figure for blacks was 31 percent. Nearly a third of all black people are officially poor. Among unrelated individuals only, 23 percent of whites and 41 percent of blacks were poor. Source: U.S. Bureau of the Census (1976b:table 673).

5. The source for the temporal data in this paragraph is the U.S. Bureau of the Census (1976a).

6. The source for these data is the U.S. Bureau of the Census (1976a:table 17).

7. A person is in the labor force when employed full time or part time, or unemployed but actively looking for a job.

8. The source for this figure is the U.S. Bureau of the Census (1976a:table 14).

9. Literature on attitudes toward the welfare poor is becoming quite extensive. See Lauer (1971), Kallen and Miller (1971), Goodwin (1972b), Ogren (1973), Williamson (1974a), and Feagin (1975). All except Ogren report highly pejorative stereotypes of the poor. I am using Feagin's study as an organizing rubric because his data are the best (a nationwide random sample).

10. These data are for individuals, not families. They do not include local relief programs.

11. See Williams (1970:438–504) for an analysis of the importance of these values in American society.

12. Coser's essay is addressed "to the memory of Georg Simmel" and enumerates a number of ideas subsequently translated in Simmel, *On Individuality and Social Forms* (1971).

13. See Skolnik and Dales (1975). They report that during the fiscal year 1965, the total social welfare expenditure by federal, state, and local governments was $77.2 million. The figure for fiscal 1970 was $145.8 million, and for 1975, it was about $286.5 million.

14. Piven and Cloward's book, *Regulating the Poor: The Forms and Functions of Public Welfare,* has generally been well received by social scientists. Obviously, however, not everyone agrees with them. For an example, see Muraskin (1975).

15. Willie (1970) argues persuasively that institutional arrangements are a far more important explanation of intergenerational transmission of poverty among blacks than whites. That is a nice way of referring to institutionalized racism. For a more thorough analysis, see below, Chapter 12.

16. The $1.27 per day is the amount available to a male-headed urban family of four living at the poverty line in 1975 (see footnote 1).

17. This is Herbert Gans's point in his foreword to Padfield and Williams (1973).

18. The single best review of the literature on poverty and the relationship between socioeconomic status and other variables remains Blum and Rossi (1969). Following their lead, I am going to phrase propositions that use "socioeconomic status" as the independent variable. Here the term is a shorthand way of asserting that as income and occupational status become lower, certain consequences are likely to follow.

19. For a qualifying note, see Greeley (1974). He argues that both religion and ethnicity are associated with political participation independently of socioeconomic status, although he does not deny the importance of SES.

20. These data are from the U.S. Bureau of the Census (1973:tables 7, 8, and 9).

21. As will be apparent, this paragraph is indebted to Stark's (1972) excellent summary of the relation between socioeconomic status and religion. Regional and ethnic variations are omitted from the analysis. Thus, the remarks in the text apply only to white non-Southerners. Inclusion of such data would clearly alter, and complicate, the findings.

22. The data on premarital pregnancy and socioeconomic status are contradictory. But Rainwater (1974:11), who relies on Coombs's (1970) findings, argues that while premarital pregnancies occur at all levels, they appear to force marriage among the poor. At higher SES levels, pregnancy often brings the engagement to a close.

9
BLUE-COLLAR
WORKERS

Descriptions of blue-collar people are dominated by two alternative theses. The first is called, somewhat awkwardly, the "embourgeoisement" thesis.[1] It focuses upon the economic characteristics of blue-collar people and attempts to generalize from them. The embourgeoisement thesis begins with the premise that there has been a long-term increase in the incomes of blue-collar people and extrapolates the following hypothesis: the greater the income equality between blue- and white-collar people, the more the social characteristics of blue collarites will resemble those of white collarites. The hypothesis argues, in short, that working-class people do not display distinctive political, religious, legal, familial, or educational attributes when their income allows them to emulate the middle class. From this point of view, a separate analysis of blue-collar people is unnecessary since most Americans, excluding the very poor and the rich, are affluent and have middle-class lifestyles. As an aside, it should be noted that many academicians see the embourgeoisement of the working class as "good" because they have a distrust for blue-collar "hard hats."

This popularized "hard-hat" image reflects the second main description of blue-collar people, the working-class authoritarianism thesis. This thesis begins from the premise that blue-collar people have unique social experiences: they are economically insecure, poorly educated, and raised in authoritarian families. As a result, it is argued that blue-collar people are a reactionary political force in the United States, intolerant of others' civil liberties, racist, antistudent, and antiintellectual.

As is obvious, these two points of view cannot both be correct. Accordingly, this chapter is a description of working-class, or blue-collar, people, largely in terms of the two theses. The chapter has three sections. The first is a brief description of the jobs blue-collar people hold. The second section is a more lengthy description of the social characteristics of blue-collar people, beginning with their numbers and economic situation, and continuing with their political, religious, legal, familial, and educational characteristics. This portion of the chapter evaluates the relative usefulness of the embourgeoisement and authoritarianism interpretations. The final section of the chapter is an examination of blue-collar alienation. This last issue is pervasive in the sociological literature, and no discussion of the working class would be complete without briefly dealing with it.

BLUE-COLLAR OCCUPATIONS

Blue-collar people are those who engage in manual rather than nonmanual occupations. They work with their hands rather than behind a desk. Some typical blue-collar occupations are listed in Table 1. As can be seen in the table, apart from the fact that their jobs require physical labor, blue-collar people have quite diverse occupational characteristics.

Table 1 Some Typical Blue-Collar Occupations

Craft Workers (skilled)	Operators (semiskilled)	Laborers (unskilled)	Service Workers
Bakers	Assemblers	Car Washers	Barbers
Bulldozer	Bus Drivers	Construction	Bartenders
Operators	Dressmakers	Laborers	Dental
Carpenters	Garage Workers	Gardeners	Assistants
Electricians	Machine	Longshore	Hairdressers
Mechanics	Operators	Workers	Janitors
Opticians	Meat Cutters	Stockhandlers	Nurse Aides
Printers	Sailors		Police Officers
Shoe	Taxi Drivers		Ushers
Repairers			
Tailors			

The diversity among the various blue-collar jobs can be captured in a number of ways. First, the amount and difficulty of physical effort varies. As Levison (1975) points out, some manual jobs are relatively dull without being arduous. Some involve heavy and dirty work but are not boring. And some involve assembly-line work that can be both arduous and boring. Second, job characteristics vary by industry. For example, some industries are automated. Automation may mean relatively interesting, highly responsible, and physically light work, as in the oil and chemical industries. Alternatively, however, automation may mean boring, meaningless, and quite arduous work, as in the auto industry. Similar variations in the nature of blue-collar work occur in the less automated industries.[2]

3) Third, with the exception of service workers, blue-collar occupations can be grouped according to skill level. This is the way the U.S. Bureau of the Census classifies occupations, and Table 1 follows its mode of organization. Craft workers are the most highly skilled blue-collar people. They constitute about one-quarter of the working-class labor force. Skilled blue-collar workers are likely to belong to craft unions (the AFL) and to have served relatively long apprentice periods learning their trades. The most salient aspect of craft occupations is that the worker defines the tasks to be done and determines solutions to them, most of the time without a great deal of direct supervision.

Operatives are often called semiskilled workers. This is because their work is more easily learned than that of the craft worker. For example, one must drive a prescribed bus route or assemble a small portion of an automobile. Operatives constitute nearly one-third of the blue-collar work force. They are more likely to belong to industrial unions (the CIO). The most important characteristic of semiskilled work is that the tasks performed are defined for those who do them by someone else. It is often the case that little independent judgment by the worker is required or allowed.

Laborers, as the name implies, are relatively unskilled workers. They constitute about 10 percent of the blue-collar work force. The most significant characteristic of unskilled work is that the tasks involved are relatively simple, although often requiring great strength and endurance.

Service workers are not classified as blue-collar workers by the Bureau of the Census. Rather, the bureau makes them into a separate occupational category. But as can be seen in Table 1, the occupations in this category clearly involve manual labor. They also involve direct and personal service to people. But, at the same time, they represent a wide range of skill and responsibility. Compare, for example, the respective tasks of police officers and ushers. Service workers make up more than one-quarter of all blue-collar workers. They are increasingly becoming unionized, mostly in industrial unions.

Finally, while not identified in Table 1, it should be recognized that farmers and farm laborers also work with their hands. Thus, they have been included in the analyses below. Farmers and farm laborers each make up about 3 percent of the blue-collar labor force.[3]

In summary, these are some of the typical occupations engaged in by blue-collar workers. They are a diverse group. But working-class jobs have one characteristic in common: they involve manual labor. As will be seen below, the people who perform them have a variety of economic and other social characteristics in common.

THE CHARACTERISTICS OF BLUE-COLLAR PEOPLE
The first issue to be dealt with is the number of blue collar people in the United States. It is often said that most Americans today are white collar and that blue-collar workers are a statistical minority (H. M. Miller, 1971). For example, Galbraith (1967:276) argues that "by 1965 there were nearly eight million more white than blue collar workers, 44.5 as compared to 36.7 million. During those years the number of professional and technical workers, the category most characteristic of the [white collar] techno-structure, approximately doubled." But Galbraith and others who describe America as dominated by white-collar workers are incorrect.

This misconception as to the number of blue-collar workers is the result of two facts. First, the census bureau does not classify farm laborers, farmers, service workers, or laborers (nonfarm) as blue-collar occupations (see H. M. Miller, 1971). When these occupations are left out, it is easy to show that white-collar workers outnumber craft workers and operatives. Second, the existence of a majority of either blue- or white-collar workers depends on whether both sexes are included in the analysis.[4] Table 2 displays the occupational distribution by sex for all workers (see also Chapter 13). When only males are considered, then blue-collar workers are clearly the majority. When only females are considered, then this situation is reversed. However, when both sexes are included in the analysis, blue-collar workers came to about half of the labor force in 1975.

Economic Characteristics of Blue-Collar Workers
A key element of the embourgeoisement thesis is the assertion that the incomes of working-class people now match that of the middle class. Popular stereotypes abound of the plumber, the teamster, and even the garbage collector as members of a new affluent working class. Unfortunately, for most blue-collar families, reality is much different. Table 3 shows median incomes by occupation for each sex and for families. Families are classified by the head of household's occupation (some of whom are women).

The table reveals that only one blue-collar occupation, craft workers, has a median income higher than any white-collar occupation. This is true for both males and families. Craft workers comprise only 26 percent of the male blue-collar labor force. Thus, the vast majority of working-class men and families earn considerably less than their middle-class counterparts and cannot be considered affluent in these

Table 2 Occupational Distribution, by Sex, 1975

Occupation	Both Sexes	Males[a]	Females[a]
White Collar			
Professionals	15%	14%	15%
Managers	10	13	5
Sales	6	6	7
Clerical	18	6	35
	49%	38%	62%
Blue Collar			
Crafts	13%	21%	2%
Operatives	16	18	13
Laborers	5	8	1
Service	14	9	22
Farm Workers	3	5	1
	51%	61%	39%

Source: U.S. Bureau of Labor Statistics, *Handbook of Labor Statistics, 1976* (Washington, D.C.: U.S. Government Printing Office, 1977), table 6.
[a]Does not add to 100% because of rounding.

comparative terms. Furthermore, examination of the median incomes of those in less skilled occupations reveals that many blue-collar families are poor. Finally, the table also displays systematic differences between male median incomes and family median incomes. These differences suggest that whatever affluence many families enjoy is often the result of both spouses working. Actually, many families stay out of poverty only because both spouses work. Among all families in which both spouses work at least part of the time, women earn 25 percent of the total income.[5]

Table 3 Median Income of Males, Females, and Families, by Occupation, 1975[a]

Occupation	Males	Females	Families
White Collar			
Professionals	$14,311	$7,862	$21,450
Managers	14,807	6,860	21,395
Sales	10,291	1,984	18,945
Clerical	10,040	5,322	15,187
Blue Collar			
Crafts	$10,870	$4,847	$16,672
Operatives	8,577	4,177	14,814
Laborers	3,991	2,645	13,420
Service Workers	4,503	1,646	13,664
Farm Workers	2,469	—[b]	10,191
Overall Median	$8,853	$3,385	$17,163

Source: U.S. Bureau of the Census, "Money Income and Poverty Status of Families and Persons in the United States: 1975 and 1974 Revisions," *Current Population Reports*, Series P-60, no. 103, tables 2 and 8.
[a]Individual data refer to all persons 14 years of age and older who had incomes in 1975. Family data are classified by head of household's occupation. The Census Bureau considers men to be household heads unless they are not present.
[b]Not available.

Regardless of the fact that blue-collar people earn less on the average than those who wear white collars, it is still possible to argue that they are relatively well off and can now afford many modern luxuries that were unavailable in the past. This argument simply suggests that yearly incomes between, say, $9,000 and $16,000 constitute a more than adequate level of affluence. One way of assessing such an argument is to compare the incomes of blue-collar people with estimated budgets calculated by the Bureau of Labor Statistics. Each year the BLS investigates the average cost of consumer items making up most families' budgets: food, housing, transportation, clothing, personal and medical care, taxes of various sorts, and a variety of other items. The bureau then divides these costs into three annual budgets for a "typical" family composed of four persons.

The three budgets are keyed to the amount necessary for a lower, intermediate, and higher standard of living in the United States. The lower-level budget was $9,198 in 1974, the last year for which data are available. This level is a practical measure of poverty in terms of the minimum amount necessary for a family to participate in American society. The intermediate-level budget was $14,333 in 1974. As its name suggests, this level is a good measure of the amount necessary for a moderate lifestyle in the United States. The higher-level budget was $20,777 in 1974. This level is a practical measure of the minimum amount necessary for a relatively affluent lifestyle.[6] When only blue-collar families are considered, fully 26 percent had incomes below the lower level in 1974, while 56 percent had incomes between the lower and higher levels, and only 19 percent had incomes at the higher level or above.[7]

The intermediate level is of primary concern here, because it is a basic working-class budget. As one writer puts it, "It constitutes the cost of living that some unions call a 'shabby, but respectable life'" (Levison, 1975:31). Yet most blue-collar families, fully 82 percent, were at or below the intermediate level in 1974. What this means in terms of a family's lifestyle can be seen from a study done by the United Auto Workers.

The BLS [intermediate] budget is much more "modest" than "adequate." It assumes, for example, that the family will own:
. . . A toaster that will last for 33 years;
. . . A refrigerator and a range that will each last for 17 years;
. . . A vacuum cleaner that will last 14 years;
. . . A television set that will last ten years.
The budget assumes that a family will buy a two-year-old car, and keep it for four years. In that time they will pay for a tune-up once a year, a brake realignment every three years, and front-end alignment every four years . . .

The budget assumes that the husband will buy one year-round suit every four years . . . and one top coat every 8 ½ years.

It assumes that the husband will take his wife to the movies once every three months, and that one of them will go alone once a year. The two children are each allowed one movie every four weeks. A total of $2.54 per person per year is allowed for admission to all other events, from football and baseball games to theater or concerts.

Finally, the budget allows nothing whatever for savings.*

Blue-collar workers as a whole are clearly not affluent, despite popular notions to the contrary. However, the embourgeoisement thesis can be stated in a more moderate way. It will be recalled from Table 3 that craft workers had a higher median income than did some white-collar workers, and that families headed by craft workers had a higher median income than families headed by clerical workers. Based on this overlap, it has been argued that craft workers and their families have experienced embourgeoisement even if other blue-collar workers have not (Mackenzie, 1967). In this moderate statement of the thesis, it is argued that only craft workers and their families should display middle-class lifestyles and values, since they are the only blue-collar people who are affluent.

But if the Bureau of Labor Statistics' measures of lower, intermediate, and higher budget levels are used, it becomes clear that not many craft workers are indeed affluent. Only 25 percent of all families of craft workers had incomes at the higher level or above in 1974. While 75 percent had incomes at the intermediate level or below.[8] The implications an intermediate level has for a family's lifestyle were noted above. Actually, what the income overlap among craft, clerical, and sales occupations means is that many white-collar families are not very affluent either (see Chapter 10).

As a final note on the incomes of blue-collar workers, the importance of moonlighting (holding more than one job) and overtime pay must be noted. The median-income levels shown in Table 3 included wages received for either moonlighting or working overtime for premium pay. Westcott (1975) found that about 20 percent of all workers labor more than 48 hours per week, and blue-collar workers are more likely to receive premium pay for overtime work. This figure has remained stable over the past few years (see Grossman, 1975; Hedges, 1975). The proportion of people moonlighting and working overtime varies by specific occupation. For example, managers and service workers are more likely than those in other occupations to either moonlight or work overtime. But, more generally, it appears that about equal proportions of blue- and white-collar people work overtime, while a far greater proportion of blue-collar

---

*Reprinted with permission of the United Auto Workers. See also Levison (1975:32–33).

workers moonlight. As Levison (1975:63) observes, in human terms this extra work "means leaving the factory at 7:00 P.M., not 5:00 P.M., or driving a cab in the evening after work; it means getting home at 8:00 P.M., having dinner and having at most one hour of 'leisure' time before going to sleep, day after day, month after month." *Summary of*

In summary, the embourgeoisement thesis is wrong in its basic premise. Most blue-collar people do not earn as much as white-collar people. Rather, based upon their incomes, it is clear that working-class people—who constitute half of the population—are far from affluence. Even when a more moderate version of the thesis is suggested, applying only to craft workers, only a minority of blue-collar people can be considered affluent. In fact, while most families can get by, they appear to live in a situation of chronic economic insecurity.

However, a potential qualifier to this conclusion must be noted. Income is a relatively narrow, although important, basis upon which to judge people's economic circumstances. It is entirely possible that a variety of market factors other than income could produce an embourgeoisementlike effect. If, for example, blue-collar workers' job security, fringe benefits, or chances for occupational mobility were as great or greater than those of white-collar workers', then blue collarites might begin to see themselves as similar to white collarites. Unfortunately, as will be shown below, in these terms working-class people are still generally worse off than middle-class people.

Job security is an important factor affecting a family's economic situation. Those who are assured of an income, even a relatively small one, can organize their lives to a greater degree than those for whom a steady income is doubtful. Bureau of Labor Statistics data clearly show that blue-collar workers have less job security than do white-collar workers. First, they are more likely to be unemployed. Among males, 81 percent of those unemployed sometime during 1975 were blue-collar workers. Among females who were unemployed during 1975, 54 percent were blue-collar and 30 percent were clerical workers.[9] Unemployment is especially unpredictable for blue-collar people because wage work is more highly affected by cyclical variations in the economy (Flaim et al., 1975). Second, when blue-collar workers are unemployed, they are likely to remain so for a longer period than white-collar workers. The BLS shows that 66 percent of those out of work for 15 weeks or more were working-class people in 1975. Further, an identical 66 percent of those unemployed 27 weeks or more were blue-collar.[10]

The real meaning of the "high salaries" paid to a few workers now becomes clear. For the plumber, electrician, and other construction workers, their wages are a hedge against periodic unemployment. It should be noted that some form of unemployment insurance does help many families through periods without work. But such insurance only covers 70 percent of the labor force, and leaves unprotected many workers who are most likely to be unemployed (Bateman and Allen, 1971). In conclusion, then, the blue-collar workers have significantly less job security than do white-collar workers. Thus, job security cannot be used as an indicator of blue-collar affluence in the embourgeoisement argument.

The availability of fringe benefits is also an important factor affecting a family's economic situation. While the fringe benefits connected to all jobs have been steadily expanding in recent years, the gap between those received by blue- and white-collar workers is still wide. Blue-collar workers often have fewer paid holidays per year. This means they work more days for the same or less pay. Similarly, working-class people generally have shorter vacations, based on length of service, than do middle-class people. For example, after one year of work, 29 percent of all blue-collar employees receive two weeks vacation. This compares to 77 percent of all white-collar employees.

Finally, by 1974, nearly all employees in private industry had access to health insurance of some sort, although in many cases the cost is still born by the employee.[11] Hospitalization, surgical, major medical, and other forms of health insurance are especially vital to blue-collar workers, who are much more likely to have work-related accidents. Estimates of the number of such accidents that result in death or disability range from 2.5 million to 25 million per year (Wallick, 1972). Blue-collar workers are more likely to be disabled and to remain so for longer periods of time (Metropolitan Life, 1975). They are more susceptible to occupational diseases.[12] And they are more likely to die from occupational injury.[13] In conclusion, the fringe benefits connected to blue-collar work are not commensurate to those received by white-collar employees. Thus, the level of fringe benefits cannot be used as an indicator of blue-collar affluence in the embourgeoisement argument.

Finally, the possibility of mobility from one job to another is also an important factor affecting a family's economic situation. There are two ways of examining career mobility: horizontally and vertically. Horizontal moves are those that occur at roughly the same level— for example, changing employers but working in a similar job. Vertical moves are those that involve changing occupational level, whether upward or downward: for example, changing from a machine operator (an operative) to a mechanic (a craft worker). The concern here is with vertical mobility. Blau and Duncan (1967) found that, among males, most occupational movement occurs between jobs that are closely related in work requirements and social status. This fact is one reason why vertical career mobility generally occurs within the blue- and white-collar hierarchies, not between them. Blue-collar workers generally have little chance to move into high-paying white-collar jobs. This finding has proven stable over time (Byrne, 1975).[14]

In conclusion, most blue-collar workers and their families are not affluent in comparison to white-collar people. They are not affluent in terms of relatively objective living budgets compiled by the Bureau of Labor Statistics. Even when the blue-collar occupation displaying the highest median income is analyzed, most people cannot be considered affluent. Finally, when a variety of other economic factors are considered, such as job security, fringe benefits, and mobility rates, blue-collar workers are not affluent. Regardless of what measure is used, most Americans have not experienced embourgeoisement and they are not middle class in economic terms. Nonetheless, the political, legal, religious, educational, and familial characteristics of blue-collar people remain of interest. It is still possible that, despite important economic differences between blue- and white-collar people, they might be quite similar in other areas. Furthermore, the fact that many blue-collar workers are relatively insecure economically is one of the premises underlying the authoritarianism thesis. The next section deals with this issue.

Blue-Collar Politics[15]

The image of blue-collar people presented in the mass media and on television is consistently negative (Levison, 1975). Archie Bunker is the prototypical blue-collar man. He is variously inept, pathetic, and even pathological. This negative public image is mirrored in the sociological literature. For some reason, the embourgeoisement thesis has not been applied to blue-collar political attitudes and behavior, where, perhaps, it is most appropriate. Rather, the "working-class authoritarianism" thesis has dominated sociological discussions. Because of its importance, this section is organized so as to evaluate the authoritarianism thesis. After the thesis is posed and some general criticisms of it noted, the political attitudes and behavior of blue-collar people will be briefly examined.

Lipset has stated the "working-class authoritarianism" thesis most forcefully.[16] He writes that the blue-collar or "lower class way of life produces individuals with rigid and intolerant approaches to politics" (1963:89). Lipset (1963:100–101) continues in the following way.

A number of elements contribute to authoritarian predispositions in lower class individuals. Low education, low [levels of] of participation in political or voluntary organizations of any type, little reading, isolated occupations, economic insecurity, and authoritarian family patterns are some of the most important.

Lipset is arguing, then, that the peculiar sociocultural experiences of blue-collar people, their relative lack of education, economic insecurity, and the like produce authoritarian personality characteristics. In turn, these characteristics are presumed to manifest themselves in the form of intolerant political attitudes and behavior on the part of blue-collar people. CRITICIZED

The working-class authoritarianism thesis has been criticized in several ways. First, the entire analysis is couched in value-laden and discriminatory terminology. As only one example, Lipset (1963:108) argues that "greater suggestibility, absence of a sense of past and future, inability to take a complex view, greater difficulty in abstracting from concrete experience, and lack of imagination" are characteristics of blue-collar people. Apart from being inaccurate, such a description hardly inspires respect for the majority of the American population (Levison, 1975).

Second, it is not clear to whom Lipset is referring. Neither the conceptual nor empirical distinction among "working class," "lower class," and "middle class" is clear. It is not unfair to require that concepts have clear theoretical and operational definitions. Third, while economic insecurity and less education can lead to intolerance, as Lipset suggests, it can also lead to greater tolerance. Being unsophisticated is not the same as being, or becoming, authoritarian. On the other hand, though being well-to-do economically and highly educated can lead to democratic values and tolerance for others, it can also lead to elitism, snobbery, and intolerance. The causal relationship that Lipset postulates is not well supported by the available data (see S. M. Miller and Riessman, 1961). Fourth, several studies have shown that the measure of authoritarianism used, the Fascism (F) Scale, is not applicable across class lines. (These studies are reviewed in S. M. Miller and Riessman [1961], and Hopple [1974].)

Finally, the main study, that by Stouffer (1955), used to support the idea that blue-collar workers would deny civil liberties to others is misleading. In an exhaustive critique, Hamilton (1972a:434–52) shows that during the 1950s blue- and white-collar people displayed few differences in levels of tolerance, as long as a person was only *accused* of being a communist (or socialist or atheist). Most citizens were quite tolerant of the rights of others to due process of law. This attitude changed, however, where an *admitted* communist was at issue. In this case, blue-collar people were indeed more intolerant. But unlike Lipset, Hamilton argues that such intolerance was not the result of peculiarities of working-class life. Rather, he suggests that the rural or southern origin of many blue collarites, along with the influence of the mass media and various respected public figures, produced intolerance for such persons during the 1950s. Today, there is little evidence that blue-collar people are more intolerant toward civil liberties than are white-collar people.

Nonetheless, it is often charged that blue-collar people have authoritarian political attitudes (Shostak, 1969). This assertion can be tested by examining two issues that can serve as examples of blue-collar attitudes in general: white working-class tolerance toward black Americans and their attitudes toward the Vietnam War. As Levison (1975:143) has observed, "the nature and extent of the prejudice and racism that exist are the most important questions about working-class political attitudes." Surprisingly, among whites there are few class-linked variations in attitudes toward blacks. This fact is shown in Table 4, where (with one exception) differences between manual and nonmanual workers are minimal. The examples included in the table have to do with job attainment and school attendance. Regardless of occupation or region, white people generally believe that blacks ought to be treated fairly in their efforts at obtaining jobs.

There are, however, regional and occupational differences in attitudes toward schooling. Among non-Southerners, whites believe that children of different races should have the opportunity to attend the same schools. But among Southerners, blue-collar workers are much less likely to favor opportunities for desegregated schooling. These findings suggest that "working-class authoritarianism" is not an adequate explanation for the political attitudes of blue-collar people. If the authoritarianism thesis were appropriate, then regional and topical variations should be much less marked. As an aside, the opinion poll data in Table 4 are not intended to suggest that white working-class people are not racist. Like most Americans, they are (see Chapter 12). Such data do suggest, however, that the attitudinal differences between blue- and white-collar people are generally not very great and, when they are, explanations other than working-class authoritarianism are probably more useful.

Support for national policies such as the war in Vietnam has been used as a test of the authoritarianism thesis in a number of studies.[17] The idea is that blue-collar people's support for the war would be congruent with their supposed authoritarian personalities. The findings, however, have not supported the thesis. For example, Wright (1972) has shown that, in 1964, blue-collar people were more likely than white-collar people to desire that the United States either pull out of Vietnam altogether or arrange a cease-fire. By 1968, the percentages had changed such that there were few differences between blue- and white-collar people over the war. Thus, working-class authoritarianism cannot be inferred on the basis of support for the war in Vietnam.

It must be recognized, however, that political attitudes and behav-

Table 4 White Attitudes Toward Blacks, by Class, Region, and Year—Selected
Issues (married white respondents, head economically active)

Year	Question	Percentage in Favor, Non-South		Percentage in Favor, South	
		Blue Collar	White Collar	Blue Collar	White Collar
1956	Federal Government should see blacks get fair treatment in *jobs* and *housing*.	73	74	63	64
1964	Federal government should see blacks get fair treatment in *jobs*.	47	45	32	33
1964	Federal government should see that white and black children go to the same *schools*.	54	60	19	36
1968	Federal government should enact fair treatment laws so blacks can be assured equal treatment when seeking *jobs*.	89	88	79	77
1968	Federal government should see that black and white children go to same *schools*.	80	89	35	64

Source: The questions from 1956 and 1964 are from R. F. Hamilton, *Class and Politics in the United States* (New York: John Wiley, 1972), p. 402. The 1968 questions are compiled from R. F. Hamilton, "Liberal Intelligentsia and White Backlash," in Irving Howe (ed.), *The World of the Blue Collar Worker* (New York: Quadrangle Books, 1972), pp. 277–38. Reprinted with the permission of the Dissent Corporation, 1971. The wording of the questions is paraphrased here. These data represent nationwide random samples and were originally collected by the Survey Research Center at the University of Michigan.

ior can often be quite different. It is possible that when behavior is examined, the authoritarianism thesis could prove applicable. When analyzing political behavior in the United States, the first consideration is clearly simple participation. As noted in Chapter 8, political participation is inversely related to socioeconomic status, regardless of the measure of participation that is used (Verba and Nie, 1972). This finding can be illustrated by looking at voting behavior. A greater proportion of white-collar than blue-collar people vote. For example, in the 1972 presidential election, 76 percent of all middle-class people voted, compared to 56 percent of the working class. Similarly, in the 1974 off-year election, 55 percent of all white-collar people voted, compared to 38 percent of all blue-collar people. In absolute numbers, this means that in each election about 7 million more white-collar people voted.[18]

Several conclusions are suggested by these data. The most obvious implication is that the American political process is clearly not dominated by hordes of authoritarian blue collarites. Rather, as Verba and Nie (1972) have concluded, white-collar people dominate all forms of political participation in the United States. Verba and Nie argue that the public policy implications of this fact are enormous, for those who do not vote generally receive less from government at all levels. The only qualifying factor to this conclusion involves membership in politically active voluntary associations, such as those based on ethnicity or religion (Greeley, 1974), or unions. However, the political impact of unions is probably overrated (Levison, 1975).

Apart from simple voting participation, additional evidence applicable to the working-class authoritarianism thesis can be gleaned from voter preferences. Ballet box choices represent a decisive step beyond the mere expression of opinion. Blue-collar voters generally support the Democratic Party, although they cannot be counted on in any mindless fashion (Levison, 1975).[19] Working-class people tend to avoid right-wing candidates. Ironically, in view of the authoritarianism thesis, such candidates gain their greatest support from more affluent segments of the population. The obvious possible exception to this statement is the George Wallace campaign of 1968. However, after analyzing the Wallace vote, Hamilton (1972b:143–47) concludes that "outside the South there was no significant difference between" manual and nonmanual workers in the vote for Wallace. In sum, then, in terms of their votes for political candidates, it cannot be concluded that working-class people are authoritarian.

In addition, during the 1960s, several ballot box issues arose that also provide good indicators of the degree of working-class authoritarianism. Only one such issue will be noted here: fair housing referenda. Fourteen such referenda took place during the 1960s. All but four were defeated, mostly by substantial margins. However, as with attitudes, these referenda show that, when faced with a clear choice, working-class people are no more intolerant toward blacks than are middle-class people. Among whites, it was found that, "the highest incidence of antagonism to open housing is among white collar–low income workers not the 'working class'" (H.D. Hamilton, 1970:728; Hahn, 1968).[20] Voters rarely have the chance to make explicit choices about specific public policies. But white people's votes on housing referenda clearly reveal that, when such a chance does occur, blue-collar people are no more, and often considerably less, intolerant than are white-collar people.

In summary, the working-class authoritarianism thesis argues that the sociocultural milieu in which blue-collar people live produces authoritarian political attitudes and behavior among them. This argument is plainly false. As noted above, there are a variety of criticisms that suggest that the thesis is not clearly focused. More specifically, in regard to attitudes toward blacks and toward the war in Vietnam, there are few differences among white people, whether they wear blue or white collars. Similarly, while working-class people generally vote less, when they do participate in the political process, they are little different than middle-class people. One might speculate that the embourgeoisement thesis may be a more viable means of explaining blue-collar politics than one attributing an ill-defined authoritarianism to them.

Religious Affiliation and Belief

The embourgeoisement thesis would suggest that there are few differences among the various social strata in terms of religious affiliation and beliefs. However, despite the fact that good data are relatively difficult to obtain, there appear to be striking differences between working- and middle-class people in both areas.[21] Church membership will be considered first. Contrary to popular beliefs, many Americans do not belong to a church. In 1973, only 62 percent of all Americans were carried on church rolls, and this figure undoubtedly overestimates the actual proportion of church members.[22] As noted in Chapter 8, in the United States, church membership is postively related to social strata. That is, the lower the social class, the lower the rate of church membership (Stark, 1972).[23] Stark argues that among white non-Southerners, blue-collar people are less religious on every measure of religiosity. They are less likely to attend church, have less knowledge of church doctrine, participate less in church activities, have less orthodox beliefs, are less likely to have had religious experiences, pray less often, and have lower levels of communal involvement. It is not clear whether these findings are true for white Southerners and blacks, but a reasonable hypothesis would be that the relationship holds, although differences by class are lessened (see Chapter 12). Stark concludes that, in the general population, class-related "differences in religious commitment are of degree rather than kind." Blue-collar and poor people are simply less involved in organized religion. *✻ Very Important*

The nature of religious belief and its relationship to stratum membership can now be considered. In this case, the focus is on church members only rather than on the general population. Again, there are great differences between blue- and white-collar people. Working-class people who are members of a church are much more likely to have highly orthodox beliefs, to engage in "private devotional activities such as prayer," and to concentrate their social activities and friendships within the church. Conversely, middle-class church members are more likely to attend church and generally display "public ritual involvement," to have a working knowledge of church doctrine and the Bible, and to participate in various church organizations (the Deacons, for example). On this basis, Stark (1972:490) concludes, "among church members class differences in piety are of kind rather than degree." In a phrase, it appears that blue-collar church members feel their beliefs, whereas white-collar members display theirs.

A number of important qualifications must be made regarding the generalizations above (Mueller and Johnson, 1975). First, the relationship between socioeconomic status and religious beliefs varies by church affiliation. For example, there appears to be no such relationship among Jews. Further, it is probable that considerable variation exists among the various Protestant denominations. Second, the socioeconomic status–religion relationship appears to vary by sex. Among church members, women are more likely to participate in all ways regardless of socioeconomic status. Finally, the nature and frequency of religious participation varies according to marital status and the presence of young children, again regardless of socioeconomic status. Both marriage and young children in the family stimulate religious involvement.

In summary, the embourgeoisement thesis is clearly not applicable to blue-collar religious affiliation and beliefs, for working-class and middle-class people differ substantially in this area. Blue-collar people are less likely to belong to a church or to display church-oriented religiosity. However, when they do become members, blue-collar people are more likely to share the fundamental tenets of the church and to participate in the more private aspects of devotion.

Blue-Collar People and the Criminal-Justice System

Once again, the embourgeoisement thesis would suggest that there are few differences between blue- and white-collar people in terms of the legal system. The complex nature of this relationship can be seen by examining three topics: (1) criminal behavior on the part of blue-collar people, (2) the extent to which working-class people are victimized by crime, and (3) their attitudes toward the police and law.

In Chapter 8 it was noted that there is no relationship between the amount of criminal behavior and class. However, blue- and white-collar people commit different types of crime. That is, the lower the socioeconomic status, the greater the arrest rate for crimes against property and violent crimes.[24] Green (1970), for example, found that, among white people, white-collar and craft workers had an average annual arrest rate of 3.1 per 100,000 people. This compares with a rate of 62.5 per 100,000 people among operatives and laborers. Lower-skilled (and poorer) blue-collar people have a much higher arrest rate.

However, it is also significant that among unemployed workers (most of whom are blue collar, of course) the average rate was 183.8 per 100,000 people. This rate is nearly three times as high as that among less skilled blue-collar workers. These variations point toward the necessity of making a clear distinction among the poor, blue-collar, and white-collar people. Although the data clearly reflect a negative relationship between socioeconomic status and crime rates (at least as revealed by arrest data), it can also be hypothesized that those who commit and are arrested for crimes of violence or against property are socially marginal individuals. As Hirschi (1972:505) argues, for some kinds of criminal behavior "the important dividing lines are between the self-sufficient and the economically dependent, between those regularly and those irregularly employed." For example, the Law Enforcement Assistance Administration (1972) found that only 11 percent of all inmates in local jails had prearrest incomes above $7,500. As noted in Chapter 8, jail inmates are poor, irregularly employed, young (59 percent are less than 30 years old), and not married (76 percent).[25]

Blue- and white-collar people also differ in the extent to which they are victimized by crime. The relationship can be clearly seen in Table 5, where income is used as an indicator of socioeconomic status and the incidence of violent crimes against persons reflects victimization rates. Phrased formally, the finding is that the lower the socioeconomic status, the higher the rate of criminal victimization. More generally, this relationship appears to hold regardless of what kind of crime against persons or property is considered.

Table 5 Income and Violent Crimes Against Persons, 1974

Income	Violent Crimes Against Persons (rate per 1,000, age 12 or over)
$3,000 or Less	54.3
$3,000–7,499	36.1
$7,500–9,999	35.2
$10,000–14,999	27.6
$15,000–24,999	28.0
$25,000 and Over	25.3

Source: Law Enforcement Assistance Administration, *Criminal Victimization in the United States* (Washington, D.C.: U.S. Government Printing Office, 1976).

Despite these differences in official crime rates and in rates of victimization, blue- and white-collar people do not differ very much in their attitudes toward the police and crime. This fact is revealed in Table 6. In nationwide surveys there are few differences in attitudes toward the police. Regardless of social class, most people believe that law-enforcement officials are doing a good job and should be tougher on criminals. These are safe, and stable, attitudes. Getting mugged is no fun, regardless of stratum. Similarly, while the population is clearly divided over the usefulness of the death penalty, there are few differences by socioeconomic status.

It should be recognized, however, that there are class differences in attitudes about certain kinds of criminal behavior. For example,

Table 6 Attitudes Toward the Police and Crime by Socioeconomic Status

Percentage of Favorable Evaluations of Law-Enforcement Officials, 1970

Income	Federal	State	Local
$ 5,000 or less	60%	59%	58%
5,000–9,999	62	64	64
10,000 and over	59	64	68

Percentage Believing Police Should Be Tougher in Dealing with
Crime and Lawlessness, 1972

Occupation	Yes	No	Don't Know
Professional and Business	80%	15%	5%
White Collar	81	15	4
Manual	84	14	2
Farmers	93	7	—

Percentage Favoring the Death Penalty, 1972

Occupation	Yes	No	Don't Know
Professional and Business	51%	44%	5%
White Collar	48	40	12
Manual	48	43	9
Farmers	46	40	14

Source: Adapted from M. J. Hindelang, *Public Opinion Regarding Crime, Criminal Justice, and Related Topics* (Washington, D.C.: Law Enforcement Assistance Administration, 1975), tables 2, 3, and 5. The occupational categories are Hindelang's. The data were originally collected in nationwide random samples by the American Institute of Public Opinion (The Gallup Poll, Princeton, N.J. 08540).

although not shown in the table, blue-collar people are much less in favor of lighter penalties for possession of marijuana (Hindelang, 1975). It is worth noting that these data can be applied to the working-class authoritarian thesis. From that point of view, one might expect that, because of their higher rates of victimization, blue-collar people would display "tougher" attitudes toward crime (especially violent crime) and expect more "toughness" from the police in dealing with offenders. In fact, working-class authoritarianism cannot be inferred from the data in Table 6. Rather, those areas where class differences do appear involve emotionally charged but nonviolent and nonaggressive crimes, such as marijuana possession.

In summary, then, blue-collar people are more likely to commit crimes against property and crimes involving violence than are white-collar people—at least when arrest and incarceration rates are considered. But those individuals who are arrested and kept in jail are generally socially marginal people: young, single, poor, uneducated, low skilled. This finding partially vitiates the relationship between socioeconomic status and crime rates. Blue-collar people are more likely to be victimized by criminals. This finding is stable and shows clear differences between working-class and middle-class people. But, somewhat surprisingly in light of the authoritarianism thesis, blue-collar people do not differ very much in their attitudes toward the police or toward many legal issues. However, this last finding must be qualified somewhat, for there are some issues over which stratum differences emerge. Neither the embourgeoisement nor the working-class authoritarianism thesis provides an adequate explanation for the relationship between socioeconomic status and the law.

Blue-Collar Family Life

This section deals briefly with three topics: (1) attitudes toward marriage on the part of blue-collar men and women, (2) mating behavior, and (3) family relations.

Attitudes toward marriage are very difficult to generalize about. Nonetheless, a few (perhaps controversial) comments are in order. Blue-collar men and women often have quite different views about marriage (LeMasters, 1975; Komarovsky, 1967). As LeMasters observes, for many working-class men, marriage is a stabilizing force. Because they are married, they obtain emotional support, material support (in the form of housewifery), keep their jobs, do not drink too much, and have a steady source for sexual relationships. However, if one can believe their own assertions, many blue-collar men really do not like women—except for sex—but do not believe there are any realistic alternatives to marriage (LeMasters, 1975). Partly for this reason, the male's familial role is often very narrowly defined, as the economic provider. Conversely, many women appear to believe that marriage is a "raw deal," since men gain most of the benefits (Bernard, 1971). One of LeMasters's blue-collar respondents puts the problem this way: "My husband is not perfect, but he's a lot better than some of the men I know. I would say he's a real nice bastard."

Despite such oft-expressed comments, most Americans do marry, and there does not seem to be much variation by strata. However, as noted in Chapter 8, there are variations by age. That is, the lower the socioeconomic status, the younger the age at marriage (Rainwater, 1974). One of the most important reasons for this relationship is that children of blue-collar parents attend college at much lower rates than do the children of white-collar parents (see below). As a result, working-class children generally enter the blue-collar work force, become financially independent of their parents, marry, and hence assume adult status at a younger age. Another reason for the relationship between marriage age and class is premarital pregnancy. Such rates clearly vary by class. That is, as indicated by the husband's occupation, the lower the socioeconomic status, the higher the rate of premaritally conceived children. Furthermore, although white-collar families conceive children out of wedlock at a lower rate than do blue-collar families, a higher proportion of white-collar people get married prior to the birth of the child.[26] Once again, as noted in Chapter 8, much of the variation in illegitimacy is a result of ignorance and lack of available contraceptive devices.

After they marry, working-class couples tend to have more children and sooner than do middle-class couples, although the differences are not great (Cutright, 1971a)[27] Stated more formally, the lower the socioeconomic status, the greater the number of children and the more rapidly they arrive. Within the marriage, it appears that the lower the socioeconomic status, the greater the role segregation between spouses (Rainwater, 1964; Komarovsky, 1967). Women married to blue-collar men tend to have a wider range of roles, even when they work. As will be shown in Chapter 13, female roles can be grouped into three areas of work: economically productive occupations, housewifery, and child raising.[28]

Whether or how blue- and white-collar families differ in their child-raising tactics is a subject of some controversy. The sociological stereotype has been that since the mid-1940s middle-class parents have been more permissive in their child-raising practices, whereas working-class parents have been less permissive (Bronfenbrenner, 1958). However, this point of view has recently been challenged by Erlanger (1974), who reviewed the historical data cited in Bronfenbrenner's classic paper along with several more recent studies. By focusing on one child-rearing technique, corporal punishment, Erlanger calls Bronfenbrenner's findings into question. Put plainly, nearly all parents spank their children in varying ways and at varying times. There are no differences between blue- and white-collar families in this regard and there probably never have been.[29]

This finding has important implications. It will be recalled that Lipset argues that "authoritarian family patterns" contribute to the development of working-class authoritarianism. Based in part on Bronfenbrenner's findings, Lipset (1963:114) argues that "the lower-class individual is likely to have been exposed to punishment, lack of love, and a general atmosphere of tension and aggression since early childhood—all experiences which tend to produce deep-rooted hostilities expressed by ethnic prejudice, political authoritarianism, and chiliastic transvaluational religion." Erlanger's findings cast doubt on Lipset's premise.

The final topic of concern here involves marital stability. Cutright (1971b) has concluded that the lower the socioeconomic status, the higher the rate of marital instability, as shown by separation, desertion, or divorce rates. LeMasters (1975) argues that blue-collar men's emphasis on role segregation and their desire for "freedom and independence and their right to spend time with their male buddies when they feel like it" are important sources of stress on blue-collar marriages. According to LeMasters, there are three major sources of strength in blue-collar marriages: (1) many blue-collar people do not believe in divorce; (2) many women are from rural and small-town backgrounds, and their early lives have prepared them for what they get; (3) blue-collar craft workers are seen as "good catches" by many women. Under these conditions, LeMasters believes that, when one is assessing whether blue-collar marriages are successful, two different criteria must be used (LeMasters, 1975). If the criterion is survival, then many marriages are successful. If the criterion is some measure of marital satisfaction, then the results would be "dubious."

Blue-Collar Education

On the average, blue-collar workers are less well educated than are white-collar workers. More formally stated, the lower the level of education, the lower the socioeconomic status. This generalization can be seen in Table 7, which displays the educational attainment for both sexes at each occupational level. For both males and females, the less well educated tend to have blue-collar jobs. They also tend to make less money, both yearly and over their lifetime. Similarly, the lower the level of education, the greater the likelihood of unemployment. This last problem is worse for both blacks and women (see McEaddy, 1975:Table L).

The relationship between education and socioeconomic status is not accidental. As noted above, the schools sort and allocate students into the adult labor market. They accomplish this goal by testing, "tracking," and counseling. Students from white-collar backgrounds often have higher test scores, are placed in "advanced"

Table 7 Education and Occupation, 1974

Occupation	Males		Females	
	Less Than High School[a]	High School or More	Less Than High School	High School or More
Professional	1.4%	19.7%	1.6%	20.7%
Managerial	6.2	17.5	3.4	5.6
Sales	3.1	7.5	7.4	6.5
Clerical	4.1	7.8	16.3	41.5
Crafts	24.4	19.5	2.3	1.5
Operatives	27.0	14.0	25.8	8.1
Laborers	13.2	4.7	1.5	.6
Service	12.1	6.4	39.2	14.8
Farm Workers	8.6	3.0	2.4	.9
	100%	100%	100%	100%

Source: B. J. McEaddy, *Educational Attainment of Workers, March 1974,* Special Labor Report 175 (Washington, D.C.: U.S. Department of Labor, 1975), p. 68.

[a]Includes all those who have less than a high school diploma.

courses, and are advised to plan on college. For the children of blue-collar workers, the public schools often serve as training for factory work (Bowles, 1972). As a result, the higher the parent's socioeconomic status, the greater the likelihood that a child will graduate from high school, plan to attend college, and attend and graduate from college.[30]

SUMMARY

In conclusion, the economic differences between blue- and white-collar people are very clear. The embourgeoisement thesis is wrong in its premise. Neither the embourgeoisement nor the working-class authoritarianism thesis adequately accounts for stratum differences in any other area. The relationship between working-class and middle-class people in political, legal, religious, familial, and educational terms is complex and variegated. In some areas, there are clear differences but not where either of the two theses would predict. Conversely, it is often the case that just where the two theses would predict blue- and white-collar differences, none appear. The final topic of concern in this chapter is one most observers believe is a peculiarly working-class phenomenon—the "blue-collar blues," or levels of alienation and job satisfaction.

BLUE-COLLAR ALIENATION AND JOB SATISFACTION

The nature and level of alienation among blue-collar workers is a matter of some controversy. Alienation has generally been inferred from indexes designed to measure people's perception of their powerlessness, meaninglessness, isolation, and self-estrangement (see Kohn and Schooler, 1973). These items are used as measures of people's personal experiences and feelings. Those who score high are judged to be more alienated. Feelings of alienation are then linked to the level of technology (automation) and social structure (the division of labor) in order to identify the conditions under which workers will feel alienated.

The general conclusion is that the more closely one is supervised, the more routinized the work, and the less complex it is, then the greater the level of alienation (Kohn, 1976). Although there is great diversity among blue-collar occupations (Blauner, 1964), under this criterion working-class people are generally more alienated than middle-class people. For example, Binzen (1970:199) notes that "only 5% of all office workers are subject to work-measurement standards in contrast to 80–85% of production workers." As a result, blue-collar people are often less able to regulate the pace of work, to have relatively free physical movement, to control the quantity and quality of work, or to select work methods. The archetypal example of such powerlessness is, of course, automobile workers (see Chinoy, 1955). It must be emphasized, however, that many blue-collar occupations are not alienating. Craft workers, for example, are least likely to be alienated. Further, neither the construction workers described by LeMasters (1975) nor the printers and chemical operators portrayed by Blauner (1964) are alienated. Nonetheless, in the literature on alienation, it is generally asserted that the lower the socioeconomic status, the higher the level of alienation.

Another way of inferring alienation involves studies of job satisfaction. This topic has been of special concern to policy makers in recent years. One result was a highly controversial Special Task Force Report to the Secretary of Health, Education, and Welfare (1973:x). Titled *Work in America,* it inferred that "a general increase in their educational and economic status has placed many American workers in a position where having an interesting job is now as important as having a job that pays well." The report asserts that, as a result, workers' discontent has increased in recent years. The solution proposed by the task force is to reorganize the work process so as to allow workers more autonomy, make tasks more interesting, and the like. However, the usefulness of the report is doubtful for the following reasons.

First, one of the premises on which the report is based is a variation on the embourgeoisement argument. As has been shown, blue-collar people have not made appreciable economic advances. It is simply wrong to suggest that such advances have altered manual workers' attitudes, toward their work or anything else. While blue- and white-collar people have roughly similar occupational interests, their rankings of the most important facets of their jobs vary radically. These differences are displayed in Table 8, which shows what workers perceive to be the 10 most important aspects of their jobs. Among blue-collar workers, most people rank high pay as the most important job characteristic. Among white-collar people, having an interesting job is ranked first, while high pay is ranked last. In their study of embourgeoisement in England, Goldthorpe et al. (1969) found that craft workers would often leave their more interesting jobs for less skilled work that carried higher pay. Blue- and white-collar workers have quite different priorities in evaluating their jobs.

The second reason that the task force report is not useful is that its major finding, increasing work dissatisfaction among blue-collar people, is quite doubtful. Based on a review of about 2,000 surveys of job satisfaction, Kahn (1972:173) concludes that most people, regardless of occupation or stratum, are relatively satisfied with their jobs. "Few people call themselves extremely satisfied, but still fewer report extreme dissatisfaction. The modal response is on the positive side of neutrality—'pretty satisfied.' " By the way, this finding is

Table 8 Ten Most Important Facets of Jobs, by Occupations

	Percentage Rating This Facet as "Very Important"
Blue Collar Workers	
1. The pay is good.	73%
2. I receive enough help and equipment to get the job done.	72
3. The job security is good.	72
4. I have enough information to get the job done.	69
5. The work is interesting.	68
6. My responsibilities are clearly defined.	65
7. I can see the results of my work.	64
8. I have enough authority to do my job.	64
9. My supervisor is competent in doing his job.	63
10. My fringe benefits are good.	62
White Collar Workers	
1. The work is interesting.	79%
2. I have an opportunity to develop my special abilities.	69
3. I have enough information to get the job done.	67
4. I have enough authority to do my job.	67
5. I receive enough help and equipment to get the job done.	65
6. My coworkers are friendly and helpful.	61
7. I can see the results of my work.	60
8. My supervisor is competent in doing his job.	60
9. My responsibilities are clearly defined.	58
10. The pay is good.	57

Source: R. P. Quinn et al., *Job Satisfaction: Is There a Trend?* Manpower Research Monograph no. 30, U.S. Department of Labor (Washington, D.C.: U.S. Government Printing Office, 1974), table 6. The data are based on a nationwide random sample collected in 1969–70. In this table, farm workers are excluded from the analysis.

also true for automobile workers (Form, 1973). It should be emphasized, however, that there are variations in level of job satisfaction according to socioeconomic status, age, and education. Among blue-collar workers, there are variations by skill level, industry, and societal level of industrialization. The findings can be summarized as follows. (1) The higher the socioeconomic status, the greater the level of job satisfaction. White-collar people are generally more satisfied than are blue-collar people. (2) The older one is, the greater the level of job satisfaction. (3) The higher the level of education, the greater the level of job satisfaction, unless one is underemployed.[31] (4) Among blue-collar workers, the higher the skill level, the greater the level of job satisfaction. (5) Among blue-collar workers, those in the auto industry are generally less satisfied with their jobs than those in other industries. (6) The greater the industrialization in a society, the more satisfied are skilled workers and the less satisfied are unskilled workers.[32]

The findings about alienation and job satisfaction seem opposed to one another: blue-collar people are alienated, yet like most other people, they are also relatively satisfied with their jobs. The reason workers can be both alienated and relatively satisfied is that people evaluate their jobs and their life experiences through a prism shaped by their major points of reference. The most important such references appear to be parents' occupations and siblings' occupations (Form and Geschwender, 1962). People evidently ask themselves, "How well have I done in comparison to my brothers and parents?" Thus, people may be alienated because their jobs are constricting and meaningless. Nonetheless, the same people may also be relatively satisfied because, in relation to their realistic expectations, they have done as well as they could.

One final (editorial) comment is in order here, and it also deals with the idea that people use their own life experiences as a means of evaluation. Form (1973) has noted that "intellectuals hate machines." From Marx to Marcuse, academicians and intellectuals have seen machines as somehow intruding upon the pristine nature of work. From this point of view, industrialization has meant the destruction of the beauty and inherent creativeness of labor. Such attitudes are foolish. At all times and places, some manual labor has been creative and self-fulfilling, while most of it has been just plain work. It is not wrong or bad to view one's job in such instrumental terms as wages or salaries. Academicians have an obsessive concern with blue-collar alienation, and they are constantly devising studies that show it. It is sheer speculation, but this concern may stem from the fact that most white-collar people cannot operate or repair anything but the most simple mechanical device. This is especially true of academicians. Among those who do not labor physically, machines are alienating. Hence, blue-collar people who must labor must also be alienated. As was suggested above, however, the situation is more complex than that.

SUMMARY AND CONCLUSION

This chapter is a description of blue-collar people in the United States. The first section identified some typical blue-collar occupations and suggested that, despite the diversity of job tasks, all blue-collar occupations involve manual labor of some sort. The second section of the chapter described the social and economic situation of blue-collar people at some length. Blue-collar people are about half of the population, but neither of the dominant theses purporting to describe them is useful. The embourgeoisement thesis is not useful because most blue-collar people are not particularly affluent. In economic terms, most manual laborers and their families are managing, but barely. Further, neither attitudinal nor behavioral predictions based on the thesis are borne out by the data. In many crucial ways, blue- and white-collar people are very different from one another. Paradoxically, however, one area in which there appears to be little difference is in political attitudes or behavior. Contrary to the working-class authoritarianism thesis, blue-collar people are no more authoritarian than white-collar people.

The third section of the chapter dealt briefly with alienation and job satisfaction among manual laborers. Blue-collar workers are relatively alienated and less satisfied with their jobs than are white-collar workers. However, it appears that nearly all workers are relatively satisfied with their jobs, once their realistic opportunities and expectations are taken into account.

As a final note, a subtheme in the chapter has been the idea that traditional sociological descriptions of blue-collar people are not very accurate. Although it cannot be shown definitively, this low level of theoretical acuity may result from a lack of contact with or simple dislike of working-class people.

NOTES

1. "Embourgeoisement" is a somewhat unwieldy term. It stems from Marxian attempts at explaining why workers in industrial societies have not become revolutionary. The argument is that workers have come to support capitalism as the principle means of improving their lifestyles. In this sense, they have become like the bourgeoisie. Phrased another way, they have experienced embourgeoisement. The best review of the literature on embourgeoisement is Rinehart (1971). See also Goldthorpe (1969), and Dalia and Guest (1975).

2. See Blauner (1964) for a good analysis of the differences among various blue-collar occupations. See Terkel (1972) for blue-collar workers' own poignant descriptions of their jobs.

3. The actual breakdown of the blue-collar work force in 1974 is as follows:

Occupation	Number (in millions)	Percentage
Craft Workers	12.0	26
Operative	15.0	32
Laborers	4.9	10
Service Worker	12.1	26
Farmer	1.6	3
Farm Laborers	1.4	3
	47.0	100

4. See Levison (1975) for a somewhat different view. His book is probably the best single source on the characteristics of the blue-collar workers.

5. Family income is also increased as a result of other members working: children and various extended kin who may live in the same family. Thus, the family-income data in Table 3 do not necessarily refer to incomes received by the husband and wife alone. The source for the figure in the text is the U.S. Bureau of the Census (1976a:table 79).

6. The source for these budgets is the Bureau of Labor Statistics (1977: tables 128, 129, 130).

7. These figures were calculated from U.S. Bureau of the Census data (1976: table 41).

8. These figures were calculated from U.S. Bureau of the Census data (1976i: table 41). The budget levels used are, of course, the same as reported above.

9. These figures were calculated from Bureau of Labor Statistics data (1977: table 60).

10. These figures were calculated from Bureau of Labor Statistics data (1977:table 68).

11. The basis for the argument above is in Bureau of Labor Statistics data (1977: tables 108, 109, and 110).

12. Wallick (1972) cites only a few such diseases: black lung (mining), brown lung (textiles), asbestosis (factories and shipyards), gas and fume poisoning (auto factories), and many more.

13. Sexton and Sexton (1972:103) have put the problem of industrial deaths in perspective: "In 1968, a total of 14,300 people died in industrial accidents in our country—almost exactly the same as the number of American servicemen who died in Vietnam that year. Between the beginning of 1961 and the end of 1969, about 46,000 Americans were killed in Vietnam. During that same period, 126,000 American workers were killed in industrial accidents."

14. Female mobility patterns generally parallel male patterns. See Tyree and Treas (1974) and Byrne (1975). For a more detailed analysis of occupational mobility, see Chapter 14.

15. Levison (1975:133-71) brings the literature on blue-collar political attitudes and behavior together in a nice way. As he notes, the best single study is clearly R. F. Hamilton's *Class and Politics in the United States* (1972a), along with two articles by him (1972b; 1972c). For data on the South, see Davidson (1972).

16. Lipset's arguments are contained in his article "Democracy and Working Class Authoritarianism" (1959) and reprinted in his *Political Man* (1963:87-126). All citations in the text are from the latter source. The literature criticizing the thesis is now fairly long. In addition to sources cited in the text, see Lipsitz (1965), Davidson (1972), and Wright (1972). Lipset has replied to his critics in (1961) and in Lipset and Raab (1970). A more general critique of "authoritarianism as a world view" is in Gabennesch (1972).

17. There is some dispute as to whether support for the Vietnam War can be construed as a partial test of the authoritarianism thesis. Wright (1972) reviews this issue at some length and concludes that opinions on this issue are useful as a partial test of the thesis.

18. In 1972, 7.3 million more white-collar people voted. In 1974, 6.8 million more white-collar people voted. These data were compiled from U.S. Bureau of the Census (1973:table 9; 1976e:table 7). By the way, voter participation is always lower in off-year elections.

19. It should be noted that class-based voting does not occur in the United States nearly as much as it does in other nations, such as Great Britain and Australia. Many blue-collar workers do support Republican candidates, just as many white-collar workers support Democrats (see Alford, 1967).

20. Davidson (1972) has studied a variety of segregationist referenda in the South and concludes that lower-income people are generally more tolerant than those with higher income.

21. Unfortunately, the Bureau of the Census does not collect data on Americans' religious beliefs. See Peterson (1964) for a commentary on this problem.

22. The source for this figure is the U.S. Bureau of the Census (1975c:table 64). However, its source is church rolls as compiled by the National Council of Churches, and such membership rolls are generally inflated.

23. There has been some suggestion that differences in church membership by class reflect more general differences in voluntary organization membership (Goode 1966). Stark persuasively rejects this argument. Even when membership in voluntary

organizations is controlled, blue-collar people are church members at lower rates than are white-collar people. This finding is especially true when church attendance is taken as an indicator of membership (see Glock and Stark, 1965:188).

24. However, it must be emphasized that official crime rates reflect those persons the police choose to arrest (Black, 1970). Such official rates may have little relationship to the actual incidence of criminal behavior. By the way, Green's data below are presented by him in such a way that white-collar and crafts workers cannot be separated here.

25. The source for these data is Law Enforcement Assistance Administration (1972).

26. These statements are based upon data from the U.S. Bureau of the Census (1976c:table 13). The data refer to first births of women living with an employed husband between 1965 and 1969. There are variations by race: blacks have higher rates of premarital pregnancy than do whites. However, like whites, a greater proportion of white-collar blacks get married prior to childbirth.

27. While most marriages are hypogamous (that is, within strata), many are not. It has been common to argue that status inequality between mates can produce marital stress. However, Glenn et al. (1974) have correctly argued that many hypergamous marriages are successful ones. It is now becoming clear that status inequality within a marriage is only important when it is accompanied by status consciousness on the part of the mates (Pearlin, 1975). When the latter occurs, mutual reciprocity, communication, affection, and value consensus become more difficult to maintain.

28. LeMasters notes that males strongly desire this sort of role segregation and it produces great stress in many marriages. This argument disagrees with Goldthorpe et al. (1969), who found working-class British families have adopted "companionate" marriages that appear to involve less role segregation.

29. It must be noted that Erlanger did find significant differences by race. Among whites, there are no variations by social strata in the use of corporal punishment. However, among blacks, it appears that the lower the socioeconomic status, the higher the rate of corporal punishment. The reason for this finding is not altogether clear.

30. This argument is based on data from the U.S. Bureau of the Census (1975b; 1976d).

31. On these three findings, see Quinn et al. (1974).

32. These second three findings are based on Form (1973). They are still speculative.

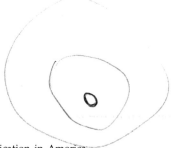

10
WHITE-COLLAR WORKERS

Sociological descriptions of white-collar workers are sparse. Apart from small-town community studies done in the 1930s and 1940s, which are of limited use today, there are few studies of middle-class people and no overarching theoretical interpretations of them.[1] Rather, as Mills (1951:ix) observes, it seems that "the white collar people slipped quietly into modern society . . . [and] before an adequate idea of them could be formed, they have been taken for granted as familiar actors of the urban mass."

Nonetheless, despite the paucity of studies focusing only on white-collar people, a great deal is known about their social characteristics. Much of that knowledge was reviewed in Chapter 9, in an attempt to compare blue- and white-collar people. That material will not be repeated here. This chapter is organized into two sections. The first is a description of the jobs white-collar people hold. The second section is a more lengthy description of the social characteristics of white-collar people, with special emphasis on some topics not covered earlier.

WHITE-COLLAR OCCUPATIONS

Description

White-collar people are those who engage in nonmanual rather than manual occupations. They generally sit behind a desk rather than work with their hands. Some typical white-collar occupations are listed in Table 1. As can be seen in the table, apart from the fact that

Table 1 Some Typical White-Collar Occupations

Professional and Technical	Managers and Administrators	Sales	Clerical
Accountants	Assessors	Advertising Agents	Airline Stewardesses
Engineers	Bankers	Hucksters and Peddlers	Bank Tellers
Lawyers	Corporate Executives	Insurance Agents	Cashiers
Librarians	Government Officials	Newsboys	Mail Carriers
Physicians	Office Managers	Real Estate Agents	Office-Machine Operators
Nurses	Proprietors	Sales Clerks	Receptionists
Scientists	Purchasers		Secretaries
Social Workers	Sales Managers		Telephone Operators
Teachers	School Administrators		
Writers	Store Managers		

their jobs generally do not require hard physical labor, white-collar people have quite diverse occupational characteristics.[2]

The diversity of white-collar occupations can be seen in a number of ways. First, varying amounts of formal education are required. Some jobs require several years of postgraduate training, while others do not require a high school diploma. Second, although some white-collar people are self-employed, most are salaried employees of governments or corporations. This last category can be divided into those people who work on a commission basis and those who do not. Finally, some white-collar jobs are highly interesting and challenging, but others are alienating in that those who fill them are relatively unable to control their environment, experience their work as relatively meaningless, are socially isolated from others, and often have low levels of self-esteem. In this regard, such jobs resemble many blue-collar occupations.

The occupations listed in Table 1 are grouped according to their census classification. Despite the fact that they comprise only 29 percent of the white-collar work force, the professions are the single occupational class most clearly identified by the public at large (Hall, 1975).[3] This recognition is largely a result of the great training needed to fill such positions, their high level of occupational prestige, and the great power many professionals have. This last point suggests the most important characteristic of professional occupations: to some degree they are self-directed in their jobs. For example, the doctor makes a diagnosis of (or guesses at) one's illness and the social worker determines a family's eligibility for welfare benefits.

However, while they are self-directed, professionals perform in three distinct settings, each of which circumscribes the worker in different ways. The smallest group is comprised of self-employed practitioners, the so-called "free professionals" in Mills' (1951) term, but among professional workers, these individuals are economically and socially marginal. The second group is made up of those professionals who have organized or participate in specialized service organizations such as law firms or medical clinics. Finally, the majority of professionals are employed in a specialized department of large organizations—for example, those doctors, lawyers, social workers, engineers, and scientists who work for corporations or government at all levels.

Managers and proprietors are those white-collar workers who "occupy middle to high positions in organizations of all types" (Hall, 1975: 137). Although together they comprise 21 percent of the white-collar work force, managers and proprietors are a diverse group. Managers are business executives or government officials at all levels, from top executives in corporate conglomerates to minor specialists (such as sales representatives). In most cases, proprietors are the owners and managers of small businesses. Such operations are occasionally quite lucrative, but most are economically marginal businesses. Despite these differences, the most important characteristic of managerial work is that, to some degree, such persons make and enforce policy in their domain, narrow or wide as it may be.

Sales workers are the smallest white-collar occupational category, only 13 percent of all middle-class workers. They are nearly all employees of businesses and charged with dealing with individual customers. Income from many sales jobs is based partly or wholly on commissions earned, so that a great deal depends upon a person's ability to attract and persuade customers to purchase goods. In such a context, the need for individual initiative becomes the most important characteristic of the job. Unlike professional and managerial occupations, sales is the first white-collar group that has a high representation of women. Roughly half of all sales persons are female.[4] Not surprisingly, sales is also the first white-collar occupation in which it is generally the case that organizational decisions are followed and not made. Apart from the ability to sell customers goods, sales people have relatively little power.

Clerical workers are the largest white-collar occupational category, comprising 37 percent of all middle-class workers. It is dominated by women. Four out of five clerical workers are female. The most important characteristic of clerical work is that it is often relatively standardized and routinized. With the increasing use of office machinery, many clerical jobs have come to resemble factory production processes.

Clerical workers perform in two different settings (Hall, 1975:172). Some people, such as bank tellers, receptionists, or mail carriers, have direct contact with the public. For many people, such employees represent their only contact with the large organizations that affect their lives. On the other hand, many clerical workers never see the public and have contact only with others performing the same or similar tasks. These people are the unnamed and often unknown keypunchers, clerks, secretaries, and others whose services are vital to most large organizations. Nonetheless, as will be shown below, such individuals are generally paid at very low rates. They are also, like sales workers, required to follow rather than make decisions. Furthermore, like the semi-skilled blue-collar workers described in Chapter 9, clerical personnel generally have their job tasks defined for them by someone else. Little independent judgment by the worker is either expected or allowed.[5]

These are some of the typical occupations engaged in by white-collar workers. Although they are a diverse group, they have one characteristic in common: they generally do not engage in manual labor. As will be seen below, people who perform in such middle-class jobs also have a variety of economic and other social characteristics in common.

THE CHARACTERISTICS OF WHITE-COLLAR PEOPLE

The occupational distribution in the United States was shown in Table 2 in Chapter 9. The concern there was with the current proportion of people in the blue- and white-collar work force. It was shown that blue- and white-collar workers are each about half of the population. Here the concern is with the number and proportion of white-collar people in a historical context. This issue is summarized in Table 2. As can be seen in the table, both the number and proportion of the work force engaged in white-collar occupations, especially clerical and professional jobs, has been expanding steadily since 1900. On the other hand, although the number of blue-collar workers has increased since 1900 because of population growth, the proportion of the work force engaged in blue-collar occupations, especially farmers and laborers, has been contracting just as steadily.[6] Although not shown in the table, the historical distribution of occupations by sex shows a similar pattern.

A significant problem involves the interpretation of these data. C. Wright Mills (1951:30–76) offers the most arresting analysis, and a brief description of his classic book, *White Collar*, is appropriate here.[7] Mills contrasts those who make up what he calls the Old Middle Class (farmers, businessmen, and "free professionals") with the New Middle Class (managers, salaried professionals, sales people, and office workers). He argues that during the nineteenth century the vast majority of white-collar workers were independent, self-employed, and self-sufficient. According to Mills, these were

Table 2 Civilian Labor Force, by Occupation and Year

	1900[a]	1920[a]	1940[a]	1960[a]	1975
Professionals	4%	5%	7%	11%	15%
Managers	6	7	7	11	10
Sales	5	5	7	6	7
Clerical	3	8	10	15	18
Total White Collar	18%	25%	31%	43%	50%
Crafts	11%	13%	13%	13%	13%
Operatives	13	16	18	18	15
Laborers	12	12	9	5	5
Service	9	8	12	12	14
Farmers	38	27	17	8	8
Total Blue Collar	83%	76%	68%	56%	50%
Number (millions)	29.0	42.4	51.7	65.8	83.5

Sources: Data for 1975 and 1960 are from U.S. Bureau of the Census, *Statistical Abstract of the United States, 1976* (Washington, D.C.: U.S. Government Printing Office, 1975), table 586. Data for 1940, 1920, and 1900 are from U. S. Bureau of the Census, *Historical Statistics of the United States, Colonial Times to 1970* (Washington, D. C.: U. S. Government Printing Office, 1975), p. 139.

[a]Does not add to 100% because of rounding.

the halcyon days when men were "ready and eager to realize the drive toward capitalism." The Old Middle Classes owned and worked their property. Society was self-balancing, not dominated by centralized authority. These bygone days were somehow better, Mills suggests. He argues that with industrialization has come "the transformation of property" and the rise of the New Middle Class to a position of numerical predominance. The New Middle Class is composed of "white-collar people on salary." These new white-collar people are propertyless and, hence, little more than modern proletarians, regardless of their occupations. They are no longer self-sufficient or independent. As a result, Mills claims they are alienated, politically powerless and apathetic, and status conscious to an increasing and piteous degree. This new and more bureaucratized society is not nearly as exciting as that of the past. And, in Mills's hands, its people are objects of scorn.

White Collar remains the most provocative description of middle-class people ever written. It is, as Dennis Wrong (1952) has observed, an "attempt to formulate a broad view of society as a whole and to plot the direction in which it is moving in the muddy river of history." Nonetheless, Mills's interpretation is not without flaws. His analysis is Weberian in origin, for he is most interested in the process of bureaucratization—what Weber called rationalization. He argues, and Table 2 implies, that economic activities in industrial societies increasingly take place in large formal organizations. As a result, one kind of (ideal type) white-collar group, the Old Middle Class, has been replaced by another, the New Middle Class. This historical process is tragic, according to Mills. He believes that modern white-collar workers are unable to realize their potential as human beings, either in work or in leisure. They are, in Raymond Aron's pithy phrase, "mutilated by the division of labor."

Mills is an intellectual who does not like the "little people" about whom he writes, for they are oppressed and uncreative. This attitude is the major flaw in the book. It leads Mills to create an idyllic nineteenth-century world that never existed. The free and independent Old Middle Class he prefers—the country doctor, the struggling farmer, the general-store owner—was, as Table 2 shows, a very small proportion of the population. Further, those who made it up were not nearly as free or creative as Mills suggests. Most people, then and now, struggle to make a living. Only the social context has changed.

In summary, the proportion of the population engaged in white-collar occupations has been expanding between 1900 and 1975. Although not shown in Table 2, this general tendency is true even when sex is controlled. C. Wright Mills's portrayal of white-collar people is brilliant and provocative, but it is also too harsh.

Economic Characteristics

As was shown in Chapter 9 (Table 3), the median income of most white-collar workers is higher than that of most blue-collar workers. This difference results mainly from the high incomes enjoyed by particular occupational groups. Engineers, lawyers, physicians (including dentists), and airplane pilots are the specific occupations with the highest median incomes in the United States. For example, in 1973, the median income for physicians and surgeons was in excess of $23,000 and that for engineers was $17,924. Plainly, these occupations are highly remunerative. On the other hand, sales clerks, bank tellers, restaurant managers, and secretaries of all sorts are in white-collar occupations with relatively low median incomes. The 1973 median income for secretaries, for example, was $6,631 and that for retail sales clerks was $8,885 for males and $4,269 for females.[8] People in these occupations are considerably less well off economically and have considerably lower incomes than do many blue-collar workers.

The income differences between blue- and white-collar people can be seen in another way, as well, by examining the proportion of workers in each occupational category at each income level. Table 3 displays these data. Most generally, the proportion of white-collar families is relatively low at the two lowest income levels and increases steadily as income rises. At the highest income level, those families that earned more than $25,000 in 1974, more than three-fourths of all families are white collar. Clearly, however, most of the families at the higher income levels have household heads in only two occupational categories: professionals and managers.

Table 3 Percent Distribution of Families, by Occupation and Income, 1974

Occupation	$4,000 or Less[a]	$4,000– 6,999	$7,000– 9,999	$10,000– 14,999	$15,000– 24,999	$25,000 and Over
Professionals	6%	7%	9%	11%	19%	29%
Managers	8	7	8	12	17	33
Sales	5	4	5	5	6	9
Clerical	10	10	11	9	8	5
Total White Collar	29%	28%	33%	37%	50%	76%
Crafts	10%	15%	19%	25%	24%	12%
Operatives	14	20	23	21	15	6
Laborers	8	8	8	5	3	1
Service	21	18	12	8	6	3
Farmers	16	7	3	2	2	2
Farm Laborers	3	4	2	1	—	—
Total Blue Collar	72%	72%	67%	62%	50%	24%

Source: U.S. Bureau of the Census, "Money Income in 1974 of Families and Persons in the United States," *Current Population Reports*, Series P-60, no. 101, table 19.

[a]Does not add to 100% because of rounding.

The income distribution shown in Table 3 suggests that white-collar people are more likely to be affluent than blue-collar people. Affluence is best measured in one of two ways, although in either case the results are startling. The first method is divide the population into fifths, with the top of 20 percent of the population being considered relatively affluent. By this measure, all those families with incomes above $22,037 were affluent in 1975. If the level of affluence is restricted to the top 5 percent of all families, then those with incomes above $34,144 were affluent, in a statistical sense, in 1975.[9]

A second way of measuring affluence, and showing the relative economic benefit of being a white-collar worker as well, is to compare the incomes of blue- and white-collar people in terms of the estimated annual budgets of the Bureau of Labor Statistics. It will be recalled that the BLS computes standard budgets based upon the cost of various family needs (food, shelter, clothing, medical care, entertainment, taxes, and so on) at three levels, which it calls low, intermediate, and high. The most recent year for which such data are available is 1974. During that year, the BLS calculates, a typical family of four needed an income of $9,198 to live at a low level, $14,333 to live at an intermediate level, and $20,777 to live at a high level.

Table 4 presents the percentage of blue- and white-collar families and unrelated individuals who had incomes at each level in 1974. The table reveals that, if some degree of affluence is indicated when a family has an income above the BLS's high level, then a far greater proportion of white-collar families are affluent. Fully 39 percent of all white-collar families had incomes above the high level in 1974, compared to 19 percent of all blue-collar families. Similarly, white-collar families are considerably less likely to have incomes below the low level established by the BLS. Fully 27 percent of all blue-collar families are poor by this measure, compared to only 13 percent of white-collar families. Thus, it is clear that in terms of income, it is generally better to be a white-collar worker. In summary, if one is willing to describe as affluent those who are either in the top fifth of the income distribution or those who earn more than the BLS's high level of income, then a far greater proportion of white- than blue-collar people are indeed affluent.

As an additional note on the economic characteristics of white-collar workers, it will be recalled from Chapter 9 that white-collar people are also better than blue-collar people in terms of a variety of economically important non-income measures. They have greater job security in that they are less likely to be unemployed and, when it does occur, are likely to be without work for shorter periods. Similarly, such fringe benefits as the number of paid holidays and longer vacations (based on length of service) also benefit white-collar people

Table 4 Proportion of Families at Each Bureau of Labor Statistics Budget Level, by Occupation, 1974[a]

BLS Budget Level	Blue Collar[b]	White Collar	Total[b]
Above $20,777 (high)	19%	39%	23%
$14,333–$20,777 21 (intermediate)	23	26	
$ 9,198–$14,333 (intermediate)	30	22	25
Below $9,198 (low)	27	13	32
	99%	100%	101%
Number (millions)	21.9	18.5	40.4

Sources: Budget levels are from Bureau of Labor Statistics, *Handbook of Labor Statistics, 1976* (Washington, D.C.: U.S. Government Printing Office, 1977), tables 128, 129, 130. Percentages were calculated from U.S. Bureau of the Census, "Money Income in 1974 of Families and Persons in the United States," *Current Population Reports*, Series P-60, no. 101, table 41.

[a]These data do not include families and individuals classified as unemployed, in the armed forces, or not in the labor force.

[b]Does not add to 100% because of rounding.

more than blue collar. Finally, intragenerational mobility is more likely to occur to white-collar workers.

However, two more disquieting observations must be added to this description of middle-class economic characteristics. The first is that, contrary to popular stereotypes, most people in America are not affluent. As Table 4 shows, 78 percent of all families earn less than the BLS's high-level budget. Further, by this same measure, a majority (61 percent) of all white-collar people are not affluent either. Yet another interpretation of these data is also possible. That is, it can be argued that many people are quite well off in America. After all, 23 percent of the population is affluent by the BLS measure, and about 26 percent is well off if the top fifth of all families is used as the criterion. In describing the income distribution in the United States and the relative proportion of blue- and white-collar people at each level, a lot depends on one's point of view: one can say *only* 23 percent are affluent or *fully* 23 percent are affluent.

This descriptive problem points to the second observation. That is, the analysis above is a statistical one and its relevance to people's own perceptions of their situation is sometimes dubious. The term "affluent" has been used to describe families earning more than $20,000. Among those people who live on less than that amount, such a description is probably fairly apt. To a family getting along on $9,000 annually, and it is clear there are many, $20,000 seems like a lot of money. In this case, then, the statistical and the linguistic description make subjective sense. However, it is unclear whether many of those families described as affluent in this chapter think of themselves in that way. Rather, while they clearly live better than others, such persons think of themselves as "average Americans" and feel their "needs" constantly pressing against their (hard-won) resources. No matter how accurate the numerical description, few things are so irritating to people as being told that a statistical fact refutes their feelings or their perceptions of reality. In this second case, then, neither the statistical nor the linguistic description makes subjective sense to those people being described.

In summary, while the income distribution among middle-class people is quite wide, the median income of white-collar people is higher than that of blue-collar people. Generally, then, white-collar individuals have higher incomes than do blue-collar individuals. Furthermore, a considerably greater proportion of the middle class can be described as affluent. However, whether this description makes subjective sense depends upon one's angle of vision.

White-Collar Politics

The place of middle-class people in the political process can be summarized in a single empirical generalization: the higher the socioeconomic status, the greater the rate of political participation (Verba and Nie, 1972; Milbrath, 1965). This statement also appears to be true cross-culturally (Verba, Nie, and Kim, 1971). The finding that socioeconomic status is associated with greater rates of political participation means, in short, that white-collar people participate in the political process more than do blue-collar people. For example, data showing that middle-class people vote in greater proportion than working-class people were presented in Chapter 9. However, the thrust of that analysis was to show that blue collarites were not authoritarian, or at least not any more authoritarian than white collarites. Despite the similarities noted in Chapter 9, there are some important political differences between middle- and working-class people. White-collar people are much more likely to identify themselves as Republicans. For example, Verba and Nie (1972:220) report that only 22 percent of people of lower socioeconomic status identify themselves as Republicans. This compares to 31 percent and 46 percent among people of middle- and upper-level socioeconomic status.[10] These differences carry over into actual voting behavior as well: middle-class people are more likely to vote Republican.

However, while these strata-related differences in party identification and voting are important, they are also commonplace and leave three key issues unexplored. First, voting does not exhaust the possible range of political behavior. It would be useful to know how socioeconomic status is related to other forms of political participation. Second, why is socioeconomic status related to participation? Third, what are the consequences of this relationship? The following paragraphs briefly deal with each of these issues.

In considering the range of possible political behavior, it has been found that the relationship between socioeconomic status and participation is generally true regardless of the measure used. For example, in a masterful piece of social research, Verba and Nie (1972: 118) conceptualize the range of political behavior as falling into the following six categories. (1) About 22 percent of the population is totally inactive. These people lack interest, skill, and feelings of competence. Persons from lower socioeconomic levels are over-represented in this group. (2) Approximately 21 percent of the population regularly participated in the most easily accessible form of political activity: voting. But since they also lack skills and feelings of competence, they do little else. As noted above, white-collar people are more likely to vote than blue-collar or poor people.

(3) About 4 percent of the population participates by contacting officials about particular problems (generally involving self-interest) but is inactive in other ways. This measure is the only one on which Verba and Nie (1972:132) found less of a relationship to socioeconomic status. (4) Approximately 20 percent of the population votes regularly and contacts officials about broad social issues. These people have a high sense of "community contribution," as well as some political skill and feelings of competence. However, they generally avoid partisan political campaigns. Individuals from higher socioeconomic levels are overrepresented in this group.

(5) About 15 percent of the population votes regularly and campaigns actively on behalf of candidates. These individuals are politically involved, highly skilled, and quite partisan. People from higher socioeconomic backgrounds are also overrepresented in this group. (6) Finally, Verba and Nie define 11 percent of the population as "complete activists" who participate in all possible ways. There is a heavy overrepresentation of upper-status people in this group.[11] Thus, if one either takes a particular measure or constructs an overall index of political participation, it is clear that the higher the socioeconomic status, the greater the rate of political participation.

There appear to be two reasons why socioeconomic status is related to political participation. Being of relatively high socioeconomic status seems to promote (1) the development of what are called "civic orientations" and (2) membership in voluntary associations. These two factors act as intervening variables stimulating political participation on the part of people of high socioeconomic status. "Civic orientations" refer to such things as level of concern for politics, level of political information, feelings of competence, and beliefs that political decisions are of importance both to the individual and the community (Verba and Nie, 1972:125). Verba and Nie show that "higher socioeconomic status increases political participation by increasing the civic orientations—involvement, efficacy, skills—of citizens" (1972:134–35). This finding is true for each individual measure as well as for an overall index of political participation.

Voluntary associations generally refer to those organizations of people formed to pursue some common interest of the members. Their manifest purpose may involve such things as leisure (as in a sports or hobby group), community service (as in service clubs such as the Lions or youth groups such as the Girl Scouts), religious belief, or partisan political expression. However, socioeconomic status is the most important predictor of voluntary association membership.[12] Association membership in turn stimulates political activity. This finding is especially true for those who are active members and seems to hold even for individuals who belong to manifestly nonpolitical groups (Verba and Nie, 1972:174–208; Hyman and Wright, 1971). In summary, socioeconomic status is positively related to political participation because it stimulates the civic orientations and voluntary association memberships of people.

The major consequence of the relationship between socioeconomic status and political participation can be simply stated: Political participation makes a difference because leaders at all levels—local, state, and federal—respond to those who demand attention and put them in office. In short, white-collar people benefit from public policies because they participate more in the political process. Verba and Nie (1972:302–8) show that community leaders and political participants tend to have similar political priorities.

In conclusion, because they are generally of higher socioeconomic status, white-collar people participate more in the political process than do either blue-collar or poor people. This finding is true for nearly all measures of socioeconomic status. It results from the tendency of middle-class people to have more clearly focused civic orientations and to join organizations. And it results in greater political benefits going to middle-class people.

Religion and White-Collar Status

The differences between blue- and white-collar religiosity were described in Chapter 9. Briefly, the major findings are that in the population at large, the higher the socioeconomic status, the higher the rate of church membership and the greater the religiosity, as measured by church attendance. This finding is clearly applicable to white non-Southerners, but it was speculated that the relationship lessened for white Southerners and blacks. However, when only church members are concerned, white-collar people appear to have less orthodox (and more public) beliefs than do blue-collar people. This finding must be qualified in that there are variations by church affiliation and by sex.

In this section, our concern is with a different but related topic: the relationship between religion (or religious background) and socioeconomic status. Ever since Max Weber's (1958) famous essay, *The Protestant Ethic and the Spirit of Capitalism*, this relationship has been the subject of a great deal of controversy (see Green, 1959). Although Weber was primarily interested in understanding a peculiar historical event, the rise of capitalism in Western Europe rather than elsewhere, subsequent observers have wondered whether the nature of religious beliefs are a causal factor in occupational status attainment, income, and other aspects of worldly success in industrial societies. Lenski (1963) reports data indicating there are "still" significant socioeconomic differences between Protestants and Catholics and suggests that the origin of these differences lies in religious affiliation. However, more recent work has either failed to replicate Lenski's findings (Schuman, 1971) or suggested that religious affiliation has only a minimal impact on occupational achievement (Jackson et al., 1970). These findings do not mean that socioeconomic differences by religion are nonexistent, for Gockel (1969) and Goldstein (1969) have both shown them to be fairly systematic. Rather, it means that religious beliefs (or background) do not appear to be an important cause of differences in socioeconomic status, at least in the United States.

White-Collar Crime

The differences between blue- and white-collar people in regard to the legal system were dealt with in Chapter 9. Briefly, it was argued that there are no differences in overall crime rates between blue- and white-collar people. Rather, members of each stratum commit different kinds of crime. Blue-collar people commit the more visible and frightening forms of crime—against property and of violence. Middle-class people are relatively unlikely to end up in jail. For example, according to the Law Enforcement Assistance Administration (1976b), of all the inmates in state prisons in the United States in 1974, only 15 percent were employed in white-collar occupations prior to their incarceration. This low figure is, by the way, considerably higher than the proportion of white-collar people confined in local jails. Middle-class people are considerably less likely than working-class people to be victimized by crimes. Surprisingly, however, the differences between blue- and white-collar people's attitudes toward the police and legal issues are minimal.

This section is concerned with the crimes middle-class people do commit—white-collar or occupational crimes. In his classic study, Sutherland (1949:9) referred to white-collar crime as those violations of law committed by people of respectability and high social status in the course of their occupations. By "white collar," he meant business managers and executives of large corporations. However, Newman (1958), Quinney (1964), and others have argued that this definition is too restrictive. White-collar or, as it is also called, occupational crime refers to illegal acts committed by nonphysical means (such as guile or concealment), either to avoid payment or loss of money or to obtain business or personal advantage (Edelhertz, 1970).

White-collar crimes can be classified into four types (Edelhertz, 1970:19–20). Some typical examples are listed in Table 5. The first type consists of "personal crimes." These are violations of law in a nonbusiness context by individuals acting against others (or the state) on an ad hoc basis for personal gain. As Table 5 shows, these crimes range from such simple acts as credit card fraud to violating Federal Reserve Board regulations regarding stock purchases. The second type of white-collar crime consists of "abuses of trust." This type refers to occupational crimes by those in business, government, or some professional capacity which violate duty or fidelity to employer or client. These crimes have important consequences. The U.S. Chamber of Commerce (1974) has estimated at least 30 percent of all business failures each year are the result of employee dishonesty. Recently, it was discovered that half of one state's meat inspectors were being bribed to overlook health violations in meat-processing plants (Finn and Hoffman, 1976). The third type of white-collar crime consists of "business crime." This type refers to violations of law explicitly designed to aid business operations. This form of illegality is pervasive in America. It ranges from performing bogus repairs on automobiles (Clark, 1970:23) to conspiring to keep prices high and bribing politicians. The fourth type of white-collar crime consists of "con games." These are violations of the law as a central function of business. Apart from the famous cons like Ponzi schemes,[13] medicare frauds by some doctors and medical laboratories fall into this category.

What links all these white-collar crimes together is the fact that they are willful violations of the law whose purpose is disguised. Further, unlike the more publicized crimes of violence or property, white-collar crimes rely upon the ignorance, carelessness, and (often) the active assistance of the victim. After all, someone must pay the confidence man. White-collar crimes are unique in another way as well. They rely for concealment on one of three factors: preventing the victim from realizing one's victimization, the fact that only a small proportion of victims will complain, or the creation of false records.

The crimes described above seem less prosaic than, say, burglary or auto theft, but their consequences are in many ways more serious. First, the economic consequences of white-collar crime are staggering. The public loses at least $40 billion a year (and probably more) as a direct result of white-collar crime (Finn and Hoffman; 1976). This figure is much greater than losses suffered from all forms of crime against property combined, and its consequence is more oppressive. As Clark (1970:23) observes, white-collar crime can "dig

Table 5 Some Typical White-Collar Crimes

Personal Crimes
    Credit Card Fraud
    Credit Purchases Without Intention to Pay
    Bankruptcy Frauds
    Welfare Fraud
    Home Improvement Loan Frauds
    Violation of Federal Reserve Board Regulations Regarding Margin
        Requirements in Stock Purchases
Abuses of Trust
    Commercial Bribery or Kickbacks
    Fee Splitting by Doctors or Lawyers
    Embezzlement
    Putting Unqualified Relatives on Government Payrolls
    "Sweetheart Contracts" Entered into by Union Officials
    False Travel Expenses or Per Diem Claims
Business Crime
    Antitrust Violations
    Food and Drug Violations
    Misrepresenting Credit Terms
    Collusion Between Physicians and Pharmacists to Cause Writing of
        Unnecessary Prescriptions
    Housing Code Violations by Landlords
    Deceptive Advertising
    Commercial Espionage
Con Games
    Ponzi Schemes
    Medical or Health Frauds
    Personal Improvement Schemes (diploma mills, modeling
        schools, etc.)
    Phony Accident Rings
    Money Order Swindles

deeper than the wallet in the pocket to wipe out the savings of a lifetime. The thief takes only what is in the purse or the dresser drawer at the moment of his or her crime. The embezzler may reach beyond to destroy the equity of a family, ruin a whole firm, or render corporate stock valueless."

The second consequence of white-collar crime is more difficult to measure yet probably more serious. White-collar crime can have dire effects on public health.[14] When thousands of people are maimed and killed as a result of riding in unsafe or defective automobiles, how can it be measured? When children are burned to death while wearing flammable pajamas sold in violation of laws prohibiting the sale of such garments, who can measure the cost? Or when industries subvert pollution and safety controls, and thereby kill or maim their workers, despoil the environment, and injure the health of citizens, who can measure the cost? Such events are not uncommon.

Third, white-collar crime contributes to American social malaise.

As Finn and Hoffman (1976:3) describe it, "citizens come to distrust government and business; business distrusts its employees and government; and government loses faith in the probity of business and the average citizen."

Given the seriousness of white-collar crime, it appears paradoxical that the government has not mobilized to prosecute it more vigorously. However, the reasons for lack of prosecution are fairly straightforward. First, unlike a robbery, most white-collar crime is not very obvious to law-enforcement officials. Many victims are unwilling to report such crimes or believe that such action would be futile anyway. As a result, much white-collar crime simply goes undiscovered. Second, many of the schemes used in white-collar crime are incredibly complex. As a result, it is difficult, time consuming, and expensive to prosecute them. Many law-enforcement agencies simply do not have the money to prosecute white-collar crime.

Third, even when successfully prosecuted, penalties are generally so light that neither individual perpetrators nor corporations suffer much. This fact is unfortunate, for, unlike much street crime, most white-collar criminality is not based on emotion or poverty. Rather, it is deliberate and premeditated. Thus, while the death penalty for murder has little deterrent value, the certainty of long jail sentences for corporate executives who violate the law could have a real deterrent effect. The fourth reason white-collar crime is not prosecuted is that such efforts are opposed by many powerful interests. At all levels of government, those sections of law-enforcement agencies dealing with white-collar crime must compete for funding with other sections. By simply focusing public attention on the more frightening sorts of criminality, it is relatively easy to ensure that white-collar crime is neither investigated nor prosecuted.

In summary, white-collar crimes are nonviolent efforts at obtaining economic advantage. There are four interlocking types: personal crimes, abuses of trust, business crimes, and con games. These forms of criminality have staggering economic consequences. They also affect public health and the social climate in disastrous ways. Unfortunately, however, white-collar crimes are generally not prosecuted because they are not reported, they are terribly difficult to prosecute even when discovered, and positive action is opposed by special interests.

White-Collar Family Life
In the comparison of blue- and white-collar families in Chapter 9, the following findings were reported. The higher the status, the older the age at marriage. This relationship appears to result, at least in part, from a greater rate of attendance at college and a lower rate of premarital pregnancy among middle-class youths. The children of middle-class parents tend to marry each other; that is, the norm is

marital hypogamy. The higher the socioeconomic status of the family, the fewer the children and the older the parents when they arrive. The higher the socioeconomic status, the less role segregation among the spouses. There are probably fewer differences in child-rearing tactics than have usually been attributed to blue- and white-collar people. Finally, the higher the socioeconomic status, the lower the rate of marital instability, regardless of the indicator used.

This section is concerned with a complicated problem: the relationship among socioeconomic status, family life, and achievement motivation. The literature on this topic is now fairly long (see Turner, 1970; Rosen et al., 1969). Sociologists have spent a great deal of time trying to show that middle-class people are more ambitious than working-class people. Phrased more formally, the major finding is that the higher the socioeconomic status, the higher the achievement motivation. Achievement motivation refers to people's desire to get ahead, to excel at tasks, to be ambitious. It is measured in two ways. First, Rosen (1956; 1959; 1961) ascertained the aspirations mothers held for their sons by asking what level of education and occupation the mothers would like their sons to have and what level they would be satisfied if their sons attained. Second, Turner (1970), Rosen, and many others have used a Thematic Apperception Test (TAT) to determine children's level of "need for achievement" (N Ach).[15]

The relationship between socioeconomic status and achievement motivation can be explained in the following way.[16] Compared to blue-collar jobs, a higher proportion of white-collar occupations have what are called entrepreneurial characteristics. That is, people have relative freedom from supervision and a high level of personal autonomy on the job. Although the exact causal sequence can only be inferred, it has been argued that father's occupation affects family socialization patterns, which in turn affect the development of achievement motivation in sons.

Occupation appears to affect family socialization patterns in two ways. First, several studies (Elder, 1965; Pearlin and Kohn, 1966) have suggested that occupations with entrepreneurial characteristics "result in an occupational ideology stressing achievement." This ideology is (somehow) "absorbed by the wife with the result that emphasis on achievement by both parents becomes a predominant training practice, especially with regard to sons" (Turner, 1970:161). Second, occupations that have entrepreneurial characteristics appear to be less frustrating to men, which results in less negative sanctioning of children and a greater emphasis on their development of self-control and self-reliance (McKinley, 1964). Such characteristics are presumed to lead to high achievement motivation, as indicated by aspirations or TAT scores. Therefore, Turner concludes, "to the extent that an occupation promotes achievement values in a father, while allowing few frustrations to develop, it may affect family structure and socializing in those ways conducive to [the development of] achievement motivation in sons" (1970:162).

In this way, then, sociologists have accounted for the "fact" that middle-class people are more ambitious than working-class people. But there are two real problems underlying this finding.[17] The first problem is one of omission. The literature is sexist in that it does not deal with women or the development of achievement motivation in females. Although socialization practices differ for each sex, many women nonetheless do develop high achievement motivation — often in spite of their parents' best efforts. Further, it is not clear how mothers affect the development of achievement motivation in children or how achievement values are "absorbed" by mothers from fathers.

The second problem is more serious. Whether measured indirectly with a TAT or more directly by assessing educational and occupational aspirations, achievement motivation ultimately refers to people's desire for occupational achievement. More specifically, it refers to the desire to fill high-prestige jobs. Success in other spheres of life is basically irrelevant to these studies. Yet the literature on achievement motivation does not take the "relative distance" of various occupations into account. It is not clear why the son of a physician who wants to become a physician is more ambitious than the son of a farm laborer who wants to become a skilled crafts worker. Phrased more generally, some children have greater opportunity than others to obtain high-prestige jobs, and the literature on achievement motivation simply fails to take this fact into account. Keller and Zavalloni (1964:60) state the problem this way.

Social class alters the content of what is aspired to and thus constitutes an intervening variable between individual ambition and social achievement. Any given success goal has both an absolute and a relative value, the first referring to the general consensus regarding its overall . . . desirability, the second, to its class accessibility. In order, therefore, to compare the extent of ambitiousness [between classes] one needs to know not only the absolute rank-order of a given goal and group rates of endorsement of this goal . . . but also the relative distance of each [class] from it.

In order, then, for one to assess the level of achievement motivation by socioeconomic status, the relative distance of middle- and working-class individuals from various occupational goals must be assessed. Neither Turner, Rosen, nor others perform this task.

In summary, sociologists have tried to show that the entrepreneurial characteristics of fathers' jobs influences familial socialization patterns such that sons develop a high need for achievement. Since middle-class occupations are more likely to have entrepreneurial characteristics, socioeconomic status is positively related to achievement motivation. However, this finding is problematic for two reasons: (1) it is sexist, based on research dealing only with males; (2) it does not take into account the relative distance that some youths must move in order to attain high-prestige jobs.

White-Collar Education

In Chapter 9 (Table 8), it was shown that white-collar people are often more highly educated than are blue-collar people. It has also been shown that white-collar people generally have higher incomes than do blue-collar people. These relationships are not accidental, for it can also be shown that those with higher levels of education also have higher incomes. For example, in 1974, the median income of individuals with an elementary school education was $5,398. This figure is below the poverty line for those with families. It compares with median incomes of $10,602 for those people with a high school education and $13,660 for college educated persons.[18]

The association between income and education can be further illustrated by a look at the distribution of income and level of education, as in Table 6. The table shows that, although individuals with all levels of education can be found at all income levels, those who are less well educated cluster at the bottom of the income heirarchy and those with progressively more education cluster at the middle and higher income levels. This close relationship among education, occupation, and income is why many indexes of socioeconomic status are comprised of these three variables.

Nonetheless, the causal relationship among these variables is a tangled controversy, with important implications for public policy (see Cain and Watts, 1970). At its heart the issue is this: to what extent do the schools contribute to the eventual occupational and income attainment of those students who pass through them? Historically, Americans have viewed education as a principle means of equalizing opportunity. However, there is now an impressive

Table 6 Education and Income, Males, 1974

Income	Education		
	Elementary[a]	High School[a]	College
$ 6,000 or Less	55%	21%	14%
$ 6,000–9,999	24	25	16
$10,000–14,999	15	32	28
$15,000–24,999	6	18	29
$25,000 or More	1	3	13
	101%	99%	100%

Source: U.S. Bureau of the Census, "Money Income in 1974 of Families and Persons in the United States," *Current Population Reports*, Series P-60, no. 101, table 58.

[a]Does not add to 100% because of rounding.

amount of literature which challenges that assumption (For example, Coleman et al., 1966; Jencks, 1972). In shorthand terms, the major finding of the "Coleman Report" is that schools make considerably less difference in students' cognitive skills (as measured by achievement test scores) than does their family background. This finding is more true for whites than blacks. Jencks goes even further, arguing that among individuals (not groups) the quality of education accounts for much less of the variation in adult income and occupation than was previously thought. What often does matter, according to Jencks, is how long one stays in school.[19] Because the school environment is often more palatable to the children of white-collar parents, and because such children have often learned more appropriate needs and behaviors, they stay in the educational system longer. The children of middle-class parents are more likely to graduate from high school, plan to attend college, graduate from college, and obtain postbaccalaureate degrees.[20]

Thus, despite the fact that job requirements are often unrelated to educational accomplishments (Berg, 1970), America is a credentially based society that uses education as a means of allocating individuals into "appropriate" statuses (Halsey, 1973). Thus, in summary, it appears to be the case that for many white-collar people and their children education is a means of status maintenance. Nonetheless, it also appears that education can be (and is) a means of upward social mobility for some children from blue-collar backgrounds.

SUMMARY

White-collar people are those who work in nonmanual occupations, ranging from doctors and social workers to office managers, insurance agents, and receptionists (see Table 1). As a proportion of the total work force, white-collar occupations have been steadily expanding over the past 75 years (see Table 2). Some middle-class occupations, especially among those classified as professional or managerial, are quite lucrative and involve a high amount of self-direction. Many sales and clerical occupations have precisely the opposite characteristics. Nonetheless, white-collar people are generally more affluent than are blue-collar people (see Table 3). In statistical terms, a greater proportion of middle- than working-class people are affluent (see Table 4), although this point may not be subjectively meaningful to many such persons.

White-collar people participate in all forms of political behavior at greater rates than do blue-collar people. Evidently, affluence triggers higher levels of civic orientation and membership in voluntary organizations. These factors in turn stimulate participation. The result, of course, is that white-collar people receive political benefits. Middle-class religious beliefs do not appear to cause differences in socioeconomic status. White-collar people commit occupational crimes (see Table 5) that have staggering effects on people's economic situations, their health, and the general social climate. Unfortunately, white-collar crimes are not vigorously prosecuted.

According to studies of "need for achievement," middle-class people are more ambitious than are working-class people. However, such studies are generally sexist and do not take into account the relative distance of various occupations. Finally, although middle-class people are generally more highly educated than are working-class people, the causal relationship among education, occupation, and income is unclear.

NOTES

1. The major community studies are those by Warner (1963: 1949) and the Lynds (1929; 1937). These classic pieces are reviewed by Gordon (1963) and Stein (1960). See also Mills's (1972) caustic analysis of Warner's work.

2. Mills (1951:63–214) provides the most provocative account of the various white-collar occupations. His book still ought to be required reading for sociologists. Hall (1975:67–186) provides a current analysis and some of the more recent citations relevant to white-collar occupations.

3. The figures here and below referring to the proportion of the white-collar work force in each occupation are calculated from Bureau of Labor Statistics (1976:table 6).

4. See Bureau of Labor Statistics (1976:table 19) and Chapter 13 below.

5. On alienation among white-collar workers, see Kirsch and Lengermann (1972) and Shepard (1971).

6. This historical trend in the occupational distribution has important implications for the analysis of social mobility. See Chapter 14.

7. Two thoughtful reviews of Mills's work are in Wrong (1952) and Reisman (1952).

8. This argument is based on data contained in U.S. Bureau of the Census (1975c: tables 589 and 603).

9. These data are from the U.S. Bureau of the Census (1976a: Table 5).

10. These figures do not refer to party membership but party identification. The two are quite different. Note that Verba and Nie use an index of education, occupations, and income as a measure of socioeconomic status. As the citations will indicate, the following paragraphs are indebted to their outstanding work, *Participation in America: Political Democracy and Social Equality* (1972).

11. About 7 percent of the population was not classifiable according to Verba and Nie's scheme (1972:118).

12. For example, see Cutler (1976), Hyman and Wright (1971), and Orum (1966).

13. Ponzi schemes are investment frauds in which individuals are promised exorbitant returns on investment (typically 100 percent). The con artist proceeds by recruiting investors and paying off some of the original investors as a means of encouraging further investment. The pattern continues until the con artist thinks as much money as possible has been invested, then she disappears.

14. For some particularly lurid, but not inaccurate, examples of the ill effects of white collar crime, see Mintz and Cohen (1971) and Lundberg (1968).

15. The TAT is a projective test in which children are shown a series of pictures and asked to tell stories about them. These stories are then scored according to a method devised by McClelland et al. (1958). On this basis, a child's "need for achievement" is inferred. See also McClelland's outstanding study, *The Achieving Society* (1961).

16. This short summary is adapted from Turner (1970).

17. For a good, though caustic, indictment of the "need for achievement" literature, see Lopreato (1970:149–61).

18. These data are from the U.S. Bureau of the Census (1976i:table 58).

19. A good review of the entire controversy surrounding Coleman's and Jencks' work is in Hodgson (1975). On Jencks, see Lasch (1975) and Coleman et al. (1973). On Coleman, see Cain and Watts (1970).

20. These assertions are based on data available from the U.S. Bureau of the Census (1976h; 1976i) and the U.S. Department of Health, Education, and Welfare (1976a).

11
THE RICH

While the poor are defined largely by their relative lack of money, the rich are defined mainly in terms of their possession of a great deal of money or economically important assets. This chapter is divided into five sections. The first identifies alternative measures of wealth and their strengths and weaknesses. In the second, in order to provide a setting for the discussion of more recent data, historical trends in the distribution of wealth are described. The third presents detailed recent data on the distribution of wealth in the United States. The fourth analyzes the manner in which wealth is protected. As will be shown, this issue involves the politics of the rich. The fifth notes other social characteristics of the rich.

However, as a prelude to these topics a qualifying note must be appended. Being poor is regarded as a social problem worthy of research. As a result, scholars can obtain grants from government agencies in order to do that research. However, being rich is not regarded as a social problem, and because the rich can protect themselves from social-scientific voyeurs, there is a paucity of systematic data available about them. Generally, the lower the socioeconomic status of people, the greater the amount of research on them by sociologists. As a result, sociologists simply do not know as much about the rich as they should.

ALTERNATIVE MEASURES OF WEALTH
There are three ways of measuring economic inequality. The first, which is also the easiest and most common, is to examine the dis-

tribution of income in the United States. From this angle, the rich are simply those with the highest incomes. The second way is to examine the distribution of wealth in America. Total wealth is comprised of all the economic assets people have—for example, automobiles, home equity, stocks, bonds, trusts, land, and all other items that can be converted to money. Individual wealth or the wealth of aggregates of people (such as each fifth or the top 1 percent of the population) is obtained by subtracting from the value of their assets the value of all asset-secured loans. For example, one may borrow money and secure the loan by giving a bank a lien against one's automobile. The third way of identifying the rich is to look at the distribution of net worth. Net worth refers to the economic assets people have minus all debts, including both secured and unsecured loans.

All three measures will be used in various ways in this chapter. However, the well-to-do are such a small proportion of the population that the distribution of income does not adequately portray their economic situation. This is so for four reasons. First, the rich are better able to hide their income and more prone to do so in order to escape high taxes. Kolko (1962:21) notes that only about 91 percent of personal money income is reported and that "nonreporting is almost exclusively confined to the upper brackets," which receive income other than wages. Second, unlike the vast majority of the population, the rich receive a great deal of nonearned income based upon their possession assets. The value of such assets is not accounted for in distributions of income. For example, stocks worth millions of dollars may produce several hundred thousand dollars of income in the form of dividends. If income is used as a measure of inequality, then the value of the stock is ignored and the true economic situation of the rich is left obscure.

Third, the wealthy are able to defer their income in various ways. For example, a company may hold back dividend payments until a person is in a lower tax bracket, perhaps after retirement. Alternatively, those who control a company by virtue of stock ownership may declare no dividends and simply reinvest the company's profit. In such a situation, the value of their stock might increase greatly at the same time their income dropped. Fourth, the rich have greater access to tax-free expense accounts and various other forms of income in kind, which drastically reduce their incomes. Income in kind is a form of indirect payment. For example, Kolko (1962:19–20) reports that in one year 80 percent of the checks in the most expensive restaurants in New York City and 30 to 40 percent of the Broadway theater tickets were covered by expense accounts.

Thus, the use of income alone as a measure reduces the level of observed inequality. As shown in Table 1, when the distribution of income is examined, the poorest fifth of the population has 7 percent

**Table 1 Percent of Total Wealth and Income Held,
by Fifths of Consumer Units, 1962[a]**

Fifths of Units	Percentage of Total Wealth	Percentage of Total Income
Lowest Fifth	0.2%	7.2%
Second Fifth	2.1	8.6
Middle Fifth	6.2	11.4
Fourth Fifth	15.5	15.6
Highest Fifth	76.0	57.2
	100.0%	100.0%

Source: Office of Management and Budget, *Social Indicators, 1973* (Washington, D.C.: U.S. Government Printing Office, 1973), p. 182. These figures are calculated from D. S. Projector and G. S. Weiss, *Survey of Financial Characteristics of Consumers* (Washington, D.C.: Board of Governors of the Federal Reserve System, 1966).

[a]Consumer units are families and unrelated individuals.

of the total income, while the richest fifth has 57 percent. However, when the distribution of wealth is examined (and the value of economically important assets is taken into account), then the poorest fifth of the population has less than 1 percent of total wealth, while the richest fifth controls 76 percent. The distribution of wealth reveals considerably more inequality because it shows that the poorer segments of the population control less of the total available economic assets.

Because both net worth and wealth take into account the assets and debts people have, they are especially useful in depicting the range of inequality in a way that more fully identifies the rich. However, as seen in Table 2, the two distributions are slightly different in that net worth shows a greater proportion of the population falling into the negative money class, while leaving the upper portion of the array virtually unchanged. Close perusal of the table will reveal that, for both wealth and net worth, the first four levels ($ negative through $4,999) comprise 45 percent of the population. When net worth is used, many people shift from having low levels of wealth to a negative net worth. This is because poorer persons are more likely to have unsecured debts. All signature loans, such as credit cards, are unsecured debts. Rather than a lien against property, poorer people are more likely to have a lien against their labor (Turner and Starnes, 1976:21).

However, an explanatory note must be added. The amount of inequality shown in Table 2 does not seem right to many people, for analysis of their own (or their family's) economic situation suggests they have little or no net worth. Yet such blue- and white-collar people—even some labeled affluent in Chapter 10—do not reasonably feel poor. After all, although some economic insecurity always exists, they think of themselves as doing all right because they possess all the accoutrements of American life: cars, color television,

Table 2 Percentage Distribution of Consumer Units, by Wealth and Net Worth, 1962

Money Class	Wealth[a]	Net Worth
$ Negative	2%	11%
$0	8	5
$1–999	16 } 45%	12 } 45%
$1,000–4,999	19	17
$5,000–9,999	16	15
$10,000–24,999	23	23
$25,000–49,999	11	10
$50,000–99,999	4	4
$100,000–199,999	1	1
$200,000–499,999	1	1
$500,000 and Over	–[b]	1
	101%	100%

Source: D. S. Projector and G. S. Weiss, *Survey of Financial Characteristics of Consumers* (Washington, D.C.: Board of Governors of the Federal Reserve System, 1966), tables A1 and A2, pp. 96–99.

[a]Does not add to 100% because of rounding.

[b]Less than one-half of 1%.

homes, and the like. But because of the availability of credit, they are always in hock: to the bank, the credit union, the loan company, and the department store—all of which are owned by the rich. Those who have very little or no net worth (and they comprise almost half the population) are not accumulating an estate.

The fact that only a few people in the United States are able to accumulate wealth is the real significance of the data in tables 1 and 2. The stunning fact is that 20 percent of the population controls 76 percent of the total wealth in America, and less than 1 percent have estates worth $500,000 or more. There are not a lot of rich people out there but, as will be shown, they are very powerful and some are extraordinarily wealthy.

In summary, there are three ways of measuring economic inequality: by examining the distributions of income, wealth, and net worth. Income is the least useful because it does not capture economically important assets held by the rich. Use of either wealth or net worth reveals that riches are very concentrated in the United States (see tables 1 and 2). As a qualifying note, it should be added that the possession of assets (such as stock) makes sources of income other than wages available to the wealthy. These sources of income will be of interest in later sections.

HISTORICAL TRENDS IN THE DISTRIBUTION OF WEALTH

Based upon Tocqueville's often prescient observations, an egalitarian thesis dominates interpretations of American history (Pessen, 1971). Tocqueville argued that "in a democracy like that of the United States the quality of conditions [that] gives some resources to all members of the community also prevent [s] any of them from having resources to any great extent." That is, it is asserted that historically there were few rich or poor people in America. Further, it is also asserted that "in America, most of the rich men were formerly poor" and when wealth was amassed it was "insecure" and circulated with "inconceivable rapidity."[1]

All of these assertions are wrong. The egalitarian interpretation of American history is a sociological and historical myth.

While the data are scanty, it appears that relative equality of condition only existed for a short time in American history, if it existed at all. For example, as early as 1693, in Chester County, Pennsylvania, the richest 10 percent owned 24 percent of the wealth. A hundred years later, in 1793, the richest 10 percent owned 38 percent of the wealth. During this same period, the share of the wealth controlled by the poorest 60 percent of the population in Chester County declined from 38 to 18 percent. The colonial era data for Salem, Boston, and Philadelphia are essentially the same (Pessen 1971:1019). Pessen concludes that in the North as a whole prior to the American Revolution, about 10 percent of the people owned 45 percent of the wealth. These are conservative estimates.

During the first half of the nineteenth century, the so-called "age of equality" in America, the available data show a sharply increasing proportion of the wealth owned by the rich. The figures for New York City are typical. In 1829, the richest 4 percent of the population in that city owned 49 percent of the wealth. By 1845, they owned 66 percent (Pessen, 1971:1022). Again, these are conservative figures. The first great fortunes were amassed during the late eighteenth and early nineteenth centuries, as a few millionaires and multimillionaires appeared. Despite this fact, many argue that America was more egalitarian in comparison to Europe, with its landed aristocracies. But Pessen (1971:1001) shows that, although the economic basis of wealth was often different, American fortunes were not paltry and the superrich in the New World were every bit as wealthy as those in the Old. He concludes as follows.

The wealth of the American rich, unlike that of the contemporary English aristocracy, derived largely from commerce and when from land, often took the form of real properties recently accumulated in speculations rather than estates held in the families for centuries. The American rich were a working class, however, only in a technical rather than an actual sense. The preference shown by many of them for attending to business rather than to pleasurable uses of leisure was a matter of taste rather than necessity and can be compared to the preoccupation shown by some peers in managing their estates. By almost any criterion opulent Americans lived lives comparable to those enjoyed by their English and Continental counterparts.

Not only was there great inequality in the United States during the first half of the nineteenth century, but most wealth was based upon inheritance and was very stable over time. Contrary to the easy generalizations of both historians and sociologists, Pessen (1971:1006–1016) argues that only a small proportion, between 2 and 6 percent, of the Jacksonian-era rich were born poor.[2] In nearly all cases, wealth was inherited. The dominant tendency was apparently for inherited wealth to be built up to higher levels with each generation. Essentially, "the extent of an individual's early wealth was the major factor determining whether he would be rich later." As will be shown below, the situation has not changed much.

During the second half of the nineteenth century, the distribution of wealth became even more unequal, especially in large cities. This fact is shown in Table 3, where three large cities and two rural areas

Table 3 The Distribution of Wealth in America, Selected Areas, 1860[a]

	Baltimore	New Orleans	St. Louis	Rural Maryland	Rural Louisiana
Richest Fifth	94.7%	92.9%	92.7%	83.7%	87.4%
Second Fifth	4.4	5.7	6.0	12.9	9.3
Middle Fifth	0.9	1.3	1.1	2.9	2.5
Fourth Fifth	0.0	0.0	0.2	0.4	0.7
Poorest Fifth	0.0	0.0	0.0	0.0	0.0
	100%	100%	100%	100%	100%

Source: R. E. Gallman, "Trends in the Size Distribution of Wealth in the Nineteenth Century," in L. Soltow (ed.), *Six Papers on the Size Distribution of Wealth* (New York: National Bureau of Economic Research, 1969), p. 23. Standard reference information with permission of NBER.

[a]Families, not individuals.

are compared in terms of population fifths for 1860. According to Gallman (1969:23), in each city the richest 20 percent of the population had more than 90 percent of the wealth, while the poorest 40 percent of the people had nothing. The situation is not much different for rural areas. There the richest 20 percent had about 85 percent of the wealth, while the poorest 40 percent had less than 1 percent. Soltow (1975) reports essentially similar data for ten other large cities in 1860. Generally, he found that about 51 percent of the people had no wealth at all. Although 49 percent had some minimal wealth, the distribution was skewed heavily toward the top.

Trend data on the distribution of wealth in America is presented in a more systematic way in Table 4. Although conventional distributions of wealth are in quintiles (fifths), such arrays conceal the extraordinary concentration of riches in a few people's hands. Table 4 shows this level of concentration by depicting the share of the wealth held by the richest 1 percent of the population. Data from a variety of sources show that the richest 1 percent of all Americans have always held between 21 percent and 32 percent of the national

Year	Percentage of Wealth Held
1810	21.0%[b]
1860	24.0
1900	26.0–31.0[b]
1922	31.6
1929	36.3
1933	28.3
1939	30.6
1945	23.3
1949	20.8
1953	27.5
1956	26.0
1958	26.9
1962	27.4–32.2
1965	29.2–34.8
1969	24.9–29.8

Sources: For years 1810–1900, R. E. Gallman, "Trends in the Size Distribution of Wealth in the Nineteenth Century," in L. Soltow (ed.), *Six Papers on the Size Distribution of Wealth* (New York: National Bureau of Economic Research, 1969), p. 6; for years 1922–1958, R. J. Lampman, *The Share of Top Wealthholders in National Wealth, 1922–1956* (New York: National Bureau of Economic Research, 1962), p. 204; for years 1962–1969, J. D. Smith and S. D. Franklin, "The Concentration of Personal Wealth," *American Economic Review* 64 (May 1974): 166. Standard reference information with permission of NBER.

[a]For years 1810–1900 the population base is 1% of all families. For all other years, the population base is 1% of all adults.

[b]Estimates are projections of 1860 estimate, based on change in rural-urban population distribution and in per capita wealth.

wealth, averaging about 25 percent. However, three specific conclusions about the distribution of wealth are also possible.

First, it appears that wealth inequality increased steadily throughout American history until the onset of the Great Depression. Both the scattered data cited above and the nationwide estimates for the nineteenth century included in the table suggest this trend. Lampman (1962) found the same tendency during the early years of this century, such that by 1929 the richest 1 percent of all Americans owned 36 percent of the wealth. Lampman argues that this level of wealth concentration reflects the tremendous increase in the value of stocks which took place during the 1920s.[3] As shown in Table 4, by 1929 the richest 1 percent of the population held a greater proportion of the wealth than it has had before or since.

Second, between 1930 and 1945, wealth apparently became less concentrated. During this period, when the economy was under great duress and World War II occurred, massive government intervention in the economy took place for the first time.[4] Partly as a result, the proportion of the total personal wealth held by the richest 1 percent of the population fell to between 23 and 31 percent (Lampman, 1962).

Third, by 1949, the rich appear to have held about 21 percent of the wealth, the lowest amount in recent history. However, they quickly recovered and held around 25 percent throughout the 1950s. Despite the variation shown in Table 4 for the postwar years, Smith and Franklin (1974:162) argue that since 1945 the distribution of wealth "has remained essentially unchanged." They believe that nearly all the variations in the estimates since 1945 result from problems with the Internal Revenue Service data, sampling errors, short-run stock-market variations, and valuation biases in the worth of stock. Furthermore, in Table 4, the two estimates each for 1962, 1965, and 1969 represent different methods of calculating the percent of wealth held by the richest 1 percent of the population. The lower figures (on the left in the table) follow Lampman's method and are designed to be comparable to his data for earlier years. However, Smith and Franklin (1974) note that these lower "figures have a downward bias of 10 to 15 percent from our best estimates of [wealth] concentration." They are unable to recompute Lampman's estimates according to newer and more accurate methods because the IRS has destroyed the original data. Thus, the figures to the right in Table 4 probably represent more accurate estimates of the concentration of wealth during the 1960s.[5]

In summary, although the available data are scanty, trends in the distribution of wealth show that throughout American history wealth has been very concentrated. The egalitarian interpretation of American history is a myth. As Pessen argues, during the colonial era, wealth concentration increased steadily. This process appears to have continued throughout the nineteenth century (see tables 3 and 4). After culminating in the 1920s, the level of wealth concentration has decreased slightly and remained relatively stable since World War II.

RECENT DATA ON THE DISTRIBUTION OF WEALTH

Systematic information on the distribution of wealth in the United States is available from only two sources. First, on at least two occasions, the Board of Governors of the Federal Reserve System has surveyed the financial characteristics of consumers and weighted the sample so as to include the very rich. Unfortunately, the most recent study was done in 1962 (Projector and Weiss, 1966).[6] Nonetheless, the information contained in this study is still among the best available because it deals with the entire population.

The second type of wealth data is tax-related information. In this case, the most recent data were compiled by the Internal Revenue Service (1973) for the year 1969. A few researchers have also had access to the 1969 IRS data (Smith, 1974). These data refer to "top wealthholders," defined by the IRS as individuals with gross assets of more than $60,000 in 1969. Information on these persons is obtained by means of the "estate multiplier technique." This technique assumes that death draws a random sample of the population.

Based upon estate-tax returns, which are required by law if the deceased had gross assets exceeding $60,000, the technique "relies on the fact that for the general population the mortality rate is known for each age and sex group" (Internal Revenue Service, 1973). As a result, the sample can be extrapolated to represent the entire population of people with assets greater than $60,000 in 1969. The analyses that follow generally rely on these two sources.[7]

Although while it is unfortunate that more recent data on the distribution of wealth are not available, there is no evidence that it has changed much in recent years. However, as Smith (1974) notes, if any changes have occurred or if better data could be obtained, it is probable that the estimates used in this chapter would be revised to show even greater inequality.

This section is organized in terms of three key questions. (1) What are the various levels of wealth and how is it distributed? (2) What is the relation between income and wealth? (3) What is the origin of wealth?

What Are the Levels of Wealth and How Is It Distributed?

Americans are a rich people, but it is not often made clear just how rich they really are. Smith (1974) notes that, in 1969, Americans held personal gross assets of $3.5 trillion. If that amount were distributed equally, it would be about $17,000 for each woman, man and child. But, of course, it is not distributed equally. From Tables 2 and 4 above, the various levels of wealth can be conceptualized in the following five ways. (1) At the lowest level are those who are *worth nothing* (including here those who, in monetary terms, are worth less than nothing). These people comprise about 10 percent of all consumer units (families and unrelated individuals). They include the poor as well as many blue- and white-collar people who have more debts than assets.

(2) At the second level are those consumer units that are *barely solvent* financially. They have wealth valued at between $1 and $24,999, and make up the vast majority of all consumer units—about 74 percent. (3) At the third level are those consumer units that have managed to acquire a financial *nest egg*, whether for their old age or to pass on to their children. These families and individuals possess wealth valued at between $25,000 and $50,000, and are about 11 percent of all consumer units. They are people who manage to live pretty well. The first three levels of wealth comprise 94 percent of all families and individuals.

(4) At the fourth level are those consumer units that can be called *rich*. After their secured debts are subtracted, they have assets worth between $50,000 and $500,000. These consumer units comprise, at most, 6 percent of the population. (5) At the very top level are the *superrich*, those individuals and families with assets worth more than

$500,000. These people comprise less than one-half of 1 percent of all consumer units, or about 200,000 families and individuals.[8]

The distribution of wealth by percentage of the population and the mean value of wealth in each category are presented in Table 5.[9] As can be seen in the table, the distribution is heavily skewed toward the top. The mean value of wealth held by the superrich is more than three times that held by the merely rich. Some perspective can be gained when it is realized that it would take 3,184 units in the lowest solvent-wealth category (those whose assets have a mean value of $396) to equal the wealth of the average superrich consumer unit.[10]

One reason for the skewness revealed in Table 5 is that even among the wealthy, riches are concentrated at the top. Table 6 reveals this fact in more detail. It focuses only upon individuals (not consumer units) with a net worth of more than $50,000 in 1969, those labeled the rich and the superrich above. As can be seen in Table 6, even though top wealthholders constitute a very small percentage of the total population, 3.5 percent, nearly all of them are clustered at the lower end of the distribution of net worth. As shown in the table, 89 percent of the rich and superrich have a net worth of less than $300,000. Really great wealth is concentrated at the top end of the continuum in the hands of only a few individuals and families. Those with a net worth of $5 million or more constitute a microscopic 3/1,000th of the total population, and only 11/100th of the rich and superrich. According to 1969 tax returns, there were

Table 5 Mean Value of Wealth and Percent of Population in Each Category of Wealth, 1962

Size of Wealth	Mean Value of Wealth	Percentage of Population[a]
$ Negative	—	2%
$0	—	8
$1–999	$ 396	16
$1,000–4,999	2,721	19
$5,000–9,999	7,267	16
$10,000–24,999	16,047	23
$25,000–49,999	35,191	11
$50,000–99,999	68,980	4
$100,000–199,999	132,790	1
$200,000–499,999	300,355	1
$500,000 and Over	1,260,667	—[b]
		101%

Source: D. S. Projector and G. S. Weiss, *Survey of Financial Characteristics of Consumers* (Washington, D.C.: Board of Governors of the Federal Reserve System, 1966), tables A2 and A8, pp. 98 and 110.

[a]Does not add to 100% because of rounding.

[b]Less than one-half of 1%.

9,330 individuals in the United States worth $5 million or more.[11] But note that Table 6 displays the same skewed configuration as does Table 5. That is, the mean value of the net worth held by the richest of the superrich ($18,403,164) is two and one-half times that of the previous level. Once again referring to the lowest solvent category in Table 5 (those with mean wealth of $396), it would take 46,472 consumer units to equal the net worth of the average person worth more than $10 million. When one is confronted with these facts, it is hard to argue that wealth is evenly distributed in the United States.

Table 6 Distribution of Top Wealthholders and
Mean Value of Their Net Worth, 1969

Size of Net Worth	Percentage of Top Wealthholders	Percentage of Total Population	Mean Value of Net Worth
$50,000–99,999	48.6 %	1.7 %	$ 74,065
$100,000–299,999	40.8	1.4	157,804
$300,000–999,999	8.9	0.3	488,068
$1,000,000–4,999,999	1.5	0.05	1,730,448
$5,000,000–9,999,999	0.07	0.002	7,221,057
$10,000,000 or more	0.04	0.001	18,403,164
	100.00%	3.5 %	

Source: Calculated from Internal Revenue Service, *Statistics of Income—1969, Personal Wealth* (Washington, D.C.: U.S. Government Printing Office, 1973), table 1, p. 19.

As a qualifying note, it should be emphasized that the wealth levels shown in Table 6 grossly understate the true amount of inequality in the distribution of wealth. These data are based upon estate-tax returns, which for the most part have been reduced to as low a level as possible by a variety of (quite legal) measures to avoid taxes. In addition, the data are for individual tax returns. They do not take into account what assets people hold in nontaxable trusts, foundations, bonds, and many other items. Further, the focus on individuals ignores the manner in which families pyramid their wealth (and power). For example, Lundberg (1975:42) estimates that the 54 members of the Rockefeller family are worth about $5 billion.[12] Assets like these give one of them, Nelson Rockefeller, an annual income (not net worth) of around $5 million dollars per year, even after all means of legally hiding income have been exhausted (Lundberg, 1975:87).[13]

In summary, the distribution of wealth can be conceptualized in terms of five levels: (1) those who are worth nothing, (2) those who are barely solvent, (3) those who have a nest egg of wealth, (4) the rich, and (5) the superrich. Data on the distribution of wealth show that it is quite unequally distributed. The rich and the superrich comprise only about 6 percent of all consumer units in the United

States (Table 5). However, even among this elite group, wealth is concentrated at the top (Table 6). The wealth levels shown for top wealth-holders greatly understate the true amount of inequality.

What Is the Relation Between Income and Wealth?
To answer this question in a reasonably systematic way, one must consider the following topics: (1) the overall relationship between income and wealth, (2) the different sources of income characterizing each level of wealth, (3) the value of assets held by people at each level of wealth, and (4) the income and assets for the top wealth-holders.

Table 7 displays the relationship between net worth and income. The table reveals just what one would suspect: those consumer units with greater assets as indicated by their net worth have higher incomes. More specifically, the vast majority of those consumer units with a net worth of less than $25,000, which constitute about 84 percent of all families and individuals, also have relatively low incomes. Conversely, those few consumer units classified as either rich or superrich in terms of their net worth, about 6 percent of all families and individuals, have very high incomes as well.

From another angle, Table 7 shows that, of those with incomes between $25,000 and $50,000, 86 percent have assets that classify them as rich or superrich. All of those families and individuals with incomes above $50,000 were either rich or superrich. Unfortunately, the government data used here do not permit analysis of incomes above $100,000. Nonetheless, there is a major question raised by these data. What is the basis for the higher incomes received by those with high levels of net worth?

The answer to this question can be found when the distribution and value of assets among consumer units at various levels of wealth are analyzed. The reason for the focus on assets is that the less wealthy have a higher proportion of what wealth they do possess tied up in non-income-producing items. They rely for income on wages and salaries (Ackerman et al., 1971; Kravis, 1968). As will be shown below, those who are more wealthy have the majority of their assets in income-producing items. As a result, they receive a great deal of nonearned income.

The distribution of assets and the importance of those that produce income can be seen in Table 8. Before the table is analyzed, it should be recalled that wealth is essentially asset equity—assets minus secured debts. For purposes of this analysis, the assets people hold can be divided into six groups: (1) liquid assets, such as cash and savings; (2) equity in one's car; (3) home equity, both one's main residence and vacation home or homes; (4) equity in one's business or profession, such as a store, professional practice, or farm; (5) investment assets, such as stocks, securities, real estate, and mort-

Table 7 Income and Net Worth Among Consumer Units, 1962

			Net Worth			
Size of Income	$0[a]	Solvent, $1–24,999	Nest Egg, $25,000–49,999	Rich, $50,000–500,000	Superrich, $500,000 and Over	Total
$0–2,999	30%	63%	7%	1%	—%	101%[b]
$3,000–4,999	23	66	8	3	—	100
$5,000–7,499	13	75	7	5	—	100
$7,500–9,999	5	77	13	5	—	100
$10,000–14,999	3	63	20	13	—	99%[b]
$15,000–24,999	—	37	27	35	1	100
$25,000–49,999	—	6	8	75	11	100
$50,000–99,999	—	1	—	63	36	100
$100,000 and Over	—	—	—	7	93	100

Source: D. S. Projector and G. S. Weiss, *Survey of Financial Characteristics of Consumers* (Washington, D.C.: Board of Governors of the Federal Reserve System, 1966), table A1, p. 96.

[a]Includes those with negative net worth.

[b]Figures do not add to 100% because of rounding.

Table 8 Percentage of Consumer Units with Some Equity in Specific Types of Assets, by Size of Wealth, 1962

| | Type of Asset | | | | | |
| | Non-Income Producing | | | Income Producing | | |
Wealth Size[a]	Liquid[b]	Auto	Home[c]	Business and Profession[d]	Investments[e]	Miscellaneous[f]
All Units	79%	73%	57%	17%	31%	8%
$1–999	70	74	9	3	4	3
$1,000–4,999	78	76	54	8	14	6
$5,000–9,999	85	77	78	16	30	7
$10,000–24,999	96	82	84	19	42	11
$25,000–49,999	97	88	80	38	64	15
$50,000–99,999	98	89	72	54	89	15
$100,000–199,999	100	93	86	53	93	16
$200,000–499,999	97	84	84	57	95	12
$500,000 and Over	100	79	81	66	99	52

Source: D. S. Projector and G. S. Weiss, *Survey of Financial Characteristics of Consumers* (Washington, D.C.: Board of Governors of the Federal Reserve System, 1966), table A8, p. 110.

[a]Excludes those with negative wealth.
[b]Liquid assets: checking and savings accounts, U.S. savings bonds.
[c]Home: principal residence and vacation homes.
[d]Business and profession: equity in family-owned and -operated businesses, professional practices, farms.
[e]Investment assets: marketable securities, investment real estate, and mortgages.
[f]Miscellaneous assets: largely assets held in personal trusts.

gages; and (6) miscellaneous assets, nearly all of which are trust funds. Table 8 is arranged in these terms, with the three types of non-income-producing items to the left (liquid, auto, home) and the three income-producing assets to the right (business, investments, miscellaneous).

Table 8 refers to the percentage of consumer units in each wealth class possessing assets in each category, regardless of their value. Nearly all families and individuals have some liquid assets and an automobile (although those with negative wealth have been excluded from this table). One must have cash to buy food and, usually, a car in order to work. It is interesting to note that a decreasing proportion of the wealthy have auto equity. This tendency merely suggests a reliance on commercial or forms of private transportation other than the car. Most people have some equity in a home, although the proportion drops radically among those with low levels of wealth ($1–$4,999). The real difference between the very rich and the majority of the population becomes apparent when income-producing assets are considered. To repeat, most of the rich have assets in income-producing items, and this fact can be clearly seen in Table 8. Among those families and individuals who are least solvent, only 3 or 4 percent have assets tied up in a business, in investments, or in the miscellaneous category. These proportions increase steadily until among consumer units worth more than $500,000 it be seen that 66 percent have assets in business, 99 percent have investments, and 52 percent benefit from trust funds. All these items produce income.

As a qualifying note, it can be seen that although virtually all of the rich and superrich have investments of various sorts, a significant minority of less well off families and individuals do also. This fact has often been used to suggest that economic equality in the United States has increased. Unfortunately, when the value of people's investments and other assets is considered, it becomes clear that ownership of a few stocks or other investment items does not alter the overall structure of inequality in this country.

Table 9 displays the mean dollar value of equity in assets possessed by families and individuals. Once again, the table is set up so that the three non-income-producing assets are to the left and those that generate income are on the right. As might be suspected, for each type of asset there are clear differences according to wealth: those with greater wealth have assets that are worth more. For example, among those consumer units that are barely solvent, average liquid assets amount to $134, auto equity $190, and home equity $40. Among the superrich consumer units worth more than $500,000, liquid assets amount to $46,094 on the average, auto equity $2,679, and home equity $56,232. These differences among nonincome producing assets are quite stark. However, among the barely

Table 9 Mean Dollar Value of Equity in Assets Held by Consumer Units, by Wealth Size, 1962[a]

Wealth Size	Non-Income Producing			Income-Producing			Total Mean Wealth
	Liquid	Auto	Home	Business and Profession	Investments	Miscellaneous	
All units	$ 2,675	$ 644	$ 5,653	$ 3,881	$ 7,013	$ 1,116	$ 20,982
$1–999	134	190	40	9	14	9	396
$1,000–4,999	701	445	1,298	83	170	25	2,721
$5,000–9,999	1,227	614	4,260	625	440	100	7,267
$10,000–24,999	2,624	850	8,852	1,499	2,054	168	16,047
$25,000–49,999	6,371	1,134	12,991	6,644	7,518	533	35,191
$50,000–99,999	10,858	1,499	14,167	16,719	24,556	1,181	68,980
$100,000–199,999	18,808	2,232	22,790	22,938	64,127	1,894	132,790
$200,000–499,999	21,007	2,326	25,889	72,516	169,052	9,564	300,355
$500,000 and Over	46,094	2,679	56,232	295,035	628,271	232,355	1,260,667

Source: D. S. Projector and G. S. Weiss, *Survey of Financial Characteristics of Consumers* (Washington, D.C.: Board of Governors of the Federal Reserve System, 1966), table A8, p. 110.

[a] All figures are *mean* dollar values. They are based on the "total mean wealth" (see Table 5). Definitions of asset types are the same as in Table 8.

solvent consumer units, the figures above constitute 92 percent of all their assets.[14] Apart from their wages and whatever is paid on a home or car, these people have few sources of income. The situation is quite different among those with higher incomes. Among the superrich, the figures cited above for liquid assets, housing, and automobiles constitute only 8 percent of their total assets. The remaining 92 percent of assets held by the superrich are income producing. The figures for other wealth levels are between these two extremes but skewed toward the top.

Table 9 can be examined in another way as well. Consider the investments made by consumer units in the $10,000–$24,999 bracket. They total $2,054 on the average. The families and individuals in this bracket would receive an income of about $144 per year if the investments (in stocks, bonds, and so on) paid at a rate of 7 percent. It can also be seen that the average value of investments is about one-fourth that of housing equity among those in this bracket. Turning again to the superrich, it can be seen that, based upon the same rate of return, these consumer units would receive a yearly income of $43,978 on their investments alone. Furthermore, it should be noted that people with more money have access to higher yielding stocks, bonds, securities, and other investments such that their rate of return is likely to be much higher. Finally, despite possessing a tremendous amount of housing equity, the average value of investments to the superrich is eleven times that of their home assets.

One final note regarding Table 9 is important. Again, a look at the bottom line, those worth $500,000 and over, shows that a real leap in wealth occurs between these consumer units and those just below. Their total wealth is four times that of the previous level. Their average income from trusts is 24 times the previous level. Their income from business and investments is four times greater. This skewness results because the distribution of wealth given by Projector and Weiss stops at such a low level ($500,000 and over). The difference between the superrich and other consumer units reflects the impact of really great wealth. In statistical terms, the tail of the distribution of wealth is quite long.

Although the data are still inadequate, the tail of the distribution of wealth can be examined by a look (as above) at only top wealthholders. The major problem here is that the data are based upon individual tax returns. So besides reflecting the extremely large understatement of wealth typical of such returns, they fail to take into account the assets held or controlled by a few extraordinarily rich families.[15] Nonetheless, with the use of IRS data on top wealth-holders, it is possible to obtain an approximate idea of the distribution of assets among the rich and superrich. Table 10 displays the mean value of assets held by top wealthholders in terms of their net worth. Except for cash, non-income-producing assets are not available for this table. Nor are they especially necessary because they constitute such a small proportion of assets held by the rich. The real basis for great wealth can be clearly seen in Table 10.

Rich & *Super Rich* — There are four fundamental divisions in the table which clearly separate those with a little wealth from those with a lot (sometimes truly extraordinary amounts). The first involves the ownership of corporate stock. The rich own stock but in relatively small amounts in comparison to some of their other assets, such as real estate. The superrich, however, own a great deal of stock. Among those persons with an average net worth of more than $300,000, corporate stock accounts for between 45 percent and 56 percent of their average total net worth. Personally owned real estate is relatively unimportant to these people, in terms of their overall assets. Stock increases in importance so that among the richest of the superrich, those individuals whose net worth exceeds $10 million, the average value of their corporate stock alone amounts to $10.3 million.

The second real division involves assets tied up in noncorporate business ventures. For virtually all levels of net worth among the top wealthholders, this category is relatively insignificant. Only among those whose worth exceeds $10 million does it become vitally important—the second most valuable item in their financial portfolio.

The third type of asset that clearly separates the superrich from the merely rich is the possession of trust funds, located in the category euphemistically titled "other" in Table 10. Although those whose net worth is less than $1 million do have access to inherited wealth, the amounts are quite small in comparison to their financial betters. Among those worth between $5 million and $9 million, their legacy was five times that of those persons at the previous level. Among those individuals whose worth was $10 million or more, their inherited legacy was twice the previous level's (the $5 million—$9 million group).

Finally, the possession of government bonds of all sorts separates great wealth from mediocre wealth. Government bonds are useful because, even though their official rate of return seems low (around 5 percent), all income so derived is tax free—making the real rate of return about 16 percent (see Stern, 1974). As can be seen in Table 10, the average value of bonds increases greatly as net worth goes up.

As a final note on Table 10, the bottom line comprising those with more than $10 million once again skews the distribution. Among the 3,413 individuals in this category are some fantastically wealthy persons. And, once again, it should be emphasized that these data on individuals do not take into account the way in which families pyramid their wealth (and power). Nor do these data account for

Table 10 Mean Value of Assets Held by Top Wealthholders, by Size of Net Worth, 1969

Size of Net Worth	Cash	Corporate Stock	Corporate and Foreign Bonds	Government Bonds[a]	Life Insurance Equity	Mortgages and Real Estate	Noncorporate Business	Other	Total[b]
$50,000–99,999	$15,834	$15,931	$617	$2,507	$2,498	$37,379	$4,840	$6,677	$86,283
$100,000–299,999	26,999	18,970	1,823	5,547	3,221	62,753	9,100	13,841	142,254
$300,000–999,999	52,446	253,638	6,664	27,794	5,652	133,001	26,003	50,713	555,911
$1,000,000–4,999,999	93,288	1,076,166	25,035	129,256	10,007	248,073	72,870	249,537	1,904,237
$5,000,000–9,999,999	207,369	4,333,277	61,349	950,482	20,450	569,207	231,367	1,128,950	7,502,451
$10,000,000 or More	382,655	10,340,755	96,689	1,873,132	24,611	869,909	3,409,317	2,547,905	19,544,973

Source: Calculated from Internal Revenue Service, *Statistics of Income—1969, Personal Wealth* (Washington, D.C.: U.S. Government Printing Office, 1973), table 1, p. 19.

[a]Includes federal, state, and local bonds.
[b]Amounts are slightly different than in Table 6 because debts have not been subtracted.

extraordinary amounts of money tied up in tax-free foundations worth hundreds of billions of dollars (see Gaulden, 1971).

In summary, data on the relationship between income and wealth clearly illustrate the truth behind the old saying that money begets money. Those consumer units classified as rich and superrich have exceedingly high incomes compared to those of others (Table 7). Their high incomes are based upon income-producing assets (tables 8 and 9), the ownership of which clearly separates top wealthholders from the rest of the population. There are differences, however, among top wealthholders in terms of the type of income-producing assets that are most important (Table 10). At the lower levels of wealth, real estate is the most important asset. At the higher levels, corporate stocks, noncorporate business ventures, trust funds, and government bonds are of greatest importance. These four types of assets comprise 93 percent of the financial portfolio held by those individuals worth more than $10 million. The fact that superrich people rely on these items leads directly to the final question of concern in this section: the origin of wealth.

What Is the Origin of Wealth in America? — *Birthright*

It will be recalled that Pessen (1971) argues that throughout American history most wealth has been inherited. During any era, those persons identified as rich usually had rich parents.[16] The modern period has not changed much in this regard, as can be seen in Table 11. The table reveals several points. First, among those consumer units identified above as barely solvent (that is, worth between $1 and $25,000), what little wealth they have is obtained during their own lives as a result of hard work, wages and salaries, saving, and an occasional judicious investment. As noted above, nearly all their assets are tied up in non-income-producing items. Their pittance of wealth is not inherited.

Second, among those consumer units identified as having a finan-

Table 11 Inherited Assets and Wealth, 1962

Wealth Size	Proportion Inherited Assets				Total
	None	Small	Substantial	Not Available	
$1–999	95	5	—	—	100%
$1,000–4,999	87	9	4	—	100%
$5,000–9,999	82	12	6	—	100%
$10,000–24,999	77	17	6	—	100%
$25,000–49,999	75	16	9	—	100%
$50,000–99,999	74	12	12	2	100%
$100,000–199,999	46	32	22	—	100%
$200,000–499,999	59	28	13	—	100%
$500,000 and Over	39	24	34	2	100%

Source: D. S. Projector and G. S. Weiss, *Survey of Financial Characteristics of Consumers* (Washington, D.C.: Board of Governors of the Federal Reserve System, 1966), table A32, p. 148.

cial nest egg of between $25,000 and $50,000, the situation is the same. While a few (9 percent) report substantial inheritance, it is still the case that most of their assets are non-income producing. For nearly all of these individuals and families (91 percent), their relatively low level of wealth results from the same hard work as those in the solvent category. However, it is possible that the real basis of these consumer units' somewhat better financial situation is occupational inheritance (see Chapter 14). This is a speculative point, however.

Third, as shown in Table 11, many of those consumer units identified as rich (worth between $50,000 and $500,000) benefit from a financial legacy of some sort. The available data do not allow researchers to know the type of assets inherited. However, from tables 8 and 9, it will be recalled that successively higher levels of wealth are accompanied by a higher proportion of assets in income-producing items. It is reasonable to speculate that many of the assets inherited at this level are income-producing ones.

Finally, among those consumer units identified as superrich (worth $500,000 or more), 58 percent report at least some inheritance. It is safe to assert that most of the inherited assets are of the income-producing sort.

Once again it must be noted that the wealth distribution based on the 1962 Federal Reserve System study stops at a relative low level. These data do not get at really great wealth, which is nearly all inherited. For example, Lundberg (1968) identifies the four richest families as follows, with his best guess as to their total wealth: the du Ponts, $7.6 billion; the Mellons, $4.8 billion; the Rockefellers, $4.7 billion; and the Fords, $2 billion.[17] These are extended families, of course, with wealth distributed among the members. The point here, however, is that all this wealth is inherited. And the same point would be made if the 20 or 40 richest families were examined. By means of clever stock manipulations, family holding companies, trust funds, and other devices, many large fortunes have been held together. It is simply not true that families proceed "from shirtsleeves to shirtsleeves in three generations."

Lundberg (1968) argues, and he is probably correct, that the last truly great fortunes were made or originated in the latter portion of the nineteenth century. They were based upon technological advances in oil, communication, and transportation. And their results are concentrated today in the hands of a few "great" families. The significance of this fact for those who do not own capital-producing property is that "they will never lay their hands on any of this property no matter how they perform, short of overturning the legal system and the military forces behind it" (Lundberg, 1968:232). Discounting some extraordinary technological breakthrough, truly great wealth is now very hard to obtain in America.

THE POLITICS OF THE RICH AND THE PROTECTION OF WEALTH

It is possible to ascertain who has power in a society by analyzing who benefits most from the distribution of valued resources. It has been shown in this chapter that an extremely small proportion of the population has a vastly disproportionate share of the wealth. It is reasonable to infer, then, that the rich also have a great deal of power. But it is also important to discover some more direct indicators of their power and the political conditions that make it possible—especially in a democratic context. In order to do that, a preliminary conceptual distinction must be made.

Aron (1966) distinguishes between what he calls a political class and a ruling class. By "political class," he means the small minority of people who actually run the government—in the United States, those elected and appointed officials in the legislative, executive, and judicial branches of government. By "ruling class," he refers to "those privileged people who, without exercising actual political functions, influence those who govern and those who obey, either because of the moral authority which they hold, or because of the economic or financial power they possess." No better statement of the role of the rich in America is possible, for the wealthy participate in the political process by using their wealth. On many issues, although by no means all, they constitute a "ruling class," as Aron uses the term.

To illustrate this fact, two issues are dealt with in this section. First, the relationship between tax rates and levels of wealth is examined. In this way the legal basis for the protection of wealth can be seen. Second, the political conditions responsible for the generation of tax laws is noted. These two issues do not exhaust the way or extent to which the wealthy influence politics in America. But they do serve as indicators of their enormous political power, at least regarding certain issues.

The argument here is not that the rich constitute a single, closed, and all-pervasive "power elite" of the sort Mills (1956) suggests.[18] It can be easily shown that on many issues the rich are either unconcerned or their influence is circumscribed—although these issues tend to be those with which the public is passionately concerned (see Rose, 1967). Nonetheless, it remains the case that the wealthy benefit disproportionately when resources are distributed. The only way of accounting for that fact is to show that they constitute a "ruling class" in America.

Tax Laws and Wealth

There are two kinds of taxes: regressive and progressive. Regressive taxes are those that take a steadily smaller proportion of income as it increases. Progressive taxes are those that take a steadily greater proportion of income as it increases. Examples of regressive taxes are Social Security, sales, property, gasoline, and liquor taxes. The way they work can be seen by using Social Security taxes as an example.

Many people believe that everyone pays Social Security taxes at the same rate, but this is not true. The Congress has decreed that Social Security taxes are withheld from wages and salaries at a rate of 5.85 percent only on the first $15,300 of income a person receives.[19] About 56 percent of the population earned less than this amount in 1976, so they had social security withheld from every check they received. Because the government stops withholding these taxes as soon as people's earnings reach $15,300, those who earn more than that amount pay a steadily smaller proportion of their total income into the Social Security system. As result, of course, those earning more than $15,300 receive a raise in take-home pay (a gift from Congress) as soon as their income reaches that level. People who earn $25,000 per year pay 3.58 percent of their income in Social Security taxes; and those earning $50,000 in wages and salaries pay only 1.79 percent of their income into the Social Security system. The principle is the same for all regressive taxes: as earnings increase, the proportion of income paid out in taxes decreases.[20]

Most of the rich, and many of the not-so-rich, clearly favor the use of regressive taxes, which allow them to keep a greater proportion of their income. This is one reason for its prevalence among state and local governments. As a result, Herriot and Miller (1971) show that, in 1968, people with incomes of less than $2,000 paid 27 percent of their meager earnings in state and local taxes, nearly all of which are regressive. This percentage decreases steadily until those with incomes exceeding $50,000 paid only 7 percent of their earnings in state and local taxes. There is no reason to believe that these figures have changed much.

Virtually the only progressive tax in the United States is the federal income tax. But while the income tax appears to be quite progressive, it is not. The published tax rates are highly misleading. For example, the theoretical tax for a married couple with a 1976 income of $5,000 is $815, or a tax rate of 16 percent. For a couple with an income of $20,000, the tax is $4,380, or 22 percent. The theoretical tax rates continue to climb as income rises until the rate for a couple with an income of half a million dollars is 64 percent, or $320,980. However, that hefty amount is rarely if ever paid.[21]

The theoretical versus actual tax rates for various income levels are compared in Table 12, this time using 1972 data.[22] The definition of income used in the table is more comprehensive than that used above, which results in lowering the theoretical tax rate at the lower income levels. Nonetheless, Table 12 clearly shows that the theoretical tax rate is heavily progressive. However, people actually pay

Table 12 Theoretical Versus Actual Tax Rates, by Income Level, 1972[a]

Income Level	Theoretical Tax Rate	Actual Tax Rate	Differences
$2,000–3,000	1.9%	0.5%	1.4%
$5,000–6,000	7.5	2.8	4.7
$10,000–11,000	12.4	7.6	4.8
$20,000–25,000	20.8	12.1	8.7
$75,000–100,000	46.0	26.8	19.2
$200,000–500,000	58.0	29.6	28.4
$500,000–1,000,000	60.5	30.4	30.1
$1,000,000 and Over	63.1	32.1	31.0

Source: Calculated by P. M. Stern, *The Rape of the Taxpayer* (New York: Vintage, 1974), p. 11. Copyright © 1972, 1973 by Philip Stern. Reprinted by permission of Random House, Inc. Based upon data in J. A. Pechman and B. A. Okner, "Individual Income Tax Erosion by Income Classes," in Joint Economic Committee of the 92nd Congress, *The Economics of Federal Subsidy Programs: A Compendium of Papers*, Part I (Washington, D.C.: U.S. Government Printing Office, 1972), pp. 13–40.

[a]The theoretical tax rates differ from those in the text because the Pechman-Okner definition of income is considerably more comprehensive.

their taxes at a much lower rate. For example, on an income of $1 million, people do not pay the 63 percent it seems they should but only pay at a rate of 32 percent. This means that the income-tax system is, in fact, only mildly progressive.

People do not pay the theoretical tax rates because of the existence of various loopholes in the law. These loopholes benefit all citizens to some degree. However, as Stern (1974:11) observes, "the loopholes save families a greater percentage of their income as they grow richer, but . . . at the top of the [income] pyramid this is a greater percentage of an astronomically larger income than is true at the bottom of the heap." For example, Table 12 shows that loopholes save a family 1.4 percent of their income tax at the $2,000–$3,000 income level. Assuming the income is $2,500, this is a saving of $35. But on an income of $1 million the loopholes save a family 31 percent. Thus, the millionaire receives a $321,000 gift from Congress. Put another way, loopholes allow the millionaire to retain 9,171 times as much income as one who earns $2,500 a year.

The unkind call these differences in tax rates a form of welfare for the rich. And, regardless of the term used, these differences in tax rates are clearly a form of governing spending ("tax expenditure" is the formal term), just as if the Congress gave all millionaires a gift or subsidy of $321,000. Essentially, Congress tinkers with tax laws so as to let a few favored (and rich) taxpayers keep great amounts of money and makes up for the loss in revenue by collecting more from everyone else.

Two fundamental facts account for the difference between the theoretical tax rates publicized each year and the actual taxes people pay. The first is that all income is not taxed in the same way. The

Sixteenth Amendment to the U.S. Constitution asserts that taxes on income should be obtained "from whatever source derived." Nonetheless, Congress has declared that various sources of income are to be treated quite differently. This difference occurs despite the fact that a dollar of income will buy the same amount regardless of its source. Essentially, as Stern (1974:346) observes, tax law provides great benefits for those few who receive unearned income based on assets and penalizes the majority of the population, which only works for a living.

Two examples can be used to show the effect of not taxing income in the same way. Table 10 (above) shows that government bonds account for a large proportion of the income-producing assets held by the rich and superrich. Income from nearly all these bonds is tax free. Stern (1974) recounts that one person acquired so many tax-free bonds that she realized an income of $1,000,000 each year, and did not even have to file income-tax forms. Here is income that is not income, at least for tax purposes. Based on a Treasury Department study, Mondale (1975) shows that tax-exempt state and local bonds provide individuals with $1.1 billion in government subsidies to individuals. Over 88 percent of this amount goes to the 6 percent of the population that is rich or superrich.

[margin note: GET OUT OF TAXS]

[margin note: Govt ← Bonds]

Capital gains are another example of the way in which all income is not taxed in the same way. Capital gains are profits made on the sale of stocks, buildings, land, or some other investment. For example, if a person buys a parcel of land for $1,000 and sells it for $5,000, the capital gain is $4,000. Tables 9 and 10 above show that investments are the single most important type of asset held by the rich and superrich. Part of the reason for this is that capital gains are not taxed as ordinary income. To begin with, half of a person's income from capital gains is tax free. The other half is taxed at a maximum rate of 50 percent on the first $50,000 of capital gains. A 50 percent tax on half the gains means that the maximum tax rate on profit is 25 percent. Thus, on capital gains of $100,000, a person pays a maximum of only $25,000 in taxes. Other loopholes often allow people to reduce their capital gains rates even further. On the amount above $50,000, the capital gains tax is 70 percent on half the total, or 35 percent. Thus, on an income of $1 million (all of which is capital gains) the maximum tax is $340,000. This amount is fairly close to the actual rate of taxation displayed in Table 12, and far below the theoretical rate a person with this income should pay. Again, because of the existence of many other loopholes, people can reduce their 35 percent capital-gains tax even further.

[margin note: CAPitAL GAiNS]

Mondale (1975) shows that by treating capital gains as a special income category, Congress supplies individuals with $6.7 billion in subsidies. These are tax expenditures, 62 percent of which go to the rich and superrich. These estimates are probably low. The effect of special rates on capital gains is to ensure that those with higher incomes pay taxes at rates comparable to those with much lower incomes. Stern (1974:96) shows that the higher the family income, the greater the proportion of income that results from the more lightly taxed capital gains. For example, of those with incomes above $1 million, 82 percent of their income results from capital gains. Stern concludes that the gentle tax on capital gains is the single most unfair aspect of the income-tax system.

The second fact accounting for the difference between theoretical and actual tax rates is the existence of numerous deductions from income. Although almost everyone gets some deductions, people with wealth get a great deal more and, again, the key lies in their possession of income-producing assets. Because such assets wear out, the law allows people to claim that their value depreciates over time and to deduct the amount of the depreciation from their income tax. However, rather than depreciating the value of, say, a machine or a building, over the entire useful life of the asset, the law allows "accelerated depreciation"—very high deductions in the early years. The tax advantages of such deductions combined with capital gains and other loopholes can be graphically illustrated with a simple example.

Assume you invest $10,000 in an apartment building worth $100,000, borrowing the remainder from the bank. The law allows you to claim the building is depreciating at a rate of 20 percent a year for five years. As a result, you can deduct from your tax not only the $10,000 down payment but also the $90,000 borrowed from the bank. Thus, each year for five years you have a tax deduction of $20,000. Furthermore, you may also deduct the interest payments on the loan. Assume that after five years the building really increases in value by 50 percent, not an unusual event. At that time, you sell the building for $150,000 and pay only capital gains taxes on half of the $50,000 profit. Thus, on an original investment of $10,000 you get back (1) $100,000 in tax deductions, (2) tax deductions on the interest paid on your loan, and (3) a minimum of $37,500 in capital gains. Interestingly, the buyer of your apartment building can use the tax laws in precisely the same way as you have, as can each subsequent buyer.

More generally, Stern (1974:6–9) calculates that in 1972 there were some 6 million families in the United States with incomes (from all sources) of less than $3,000. These poor families received tax deductions— or "tax welfare"—totaling $92 million, or about $16 per family. At the other extreme, there were about 3,000 families with incomes greater than $1 million in 1972. These rich families received tax deductions of $2.2 billion, or about $720,490 per family. Faced with this level of "tax welfare" for the wealthy, it is hard for one to worry about the meager "welfare" received by the poor.

In summary, the difference between theoretical tax rates and actual tax rates (Table 12) identifies the extent to which great wealth is protected by tax laws. The rich have sources of income which are treated differently than are the wages and salaries most people earn and they have access to deductions that enable them to greatly reduce their income. These differences suggest that the wealthy constitute a "ruling class" in that they are able to influence those who actually make the decisions.

Tax Laws and Politics[23]

The analysis of tax rates provides some evidence that there is a "ruling class" in the United States. Otherwise it seems fair to assume that the government (the "political class") would not subsidize one group to such a great extent. A key issue, then, involves the political conditions under which it is possible to maintain the structure of inequality in a democratic context. Tax laws are written so as to favor the wealthy for four reasons.

The first, and most important, reason is because of the way political campaigns are financed. Now superficially it would seem that the voters elect the members of Congress and that those who run (or at least influence) Congress are those who elect its members. But it turns out that those who really elect members of Congress are those who finance political campaigns (Green et al., 1972). Without adequate financing, no one can run for or be elected to Congress. These people are predominantly wealthy. Nearly all political donations, 90 percent, come from just 1 percent of the population (Stern, 1974:382). Further, nearly all candidates are dependent upon such contributions in order to finance their campaigns. Between 1948 and 1968, about 60 percent of all individual contributions to Presidential election campaigns came from donations of $500 or more. As Stern observes, very few American families can afford to contribute that amount and more. Because the costs of primary and general election campaigns keep rising, candidates for the House of Representatives and the U.S. Senate are forced to raise hundreds of thousands of dollars every two years and every six years, respectively. A candidate generally cannot raise these sums of money without the help of the wealthy. Those candidates who desire to reform taxes by, say, taxing capital gains as regular income are swiftly denied the support of wealthy contributors.

Contributors do not necessarily gain tax advantages for themselves as individuals, although tax relief for specific wealthy individuals or corporations occasionally occurs. More generally, the tactic used is to provide tax benefits for specific classes of individuals or corporations—for example, all those individuals who make capital gains or all those corporations extracting minerals from the environment. Furthermore, one can then lobby to have more and different kinds of income declared to be capital gains or to have more expenses declared deductible. Campaign contributions are not, then, bribes. They do, however, help to ensure that the donors will have access to members of Congress in order to plea for the benefits of their particular bill. As a result, tax loopholes proliferate to the benefit of the "ruling class."

The second reason tax laws favor the rich is because they have nearly always been written in secret. Tax laws are written in the House of Representatives by the Ways and Means Committee and in the Senate by the Finance Committee. Prior to 1973, these two committees nearly always met in strict secrecy, barring not only the press and public, but also members' personal staff (Stern, 1974:392). In this context, special-interest tax laws were freely introduced and written into law, with no public accountability. However, since 1972, new and more stringent rules have been in force which encourage open meetings of the entire Congress. As a result, in the House, "only" 5 percent of all Ways and Means Committee meetings were closed during 1974. In the Senate, "only" 37 percent of the Finance Committee meetings were closed during that same year (Congressional Quarterly, 1975). Nonetheless, it is still the case that many of those laws that touch every American's life are written behind closed doors. In this context, there is every reason to make sure that the tax needs of those who contribute to political campaigns are satisfied. And loopholes abound.

The third reason tax laws favor the rich is because they are so hideously complex. Not even the members of Congress, most of whom are lawyers, can understand many of the provisions in the tax code. The following excerpt (cited in Stern, 1974:394) is typical of the tax code.

For purposes of paragraph (3), an organization described in paragraph (2) shall be deemed to include an organization described in Section 501 (c) (4), (5) or (6) which would be described in Section 501 (c) (3).

Trying to read and understand the tax code is nearly impossible for all but the specialists. The arcane language used in writing tax laws greatly benefits the rich, for it makes the opening of loopholes possible and ensures that only the experts can understand them.

The fourth reason tax laws favor the rich is because the mass media and the educational system fail to inform the public "just who is doing what to whom." Public ignorance and apathy about tax laws and the way they are set up to aid the wealthy helps to prevent tax reform.

In summary, four political conditions—campaign financing, secrecy, arcane language, and lack of public awareness—allow a "ruling class" of wealthy people undue influence over the American "political class." The members of Congress are clearly caught in the middle. On the one hand, they are elected by the voters and have an obligation to represent their interests. On the other hand, their campaigns are financed by the rich, with the consequences noted in this chapter.

CONCLUSION

This chapter has focused upon the wealth of the rich—the historical trends in wealth distribution, how rich the rich are today, and how wealth is protected. This emphasis means several other issues have been ignored, the most important of which involves social status, discrimination, and the existence of an American aristocracy. Among wealthy people there are important differences between those who are just rich and those who are wellborn. Although the wellborn are not a completely closed status group, they do have the following characteristics. They are generally inheritors of large fortunes, Anglo, native born, and Protestant. The wellborn tend to intermarry a great deal, thereby excluding those with "new money" as well as Jews and blacks from entry into their ranks.

While they are well educated, the mark of these aristocrats is not a college degree—even from Harvard or one of the other Ivy League colleges. From their point of view, "anyone can attend Harvard" these days. Rather the educational mark of aristocratic origin is attendance at one of several (usually northeastern) private prep schools. The members of the American aristocracy belong to a variety of exclusive "gentlemen's" clubs, which are also a primary means of discriminating against those of humble origin and diverse background.

Baltzell (1958; 1964) argues that a man's position in high society is indicated by the clubs to which he belongs (women, even those of proper origin, are often excluded from these clubs). He argues further that the existence of an aristocracy is useful and important, even in a democratic context, because such an aggregate of people values, among other things, service to the society. As a result, the aristocracy supplies many of the society's leaders. However, it is vital that such an aristocracy be open, so that those who are extremely upwardly mobile (or at least their immediate descendents) are incorporated into the elite status group and taught its values and lifestyle. Baltzell believes this process of assimilation has broken down in this century, mainly along ethnic and racial lines. As a result, he believes, the American aristocracy has become too closed and too self-centered. The consequence is a crisis of moral authority in the United States.

NOTES

1. The quotations are from Tocqueville (1969) as cited by Pessen (1971:992, 1004, 1015). The Pessen article is an excellent summary of the historical literature on inequality and wealth.

2. See Perkins and Van Deusen (1968:446) and Lipset and Zetterberg (1966:561) as examples of those who buy the rags-to-riches myth. For an exceptional study that rejects the myth, see Thernstrom's (1964), *Poverty and Progress.*.

3. Some have argued that the increasing inequality during much of the period between 1850 and 1929 can be accounted for by an expanding labor supply—rural to urban migration, women and children in the labor force, and foreign immigration. Williamson (1976) shows that supply factors fail to account for the extremes of inequality after 1896. It is plausible that they also do not account for the extremes of inequality prior to 1896, but such data are not available.

4. Kolko (1962), however, argues that New Deal policies were specifically designed to avoid redistributing the wealth.

5. These figures were computed by Turner and Starnes (1976:19).

6. Bach and Stephenson (1974) report survey data for 1969, but there is reason to believe they seriously underestimate the extent of wealth inequality (see Turner and Starnes, 1976:36).

7. Projector's (1964) early article uses the same 1962 data but, as she notes, it contains some inaccurate estimates because all the data had not yet been analyzed. Thurow and Lucas (1972) are often cited, but they rely on Projector's early analysis. The best source for the 1962 Board of Governors data is the summary report prepared by Projector and Weiss (1966).

8. The source for this assertion is Projector and Weiss (1966:table A36, p. 151).

9. For breakdowns of the distribution of wealth by sex and marital status, see Smith (1974) and Internal Revenue Service (1973).

10. This figure was calculated by Turner and Starnes (1976:22).

11. This figure is from Internal Revenue Service (1973:table 1).

12. Abels's (1965) estimate is slightly lower. He calculates the Rockefeller family as worth only about $4 billion.

13. Lundberg (1975:87) notes that on his $5 million income Nelson Rockefeller generally pays taxes in the 25 percent bracket "or at about the level of someone with an income of $12,000 to $16,000."

14. The percentage is obtained by adding the amount in the non-income-producing columns and dividing by the total. Turner and Starnes (1976:27) have performed all these calculations.

15. Lundberg (1968) portrays some of these families and their power in great detail. His *The Rich and the Super-Rich* is probably the best single description of these people. Lundberg (1975) also shows the way and extent to which the Rockefeller fortune was systematically understated during Nelson Rockefeller's confirmation hearings as Vice-President. By the way, Lundberg's definition of the "rich" and "superrich" are considerably different from those used here.

16. See also the collection of papers in Pessen (1974) and Thernstrom's (1964) study of Newburyport, Mass. (Yankee City).

17. The difference between Lundberg's 1968 estimate of Rockefeller wealth ($4.7 billion) and his 1975 estimate ($5.4 billion) reflects better data that are now available. The 1968 estimates for the other three families are also probably low.

18. Of the long literature on Mills's controversial book, see Domhoff and Ballard (1968), Biderman and Sharp (1968), and Lieberson (1971). See also Rose's analysis (1967).

19. The source for these data is the U.S. Bureau of the Census (1976c:table 469).

20. For data on the relative importance of regressive taxes at various income levels, see Stern's excellent *The Rape of the Taxpayer* (1974:24). This book is by far the best and most easily accessible analysis of the tax system.

21. The source for these data is Internal Revenue Service (1976:28–31).

22. Stern's calculation of the actual tax rates by income level is mirrored in *U.S. News & World Report* (1975:90), using 1973 Internal Revenue Service data. *U.S. News* found that those with incomes greater than $1 million pay at a rate of 32.1 percent, while those with incomes between $500,000 and $1 million pay at a rate of 33.2 percent. These figures are comparable to Stern's 31 percent and 30.1 percent.

23. This section is adapted from Stern (1974:381–97).

12
RACIAL
INEQUALITY

In the United States, adults obtain positions in two interrelated ways: by ascription and by achievement. As noted in Chapter 6, ascription refers to the process of assigning individuals to positions on non-performance-related grounds, based on their membership in certain categories or their inherited characteristics. These categories or characteristics can be age, sex, race, religion, family background, and region of birth, and many more. The two most important bases of ascription in the United States are race and sex. Chapters 12 and 13 deal with each of these topics in turn.

In the aftermath of tumultous violence in our cities, the National Advisory Commission on Civil Disorders (1968:4) forecast that "our nation is moving toward two societies, one black, one white— separate and unequal." Such a situation is the essence of a caste relationship. In light of that chilling assessment, an important question is whether relationships between blacks and whites have changed much in recent years. This chapter describes some of the dimensions of racial inequality in the United States. The analysis begins with an assessment of black and white economic characteristics, mainly their respective occupations and incomes. Then the political, legal, religious, familial, and educational characteristics of the two races are compared. In all cases, the emphasis is on assessing the extent to which racial inequality has lessened in recent years. In those areas where inequality continues to exist, an attempt is made to suggest why this is so.

THE ECONOMIC CHARACTERISTICS OF BLACK AND WHITE AMERICANS

There are 25 million black Americans in the United States. They constitute the country's largest minority group, making up 11 percent of the total population. This proportion has not changed much in recent years. Neither, as it turns out, has the economic relationship between blacks and whites. The essential nature of this relationship can be seen by examining data dealing with income and occupational differences by race. Accordingly, this section is divided into three sections, each of which illustrates an important aspect of economic welfare: (1) trends in the distribution of income for each race, (2) trends in the occupational distribution for each race, and (3) trends in unemployment rates for each race. Analysis of these trends will reveal that great economic differences continue to exist between blacks and whites in the United States.

Trends in the Distribution of Income

Table 1 displays trends in the distribution of income for white and nonwhite families for the years 1960 to 1975. There are two important aspects of the table which should be noted. First, the inclusion of other nonwhite races in addition to blacks alters the figures so as to slightly underestimate the differences between blacks and whites. If only blacks were included in the table, the racial differences would be slightly greater.[1] Second, all the figures in the table are calculated in terms of the value of 1975 dollars. In this way, the effects of inflation are controlled statistically.

In examining the data in Table 1, note first the differences in median incomes. On the average, nonwhite families earn less than white families. In 1975, the average nonwhite family's income was only 65 percent of the average white family's income, and this figure is an all-time high.[2] Although it is not shown in the table, since World War II, nonwhite family income has been steadily, albeit slowly, increasing in relationship to that of white families.

The table also shows the percentage distribution across income categories for each year. In all years, the general pattern is for nonwhites to be concentrated at the lower income levels while whites are more evenly spread. Nonetheless, some changes have occurred during the period covered by the table. A much smaller proportion of nonwhites earned less than $3,000 in 1975, as compared to 1960. Further, the entire nonwhite income distribution has "moved up" over the years. Much greater proportions of nonwhites can be found at the highest three income levels in 1975 than in any earlier year. However, the cruel fact remains that the nonwhite distribution of income in 1975 almost duplicates the white distribution of 1960—15 years earlier. Because the white income distribution has also "moved up" over the years, nonwhites have not gained very much.

Table 1 Family Income, by Race, 1960–75 (in constant 1975 dollars)

	1960	1965	1970	1975
Nonwhites				
Under $3,000	26%	18%	13%	11%
$3,000–4,999	17	17	13	15
$5,000–6,999	15	17	12	12
$7,000–9,999	17	18	18	15
$10,000–11,999	9	8	9	9
$12,000–14,999	7	10	12	11
$15,000–24,999	8	11	19	20
$25,000 and Over	1	2	5	6
Median Income	$ 5,871	$ 6,812	$ 9,032	$ 9,321
Whites				
Under $3,000	9%	6%	4%	4%
$3,000–4,999	9	8	6	7
$5,000–6,999	10	8	7	8
$7,000–9,999	19	15	13	13
$10,000–11,999	16	11	10	9
$12,000–14,999	13	17	15	14
$15,000–24,999	20	27	32	32
$25,000 and Over	5	9	14	15
Median Income	$10,604	$12,370	$14,188	$14,268
Black % of white	55%	55%	64%	65%

Source: U.S. Bureau of the Census, *Statistical Abstract of the United States, 1977* (Washington, D.C.: U.S. Government Printing Office, 1977), tables 648 and 650, pp. 404–405.

As can be seen in Table 1, income parity between blacks and whites is still a long way off. On the average, blacks earn less than two-thirds of what whites earn. Although the figures will vary to some degree, this assertion is true regardless of region of the country, characteristics of the family (number of children present, male or female headed), or the occupation of the parents.

Trends in Occupational Distribution

Nearly all measures of socioeconomic status use occupation in some way, either by itself or jointly with other variables. For example, Duncan's (1961) "socioeconomic index scores" combine education and occupation into a single index of socioeconomic status. On the basis of the Duncan measure, Featherman and Hauser (1976:627) conclude that, between 1962 and 1973, "black men enjoyed larger absolute and relative upward shifts in current occupational status than did whites." Similarly, Farley (1977:196) argues that over the past few years "there has been a . . . dramatic shift into higher status jobs" among nonwhites. Thus, it appears that some significant changes have occurred. However, these conclusions must be interpreted with some caution because they hide the fact that the occupational structure is quite different for blacks and whites.

Table 2 displays the occupational distribution for each race for the years 1960, 1970, and 1975. During this period the white work force

Table 2 Occupational Distribution, by Race, 1960–75

	1960		1970		1975	
	Black[a]	White	Black	White[a]	Black	White
Professionals	5%	12%	9%	15%	11%	16%
Managers	3	12	4	11	4	11
Sales	2	7	2	7	3	7
Clerical	7	16	13	18	15	18
Total White Collar	17%	47%	28%	51%	33%	52%
Crafts	6%	14%	8%	14%	9%	13%
Operatives	20	18	24	17	20	15
Laborers	14	4	10	4	9	4
Service	32	10	26	11	26	12
Farming	12	7	4	4	3	4
Total Blue Collar	84%	53%	72%	50%	67%	48%

Source: U.S. Bureau of the Census, *Statistical Abstract of the United States, 1977* (Washington, D.C.: U.S. Government Printing Office, 1977), table 601, p. 373.

[a]Does not add to 100% because of rounding.

remained relatively stable. About half of all whites work in blue- and white-collar jobs, respectively. But as the authors cited above assert, significant changes have occurred among blacks. First, between 1960 and 1970, blacks moved out of farming occupations. There are now no differences between the races in this category. Although it is not shown in the table, when farming occupations are broken down into farmers and farm laborers, there remain important racial and ethnic differences. Farm laboring occupations are dominated by Chicano and black Americans. Few whites other than Chicanos engage in them. Among farmers, blacks tend to own or operate smaller, less productive farms. Disproportionate numbers of them are located in the southern United States. Nonetheless, Table 2 reveals that, in response to changing opportunities, blacks have clearly redistributed themselves to some degree. A far greater proportion of blacks were working in white-collar jobs in 1975 than in 1960, especially in clerical and professional occupations. It is this movement into white-collar jobs that leads Farley, and Hauser and Featherman, to conclude that significant changes have occurred.

However, their conclusion is based upon socioeconomic index scores, not the actual occupations that blacks and whites hold. When changes in the occupational distribution are analyzed more carefully, using census categories, it becomes evident that only a little progress has been made. Thus, examination of the occupational distribution in 1975 shows that there are three job categories into which blacks have not moved: skilled craft work, sales, and managerial jobs. Craft occupations are the highest paying and most prestigious blue-collar jobs. Blacks have been relatively unable to move into these occupations because of union opposition and corporate acquiescence. It is important to distinguish between industrial and craft unions.

Industrial unions are organized on an industry-wide basis (for example, automobile workers) and their members generally, although not necessarily, work in operative and laboring occupations. As Levison (1975:185) observes, industrial unions constitute one of the "most integrated institutions in the country," and this fact is reflected in Table 2. As an aside, it should be noted that in industrial unions, blacks are still confined to the lower-paying, less prestigious blue-collar jobs. They are also denied access to union apprenticeship programs. As for craft unions, as the name implies, such unions are generally made up of more skilled blue-collar workers. One of the most significant facts about craft unions is that they are organized such that the unions control the hiring and firing of workers. As a result, blacks have been unable to move into many better paying blue-collar occupations. For example, Levison (1975:187–88) reports that only 4 percent of all unionized boilermakers are black, only 2 percent of all electricians, and only 1 percent of all sheet-metal workers.[3] He adds that "the problem of discrimination remains today the saddest failure of American unionism to live up to its own ideals."

As Table 2 shows, blacks have also not moved into sales and managerial occupations. Both sorts of jobs are often ones in which whites and blacks can meet on equal bases or in which blacks may be superordinate over whites. As Anderson (1970:54) has argued in regard to public utility companies, many businesses are concerned with maintaining a favorable public image among whites and, hence, are still unwilling to employ blacks in "nontraditional public contact jobs" such as sales.

This problem is exacerbated when blacks enter managerial and professional occupations in the corporate world. Fernandez (1975) has shown the subtle and sophisticated forms of racism practiced in large corporations. Such businesses are run by and for whites. Although some have "affirmative action programs" in name, in most cases there are no explicit goals and the corporate officers in charge of them are not held accountable for failure to hire minority-group persons. As a result, few blacks are recruited into management positions. In those relatively rare cases in which minority recruitment goals are established and supervisors held accountable, qualified (often over-qualified) blacks are found. However, even after they are hired, black managers have great difficulty in "making it" up the corporate ladder. Part of the reason for this difficulty is captured in the following quotation from Fernandez's (1975:1) account.

A black manager in one of the companies in this study was so light skinned that, unless people had been told otherwise, they considered him white. His credentials were impeccable, and at work he was completely accepted. However, when his colleagues discovered that he was black, their behavior changed completely. They no longer spoke to him freely or invited him to join them for lunch or a drink. In short, he was isolated and ignored. And this was not the first job on which he had experienced such reactions. This anecdote, a true one, reflects the situation of many blacks in the business world today.

At best, black managers are left out of the informal social networks in which information is shared, contacts made, and much business conducted. At worst, black managers are harrassed in many small ways and prevented or discouraged from doing their job. According to Fernandez, blacks are judged to be culturally different and hence unable to interact effectively with whites. As a result, blacks who do move into managerial positions in large corporations, do so at the lowest levels, exercise little formal power compared to that of whites in similar positions, and find it difficult to get promoted.

However, as noted above, Table 2 does show that blacks have moved into two types of white-collar jobs, professional and clerical work, between 1960 and 1975. It is this change that has produced significant differences in socioeconomic index scores. Clerical jobs are often among the most menial white-collar jobs available. Nearly all the movement into these occupations has been among black women (see Chapter 13.) The greater prestige of clerical jobs results from the fact that the work is not dirty. More significant are black professionals, who comprised 11 percent of the black work force in 1975. Unfortunately, when the occupational composition of this category is broken down it can be seen that blacks still have not become doctors, lawyers, or engineers or have entered other technical fields. In fact, as Snyder and Hudis (1976) conclude, black Americans are still systematically excluded from higher-paying occupations. The movement of blacks into the professions has been concentrated in those occupations that are directly dependent upon the continued existence of the black poor, such as "social and recreation workers."[4]

In summary, some occupational redistribution has occurred over the past few years. Blacks have moved out of farming occupations to such a degree that similar percentages of each race now engage in them. In addition, some blacks have moved into professional and clerical occupations. As an aside, it should be noted that these people are generally not the same ones who moved off of the farm (see Chapter 14). However, the occupational structure of blacks is still quite different from that of whites. Blacks are much more likely to be in blue-collar jobs and those who have moved into the white-collar category have done so in selective occupations.

Trends in Unemployment Rates

Unemployment is, first of all, an economic problem. People are de-prived of income when they are unemployed. Table 3 displays differences in unemployment rates by race between 1960 and 1975. As can be seen in the table, year in and year out, during periods of prosperity and during periods of recession, black people are about twice as likely to be unemployed as are white people. Although not shown in the table, this tendency has been true since World War II. Furthermore, this racial difference in the probability of unemployment exists regardless of educational attainment or skill level. For example, among those who have some college education, 4.7 percent of all whites were unemployed in 1975, while 7.2 percent of all nonwhites were without work (Congressional Budget Office, 1976:20).

However, the figures in Table 3 are conservative, for they do not take into account those individuals who have become so discouraged that they have stopped looking for work and have dropped out of the labor force.[5] For example, the National Urban League reports that during 1974 the true unemployment rates among blacks (counting those who had "dropped out") stood at 25 percent (Johnson, 1976). In addition, unemployment rates refer to the average number of persons who were unemployed during any one year, not to the duration of time without a job.

When black people lose their jobs, their average duration of unemployment is much greater than that of whites.[6] As a result, blacks are more likely to give up and stop looking for a job. They are also more likely to take a short-term or unstable job, or one at a lower salary than their skills or education might merit. As a result, they are likely to be unemployed again and again. Unemployment, especially when it is long term or not ameliorated by supplemental compensation of some sort, breeds desperation. It can result in severe economic hardship. But more than that, it can lead to loss of seniority, deterioration of skills, and loss of pride and self-esteem. It can also lead to crime, to family break-up, to mental illness. The longer the period of time one goes without a job, the more serious are the economic and personal problems an individual faces. Blacks are much more likely to suffer these sorts of problems than are whites.

The data in Table 3 indicate, as Thurow (1976:4) has argued, that "we are dealing with a long-run, deeply embedded, structural relationship in the economy." Two interrelated reasons for this relationship can be adduced. First, it has been argued that American society can be divided into two distinctive labor markets. The primary labor

Table 3 Unemployment Rates, by Race, 1960–75

Year	Nonwhites	White	Ratio Black/White
1960	10.2%	4.9%	2.1
1961	12.4	6.0	2.1
1962	10.9	4.9	2.2
1963	10.8	5.0	2.2
1964	9.6	4.6	2.1
1965	8.1	4.1	2.0
1966	7.3	3.3	2.2
1967	7.4	3.4	2.2
1968	6.7	3.2	2.1
1969	6.4	3.1	2.1
1970	8.2	4.5	1.8
1971	9.9	5.4	1.8
1972	10.0	5.0	2.0
1973	8.9	4.3	2.1
1974	9.9	5.0	2.0
1975	13.9	7.8	1.8

Sources: U.S. Department of Labor, *Handbook of Labor Statistics, 1975—Reference Edition* (Washington, D.C.: U.S. Government Printing Office, 1975), table 60, p. 146; U.S. Bureau of the Census, *Statistical Abstract of the United States, 1977* (Washington, D.C.: U.S. Government Printing Office, 1977), table 582, p. 361.

market is seen as consisting of "the most rewarding, steady, and preferred jobs. Employees in this sector are secure, receive job promotions regularly, and enjoy regular working conditions" (Congressional Budget Office, 1976:21). Unemployment in this sector is low. When it does occur, it is temporary and its effects are generally alleviated by unemployment compensation. Whites are disproportionately in the primary labor market.

The secondary labor market, as the Congressional Budget Office (1976:21) describes it, is "characterized by low-paying jobs, limited advancement, and unstable employment. Layoffs, discharges, and resignations are frequent, and unemployment may be high even when the economy is operating close to its potential." In this context, there is little incentive for workers to remain on the job, develop good work habits, or obtain valuable work experience. These jobs involve low skill and high turnover rates, and both employers and employees know it. Blacks and other minority group members are disproportionately in the secondary labor market.

The second reason for high black unemployment rates is racial discrimination. "At the most blatant level", says the Congressional Budget Office (1976:22), "employers may make observations about nonwhites as a group, relative to whites, and then on that basis hesitate to hire individual nonwhites. At a more subtle level, employment tests may contain sections that are not precisely relevant to the job for which the applicant is applying and the scores on these tests may reflect socioeconomic or racial background rather than potential job performance." Such discriminatory practices are often not easily recognized or alleviated. They are an example of what Carmichael and Hamilton (1967) call institutionalized racism. For these two reasons, then, black unemployment rates are much higher than those for whites.

High levels of unemployment mean that, even when they are employed, blacks face a more uncertain future than do whites. For many blacks, long-run planning is more difficult simply because continued employment is not certain. As Hodge (1973:22) observes, even when long-term plans are made, they may be difficult to realize because the same employment insecurity that makes planning more difficult also makes many blacks appear to be poor credit risks and increases the interest rates on financing they are able to obtain. This problem affects all blacks because financial institutions often try to simplify procedures, with the result that all blacks are treated in the same way regardless of their individual situation.[7]

In summary, regardless of the measure used, it is clear that the economic situation of blacks has not changed much in recent years, at least in comparison to that of whites. Blacks continue to earn less, on the average, than do whites. Blacks are still concentrated in lower-skilled jobs, in both the white- and blue-collar categories. Although significant numbers of blacks have moved into some professional occupations, they are often in those jobs designed to serve the poor, especially the black poor. There are still very few black doctors, lawyers, professors, engineers, airline pilots, and the like. Finally, blacks are about twice as likely to be unemployed as are whites. A key issue is why these differences continue to exist, and that is the topic of the next section.

ALTERNATIVE EXPLANATIONS FOR BLACK ECONOMIC SUBORDINATION

A variety of hypotheses have been offered to explain the continued economic differences between black and white Americans. Four of them are as follows. (1) It has been argued that the migration of southern blacks to northern cities causes much of the racial difference in income, at least in the North. A more general variation of this argument is that black rural-to-urban migration causes most of the income differences. (2) It has been asserted that housing segregation causes the income gap between blacks and whites. (3) Another suggestion has been that differences in educational attainment between blacks and whites causes the income gap between the races. (4) The most widespread argument is that racial discrimination on the part of whites continues to keep blacks in economically subordinate positions in American society. This section explores each of these hypotheses.

Migration and Income

During this century, blacks have moved out of the South in great numbers,[8] and today about half of all blacks now live outside the South. Three-quarters of all blacks live in metropolitan areas. Of those still living in rural areas, nearly all are in the South (see U.S. Bureau of the Census, 1975a). In a controversial book, Banfield (1968) asserts that one of the major causes of racial differences in income has been the migration of unskilled and uneducated southern blacks to northern cities. A variation on this theme has been picked up by both the popular press and some social scientists. That is, it has been argued that southern blacks moved into northern cities in order to acquire the greater welfare benefits that are available there (see Long, 1974, for a review). There is evidence that many Americans believe "a lot of people" are moving north in order to obtain welfare (see Chapter 8). Banfield's well-known assertion is as follows (p. 68).

Today the Negro's main disadvantage is the same as the Puerto Rican's and Mexican's: namely, that he is the most recent unskilled, and hence relatively low-income, migrant to reach the city from a backward rural area. The city is not the end of his journey but the start of it. He came to it not because he was lured by a cruel and greedy master but because he was attracted by job, housing, school, and other opportunities that, bad as they were, were nevertheless better by far than any he had known before. Like earlier immigrants, the Negro has reason to expect that his children will have increases of opportunity even greater than his.

Banfield's argument is that the economic problems facing blacks are concentrated among southern migrants to northern cities. Yet there has never been any persuasive evidence for this assertion. Banfield offers none. Rather, an impressive body of data now show that, as Long and Heltman show (1975:1395), black migrants from the South "earn higher incomes on the average after having lived in the North for five years" than those blacks who are native to the North. Furthermore, they assert, black migrants to the north "more successfully avoid falling into the lowest income category than blacks who are of the second and later generations." For example, Long and Heltman found that the median income of northern-born black men, aged 25 to 34, was $6,129 in 1970. However, among southern-born black men aged 25 to 34 who had migrated to the North prior to 1965, the median income was $6,804 in 1970. Even among the most recent young male migrants, those who had left after 1965, the median income of $6,244 in 1970 exceeded that of northern-born blacks. Similarly, among northern-born black men aged 25 to 34, 20 percent had incomes below $3,000 in 1970. Among migrants from the south of the same age, only 13 percent of those who had left prior to 1965 and 15 percent of those who had left after 1965 had incomes below $3,000 in 1970.[9] Long and Heltman's findings agree with those by Bacon (1971), Weiss and Williamson (1972), Cutright (1974), Masters (1975), and Adams and Nestel (1976).

In sum, Banfield is wrong. The earnings of young black men who migrate from the South to the North are on the average, greater than those of young blacks born in the North. In all cases, of course, the earnings of blacks are less than those of whites. Migratory status has no effect on the racial differences in income displayed above (see Long and Heltman, 1975; Adams and Nestel, 1976). Three reasons have been advanced to account for this finding. All are speculative. First, it is possible that black migrants are more highly motivated, ambitious, or intelligent than nonmigrants who have stayed behind. It is possible, in short, that "migration has provided southern blacks with a visible means of changing their lives and has been undertaken by the most able and those with the most initiative" (Long and Heltman, 1975:1406). It is also possible that migrants who are less able or ambitious quickly return to the South, where the social environment is more familiar. Whether this line of reasoning is appropriate is unknown at the present time.

Second, and related to the first, it is possible that black migrants have different attitudes toward working and welfare than those born in the North. There are some preliminary data on this point. Adams and Nestel (1976:163) report that black migrants from the South have a somewhat stronger commitment to work and are more interested in good wages on the job than in working conditions. Following this line of reasoning, it is possible that recent migrants take jobs that are seen as "unacceptable" by others, because of the regimentation involved, discrimination against blacks, and other undesirable or oppressive characteristics. But because of their greater commitment to the labor force, migrants end up with higher incomes than native-born northerners.

Third, and related to the two above, life in northern ghettos may be more discouraging for many of those born and raised in them. The quality of life in some ghetto areas may be such that "blacks born and raised there experience severe handicaps in planning and pursuing orderly occupational careers" (Long and Heltman, 1975:1407). As a result, southern-born blacks who migrate may experience difficulty in passing on their higher incomes to their children. While all these reasons are speculative, they are a step toward accounting for the income differences between black migrants and nonmigrants in the North. More generally, however, as Masters (1975:51) argues, the low incomes of northern-born blacks appear to represent a long-run equilibrium position resulting from discrimination by whites. The effects of migration cannot be used to account for racial income differences.

Housing and Income

Housing segregation is one of the nation's most intractable civil rights problems. According to the Fair Housing Act of 1968, it is illegal to discriminate in the sale or rental of living accommodations. Yet black and white Americans still live in different neighborhoods. Indexes of housing segregation are high in virtually all American cities (Van Valey et al., 1977), just as they have been for many years (Taeuber and Taeuber, 1965). It has been estimated that 83 percent of all black families would have to move from an all-black block to a white one to achieve a racially random pattern of housing.[10]

The issue of housing segregation is important in its own right, at least among those who see an integrated society as a better one. However, it has been asserted that housing segregation also has implications for income differences among blacks and whites, and that is the concern here. In a series of articles, Kain (1968; 1974) has argued that the "ghetto has isolated the Negro economically as well as socially [through] inadequate access to the job market" (Kain and Pesky, 1969:77). According to Kain, and several others, the relationship between housing and income occurs mainly because (1) jobs are more and more located in suburban areas and blacks have greater difficulty in reaching such areas, and (2) those jobs that are available in central cities are predominantly for those with skills greater than many blacks possess. Low-skill jobs have moved to the suburbs. The policy implications of this argument involve providing blacks and other inner-city residents with mass transportation to suburban areas and, of course, providing low-cost (often federally subsidized) housing in suburban areas.

However, based upon a review of the available data, Harrison (1974) concludes that there is little support for this argument. First, while the number of jobs in suburban areas clearly has increased, employment opportunities in central cities have been increasing as well. There are plenty of jobs where black people live. Second, the "mismatch hypothesis," that low-skilled jobs are available in the suburbs and not in central cities, appears to be false. In one study of the eight largest standard metropolitan statistical areas (called SMSAs), it was found over a two-year period that 70 percent of the new jobs within the central cities were not for highly skilled persons (Fremon, 1970).

Harrison concludes that the primary reason for high unemployment rates and low incomes on the part of blacks living in central cities is that suburban residents hold a large number of the available jobs, both skilled and unskilled. He argues that we must confront the reality of job discrimination. It appears that blacks have difficulty getting jobs in white-owned businesses, even when they are located in the ghetto itself (Aldrich, 1973). More recently, Masters (1975:91), using data that were unavailable to Harrison, also concludes that, at least as of 1970, housing segregation was "not one of the major factors accounting for the relatively low earnings of urban blacks." In summary, the argument that segregated housing is an important cause of the income differences between blacks and whites is probably not true.[11]

Education and Income

Blacks are less well educated than whites, although the differences are decreasing. For example, in 1963, the median years of schooling completed was 9 among blacks and 12 among whites. By 1975 the black population had a median of 10.9 years of education, while whites, had 12.3 years.[12] Obviously, young blacks are obtaining more years of education than their parents did. The problem of discrimination and equality of educational opportunity will be dealt with below. Of interest here is whether differences in educational attainment account for differences of income. As shown in Table 4, the answer is no. Although increasing amounts of education are monetarily rewarding for both races, at each level of education blacks earn significantly less than whites. In other words, the table shows that the economic reward for educational attainment is less for blacks than for whites. Furthermore, although the black percentage of white income is generally higher now than it was a few years ago, in both 1963 and 1973 a black college graduate earned about the same, on the average, as a high school educated white. As noted above, in many ways not much has changed in American society.

The pattern displayed in Table 4 reflects findings reported by Althauser et al. (1975). The authors analyzed matched samples of black and white college graduates who went to the same schools and graduated in the same years. Each pair of graduates had similar grade-point averages and family social status. Althauser and his colleagues show that although college graduates of both races find jobs of roughly similar social status, blacks have significantly lower incomes than do whites. Thus, differences in educational level by race

Table 4 Median Income, Education, and Race, 1963 and 1973[a]

Years of Education	1963			1973		
	White	Nonwhite	Black as a Percentage of White	White	Nonwhite	Black as a Percentage of White
Elementary (1–8)	$4,817	$2,802	58%	$8,103	$5,717	71%
High School	6,722	4,000	60	12,829	8,320	65
College	8,802	6,014	68	17,640	13,650	77

Source: Bureau of Labor Statistics, *Handbook of Labor Statistics, 1975* (Washington, D.C.: U.S. Government Printing Office, 1976), table 181.

[a]The 1963 data are for family heads, aged 14 years and over. The 1973 data are for family heads aged 25 years and older.

do not account for income differences between blacks and whites. When level of education and other background variables are controlled, differences in income remain. As will be argued below, these differences are the result of racial discrimination.

Racial Discrimination and Income

Blacks have different social characteristics than whites. Disproportionate numbers live in the South. They are, on the average, less well educated, have jobs of lower occupational prestige, work less hours (because of the likelihood of being either unemployed or forced to work part time), and have less years of experience at their occupations. A key question involves how much these differences cost, in purely economic terms. Further, after the effects of the differences noted above are taken into account, what is the cost of being black in America? This is a polite way of asking how much racism costs black Americans.

A number of sociologists have attempted to statistically "decompose" the various economic costs imposed on blacks in American society.[13] The most recent effort is that by Farley (1977), as shown in Table 5. As can be seen in the table, the cost of being black varies somewhat by sex. Males will be considered first. Table 5 shows that black men earned about $5,165 less than did white men in 1959 and about $4,295 less in 1974. By means of regression analysis, Farley illustrates the extent to which the racial differences in earnings are attributable to differing social characteristics and the extent to which they are the result of white racism. Thus, on the average, if black males had had the same characteristics as whites (in terms of regional distribution, education, occupation, hours worked, and experience), they would have earned about $2,024 more in 1974. The amount left over is the average cost of being a black male in America during that year. Put differently, on the average, white racism cost each black male about $2,749 in 1959 and $2,271 in 1974. The cost of racism is not as high for black women. In 1974, black females earned $108 less than white females, on the average. And, as the bottom portion of Table 5 suggests, black women are discriminated against more on grounds of sex than of race. In other words, the differences between black and white women are less important than the differences between men and women (see Chapter 13).

In summary, four hypotheses have been advanced to account for the economic subordination of blacks to whites. The first is that much of the racial difference in income can be attributed to the migration of unskilled and uneducated blacks to the urban North. Since black migrants earn higher incomes than do nonmigrants, this hypothesis can be shown to be false. The second proposition is that housing segregation is a significant cause of low incomes among

Table 5 Sources of Racial Differences in Earnings in Constant 1974 Dollars, 1959 and 1974

	Males		Females	
	1959	1974	1959	1974
White Median Income	$10,638	$13,432	$4,762	$5,760
Black Median Income	5,473	9,137	2,954	5,652
Difference	$ 5,165	$ 4,295	$1,808	$ 108
Earnings Difference Associated with Racial Differences in Specific Variables:[a]				
Region	650	401	331	212
Education	542	329	191	202
Occupation	941	715	989	520
Hours Worked Yearly	341	584	160	−65
Years of Experience	−57	−5	0	−1
Total	$ 2,416	$ 2,024	$1,671	$ 868
Earnings Difference Attributable to Racism	$ 2,749	$ 2,271	$ 137	−760
Total	$ 5,165	$ 4,295	$1,808	$ 108

Source: Adapted from R. Farley, "Trends in Racial Inequalities: Have the Gains of the 1960s Disappeared in the 1970s?" *American Sociological Review* 42 (April 1977): 205.

[a]That is, the change in earnings which would occur if blacks retained their own rates of return but had the characteristics of whites—were regionally distributed in the same way, had similar levels of education, etc.

blacks. This argument also appears to be false. The third hypothesis is that racial differences in educational attainment can account for differences in income. However, it can be shown that when blacks and whites of equal educational levels are compared, blacks still earn less. So this hypothesis is false. The final proposition asserts that racial discrimination causes much of the difference in income between blacks and whites. It can be shown that when blacks are assumed to have the same social attributes as whites (that is, the same regional distribution, the same levels of education, and so on), blacks still earn less. Sociologists argue that the difference between what blacks earn when they are assumed to have the same attributes as whites and what whites earn represents the economic effect of racism.

BLACK POLITICS
This section is divided into three parts. First, black and white political attitudes are briefly compared. Second, black rates of political participation are analyzed in terms of party identification and voting behavior. Third, the consequences of black political behavior are noted in terms of the election of black officeholders and the influence of political participation on patterns of racial inequality.

Black and White Political Attitudes
"No other group in American society is as distinctively liberal as American blacks" (Nie et al., 1976:255). Nie and his colleagues show

that in virtually every area—economic welfare, the size of the government, black welfare, school integration, and foreign policy, to name just a few—blacks are more liberal than the American population as a whole. The differences between the two races can be shown in terms of an overall measure of political orientation. In 1975, the National Opinion Research Corporation (NORC) asked a random sample of Americans how they would label themselves politically.[14] Among whites, 28 percent called themselves liberal, 41 percent middle of the road, and 31 percent conservative. Among blacks, on the other hand, 47 percent saw themselves as liberal, 29 percent as middle of the road, and 24 percent as conservative.

Although these figures suggest that there are significant differences between the races, they probably understate the extent of black liberalism. For it is not clear whether blacks who identify themselves as conservative are comparing themselves to whites or to other blacks. As noted above, when racial attitudes on specific issues are compared, the differences between the races are even wider (Nie et al., 1976). For example, NORC also asked members of both races their attitudes toward busing school children—an issue that affects many members of both races and one on which emotions run hot. Whites were overwhelmingly opposed to busing; 86 percent said no. Blacks, on the other hand, were split on the issue, with 53 percent opposing busing and 47 percent favoring it. Clearly, then, these examples suggest that black and white Americans have different political orientations.

Black Political Behavior

This section focuses upon three issues: (1) patterns of party identification among black Americans, (2) problems and patterns of voting registration, and (3) patterns of voting behavior. All three issues are indicators of the extent of black participation in the legitimate political system.

Table 6 displays trends in party identification among black Americans for the years 1952 through 1972.[15] The table shows that since World War II, the majority of black Americans have been consistently Democratic. This affiliation is presumably in tune with their liberal political attitudes. However, a number of interesting regional and temporal patterns can be seen in the table. During the 1950s, between 10 and 20 percent of all blacks identified themselves as Republicans. This tendency occurred in both the North and the South. It was apparently the result of many black Americans identifying the GOP as the party of Lincoln and emancipation. Further, especially in the South, the Democrats were seen by many blacks as the party of oppression.

However, during the 1950s, the black population was divided into two distinct groups: a large and apathetic mass and a small articulate activist group (Mathews and Prothro, 1966:55). This fact can be seen to some degree in the large proportion, between 21 and 31 percent, of southern blacks who were apolitical during the 1950s. Knoke (1976:42) observes that "through 1960 southern blacks have the highest rate of apolitical responses to the party identification question of any social group in the [Survey Research Center's] surveys." These apolitical responses probably reflect the harassment, intimidation, and (where necessary) the violence perpetrated on southern blacks who attempted to participate in the political process.

It is apparent, however, from the data in Table 6 that, at some point between 1960 and 1964, southern blacks became politically mobilized. As Knoke suggests, this important change probably represents the impact of national events such as the burgeoning civil rights movement, President Kennedy's assassination, President Johnson's strenuous backing of civil rights, and the presidential nomination of Senator Goldwater by the Republican Party in 1964. As a result, the level of black support for the Democratic Party increased greatly during the 1960s and 1970s in both regions, but especially in the South. Although it is not shown in the table, the extent to which blacks identify with and support the Democratic Party has continued through the election of 1976. Knoke (1976:43) concludes that "blacks of both regions remain the most Democratic of all social groups." Partly as a result, the tenacity of white southerners' support for the Democrats appears to have eroded in recent years.

In 1940, only 5 percent (or 250,000) of all blacks living in the

Table 6 Party Identification Among Blacks, by Region, 1952–72

Region and Party	Year					
	1952	1956[a]	1960	1964	1968	1972[a]
North						
Democratic	59%	56%	43%	67%	76%	71%
Independent	25	22	40	18	18	18
Republican	11	21	12	13	3	9
Other	5	2	5	2	3	3
	100%	101%	100%	100%	100%	101%
South						
Democratic	48%	46%	44%	78%	92%	65%
Independent	12	6	16	13	3	27
Republican	15	17	19	3	1	6
Other	25	31	21	6	4	2
	100%	100%	100%	100%	100%	100%

Source: David Knoke, *Change and Continuity in American Politics* (Baltimore, Md.: Johns Hopkins University Press, 1976), p. 41.

[a]Does not add to 100% because of rounding.

eleven southern states were registered to vote. At that time, the majority of blacks still lived in the South. Violence and the fear of violence successfully kept nearly all blacks from participating in the political process. By 1960, only 28 percent of all blacks were registered to vote in the South.[16] Further, there were many areas in which virtually no blacks were allowed to vote. For example, in Dallas County, Alabama (the county seat of which is Selma), only 2 percent of all blacks were registered to vote in 1965 (Wells, 1975). This situation was not unusual, especially in those counties where blacks constituted the majority of the population.

Historically, political participation by means of the vote has been seen as one of the keys to black equality. Whites, especially in the South, have used a variety of machinations to prevent blacks from registering. Legal mechanisms involved such tactics as "grandfather clauses," white-only primaries, poll taxes, and literacy tests. These laws were all eventually struck down by the courts (see Bardolph, 1970). More fundamentally, the level of violence and intimidation against blacks, a constant feature of southern life until recently, is difficult for most whites to understand. But the issues in many places were not minor, for blacks constituted the majority of the voting-age population in many communities and whites feared a black takeover.

The ability of whites to keep blacks disenfranchised was effectively curtailed by passage of the Voting Rights Act of 1965. In the aftermath of demonstrations, murders, and the televised spectacle of police violence in Selma, Alabama, the Congress voted to send federal examiners into seven southern states—Alabama, Georgia, Louisiana, Mississippi, North Carolina, South Carolina, and Virginia—to register voters and monitor elections. As a result, the proportion of blacks registered to vote climbed to 58 percent in the South in 1975. This figure is very close to the 61 percent of all Southern whites who were registered to vote.[17] The result has been a "quiet revolution" in the South, as blacks have elected many officeholders at all levels of government (see below) and caused a moderation in the racial stance of most candidates.[18]

In recent years, the extent of black political participation has increased markedly, a direct result of the Voting Rights Act. As can be seen in Table 7, since passage of the act, southern blacks have voted in national elections at a rate 7 to 10 percent below that of whites. In the North, 9 to 14 percent fewer blacks have voted. (It should be noted that the extent of political participation on the part of all voters drops in nonpresidential election years such as 1970 and 1974). It may be that much of the racial difference in voting participation can now be accounted for by socioeconomic factors: a greater proportion of blacks are poor and the poor participate in the political process at lower rates than do other social strata.

Table 7 Voting Participation, by Region and Race, 1968–74

	Percentage Voting			
	1968	1970	1972	1974
South				
White	62%	46%	57%	37%
Black	52	37	48	30
Non-South				
White	72	60	68	50
Black	58	51	57	38

Source: U.S. Bureau of the Census, "The Social and Economic Status of the Black Population in the United States, 1974," *Current Population Reports,* Series P-23, no. 54, table 94.

Black Political Behavior and Inequality

The impact of black votes can be easily seen in terms of the number of black officeholders at all levels who have been elected since 1964. During that year, there were five black members of Congress, all in the House of Representatives. In the entire nation, there were 94 black members of state legislatures, of whom 16 were from the South.[19] Although data for local officeholders is not generally available prior to the Voting Rights Act, it appears that the number of such officials was very low everywhere, and zero in the South. For example, the first southern black mayor, Charles Evers of Fayette, Mississippi, was not elected until the summer of 1969. At that time, a climate of fear and hostility pervaded race relations in southwestern Mississippi, and Evers's election received nationwide publicity. The situation has changed a great deal in recent years, as shown in Table 8. In 1975, there were a total of 3,503 black elected officials at all levels in the United States. Although not shown in the table, more than half (55 percent) are from the South.[20] However, it remains the case that in no region of the country and at no level does the number of black elected officials reflect their proportion of the population.

Table 8 Black Elected Officials, by Type of Office, 1975

	Number	Percent[a]
Members of Congress	18	1%
State Legislators and Executives	281	8
Mayors	135	4
County Officials	305	9
City Officials	1,438	41
Law Enforcement	387	11
Education	939	27
	3,503	101%

Source: U.S. Bureau of the Census, "The Social and Economic Status of the Black Population, 1974," *Current Population Reports,* Series P-23, no. 54, table 102.

[a]Does not add to 100% because of rounding.

Nonetheless, these figures show clearly that much progress has been made, especially at the local level. Fully 92 percent of all black officeholders serve as mayors, county and city officials, and as elected law-enforcement and educational personnel. However, this figure also suggests the limited relationship between black political participation in electoral politics and racial inequality. The major impetus for affirmative action to reduce economic inequalities between the races must come at the federal level. But only 1 percent of all black elected officials are members of the Congress. While it is not clear how many blacks serve in the executive branch of the government, the number is still not high. The ability of local politicians to change patterns of economic inequality is quite limited. However, what they can do is (1) ensure fair and equitable enforcement of the laws, (2) ensure equitable distribution of public goods and services, and (3) end discrimination in the public sector itself (see Keech, 1968).

These items are not unimportant. In most cities and towns, blacks have more limited access to public services than do whites—everything from libraries and parks to garbage disposal and paved roads. Similarly, many local governments still covertly discriminate in hiring and firing, and many make little effort to guarantee minorities access to public accommodations. Nonetheless, along with legal redress in the courts, the vote helps to ensure black civil rights by making local public officials accountable to the electorate. As one might guess, such protection is far more likely where blacks constitute a majority of the population than where they do not (Keech, 1968).

BLACKS AND AMERICAN CRIMINAL JUSTICE
Modern urban police forces originated in the nineteenth century in an effort to protect the property of the capitalist classes from the so-called "dangerous classes," mostly the poor, blacks, and immigrant groups (Silver, 1967). To a large degree, this task has not changed. Partly because many of them are poor and partly because they are not white, blacks have always been disproportionately victimized by crime and labeled as criminal. This section deals with three topics: (1) victimization rates among blacks and whites, (2) rates of arrest and incarceration for each race, and (3) a brief note on why blacks are disproportionately subjected to criminal justice in America.

Race and Criminal Victimization
Studies of criminal victimization rely on self-reports of victims obtained from survey research. They are not based on official police data and, hence, are more reliable. On this basis, it can be concluded that black Americans are much more likely to be victimized by criminals than are whites. In 1973, out of every 1,000 black persons, about

47 were subjected to a crime of violence, such as rape, robbery, or assault. In comparison, during that same year, out of every 1,000 white persons, only 32 were subjected to a violent crime.[21] In other words, every black American is one-third more likely than a white to be victimized by a violent crime.

However, contrary to popular stereotypes, most crimes appear to be intraracial rather than interracial. That is, blacks victimize blacks and whites victimize whites. For example, in 1973, black victims reported that their assailant was black 87 percent of the time. Only 8 percent of all crimes against black persons were committed by whites. Similarly, in that same year, white victims reported that their assailant was white 74 percent of the time. Only 21 percent of crimes against white persons were reported to have been committed by blacks.[22]

This general tendency for intraracial crime is also true for homicides, which were not included in the data cited above. Swigert and Farrell (1976:48) show that, over a 20-year period, 85 percent of all black homicide defendants were accused of murdering black persons. Conversely, 92 percent of all white defendants were accused of murdering whites. Calculated in a different way, Swigert and Farrell found that only 12 percent of all homicides in the urban area they studied were interracial, and in most of those cases whites were accused of murdering blacks.

In sum, blacks are more likely to be victimized by criminals than are whites and most crime is intraracial in nature. Although not shown above, the relationship between race and victimization is true even when blacks and whites of similar socioeconomic status are compared.[23] Racial differences in victimization rates along with the intraracial character of most crimes suggest that white fears of black criminality may be misplaced.

Race and Criminality

It will be recalled that black Americans comprise 11 percent of the population. Data comparing rates of arrest and incarceration between blacks and whites should be evaluated with that fact in mind. Of all those arrested for serious crimes in 1975, 65 percent were white and 33 percent were black.[24] This sort of disproportionality in arrest rates also occurs for each of the so-called seven major crimes. Of those arrested for murder in 1975, 55 percent were black. Of those accused of rape, 46 percent were black. Of alleged robbers, 59 percent were black. Among persons arrested for assault, 39 percent were black. Arrestees for larceny were 31 percent black. And finally, blacks were 26 percent of all those arrested for auto theft.

As alleged criminals move through the criminal justice process, blacks are inevitably worse off than whites. They are less likely to make bail and to have a private attorney (Swigert and Farrell, 1976).

They are more likely to be convicted and when convicted to receive longer jail sentences (Chiricos et al., 1972). This last finding is reflected in Table 9, which compares the length of prison sentences meted out to blacks and whites convicted of specific categories of crime. As can be seen in the table, blacks receive much longer sentences than do whites for crimes of violence. The racial disparity is not so great for those convicted of crimes against property. However, for blacks convicted of the sale or possession of drugs, penalties are again more severe.

Table 9 Length of Prison Sentence, by Race and Type of Crime, 1972

Type of Crime	Median Number of Months	
	Blacks	Whites
Murder or Kidnapping	66	6
Rape	11	6
Robbery	53	12
Burglary	11	11
Aggravated Assault	13	11
Grand Larceny	10	10
Auto Theft	6	5
Drug Sale	9	5
Drug Possession	11	5

Source: U.S. Bureau of the Census, "The Social and Economic Status of the Black Population in the United States, 1974," *Current Population Reports*, Series P-23, no. 53, table 116.

The different way in which blacks and whites are treated in the criminal-justice system can be graphically illustrated by examining the characteristics of those prisoners who have been placed under death sentences. In 1973, there were 160 persons of both races on death row in various American prisons, 51 percent of whom were black and 49 percent white.[25] There are significant regional variations in the assignation of the death penalty. In the South, 64 percent of those awaiting execution were black, and 36 percent were white. Outside the South, 40 percent were black and 60 percent white. In summary, at every stage of the criminal justice process, blacks are disproportionately represented. They are more likely to be arrested for crimes of all sorts, to be denied bail, to be denied a private attorney, and to serve longer jail sentences. They are also more likely to be sentenced to die.

Race and the Dispensation of Justice
In Chapter 8 it was argued that most crime is economically motivated and that the most effective way of reducing violent crime and crime against property is to eliminate poverty. Those who are poor have no way of hiding their crime. Because they lack resources they are forced to be direct and, often, violent. Because disproportionate numbers of blacks are poor, they are overrepresented in criminal statistics. For example, among jail inmates in 1972, 59 percent of

blacks and 54 percent of whites had prearrest annual incomes of less than $3,000. Using a more inclusive measure, 93 percent of black inmates and 86 percent of whites had prearrest annual incomes of less than $7,500. In other words, there are few racial differences in socioeconomic status among those incarcerated in jail. The legal system focuses upon the poor of both races.

This emphasis can be understood more clearly when the process of criminal justice is analyzed step by step and in light of the social context in which it operates. In American society, the law is seen as the institutional embodiment of the American Creed (Myrdal, 1944). Everyone is supposed to be equal before the law. At the same time, of course, the law is also an instrument of social control, oriented toward the crimes of the poor rather than those of the rich (see Chapter 10). Finally, the entire legal system is beset with a mad crush of humanity—too many crimes, too many prisoners, and too many court cases.

Within this social context, then, legal decisions are made. The fundamental characteristic of all such decisions is that they involve discretion: whether to arrest, to set bail, to plea-bargain, to convict, and the length of the sentence. In order to help make these decisions, legal personnel appear to have developed a stereotypical conception of what might be called the "normal criminal."[26] The police believe, whether rightly or not, that people they perceive as coming from backgrounds in which they believe it is normal to be violent, uneducated, disrespectful of authority, sexually promiscuous, and lack occupational achievement, among other characteristics, are likely to commit crimes of violence and crimes against property. As emphasized above, these are the main crimes that concern the police and all elements of the criminal-justice system. From the point of view of the police, many poor persons, white and black, fit this stereotype, although not all do. Thus, such persons are more likely to be arrested.

Those who appear to be "normal criminals" are also more likely to have a prior record and, hence, to be denied bail. They are more likely to have a public defender than a private attorney. As Swigert and Farrell (1976; 1977) argue, the denial of bail and the inability to obtain a private attorney lead to an assumption of guilt. From the point of view of prospective jurors, a judge would not have denied bail to an innocent person. This reaction is visceral and emotional. Jurors cannot be told to ignore it. Thus, those who languish in jail and cannot obtain private counsel are assumed to be "normal criminals." The assumption of innocence is reserved for people who are more fortunate. Those individuals who are arrested, denied bail, and lack a private attorney are also more likely to plea-bargain; that is, to plead guilty to a less serious offense than they were originally charged with.

Whether a person plea-bargains appears to have little relationship to one's actual innocence or guilt. Plea bargaining is neccessary to the continuation of the criminal-justice system, for if every defendant demanded a jury trial the courts could not function. However, the plea bargain has unintended consequences in that it confirms, in a sense, the stereotype of the "normal criminal." Those individuals who have the characteristics of the "normal criminal" and choose not to plea-bargain are more likely to be found guilty anyway (see Shoemaker et al., 1973). Finally, the "normal criminal" is likely to receive a longer sentence.

In summary, the argument presented here is that more than class and race are involved in explaining the data above, although both are clearly important. As Swigert and Farrell (1977:18) put it, "cultural stereotypes of criminality determine the decisions of legal authorities. While these stereotypes include class and race-related characteristics, they are not restricted to, nor do they include all members of these groups." Nonetheless, the effect of these stereotypes is racist and discriminating.

BLACK RELIGION

Religious Preference and Participation
With the onset of the civil rights movement in the 1960s, some observers believed that the church might lose its dominant position in the black community. The logic behind this suggestion was that blacks would increasingly reject their historic allegiance to conservative and sectarian Protestantism because of its accommodation with the existence of racial inequality. According to this view, increasing numbers of blacks would reject all religion, turn to black nationalist religions such as the Muslims, or turn to either Catholicism or the "higher status" Protestant denominations.

However, Glenn and Gotard (1977) show that none of these changes appear to have occurred, either in terms of religious preference or participation. Studies of religious preference simply ascertain the religion with which people identify themselves. Religious preference does not necessarily indicate church membership. Table 10 displays the religious preferences of black and white Americans. In 1972 through 74, as in 1957, there are clear differences between the religious preferences of blacks and whites. However, these differences are stable over this time period. Between 1957 and the early 1970s most blacks, between 55 and 60 percent, continued to identify themselves as Baptists. There has not been a massive movement into the liberal Protestant denominations. Nor have blacks converted to Roman Catholicism or Judaism. Less than 10 percent of all blacks are Catholic and less than 1 percent are Jewish. Further, the proportion of blacks identifying themselves with various non-Christian religions, such as the Muslims, continues to be very low. Finally, few blacks, less than 5 percent, say they are not religious.

However, it is possible that general religious preferences could remain stable while participation dropped. Such a change would lend support to the proposition that blacks were rejecting religion. But Glenn and Cotard (1977) also report data which suggest that black rates of religious participation have not declined, at least over the long run. In surveys conducted in 1956, 1966, and 1973, black Protestants were asked if they had attended church during the previous week. In 1956, 46 percent responded that they had. In 1966, 38 percent indicated church attendance. And in 1973, 44 percent said they had been to church during the previous week. Thus, it appears that if blacks became disaffected with religion during the 1960s, such feelings were only temporary.

Table 10 Religious Preference, by Race

	Whites		Nonwhites	
	1957	1972–74	1957	1972–74
Baptist	15.2%	15.3%	60.6%	55.2%
Methodist	13.6	13.1	17.3	15.6
Other Protestant	35.0	31.9	9.6	13.0
Total Protestant	63.8%	60.3%	87.5%	83.8%
Catholic	27.8	28.3	6.5	8.9
Jewish	3.5	3.5	.5	.3
Non-Christian Religion	1.3	1.4	1.5	2.3
No Religion	2.6	6.3	3.5	4.5
No Answer	1.0	.2	.6	.2
	100 %	100 %	100 %	100 %

Source: N. D. Glenn and E. Gotard, "The Religion of Blacks in the United States: Some Recent Trends and Current Characteristics," *American Journal of Sociology* 83 (September 1977): 444.

The Consequences of Black Religiosity

Despite the historical importance of the black church, the consequences of blacks' religious belief are not well agreed upon. The main area of interest involves the relationship between black churches and civil rights activity. In analyzing the consequences of black religiosity, Gary Marx (1967) shows that the literature on race relations is rich with impressionistic and flatly contradictory statements about the relationship between the black church and racial protest. Historians, social commentators, and civil rights leaders all see the church as either encouraging racial protest or inhibiting it. Further, in one of the few systematic studies available, Marx (1967:72) came to splendidly mixed results. "The effect of religiosity on race protest," he wrote, "depends on the type of religiosity involved."

Some black religions are "otherworldly" in orientation, seeking redress and salvation in the next world where God will judge people. Black members of religious sects often have such beliefs and tend to be less militant. In general, Marx found that high levels of religiosity and racial militancy were inversely related. At the same time, however, most black "militants" turned out to be either "very religious" or "somewhat religious." Black religion, then, has a dual orientation—as opiate and inspiration—depending upon people's background and the social situation.

More recently, Nelson et al. (1975) have argued that "the black church will expand its prophetic role as critic and moral judge of the society." They report data suggesting that as black religions become less sectarian the church's role as a stimulus for protest will increase. Whether they are correct remains to be seen.

THE BLACK FAMILY

Ever since publication of Daniel Moynihan's *The Negro Family: The Case for National Action* (1965), the nature and consequences of black family structures have been the center of much controversy. This section briefly explores that controversy. It is divided into two parts. First, the demographic characteristics of black families are described, with particular attention to the way in which black and white families differ. Second, the presumed effects of the black family structure are directly examined and the thesis contained in the "Moynihan Report" (as it is popularly known) is evaluated.

The Characteristics of Black Families

In assessing the characteristics of black families, four topics are of primary interest: (1) the marital status of the population, (2) fertility rates, (3) illegitimacy rates, and (4) the proportion of single parent households. In each case, differences by race are examined.[27]

The marital status of black and white Americans is shown in Table 11. As can be seen there, a larger proportion of blacks are single and a correspondingly smaller proportion are married. Although it is not shown in the table, this relationship is true for both sexes. There are few racial differences in the proportion of widowed individuals. However, 16 percent of all blacks are either separated or divorced, compared to only 6 percent of all whites. The data in Table 11, however, refer to all adults of both races. If the population is restricted to those who live in urban areas and who are married, divorced, or separated, then the figures are quite different. Among urban families, 29 percent of all blacks are divorced or separated, compared to 10 percent of all whites.[28] The reasons why so many black marriages dissolve are not altogether clear. Marital instability is not approved of in the black community, nor is it sanctioned by black religious beliefs (Glenn and Gotard, 1977). Some of the differences can

Table 11 Marital Status, by Race, 1976

Marital Status	Black	White[a]
Single	35%	25%
Married	40	61
Widowed	9	7
Separated	10	2
Divorced	6	4
	100%	99%

Source: Calculated from U.S. Bureau of the Census, "Marital Status and Living Arrangements: March 1976," *Current Population Reports*, Series P-20, no. 306, table 1.

[a]Does not add to 100% because of rounding. *HIGH RATE OF DIVORCE. WHY?*

be accounted for in terms of high unemployment rates, low skill levels, and low incomes of black males. One of the consequences of a chronic inability to perform traditional masculine roles, such as holding a job, is lower self-esteem and (often) marital break-up. This possibility may also account for the high proportion of single blacks.[29]

Historically, the fertility rates of black women have been higher than those of white women. It should be noted that fertility rates are dropping for women of both races, as child bearing becomes less highly valued in our society. In 1960, nonwhite women had 4.5 children, on the average. By 1970, this figure had dropped to 3.1 children. And by 1974, it had fallen to 2.4. In comparison, white women had, on the average, 3.5 children in 1960, 2.4 children in 1970, and 1.8 in 1974.[30] These differences occur even when socioeconomic status is controlled. Black women tend to have slightly higher fertility rates than do white women.

Most illegitimate children are borne by single women, rather than by widows or divorcees (Farley and Hermalin, 1971:9). Historically, illegitimacy rates among black women have been about 10 times higher than those among whites. However, the number of illegitimate births among blacks has been dropping since about 1960. During that year, there were 98 illegitimate nonwhite children out of every 1,000 births, compared to 9 out of every 1,000 white births. By 1970, 90 out of every 1,000 nonwhite births were illegitimate, compared to 14 of every 1,000 white births. And by 1974, the nonwhite rate was 82 of each 1,000 whereas that among whites was 12 of every 1,000.[31] The reasons for these differences are also not clear. Some plausible answers involve ignorance of or inability to obtain contraceptive devices, inability to obtain abortions, underreporting of white illegitimate births, and the possibility that premarital conception forces marriage among whites more than blacks. Which of these factors best accounts for high black illegitimacy rates is not known.

Racial differences in marital status, fertility rates, and illegitimacy rates results in a higher proportion of black families having only one parent, usually the female. As will be noted below, the instability of the family—particularly as reflected in the high proportion of single parent households—is an important item in the Moynihan thesis. As can be seen in Table 12, when only those families in which children are present are analyzed, 44 percent of all black households had only one parent, compared to 12 percent of white households. The table also shows that, for both races, the lower the family income, the higher the proportion with only one parent. However, black families are worse off at every income level.

Table 12 Families with Children Less Than 18 Years of Age, by Race and Income, 1974

Income	Black			White		
	Both Parents	One Parent		Both Parents	One Parent	
Less Than $4,000	18%	82%	100%	39%	61%	100%
$4,000–5,999	35	65	100	66	34	100
$6,000–7;999	53	47	100	77	23	100
$8,000–9,999	78	22	100	88	12	100
$10,000–14,999	86	14	100	94	6	100
$15,000 and Over	90	10	100	97	3	100
Average, All Income Levels	56	44	100	88	12	100

Source: U.S. Bureau of the Census, "The Social and Economic Status of the Black Population in the United States, 1974," *Current Population Reports*, Series P-23, no. 54, tables 75 and 77.

The Consequences of Black Family Structure

The "Moynihan Report" asserts that the black family structure has deteriorated, producing a "tangle of pathology" in America's urban ghettos. Moynihan develops his argument in the following way (see Rainwater and Yancy, 1967:5–6).

First, one impact of slavery and Reconstruction was to ensure that black males could not adequately provide for their families because of their perpetually high unemployment rates and low wages. This problem has not been solved and, Moynihan asserts, it is growing worse because of continued high black fertility rates. While he may exaggerate the impact of black-white differences in fertility rates, it was shown above that the problem of unemployment and low incomes continues to be a serious one among black Americans.

Second, as a result, Moynihan says, the black family has deteriorated. This deterioration can be demonstrated with a few simple facts. (a) Nearly one-fourth of all urban black marriages are dissolved. As noted above, this figure has increased slightly in recent years. (b) Nearly one-fourth of all black births are illegitimate. Moynihan transforms the birth rates cited above into a ratio of illegitimate to legitimate births. His assertion is probably a little high today. (c) As a result, nearly one-fourth of all black families are headed by females. As Table 12 shows, Moynihan's assertion is even more true today. One reason it is argued that black Americans have a matrifocal family pattern is that 44 percent of all black families are headed by one parent, usually the woman.

Third, Moynihan asserts that the breakdown of the black family has led to a startling increase in welfare dependency as well as a variety of undesirable behaviors: higher rates of deviance and delinquency among youth, educational failure, and alienation within the family. Moynihan calls such "aberrant, inadequate [and] antisocial behavior" a "tangle of pathology." In order to solve these problems, he argues, national policy should be directed toward strengthening the black family, although he does not suggest how this is to be done.

A storm of controversy followed publication of the Moynihan Report (see Rainwater and Yancey, 1967). Liberals noted the obvious fact that most black families are intact two-parent households. Black scholars showed, rightly, the adaptive strength of the black family in the face of incredible economic and social adversity (see Billingsley, 1968). Some white conservatives used the report as an ideological tool, as an argument for the dismantling of those social welfare programs that did not focus on changing the structure of the family.

However, most of the immediate reactions did not really get at the key conceptual and empirical issue raised by the Moynihan Report. Although most sociologists agree that basic skills, values, motives, and need dispositions are learned in the context of the family (Kerkhoff, 1972), the causal relationship postulated by Moynihan seems doubtful in a social context characterized by racial discrimination. However, this issue can be tested. If Moynihan is correct, then black children coming from stable families (defined as having both parents present) should display lower rates of deviance and delinquency, do better in school, and have more positive familial experiences than do black children from broken homes. It has been shown that such differences do not exist. Berger and Simon (1974) have demonstrated that in the three areas Moynihan focuses upon, virtually no significant differences exist between children coming from stable and unstable black families. For example, in terms of "normal deviance"—drinking, smoking, skipping school, and the like—it makes little difference whether a black child is from a broken or intact home. In terms of delinquent acts, such as crimes against property, family structure is not associated with differences in black adolescents' behavior. Further, broken homes are not associated with differences in teenagers' levels of educational aspirations, expectations of actual educational attainment, or grades in school.

Finally, Berger and Simon examined several dimensions of familial activity—for example, the existence of rules and rule enforcement. liking and affect toward parents—and found that there is no consistent pattern indicating the harmful nature of broken homes among black youth. This last point has been replicated by Hunt and Hunt (1975). They found that father absence can produce positive psychological effects for black children and damaging effects for white children. These findings suggest, as Billingsley (1968) and others have argued, that various forms of extended family structures aid blacks in coping with an extremely adverse environment. They also suggest that Moynihan was wrong. While there is pathology in urban ghettos, and it would be a mistake to deny that fact (Clark, 1965), it is very doubtful that the black family causes such behavior.

In summary, black Americans are more likely than whites to be both single and divorced. Black women have higher fertility and illegitimacy rates than do white women. A higher proportion of black families are headed by one parent. Despite these problems, black families have apparently evolved ways of mitigating some of the potential consequences, for there are few differences between black children from either broken or stable homes.

EDUCATION AND RACE

Blacks have lower levels of educational attainment than do whites. It was noted above that the average black person had 10.9 years of schooling in 1975, compared to 12.3 years for the average white. In general, racial differences in educational attainment have been decreasing in recent years. However, this finding is not true in regard to higher education. In 1960, 4 percent of all black adults had four-year college degrees or more. Among whites, 8 percent had completed college. In 1975, 6 percent of all black adults had college degrees, compared to 15 percent of all whites.[32] Overall, then, blacks are less well educated than are whites, especially in terms of collegiate education.

This finding has important implications, for level of education is a key variable in the process of status attainment for both races (see Chapter 14 for an analysis of this issue). Further, as Table 4 above shows, increasing levels of education are associated with higher incomes for members of both races. However, blacks receive lower monetary rewards when they have educational levels similar to whites. This section is concerned with a different, though related, topic: desegregation in the public schools.

In 1954, the U.S. Supreme Court declared that legally "separate educational facilities are inherently unequal." The Court's reasoning was as follows (quoted in Bardolph, 1970:278).

To separate [children] from others of similar age and qualifications solely because of their race generates a feeling of inferiority as to their status in the community that may affect their hearts and minds in a way unlikely ever to be undone. . . . Segregation of white and colored children in public schools has a detrimental effect upon the colored children. The impact is greater when it has the sanction of law, for the policy of separating the races is usually interpreted as denoting the inferiority of the Negro group. A sense of inferiority affects the motivation of a child to learn. Segregation with the sanction of law, therefore, has a tendency to retard the educational and mental development of Negro children and to deprive them of some of the benefits they would receive in a racially integrated school system.

The court went on to direct the cities and school sytems affected by the ruling to proceed "with all deliberate speed" in complying with its ruling. Some did (see Simpson and Yinger, 1972:549); many did not. Although the legal apparatus supporting segregated education no longer exists in any state, black and white students still do not attend the same schools. Schools are now segregated largely because blacks and whites live in different neighborhoods. In other words, residential segregation is highly correlated with educational segregation (Farley and Taeuber, 1974).

The clearest way to see the extent of school segregation is to examine the level of racial isolation in the schools in terms of the extent to which nonwhite children attend schools comprised of varying proportions of nonwhite students. Data for the years 1968 and 1972 are shown in Table 13. As can be seen there, during the past few years, about 20 percent of all public school students have been nonwhite (most of them black). This figure varies by region, with smaller proportions of nonwhite students outside the south. However, most nonwhite children attend schools that are more than half nonwhite. In 1968, 70 percent of all nonwhite students were going to public schools that were more than half nonwhite. By 1972, this figure had dropped to 60 percent.

There are interesting regional variations that account for this decrease. In 1968, southern schools were more segregated than those of any other region. Four years later, schools in the South were less segregated than those in any other region, although even there a majority of all nonwhites still attended schools that were more than half nonwhite. These data suggest two conclusions. (1) Federal efforts at stimulating school desegregation have focused mainly on the South, and some significant changes have occurred in that region of the country. (2) Many black children still attend segregated schools. This fact can be seen especially clearly in the bottom row of Table 13, which shows the proportion of nonwhite students attending schools that are 90 to 100 percent nonwhite. As shown there, 34 percent of all nonwhite children attend schools in which the student body is virtually all nonwhite. Again, there are regional variations.

The Supreme Court's mandate that racially separate schools are inherently unequal and the finding that most schools remain segregated has greater significance in light of social scientific research. In a massive study, the famous "Coleman Report" (1966), *Equality of*

Table 13 Level of Isolation of Nonwhite Students, 1968 and 1972

	U.S.[a]		North and West		Border[b]		South[c]	
	1968	1972	1968	1972	1968	1972	1968	1972
Total Nonwhite Enrollment	20%	22%	16%	18%	18%	19%	32%	33%
Nonwhites Attending Schools that Are:								
0–49% Nonwhite	30	40	38	37	32	37	21	43
50–100% Nonwhite	70	60	62	63	68	63	79	57
	100%	100%	100%	100%	100%	100%	100%	100%
90–100% Nonwhite	53%	34%	38%	37%	60%	51%	70%	26%

Sources: 1968 data, U.S. Department of Health, Education, and Welfare, *Digest of Educational Statistics, 1973* (Washington, D.C.: U.S. Government Printing Office, 1974), p. 153; 1972 data, U.S. Department of Health, Education, and Welfare, *Digest of Educational Statistics, 1975* (Washington, D.C.: U.S. Government Printing Office, 1976), p. 186.

[a]Excludes Hawaii.
[b]Delaware, District of Columbia, Kentucky, Maryland, Missouri, Oklahoma, and West Virginia.
[c]Alabama, Arkansas, Florida, Georgia, Louisiana, Mississippi, North Carolina, South Carolina, Tennessee, Texas, and Virginia.

Educational Opportunity, came to the following conclusions about the state of American education in the mid-1960s.

First, despite popular impressions to the contrary, the physical facilities, the formal curriculums, and most of the measurable characteristics of teachers in black and white schools were quite similar. Second, despite popular impressions to the contrary, when measured differences in school physical facilities, formal curriculums, and teacher characteristics did exist, they had very little effect on either black or white students' performance on standardized tests. Tests of achievement were used as measures of academic achievement. Third, many black children began their school careers with serious educational deficiencies. That is, they were behind whites in academic achievement. This problem was not caused by the schools. However, by the end of their public school careers, many black children were even further behind whites. This difference was plainly caused, at least in part, by the schools. Fourth, the only school characteristic that had a clear and consistent relationship to test performance was the family background of students' peers. Having classmates from affluent backgrounds was associated with higher academic achievement on the part of all students, black and white, as indicated by achievement test scores.

These findings have not been refuted since publication of the Coleman Report (see Mosteller and Moynihan, 1973; Jencks, 1972). They provide the educational logic behind school desegregation. Because desegregated schools are likely to contain higher proportions of students from more affluent backgrounds, many black (and poor white) children will perform better. It has also been shown, by the way, that the presence of children from lower socioeconomic backgrounds does not lower the achievement test scores of more affluent students (U.S. Civil Rights Commission, 1967).

The reasons for the relationship between socioeconomic background of the student body and academic achievement among black children is still a matter of speculation. However, there appear to be at least two reasons (U.S. Civil Rights Commission, 1967:88–89). First, students mutually influence each other, establishing what goals are seen as attainable. For example, if children's peers regard a college education as a reasonable and necessary goal, then such students may come to see it as a possibility for themselves as well. Second, teachers also operate as "significant others," by influencing what students see as reasonable goals and by establishing an educational climate that encourages or discourages academic performance (see Rosenthal and Jacobson, 1968). Teachers tend to adjust their expectations depending upon, among other things, the social class backgrounds of their students. (On the influence of "significant others" in the process of status attainment, see Chapter 14.)

Unfortunately, although the drive to desegregate the public schools has received consistent backing from the courts, many whites have resisted, especially when such desegregation involves busing. Children have been transported by bus for a variety of purposes for many years (including maintaining segregated schools), but, even so, busing for purposes of desegregation arouses special opprobrium among whites. Furthermore, in those cases where whites have options, they are inclined to remove their children from schools in which large numbers of blacks are enrolled, regardless of the mechanism of desegregation (Levine and Meyer, 1977). "White flight" from desegregated schools is a pervasive problem. Further, many large urban school districts simply cannot desegregate, since there are few whites available. Clearly, some effort must be made at raising the educational expectations and level of accomplishment of black students in the public schools. Little help can be expected from whites in this task. How it is to be accomplished is not known.

SUMMARY AND CONCLUSION

This chapter has described some of the dimensions of racial inequality in the United States. There has been the illusion of progress, buoyed by the dismantling of the formal and overt elements of American racism. Yet in economic terms the relative positions of black and white Americans have not changed much. On the averagea, blacks earn about 65 percent of what whites do. They are still excluded from the higher-paying and higher-prestige occupations in both the blue- and white-collar job hierarchies. Finally, the unemployment rate among blacks is still twice that of whites.

In the second section of the chapter, some alternative explantions for these economic differences were explored. It was shown that three hypotheses dealing with patterns of migration, housing segregation, and educational differences do not adequately account for the income differences between the races. When these differences are decomposed statistically, it can be shown that racial discrimination accounts for a great deal of the income gap, especially between black and white men.

The fourth section of the chapter dealt with political differences between blacks and whites. Black Americans are more liberal than are whites on nearly every measure of political orientation. Partly as a result, blacks overwhelmingly identify themselves with the Democratic Party. Although black political participation, especially in the form of voting, has increased markedly in recent years, it is still lower than that among whites. However, the vote has meant important political changes in the South, where black officials are being elected at the local level in increasing numbers and the racial tone of political campaigns had changed radically. But the vote has not altered overall patterns of economic inequality.

In the fifth section of this chapter, the black experience with American criminal justice was portrayed. Although blacks are more likely to be victimized, most crimes are intraracial in nature. Blacks, especially poor blacks, often resemble a "normal criminal" in the eyes of the police and others in the criminal-justice system. As a result, they are disproportionately arrested, denied bail, unable to obtain a private attorney, forced to plea-bargain, found guilty, and given longer sentences.

The sixth section of the chapter sketched black religiosity in America. Blacks are more religious than are whites and more likely to be Protestant. They are also more likely to participate in their churches. The relationship between religiosity and social action among blacks is unclear.

The seventh section of the chapter dealt with the black family. Blacks are more likely to be single and to have broken marriages than are whites. Black women have higher fertility and illegitimacy rates than do white women. A higher proportion of black families are headed by a single parent. The consequences of these differences are considerably less serious than previously thought. Although there is a great deal of crime and deviance generally in urban ghettos, it does not appear that the black family is an important causal factor. Rather, unique extended family structures appear to restrain and prevent even more serious problems from developing. The final section of the chapter limned the lack of desegregation in public schools. Black and white children still attend different schools. It is not clear how the effects of racial isolation are to be obviated.

In conclusion, black and white Ameicans still live in an essentially caste relationship. Blacks are unequal to whites in virtually every area. It does not appear that this situation is going to change much in the near future. Perhaps we have only begun to pay the consequences.

NOTES

1. For example, the median family income in 1975 for whites was $14,268. For all nonwhites the median income was $9,321. For blacks alone, the median income was $8,779. Nonwhites were used here because data for blacks only are not available prior to 1967. See U.S. Bureau of the Census (1976a:table 4).

2. Table 1 compares all families, including those in which the head of household was unemployed for all or part of the year. However, when the ratio of black to white income is compared only among year-round, full-time workers, similar results are obtained (see Thurow, 1976).

3. For a good in-depth analysis of the experience of black workers in white unions, see Gould (1977). For some statistical data, see Hammerman (1973). For an outstanding analysis of the opportunities and liabilities of unions in enforcing equal opportunity, see Hammerman and Rogoff (1975).

4. See U.S. Bureau of the Census (1976b:table 602) and Garfinkle (1975).

5. A person is in the labor force when employed full or part time or unemployed but actively looking for a job.

6. The source for this assertion is the Congressional Budget Office (1976).

7. Hiltz (1971:987) has shown that "the consumer financial system . . . operates to increase inequalities between blacks and whites in our society." For example, blacks know less about potential financial services than whites and use financial services less. A smaller proportion of blacks have savings accounts. Finally, blacks own less life insurance and obtain less insurance per dollar spent than do whites. These findings appear to hold even when income is controlled.

8. There is some indication that blacks have begun to return to the South, although remaining in urban areas, in recent years (see Campbell et al., 1974). Whether this trend will continue is unknown.

9. Older black migrants who left the South prior to 1965 also earn more than blacks born in the North. They also have a lower proportion who are poor. However, among older blacks who only recently left the South, the situation is somewhat different. In this case, migrants do earn less than natives (see Long, 1975:1393).

10. This estimate is by Thomas Pettigrew as quoted in the *New York Times* (see Rosenbaum, 1977).

11. For a debate on the issue of housing and income, in which Kain stoutly defends his position, see Furstenberg et al (1970).

12. The source for the 1963 figures is U.S. Bureau of Labor Statistics (1976:table 181). The source for the 1975 figures is U.S. Bureau of the Census (1976b:table 200).

13. See Siegel (1965), Duncan (1969), Johnson and Sell (1976), and Farley (1977).

14. The unpublished data used here are made available under the auspices of the Inter-University Consortium for Political Research.

15. The discussion in this section on party identification is indebted to David Knoke's recent book *Change and Continuity in American Politics* (1976:40–46). The data used here were obtained in nationwide surveys conducted by the Survey Research Center of the University of Michigan.

16. The source for these assertions is Simpson and Yinger (1972:392).

17. These figures are from U.S. Bureau of the Census (1976b:table 747).

18. However, Wells (1975) shows that while the level of overt violence has declined greatly, many blacks are still intimidated and prevented from registering by a variety of legal and illegal tactics.

19. The source for these figures is U.S. Bureau of the Census (1975a:table 99).

20. The source for this assertion is U.S. Bureau of the Census (1975a:table 99).

21. These figures are from U.S. Bureau of the Census (1975a:table 106).

22. These data are from U.S. Bureau of the Census (1975a:table 109). The percentages do not add to 100 because of the impact of other races.

23. This assertion is based upon data in U.S. Bureau of the Census (1975a:table 108).

24. The source for these data is U.S. Bureau of the Census (1975a:table 117).

25. These data are from U.S. Bureau of the Census (1975a:table 114).

26. This term is adapted from Swigert and Farrell's (1976; 1977) description of the "normal primitive." The analysis below is indebted to their work.

27. For a historical analysis of black and white marital characteristics, see Farley and Hermalin (1971).

28. The figures are calculated from U.S. Bureau of the Census (1977b:table 1).

29. This argument is suggested by Liebow (1967) and Schulz (1969).

30. The sources for these data are U.S. Bureau of the Census (1975a:table 78; 1976b:table 70).

31. These data are from U.S. Bureau of the Census (1976b:table 81).

32. These data are from U.S. Bureau of the Census (1976f:table D).

13
SEXUAL
INEQUALITY

Most analyses of discrimination focus on racial and ethnic minorities. In recent years, however, it has become clear that women, a 51 percent majority of all Americans, are also discriminated against. This recognition is a dramatic change in perspective, for sociologists as well as for other citizens. Until recently, most people believed that women's place was in the home, and accepted as right and proper the exclusion of females from employment, occupational advancement, and equal pay.

Males predominate in the discipline of sociology. Partly as a result of this dominance, they have only recently begun to consider sexual inequality as a topic worthy of study.[1] In the past, a set of interrelated assumptions have been made which usually precluded such an analysis (Acker, 1973:937). First, it has been assumed that the family rather than the individual is the proper unit of analysis in studies of social stratification. For example, it is generally families that are ranked by socioeconomic status. Second, it has been assumed that the family's social position is determined by the status of the "male head of household." Third, it has been assumed that the social status of married females is determined by that of their husbands. Wives' economic contributions, educational attainment, and occupational prestige are simply discounted as unimportant. Fourth, it has been assumed that women determine their own social status only when they are not attached to men. Fifth, although it has been acknowledged that women are discriminated against in many ways, it has been assumed that this fact is unimportant and irrelevant to the operation of the stratification system.

These misbegotten assumptions have made sociological analyses considerably easier (and misleading, because half the population was not considered). They also reflected popular conceptions of women's proper place: as wife and mother. While the peculiarly restricted roles of womanhood have been justified on a variety of biological, moral, and other seemingly benign rationales, they are essentially a means of social control. Women who are wives and mothers are economically dependent upon men. They also do not compete with men for jobs. Most sociological analyses have failed to recognize the political implications of the assumptions noted above; that is, women rarely hold direct power over their own lives.

This chapter is a description of sexual inequality in the United States. It emphasizes the inconsistency between the image of women's traditional familial roles and their economic roles. In order to underline that relationship, the chapter is divided into five sections: (1) a brief summary of traditional sex role ideology, (2) trends in female labor-force participation, (3) trends in the occupational distribution of women, (4) economic differences between employed women and men, and (5) barriers to women's occupational advancement. In each of the last four sections, the influence of traditional sex-role ideology will be shown.

TRADITIONAL SEX-ROLE IDEOLOGY
Historically, Americans have placed great value on a fairly rigid sexual division of labor. Most people have believed that adult women ought to take responsibility for three interrelated tasks, all of them centered in the family: reproduction, child rearing, and homemaking.[2] While these roles were not always filled in practice, they represent the ideal of womanhood in America. Yet, perversely, it is precisely because these roles have been deified and arbitrarily restricted to one sex that women have been kept in their place.

Reproduction
Somewhat obviously, reproduction is a task that can neither be shifted nor shared. However, as Bernard (1971) has observed, the extent to which it is a valued activity has changed greatly with industrialization. Over the past 200 years fertility rates have dropped from more than seven children per woman to less than three. This decline has occurred despite governmental pressures to increase fertility (Huber, 1976).

Huber argues that there appear to be three main reasons for the decline in fertility rates. The first is that, with industrialization, children are no longer economic assets. Because the family has become a purely consumptive rather than an economically productive unit, child labor is no longer necessary. It costs a great deal to bear and raise children. The second and third reasons for the decline in fertility are technological in origin: new methods of birth control and infant feeding. The development of safe and effective means of birth control has meant that women can have children if and when they choose. New and safe methods of infant feeding have meant that the survival of newborn infants is no longer dependent upon the mother's ability to lactate. Thus, although reproduction is a biological fact that cannot be altered, it is now a function of choice. The current context is one in which families are choosing to have fewer and fewer children. As a result, the importance of women's other two roles has diminished.

Child Rearing

Many people believe that children ought to be raised by their mothers. This belief in the overriding importance of maternal care has served as a justification for keeping women in the home and men out of it. As recently as 1973, 48 percent of the respondents in one urban sample asserted that a mother who works outside the home cannot establish a warm relationship with her children (see Mason et al., 1976). Yet there is little evidence showing that the children of mothers who work for pay are adversely affected. For example, the children of employed mothers do just as well in school and have delinquency rates similar to children of mothers who are not employed (see Nye and Berardo, 1973).

There has been some academic controversy regarding the necessity of the continuous presence of the mother for infants' mental development and health. Yet recent research indicates that it is the quality of care and attention that young children receive that is of greatest importance in their future mental health (Harbeson, 1971). Furthermore, any consistent, warm adult or set of adults can provide children with affection and nurturance (Schaffer, 1977; Bernard, 1971). Put bluntly, men or any other mother substitutes can perform childrearing tasks as well as mothers (see Heatherington and Parke, 1975). As Schaffer (1977) puts it, all the evidence shows that there is "no reason why the mothering role should not be filled as competently by males as by females. The human male's relative lack of involvement in child rearing is essentially a cultural rather than a biological phenomenon."

Homemaking

The term "homemaker" summarizes a variety of tasks that women are assigned. Prior to industrialization, when homes were economically productive units and families were unable to control births, the confinement of females in the home might have made sense. Today, however, homemakers perform essentially supportive tasks for their husbands. They raise children and chauffeur them around. They cook, clean, and maintain the home. They wash the family's clothes. In addition, however, women fill "stroking" roles. In social-psychological terms, stroking behavior involves the expression of loyalty, deference, self-denial, understanding, passive acceptance, and the like.

In her analysis of female stroking behavior, Bernard (1971:92) cites the nineteenth-century novelist Nathaniel Hawthorne's summary of women's "true place."

Woman is the most admirable handiwork of God, in her true place and character. Her place is at man's side. Her office, that of sympathizer; the unreserved, unquestioning believer; the recognition, withheld in every other manner by other men but given, in pity, through woman's heart, lest man should utterly lose faith in himself; the echo of God's own voice, pronouncing, "It is well done."

As with child rearing, there is no particular reason why these tasks must be arbitrarily assigned to women. For the most part, household tasks (including the stroking role) can be done by any competent adult and by most children. Males who feign incompetence at these tasks are dissembling. Their lack of involvement in household tasks is an ideological stance suggesting that certain tasks are beneath their dignity. Unfortunately, women who limit themselves to the three traditional roles too often end up encouraging rigidity in both themselves and their spouses. If the husband of a traditional woman suddenly became competent at her tasks, it would further demean her position and threaten her sense of purpose.

There is a myth that marital stress increases when wives leave their traditional roles and enter the labor force. This belief is an important factor preventing many women from seeking paid employment. Yet it appears that the more freedom spouses have to choose among alternative roles, the happier the marriage (see Orden and Bradburn, 1969; Whitehurst, 1977). With greater freedom to choose, both women and men can escape the limitations of traditional roles.

The roles described in this section are ideal types in the sense that they are cultural prescriptions of women's "proper place." The image of womanhood embodied in these roles has functioned to keep females out of the labor force. Nonetheless, some women have always worked for pay. For employed females, the image has been used as a justification for lower opportunities and wages. The remainder of this chapter describes women's place in the economy and the extent to which it is a result of the traditional image of women's place in the family.

TRENDS IN LABOR-FORCE PARTICIPATION AMONG WOMEN

The single most important change in women's status over the past 80 years may be the steadily increasing proportion of females who work outside the home, for it portends most of the findings reported in the remainder of this chapter (Oppenheimer, 1970; 1973:947; Waite, 1976). "In 1900," it has been reported, "if the average woman worked at all during her lifetime—and not many did—it was only before marriage and children; the proportion of employed females declined steadily with age."[3] As recently as 1940, only 27 percent of all women and 17 percent of all married women were in the labor force. The proportion of females in the labor force has increased slowly but consistently until, by 1975, 46 percent of all women were working or looking for work.[4]

Not only has the proportion of working women increased over the past few years, but their social characteristics have changed as well. This change is shown in Table 1, which focuses upon married women living with their husbands. As can be seen in the table, during the past few years increasing proportions of all married women have been entering the work force. This fact can be seen even more clearly when the distribution by age is examined. Although a majority of all young married women between 20 and 24 years work for pay, an increasing proportion of "mature" women have also been entering the labor force. Furthermore, Table 1 shows that the presence of children is less and less of a deterrent to female labor-force participation, even among married women who have children less than six years of age. During the period covered by the table, 1960 to 1975, this group had the largest percentage increase in labor-force participation, from only 19 percent to 37 percent.

Waite (1976) accounts for the data in Table 1 by showing in statistical terms that those historical factors that tended to prevent married women from entering the labor force have declined in importance—for example, women's age as a disqualification for employment and the presence of young children in the family. On the other hand, those factors that might stimulate female labor-force participation by married women have become more important in recent years—for example, the wife's earning potential, the probability of her having worked at some point in the past, the changing age distribution of the population, and greater ability to control fertility (see Waite, 1976; Darian, 1976).

Clearly, then, working for pay is an important part of the lives of married women, not merely something they do prior to finding a husband and having children. Further, demographic projections show that increasing proportions of women will continue to enter the labor force, at least through 1990 (see Fullerton and Flaim, 1976).

Table 1 Labor Force Participation Rates of Married Women, Husband Present, by Age and Presence of Children, 1960–74

	1960	1965	1970	1975
Age of Women				
All ages	31%	35%	41%	44%
20–24 Years	32	37	48	57
25–44 Years	33	36	43	50
45–64 Years	36	40	44	44
Presence of Children				
No Children Under 18 Years	35%	38%	42%	44%
Children 6–17 Years	39	43	49	52
Children Under 6 Years	19	23	30	37

Source: U.S. Bureau of the Census, *Statistical Abstract of the United States, 1977* (Washington, D.C.: U.S. Government Printing Office, 1977), tables 574, 575, and 576.

The significance of these data can be explored by considering three topics: (1) the division of labor within families when wives work for pay, (2) the impact of family migration on women's labor force participation, and (3) labor force participation and mental health among women. The first two topics suggest the incompatibility between traditional family life and labor-force participation, and the third identifies some of the positive benefits of working outside the home.

Working Wives and the Division of Labor Within Families

Women who work for pay often experience a great deal of role conflict, primarily because in most families wives are expected to fill their traditional roles even if they are employed outside the home. Thus, in a situation in which task segregation is the norm, women bear primary responsibility for child raising and housekeeping (Bernard, 1971).

In such a context, women have three options. First, they can choose not to work for pay. As shown in Table 1, more than half of all married women still do not participate in the labor force. Some do not work outside the home because of a belief that it is inappropriate behavior. For example, in 1975, 25 percent of all women in a nationwide random sample disapproved of the idea of a married woman earning money outside the home if she had a husband capable of supporting her.[5] Other housewives would prefer to be employed but feel constrained by their children or pressures from their husbands. For them, opting out of the labor force avoids the role conflict that would be generated by the combination of employment and familial responsibilities. It also minimizes familial disruptions (Coser and Rokoff, 1971).

A married woman's second option is to get a full-time job. But given traditional role expectations, this choice means that employed wives often have, in effect, two jobs—one at home and one at work. In his review of the literature, Pleck (1977:418) concludes that "the total burden of work and family roles combined is substantially greater for the employed than the nonemployed wife." Studies of how people use their time during the day show that unemployed married women spend about eight hours each day doing family-oriented work of all sorts, while employed wives spend nearly five hours per day on such tasks (Walker, 1969; 1970; Robinson et al., 1976). In effect, the requirement that women perform most household tasks means that wives who are employed full time may have to work 13-hour days on two different jobs while being paid for only one. The diminution in time spent on family work among employed women means that some tasks come to be defined as unnecessary or are simply done less often. As an aside, it is generally the case that when wives work for pay, husbands do not increase the amount of time they spend on family-oriented work. Pleck (1977:420) concludes "fully employed men still do only a fraction of the family work that fully employed women do—about one-third."

The expectation that working wives will also perform an unequal share of family tasks leads some of them to compromise by working only part time. This is their third option. In 1974, 22 percent of the female labor force voluntarily worked part time, as compared to only 5 percent of the male labor force. Of course, an important consequence of the decision to work part time is that a person's income is relatively low, job seniority or security is not possible, and promotion is rare.

It should be noted that some women do not fill traditional family roles at all—they never marry or are not currently married. Among males, labor-force participation is associated with being married. However, the reverse is true for working women. That is, among women, labor-force participation is associated with their being unmarried (Havens, 1973). Furthermore, Havens suggests that the higher the socioeconomic status of women, the lower the rate of marriage, and this position has received some tentative support (see Mueller and Campbell, 1977). Havens argues, plausibly, that some working women choose not to marry.

Family Migration and Labor Force Participation
In general, families move in response to husbands' occupational needs rather than wives' (Duncan and Perrucci, 1976; Long, 1974a). This finding appears to be true regardless of the occupational prestige of a woman's job or her contribution to the family's total income. The major factors affecting family migration are husbands' occupational prestige, occupational demands for husbands to migrate (for example, company transfers), and employment opportunities in

husbands' fields. This emphasis on men's occupational needs reflects the dominant conception that males' jobs are more important
than females', since women belong in the home.

One result is that wives are more likely to drop out of the labor
force when families move long distances. The longer the distance of
the move, the greater the probability that wives will stop working
outside the home (Long, 1974a). This finding is true even among
college-educated women. Among married couples in which both
spouses are college gradautes, Duncan and Perrucci (1976) found
that, over a four-year period, 88 percent of the wives remained in
the labor force when the couple was geographically stable. But
among those couples who moved to a new state, only 75 percent of
the wives remained employed or were looking for a job. As an aside,
it should be noted that college-educated women have a greater at-
tachment to the labor force than do less well educated women, even
when their families are geographically mobile.

A second though more indirect result of the emphasis on men's
careers is that women, and this includes college-educated women,
take the probability of migration into account in selecting their occupations in the first place. That is, they choose to develop work skills
that are easily transportable—for example, teaching. Furthermore,
the fact of migration also adversely affects the career development
and income levels of women. Females who are forced to move according to their husbands' job needs are often unable to obtain
seniority and work experience necessary to advance in their fields
and move up in salary.

Working and the Mental Health of Women
Among those women who do not participate in the labor force, 75
percent cite "home responsibilities" as their major reason.[6] Yet for
some women, remaining in the home can have deleterious consequences. For example, Whitehurst (1977:22) makes the following assertion.

*Although most young women before marriage indicate little or no positive
interest in the domestic arts, they find that this becomes their major function. Housework is menial labor, low status, unpaid, never-ending, and
dead-end in the sense that there is no way to be promoted to a higher level.
This may have a deteriorating effect on a woman's mind, and the isolation
which comes from being imprisoned in a nuclear household can lead to erratic judgments, a sense of powerlessness, and susceptibility to psychosis.*

For many women, housework does produce social isolation, and
for some the result can be debilitating. They are psychologically and
economically dependent upon their husbands. They become small
minded and petty, pursuing trifling and inconsequential topics of

interest. They lack concentration. They are given to daydreaming, brooding, fatigue, and psychosomatic symptoms.[7] The result can be seen in terms of rates of mental disorders among women.

In a series of publications, Gove and his associates have summarized the relationship among sex, marital status, and mental disorders. For present purposes, mental disorders are defined broadly so as to include all forms of neuroses and psychoses affecting both institutionalized patients as well as the general population.[8] Gove's findings are as follows: (1) Women are more likely to suffer from mental disorders than are men. (2) Married women are more likely to suffer from mental disorders than are single women, whether the latter are divorced, widowed, or never married. (3) Married women are more likely to suffer from mental disorders than are married men. (4) Never-married women are less likely to suffer from mental disorders than are never-married men.

Gove (1972a:43) explains these findings by asserting that they reflect the nature of the marital roles occupied by women. Essentially, because of the different role expectations imposed on husbands and wives, "being married is considerably more advantageous to men than it is to women. While being single is, if anything, more disadvantageous to men than to women." Furthermore, according to Gove (1972b; 1973), differences in marital sex roles can also be used to account for differences in mortality and suicide rates for each sex.

The findings reported above do not take into account the effect of labor-force participation on married women. Yet paid work is the major source of status (and independence) in American society. Those who are employed generally have a more positive sense of self-esteem than those who are not. Ferree (1976) interviewed an urban sample of women married to blue-collar workers. About half of these women were housewives, the other half were employed in blue-collar jobs (for example, as textile workers) or in low-level white-collar jobs (for example, doing clerical work). The nature of the sample is important because it is often asserted that married blue-collar women would rather be housewives than work in "ordinary" jobs. Yet Ferree's findings show the benefits of employment in a particularly striking way.

First, most of the blue-collar women in her sample would prefer to work for pay rather than in the home (or only in the home). Second, the employed women in this sample are more satisfied with their lives and have a greater sense of personal autonomy and self-esteem. For example, 57 percent of the housewives report they are not very good at family work. None of the employed women say they are not very good at their jobs. Third, in this sample, housewives are more likely to believe that what they do during the day is less interesting and that they are more isolated than are their blue-collar husbands. They are also more likely to see themselves as worse off than employed women. As a result, housewives are more likely to want their daughters to "be different" than they are. Fourth, those housewives who are intrinsically satisfied with their roles are enmeshed in social networks of various sorts—with kin or neighbors, for example. As a result, the isolation of the nuclear family is alleviated. Clearly, then, labor-force participation can have positive consequences for women, apart from whatever economic benefits are derived.

In summary, rates of labor-force participation among women have increased substantially during the past 80 years. Nearly half of all women now work for pay. These increases have also occurred among married women, irrespective of age or the presence of children. However, regardless of their employment status, most women are still expected to fill their traditional female roles—especially child rearing and housekeeping. Family migration occurs in response to men's occupational needs. Migration tends to stifle female labor-force participation. Finally, while women have higher rates of mental disorders than do men, it appears that working women are less susceptable to such problems.

TRENDS IN THE OCCUPATIONAL DISTRIBUTION OF WOMEN

Despite much rhetoric, and the sometimes anguished cries of many males, men and women still generally work at different and unequal jobs. The extent of occupational segregation by sex has not changed much during this century (see Oppenheimer, 1970; Gross, 1968; Williams, 1975). This section is a description of the jobs women hold. It is divided into four parts. In the first, the economic contributions of women who do not work outside the home are briefly described in terms of the "two-person career." The second notes recent trends in the occupational distribution of men and women. The third shows recent trends in the proportion of each sex in each occupational category. These two topics are presented in terms of the census occupational categories used in previous chapters. The fourth part analyzes recent trends in the proportion of females in specific occupations so as to show more fully the extent of occupational segregation between the sexes.

The Two-Person Career — HOUSEWIVES

Although it is not possible to describe the occupational distribution for the half of all women who do not work outside the home, they make clear economic contributions to their families by participating in what Papanek (1973) has called the "two-person career." That is, wives participate in their husbands' jobs vicariously by providing a variety of support services. These support services can be of two sorts. (First) within a traditional familial relationship "the 'two-person career' pattern is fully congruent with the stereotype of the wife as supporter, comforter, backstage manager, home maintainer, and main rearer of children" (Papanek, 1973:853). These tasks constitute economic contributions in several ways. They free husband's' time for "productive" work. For example, the lawyer can work on his case or the scholar his book rather than purchasing groceries, going to the laundry, and picking up children from school. Women can also provide a relaxing and tension-free home environment within which their erstwhile breadwinners can recover from each day's stress.

(Second) the support services wives provide may involve overt contributions to their husbands' occupational advancement. Such contributions can be especially important among upper-echelon white-collar families. For example, wives may be expected to entertain husbands' colleagues and superiors, run errands for the wives of superiors (as in the military), and perform such job-related tasks as typing or editing manuscripts. As Coser and Coser (1974:96) have noted, while these tasks are nominally optional (and often done out of "love"), "a wife who refuses to participate risks injuring her husband's career."

The two-person career embodies both the interdependence and inequality that exist between husbands and wives in traditional marriages (Papanek, 1973). The feminist Charlotte Perkins Gilman described this relationship more than 80 years ago (as quoted in Chapman, 1976:13).

For a certain percentage of persons to serve other persons in order that the ones served may produce more, is a contribution not to be overlooked. The labor of women in the house, certainly, enables men to produce more wealth than they otherwise could; and in this way women are economic factors in society. But so are horses. The labor of horses enables men to produce more wealth than they otherwise could. The horse is an economic factor in society. But the horse is not economically independent, nor is the woman.

More kindly, perhaps, Papanek, (1973:864) suggests that the two-person career is a "derailment solution" for women that is produced by the combination of relatively equal educational opportunity combined with inequalities in employment opportunity. Furthermore, the two-person career embodies cultural definitions of desirable life goals in American society precisely because it is based upon traditional female roles. In this regard, it should be noted that while many women become unhappy in such subordinate roles, many do not. In those situations where husbands earn relatively high incomes and wives have few occupational skills, it is plausible that a female would prefer to be a housewife (and identify herself as, say, "Mrs. Joe Physician") rather than work outside the home in what might seem to her to be a relatively low prestige job.

Further, a two-person career can allow a woman enough free time to develop her non-income-producing interests, whether they be raising children, talking to neighbors, learning to play tennis, or joining voluntary associations of various sorts. Incidentally, many relatively significant organizations are dependent upon the volunteer help of unemployed married women—for example, the League of Women Voters and the PTA. In addition, without the help of mothers in the classroom, many public schools would be considerably less effective.

Recent Trends in the Occupational Distribution by Sex

Table 2 shows the occupational distribution for males and females for the years 1960, 1970, and 1975. Two main conclusions can be drawn from it. First, despite the tremendous increase in the female work force in recent years, employed men and women are doing about what they have always done. The percentages of men and women in each occupational category have not changed very much between 1960 and 1975.

Second, there are striking differences in the male and female work force. In general, about 40 percent of all men are white-collar workers and about 60 percent are blue-collar. In contrast, about 60 percent of all women are white-collar employees and about 40 percent are blue-collar. These overall percentages have remained stable over time. However, within the blue- and white-collar categories, men and women clearly work at different sorts of jobs. Men are clustered

Table 2 Occupational Distribution, by Sex, 1960–75[a]

Occupation	1960		1970		1975	
	Males	Females	Males	Females	Males	Females
Professionals	10%	12%	14%	14%	14%	15%
Managers	13	5	14	4	13	5
Sales	6	8	6	7	6	7
Clerical	7	30	7	34	6	35
Total White Collar	36%	55%	41%	59%	39%	62%
Crafts	19%	1%	20%	1%	21%	2%
Operatives	20	16	20	15	18	13
Laborers	9	[b]	8	1	8	1
Service	7	25	7	22	9	22
Farm Workers	10	4	5	2	5	1
Total Blue Collar	65%	46%	60%	41%	61%	39%

Sources: U.S. Bureau of Labor Statistics, *Handbook of Labor Statistics, 1975* (Washington, D.C.: U.S. Government Printing Office, 1976), table 6; U.S. Bureau of Labor Statistics, *Handbook of Labor Statistics, 1976* (Washington, D.C.: U.S. Government Printing Office, 1977), table 6.

[a]Some columns do not add to 100% because of rounding.

[b]Less than ½ of 1%.

in occupations near the top of both the blue- and white-collar hierarchies. Women are clustered near the bottom of both hierarchies: 57 percent of all employed females are either clerical workers or service workers. Table 2 shows that the proportion of female managers and sales workers remained stable between 1960 and 1975. Among professionals, the proportion of employed females increased only slightly. In general, these are the most lucrative and prestigious occupations in American society. Similarly, there has been little increase in the proportion of women who are employed in crafts occupations, the most skilled blue-collar jobs. Essentially, traditional conceptions of woman's place are reflected in the occupational distribution of the two sexes. Some less important and less prestigious jobs are defined as "woman's work." Occupational segregation results.

Recent Trends in the Proportion of Each Sex in Each Occupational Category

A similar conclusion can be drawn when the occupational distribution is examined from a different angle, as in Table 3, which displays the percentage of males and females in each occupational category for the years 1960 and 1975. The increases in women's labor-force participation described above can be seen more clearly in Table 3, for females constitute a larger proportion of workers in every occupational category except service and farming. However, the largest gains in employment came in those occupations where women have always been more likely to work (Garfinkle, 1975). The greatest percentage increase between 1962 and 1975 was among female professionals, from 28 to 41 percent. However, as will be shown below, most of these additional workers are in specific occupations that are traditionally female.

Although not shown in the table, the greatest numerical increase in women employees was among clerical workers. By 1975, four out of five clerical workers were women. Among managers, sales, crafts, operatives, and laborers, there were slight increases in the proportion of females. However, it should be noted that it is still the case that few women become crafts workers or laborers. Among service workers, the proportion of females drops in Table 3 only because private household workers are included in this category. Private household workers are in a declining occupational role (see Coser, 1974:67–88).

Recent Trends in the Proportion of Women in Specific Occupations

Although tables 2 and 3 are suggestive, they fail to reveal the true extent of occupational segregation by sex because each category in the tables consists of a cluster of sometimes unrelated specific occupations, many of which are predominantly filled by one sex or the

Table 3 Percentage of Males and Females in Each Occupational Category,
1960 and 1975

Occupation	1960			1975		
	Males	Females		Males	Females	
White Collar						
Professionals	72%	28%	100%	59%	41%	100%
Managers	84	16	100	81	19	100
Sales	60	40	100	57	43	100
Clerical	32	68	100	22	78	100
Blue Collar						
Crafts	97%	3%	100%	95%	5%	100%
Operatives	72	28	100	70	30	100
Laborers	98	2	100	91	9	100
Service	35	65	100	38	62	100
Farm Workers	82	18	100	84	16	100

Source: Calculated from U.S. Bureau of the Census, *Statistical Abstract of the United States, 1977* (Washington, D.C.: U.S. Government Printing Office, 1977), table 600.

other. Table 4 displays the percentage of women in selected specific occupations for the years 1962, 1968, and 1974. The table shows more clearly that some jobs are defined as "woman's work" and some as "man's work." Furthermore, there has not been much change in recent years. Those jobs that have been dominated by men still are. In turn, those jobs that have been dominated by women still are. Although 41 percent of all professionals were women in 1974, most of them were in just a few of the less prestigious occupations: librarians, nurses, social workers, and elementary school teachers, for example (see Grimm and Stern, 1974). Despite rhetoric about affirmative action, there are still very few female lawyers or physicians. In other words, women are still not acquiring positions in the most prestigious professional occupations.[9]

Furthermore, in those occupations that are dominated by women, they still do not work in the most prestigious positions. Among librarians, nurses, and social workers, disproportionate numbers of men are supervisors. In elementary schools, most principals are men. And in education generally, as the academic or administrative level increases, the proportion of women decreases.

Finally, within the more lucrative professions, women are generally relegated to the less pretigious areas of specialization. For example, few women are surgeons, and those who are tend to specialize in gynecology (see Quadagno, 1975; Jacobson and Jacobson, 1975). Among lawyers, women tend to specialize in matrimonial law rather than in corporate law (see Epstein, 1970; 1971).

Job segregation prevails whether women dominate an occupational category or form only a small segment of it. Four out of five clerical workers are women, yet there are clearly male-dominated clerical occupations: insurance adjusters and mail carriers, to name two. Although only 5 percent of all crafts workers are women, those

Table 4 Females as a Percentage of All Workers in Selected Detailed Occupations, 1962–74

Occupations	1962	1968	1974
Professionals	36%	38%	41%
Lawyers and Judges	3	3	7
Librarians	86	89	82
Chemists	9	9	14
Physicians	6	8	10
Registered Nurses	99	99	98
Social Workers	60	62	61
Elementary School Teachers	87	87	84
Drafting Technicians	4	7	8
Managers	15%	16%	19%
Purchasing Agents	11	12	18
Sales	39%	41%	42%
Hucksters and Peddlers	66	75	75
Insurance Agents	10	10	13
Clerical	69%	73%	78%
Bank Tellers	72	86	92
Bookkeepers	85	89	89
Insurance Adjusters	9	20	46
Mail Carriers	3	5	8
Secretaries	99	99	99
Shipping Clerks	8	12	16
Telephone Operators	96	98	94
Crafts	3%	3%	5%
Bakers	18	19	41
Printers	6	11	20
Decorators	50	53	62
Painters	3	2	3
Operatives	26%	30%	31%
Gas Station Attendants	2	3	5
Graders and Sorters	55	74	75
Packers and Wrappers	60	61	63
Welders	6	5	5
Delivery Workers	2	3	4
Taxi Drivers	4	4	12
Service	54%	57%	59%
Private Household	97	a	98
Bartenders	12	19	33
Cooks	64	65	59
Hairdressers	88	90	92
Guards	5	6	6
Nursing Aides	75	83	87

Source: S. H. Garfinkle, "Occupations of Women and Black Workers, 1962–74," *Monthly Labor Review* 98 (November 1975): tables 1 and 3.

aNot available.

females who do crafts work are concentrated in specific occupations—for example, decorators. A similar pattern occurs among operatives. Although women are 31 percent of this job category, they predominate in occupations classified as "graders and sorters" and "packers and wrappers." At the same time, women constitute a very small proportion of the other operative occupations, such as welders and delivery workers. A majority of all service workers are women. Yet in certain occupations they are clearly underrepresented—for example, as bartenders and guards.

In summary, while half of all married women are not employed outside the home, they nevertheless contribute to the economic well-being of their families by providing support services to their husbands. Papanek called this pattern of vicarious participation the two-person career. Among women who are employed outside the home, little change in their occupational patterns, relative to those of men, has occurred in recent years. In both the blue- and white-collar job hierarchies, men have the higher income and higher prestige jobs (Table 2). Women constitute a larger proportion of the workers in every occupational category, except service and farming. However, the largest gains have been in those categories where females have always been more likely to work (Table 3). Finally, when the sex composition of specific jobs is analyzed, the extent of occupational segregation by sex becomes even more clear (Table 4).

One important, although simple, point can be extrapolated from the data presented thus far. It is clear that the work women do is subordinate to that of men. This is true not only at home but also on the job; women are engaged in lower-prestige jobs than are men. Furthermore, when they are on the job, females are often cast into supportive, which is to say traditional, roles. The supportive nature of women's work roles can be suggested by noting a variety of complementary occupational pairs: doctor and nurse, editor and research assistant, executive and secretary, principal and teacher, academician and research assistant. In effect, employed women are often cast into jobs that are defined as extensions of maternal roles.

ECONOMIC DIFFERENCES BETWEEN EMPLOYED WOMEN AND MEN

Nearly all Americans, 98 percent, now believe that women who work at the same jobs as men should receive the same pay (Mason et al., 1976). However, in general, women are not paid at the same rates as men, whether they are in the same occupational category, the same specific occupation, the same specialization within that occupation, or actually doing the same jobs. This section describes the economic differences between women and men. These differences reflect the idea that woman's place is in the home. People have always assumed that women did not need or deserve equal pay. Presumably, they did not have a family to support and were only working for "pin money." However, as will be shown below, this stereotype is often not true. In addition to rationalizations about woman's place, it is frequently alleged that females earn less than men because they have different characteristics, what the economists would call "human capital": many do not work full time, they are less well educated, and their labor-force participation is intermittent. In the comparisons that follow, it is shown that even when these differences are taken into account women earn less than men.

Overall Income Differences by Sex

In comparing the median incomes of men and women, full-time workers constitute the proper unit of analysis. Because so many women choose or are forced to work part time, their inclusion in the analysis would artificially increase the income differences between the two sexes. In 1975, men who worked full time all year long had a median income of $13,144, while women who also worked full time for the entire year had a median income of $7,719. In other words, on the average, full-time female workers earned only 59 percent of what males earned in 1975. And these figures are very stable over time. In 1970, women employed full time also earned 59 percent of what men did. In 1960, fully employed women had a median income that was 61 percent of men's.[10] Clearly, very few gains have been made in recent years and, in fact, some ground appears to have been lost.

Income Differences by Occupation and Sex

It has been argued that the income differences between men and women can be accounted for in terms of their different occupational characteristics. However, the same general differences described above also appear when the incomes of each sex at each occupational level are examined. Table 5 displays the median incomes for full-time workers for each occupational category and sex during 1975.

As can be seen in the table, in every occupational category, women earn considerably less than do men. Among full-time professional workers, females earn 66 percent of what men do. In some perverse way, it seems just as well that there are relatively few female sales workers, for they earn only 39 percent as much as their male counterparts. Among clerical workers, nearly all of whom are women, female median incomes were only 62 percent as much as males'—$7,562 compared to $12,152. Similarly, among service workers, the majority of whom are female, women earn only 57 percent of what men do. As shown in Table 5, this percentage would be considerably lower if private household employees were included in this category. The job category where women's and men's average

Table 5 Median Income of Year-Round Full-Time Workers,
by Occupation and Sex, 1975

Occupation	Female	Male	Females as Percentage of Male
Professionals	$10,639	$16,133	66%
Managers	9,125	16,093	57
Sales	5,460	14,025	39
Clerical	7,562	12,152	62
Crafts	7,268	12,789	57
Operatives	6,251	11,142	56
Laborers	6,973	9,057	77
Service (except private household)	5,414	9,488	57
Private Household	2,413	a	—
Farm Workers	a	5,935	—

Source: Calculated from U.S. Bureau of the Census, "Money Income and Poverty Status of Families and Persons in the United States: 1975 and 1974 Revisions," *Current Population Reports*, Series P-60, no. 103, table 9.

[a]Not available because of small numbers.

incomes are closest together is among laborers—where even men's incomes are not very high. The few women in these occupations earn 77 percent as much as men. *HIGHER INCOME*

Similar findings occur when specific occupations are examined, rather than the census categories used in Table 5. For example, in 1974, male computer specialists had median incomes of $18,600, compared to medians of $16,300 for females. In this field, then, women earned a relatively "high" 88 percent of what men did. Among physical scientists, men had a median income of $20,000 compared to women's $15,000. Women earned 75 percent as much as men. And among social scientists, males earned $20,900 on the average, while females earned $16,100. Women earned 77 percent as much as men.[11] These differences exist when areas of specialization within fields are compared (see Epstein, 1970). They also exist when the various nonprofessional occupational categories are analyzed in more detail (see U.S. Bureau of the Census, 1977a:table 602).

Income Differences by Education and Sex

It has been argued that women's earnings are lower than men's because they do not obtain as much education as do men. It is true that females are less well educated than are males, especially at the highest levels. In 1975, women received 51 percent of all high school degrees, precisely their proportion of the total population. In that same year, they received 45 percent of all college degrees. It can be hypothesized that this somewhat lower figure is the result of marriage, pregnancy, the presumed need to support one's husband while he is in school, or some combination of these factors. The percentage of women who obtain advanced or professional degrees of various sorts has always been low. In 1973, while females received 42 percent of all masters' degrees, they obtained only 18 percent of all Ph.Ds. In that same year, women received only 8 percent of all law degrees and 9 percent of all medical degrees.[12] These extraordinarily low figures are clearly the result of discrimination, differing sex-role expectations, and differences in socialization by sex (see Whitehurst, 1977; Epstein, 1970; and Feldman, 1973).

However, regardless of their level of educational attainment, women earn less than do men. The income figures given above for the various professional occupations all require advanced degrees. Similar disparities exist among physicians and lawyers. Table 6 summarizes the income relationship between women and men at each educational level for persons 25 years of age and older who worked full time all during 1975. As can be seen in the table, men earn more than women at each educational level. Even among college graduates there is a great disparity in median income. In 1975, male college graduates earned $18,450 on the average, while females with college degrees earned only $11,359. In fact, the table shows that college-educated women not only earn less than college-educated men, they also earn less than high-school-educated men. As noted, female college graduates had a median income of $11,359 in 1975, while male high school graduates had a median income of $13,542.

Income Differences by Continuity of Labor Force Participation

It has also been argued that women earn less than men because of their intermittent labor-force participation. Women, so the argument goes, drop out of the labor force periodically in order to have children, to manage the home, or to move when their families migrate. It was shown above that family migration does have an impact of female labor-force participation. On the other hand, it is argued that women who are essentially housewives periodically enter the labor force (either full or part time) for limited periods in order to satisfy particular familial needs—during an economic crisis or to help

Table 6 Median Income of Year-Round Full-Time Workers, 25 Years and Older, by Sex and Education, 1975

Education	Males	Females	Females as Percentage of Males
Elementary (8 years)	$10,600	$ 5,691	54%
High School Degree	13,542	7,777	57
College Degree	18,450	11,359	62
Overall Median	13,821	8,171	59%

Source: U.S. Bureau of the Census, *Statistical Abstract of the United States, 1975* (Washington, D.C.: U.S. Government Printing Office, 1976), table 668.

finance a consumer item of some sort. Regardless of people's motivation, intermittent labor-force participation reduces their income because they lack seniority, job experience, and training in the latest methods or techniques of work.

However, when only those individuals who have worked all their adult lives are compared to one another, it can be shown that women still earn less than men (Suter and Miller, 1973). This is true even when education is controlled. Table 7 displays median incomes for women and men in their prime earning years who have worked all their adult lives by their level of education.

The income data in the table are for 1966 and, hence, of less interest right now.[13] However, there is no reason to believe that the overall relationship between men and women has changed very much during the intervening years. For example, as can be seen in Table 7, among people who have worked all their adult lives, women earned about 73 percent as much as men did, at least as of 1966. It will be recalled that full-time female workers earned about 59 percent of what men did in 1970, and 61 percent in 1960. If it is assumed that continuous labor-force participation has economic benefits, even in the face of discrimination, then the 73 percent figure reported in Table 7 is plausible. The table shows that, regardless of the fact of continuous labor-force participation, women earned considerably less than men did at each level of educational attainment.

Women's Incomes and Poverty

The systematic differences between men's and women's incomes have an important implication: it is very difficult for a female to be economically independent, whether from her parents or her husband. This fact can be highlighted by examining official data on poverty. It can be shown that, on the average, employed women contributed about 25 percent of the total family income among whites and about 32 percent among blacks.[14] However, this figure is misleading. Among the poor, working wives often contribute, not 25

Table 7 Median Income of Persons Aged 30–44 Years Who Worked All Adult Lives, by Sex and Education, 1966

	Men	Women	Women as Percentage of Men
Overall Median	$ 7,221	$5,281	73%
Less Than High School	5,660	3,132	55
High School Degree	7,362	5,511	75
Some College	8,310	5,608	67
College Degree	10,726	6,862	64

Source: L. E. Suter and H. P. Miller, "Income Differences Between Men and Career Women," *American Journal of Sociology* 78 (January 1973): 965.

percent, but 50 percent or more of the total family income (Bell, 1976). Without their efforts, starvation would result.

The situation is even more stark among female-headed families. By definition, such families have no adult male present. In 1975, 6 percent of all male-headed families were poor, according to the government's criteria. Nearly all of these families had two adults present, both of whom could possibly earn income. In contrast, 33 percent of all female-headed households were officially poor.[15] This percentage translates into more than three million families. Table 7 shows that excessive proportions of female-headed families are poor regardless of the characteristics of the family or its head of household. Among families headed by young women, 63 percent are poor, compared to 12 percent of those headed by young men. Even among women in their prime working years (ages 25 to 44), when children are most likely to be in school, female-headed families are eight times as likely as male-headed families to be poor—41 percent compared to 5 percent.

These same relationships exist when size of the family, education of the head, work experience of the head, occupation of the head, or race of the head is taken into account. For example, 11 percent of those families headed by college-educated women are poor, compared to 2 percent of families headed by college-educated men. Similarly, among families whose head worked all during 1975, only 3 percent of those led by men were poor, compared to 8 percent of those led by women. It should be noted that federal welfare policy continues to assume that women with young children "cannot" work. Actually, many of these women and their families are kept poor simply because adequate day-care facilities are not available.

In summary, it was shown that women work in occupations that are subordinate to those of men. This occupational difference is reflected in female incomes, which are generally less than those of men. When the incomes of each sex are compared while controlling for occupation (Table 5), education (Table 6), and continuity of labor-force participation (Table 7), it is still the case that women earn less than do men. Further, the economic subordination of women can be vividly shown by comparing poverty rates of female- and male-headed families (Table 8).

In general, despite much rhetoric about affirmative action in order to end discrimination, it remains the case that most American women are economically dependent upon the men with whom they are associated, whether these men be fathers, husbands, ex-husbands, or simply benefactors. As an aside, the data in this chapter suggest an important relationship between women's economic status and their marital status. Although there are few studies to support this assertion, it is plausible to argue that women recognize their economic dependence and that this dependence is a major incentive for staying married. Certainly the data in Table 8 suggest (on one level) that a woman who is living reasonably well ought to stay married even if she is unhappy in the relationship. Most people do not want to live, or have their children live, in poverty. Furthermore, the fact that "after four years only 33 percent of court-awarded child support payments are made, and after 10 years practically none," is probably suspected by many women (Chapman, 1976:20). Put bluntly, many marriages are probably kept together mainly because women are economically dependent, whether because they lack skills or experience, are discriminated against on the job, or because of more intangible differences in the socialization of the two sexes (see Whitehurst, 1977; Chapman, 1976).

Table 8 Selected Characteristics of Male and Female Headed Families, by Poverty Status, 1975

	Percentage Below Low-Income Level	
	Male Head	Female Head
Age of Head		
14–24 Years	12%	63%
25–44 Years	5	41
45–64 Years	5	20
65+ Years	8	13
Size of Family		
2 Persons	6%	23%
4 Persons	5	45
6 Persons	10	57
7+ Persons	19	67
Education of Head		
8 Years or Less	14%	38%
High School or Less	5	31
College	2	11
Head's Work Experience Last Year		
Worked 50 Weeks or More	3%	8%
Worked 1–49 Weeks	11	40
Did Not Work	15	50
Major Occupation of Head		
Professional and Managerial	2%	5%
Clerical and Sales	2	12
Craft	4	[a]
Operatives	5	25%
Service	7	37
Laborers	10	[a]
Farm Workers	21	[a]
Race of Head		
Black	14%	50%
White	6	26

Source: U.S. Bureau of the Census, "Money Income and Poverty Status of Families and Persons in the United States: 1975 and 1974 Revisions," *Current Population Reports*, Series P-60, no. 103, table 19.
[a]Not available because numbers are too small.

SEX-ROLE IDEOLOGY AND JOB DISCRIMINATION
The data presented above show clearly the extent of economic discrimination against women. The process of discrimination can be briefly sketched by considering three interrelated topics: (1) socialization and job discrimination, (2) public policy and job discrimination, and (3) work behavior and job discrimination. The impact of Americans' belief that women ought to be wives and mothers can be seen in each case.

Socialization and Job Discrimination
The occupational and income differences between women and men stem initially from differences in sex-role socialization. Socialization is the process by which people acquire appropriate values, motives, skills, and need dispositions (Brim, 1966). Teaching girls that their major adult responsibilities ought to revolve around child rearing and homemaking impedes women's economic advancement in three ways. First, many women are ambivalent about their job roles. As a result, they often work "overtime" at home and place their familial obligations ahead of occupational ambition. Second, those who do work for pay seek and are trained for "nonladder jobs"; that is, jobs in which the possibility for occupational advancement is relatively low. As Huber (1976) observes, it is still the case that "little girls want to be school teachers. Little boys want to be business executives." Third, women often adopt behavior patterns that prevent occupational advancement (Weitzman, 1975). For example, women frequently shy away from overtly competitive situations, partly because they have no experience with them. Here is one of the latent consequences of boys' participation in organized sports at very young ages. They learn to compete, while girls do not. In effect, then, by socializing girls to be wives and mothers, occupational success is made more difficult for women.

Public Policy and Job Discrimination
Job discrimination against women is illegal according to the Equal Pay Act of 1963 and the Civil Rights Act of 1964. Nonetheless, women are arbitrarily excluded from training and employment for many jobs. One way in which sex-role ideology produces job discrimination (and subverts public policy) is revealed in a study by Levinson (1975). He had college students of both sexes answer 256 classified advertisements for jobs. It was found that 35 percent of the potential employers responded in a clearly discriminatory way. For example, a "sex-inappropriate" caller (say, a male inquiring about a secretarial job or a female inquiring about a telephone lineman's job) would be told that the person responsible for hiring was not available that day. However, a few minutes later a "sex-appropriate"

caller who claimed similar credentials would be told to come for an interview. This tactic is only one of many that are used by employers. Furthermore, Levinson found that many employer responses were discouraging but not overtly discriminatory. For example, males would be told that stereotypically female jobs were too simple, dull, or low paying. Females would be told that stereotypically male jobs were too difficult, required too much strength, or demanded long hours.

Interestingly, some employers attempted to use potential applicants in affirmative action games. Such callers were told that since job discrimination by sex is illegal they should come for an interview—with the clear implication they would not be hired. Thus, federal laws prohibiting job discrimination have been circumvented, and the Levinson study only suggests some of the cruder ways of keeping women in their place. The laws have been violated with impunity because the men who run corporations and the men who write the laws do not wish them enforced. For example, the federal Equal Employment Opportunity Commission, the agency that is supposed to protect minorities and women, has never been adequately funded. The EEOC currently has a backlog of more than 9,000 cases (Griffiths, 1976). In effect, federal policy supports job discrimination against females despite laws designed to prevent such behavior.

Three other elements of federal policy also reinforce the idea that a woman's place is as wife and mother. First, federal income-tax laws are based on the assumption that women belong in the home. The tax laws penalize families in which both spouses work and provide advantages to married couples with only one income (see Stern, 1974). Second, social security laws also assume that women belong in the home, since working wives receive no more social benefits than if they had never worked (Griffiths, 1976).[16] Third, federal employment policy is also directed toward the needs of men, on the assumption that wives must tend to their families. For example, despite the fact that most able-bodied recipients of Aid to Families with Dependent Children (AFDC) are female, federal law gives priority to men who volunteer for work-incentive programs. Day-care centers would be more helpful to many families. In short, the federal government "discourages women from working outside the home and treats them as second-class citizens when they do so. Public policy fails to assure equitable reward for women's employment" (Griffiths, 1976:26).

Public policy at the local level also operates against women. This occurs especially in the schools, which are an important socializing agency. Textbooks, classroom practices, and educational curriculums all suggest that women ought to remain in the home or, when they do work for pay, they ought to be employed in sex-appropriate jobs (see Whitehurst, 1977). For example, in New York City's vocational high schools, women are trained for and referred to occupationally segregated jobs. Baker and Levenson (1975:17–18) make the following observation about the New York City schools.

Over 90 percent of the female vocational school students are trained in cosmetology, office skills, low-level health occupations, distributive education, and apparel manufacturing; less than 4 percent of the male vocational students are trained in these same areas. In contrast, over 80 percent of the males are enrolled in training for technical, mechanical or repair skills (e.g., computer technology, TV broadcasting technology; auto, aviation, business machine, radio-TV mechanics); skilled crafts (e.g., carpentry, plumbing, printing); and other skilled work (e.g., computer programming, drafting, sheet metal work). Less than 3 percent of the women are enrolled in these training programs.

It should be noted that the New York school system is not the only one with such educational policies (see Sullerot, 1971).

Sex-Role Ideology and Work Behavior

It is often asserted that women's relative lack of occupational success is simply a result of the sex differences between men and women. In this way, traditional sex-role ideology is reaffirmed. However, it is a general sociological principle that people's behavior is decisively influenced by the social situations in which they find themselves. This idea can be applied to the work behavior and experiences of women in order to show that sex-role ideology has less to do with women's lack of achievement than does simple discrimination. Following Kantor's (1976; 1977) recent work, two topics are dealt with here. First, the impact of the range of job opportunity on work orientation is examined. Second, the effect of skewed sex ratios on work behavior is described in a context in which job opportunity is great. These two topics also serve to identify some of the informal but very significant barriers to women's occupational success.

It is often asserted that women and men have differing orientations toward their jobs. Men are seen as being more ambitious and less concerned with interpersonal relations, such as getting along with colleagues, than are women. This argument has been used to "explain" why men are more occupationally successful than women. It implies that there are "sex differences" in work orientation which reflect their traditional roles in society. However, Kantor (1976) argues that differences in women's and men's orientations toward their jobs can also be explained by applying the general principle identified above. That is, she shows that, for both sexes, the greater the opportunity for promotion, advancement, and so on, then the higher the occupational aspirations and the less concern with interpersonal relations—and vice versa.

The data presented above indicate that most women end up in jobs in which the distance a person can be promoted is fairly short. Those females in clerical, service, and some professional occupations (such as nursing) are examples. As a result, they have little possibility for career mobility or economic advancement. In this social context, women do tend to be less ambitious and more concerned with interpersonal relations (Langer, 1970). However, many males also work at jobs in which the possible range of promotion is fairly short. Many assembly-line workers and others in laboring, operative, and service occupations are examples. In this context, it has been found that men also tend to be less ambitious and more concerned with interpersonal relations (Chinoy, 1955; Purcell, 1960). However, it is generally the case that those jobs where there is the least possibility for advancement are dominated by women (Grunker et al., 1970; Kantor, 1976:418).

In other words, work orientations that are stereotypically imputed to each sex are, in reality, largely a result of the social situation in which people find themselves. This fact can be seen more clearly when men and women who work in achievement-oriented occupations are compared with one another. Kantor (1976:419) studied sales personnel in a corporation in which the range of promotion was great and individuals regularly moved up into executive positions. She found that when individuals of either sex "are advantageously placed in a high-mobility opportunity structure . . . they are highly motivated and aspire to top management positions." More generally, then, it can be argued that the pattern of occupational discrimination described above is one important reason for differences in work orientation by sex.

As shown in Table 3, during recent years there have been increases in the proportion of women in professional, managerial, and sales jobs. Many of these occupations are ones in which aggressiveness and ambition can pay off in promotion. The presence of women in such jobs is fairly recent. Further, there are still few women in these types of positions. As a result, the work environments are often characterized by skewed sex ratios: large numbers of men and small numbers of women. In these situations, women are "tokens" in the sense that "they are often treated as representatives of their category, that is, all women, as symbols rather than individuals" (Kantor, 1977:966).

The presence of token women decisively alters the social situation and disrupts ongoing modes of behavior. Kantor argues that token women generally have greater difficulty than do men in advancing occupationally for three reasons. First, token women are highly visible to peers and supervisors. This visibility creates performance pressures. Yet because tokens must do their jobs in public, mistakes cannot be hidden. As Kantor notes of the women she studied, "it was impossible for them to have any privacy within the company" (1977:973). This lack of privacy makes it easier to fire or at least not promote women, while appearing to adhere to universalistic standards. Further, because token women are viewed as being symbolic representatives of all women, their success and, especially, their failures are held up as examples to others. In many cases, a self-fulfilling prophecy occurs. Women are expected to fail and they do, often with a little help from their male "friends" and supervisors. Token women in a competitive work environment are faced with a serious dilemma.

Furthermore, even in a competitive situation, women are not expected to make men look bad or show them up (recall the stroking role). Peers as well as supervisors can and do retaliate. As one might expect, token women often respond inconsistently to these contradictory expectations, which makes their behavior unpredictable and social relations more difficult. An inability to get along with colleagues can also be used as a rationale for firing a person. Women in this situation have two options. They can overtly eschew the stroking role and try to overachieve, or they can be more covert in their efforts while limiting their visibility. Kantor speculates, plausibly, that the so-called "fear of success" among women in achievement-oriented occupations is really an attempt at keeping a low profile within a threatening environment, and thus preventing retaliation (see Levine and Crumrine, 1975).

The second reason women have difficulty advancing occupationally is that the "presence of a token makes [male] dominants more aware of what they have in common at the same time that it threatens that commonality" (Kantor, 1977:975). Thus, boundaries are established and maintained in order to isolate the female intruder. Males do this by means of sexual innuendos, dirty jokes, displays of macho, sexual teasing, and telling war stories (most of which are fictional). Another tactic is to interrupt the flow of group events in artificial ways that serve to emphasize the token woman's differentness and isolation. For example, men may ask, "Can we still swear?" "Can we use technical jargon?" Token women generally know the curses and the jargon just as well as men do and they rarely wish to inhibit what males consider (or say they consider) normal behavior. Yet tokens have been made excruciatingly aware that behavior is not and cannot be normal merely by their presence.

Apart from these and other forms of psychological harassment, the establishment of boundaries has more serious consequences for women's occupational achievement. In such situations, women rarely have sponsors or role models who can guide and protect them. Further, occupational success is often dependent upon inclusion in informal gatherings where information is exchanged, contacts made, and bureaucratic maneuvers decided upon (see Epstein, 1971). Women are often excluded from such gatherings.

Token women have three possible responses, none of which is really satisfactory. (1) They can accept isolation. Of course, the risk here is that they will be excluded from important information and events. (2) They can try to become insiders by proving their loyalty—in effect, breaking down or crossing over the sexual boundary. This tactic often means turning against the other women in various ways. Kantor suggests, again plausibly, that this reaction is an example of the so-called "queen-bee syndrome"; that is, women being prejudiced against other women. She argues that this reaction often has structural rather than sexual origins (see Ferber and Huber, 1975). (3) Finally, token women can try to be loyal to the work group without being overtly disloyal to other women. They simply do not participate in prejudicial conversations or actions. This tactic is very difficult because male colleagues must acquiesce by ignoring women's nonparticipation. Males can force a token to choose sides.

The third reason women have difficulty advancing occupationally is that, even when they are assimilated into a male-dominated work group, it is often on the males' terms. These terms may preclude rising to the top because of the job roles forced on a female token. For example, a woman may be expected to be nurturant toward her male colleagues. She may be treated as a seductress (regardless of her actual intentions or behavior). She may be treated as the group's pet. An independent stance on the part of a woman may result in her being treated as the "iron maiden," the tough woman, with all the unflattering connotations that phrase conveys. This often occurs when a talented woman succeeds despite male opposition and, as Kantor puts it, demands "treatment as an equal in a setting in which no person of her kind has previously been an equal" (1977:984).

This section has described some aspects of the process of discrimination against women. The basis for sex discrimination is traditional sex-role ideology that suggests that women belong in the home. This ideology affects socialization practices and makes females ill-equipped for occupational success. Although federal laws seem designed to prevent discrimination against women, these laws are ineffective because they are not enforced. At the local level, the schools not only socialize women as to their proper place, they also actively discriminate. Finally, while the dynamics of discrimination on the job are subtle, they essentially involve placing women in situations where contradictory role expectations serve to prevent occupational success.

SUMMARY

This chapter has described patterns of sexual inequality in the United States by considering five interrelated topics. First, traditional sex-role ideology emphasizes that women's most important roles involve reproduction, child rearing, and homemaking. Many people believe that women belong in the home. Second, women are participating in the labor force in greater numbers than ever before. This increase has occurred regardless of age, marital status, or the presence of young children in the home. Nonetheless, women who work outside the home still experience role conflict because of the concurrent demands that they feel as a result of their child-rearing and homemaking responsibilities. There is some evidence that family migration increases the possibility that married women will drop out of the labor force and return to their traditional roles. However, staying home does not have many benefits, for it also appears that married women who are not in the labor force are more susceptible to a variety of mental disorders.

Third, occupational segregation is still the norm in America, and women's jobs are generally less prestigious than are those of men. Half of all women still fill their traditional roles within the family, participating in what has been called the two-person career. Of those who work for pay, the occupational distribution has remained very stable in recent years, even though the proportion of women in each occupational category has increased. When specific occupations are examined, it is clear that most jobs are dominated by one sex or the other. Women's jobs are often extensions of maternal roles in that they are supportive of men. Fourth, the economic differences between men and women remain great. Women earn less than men do regardless of similarities in occupation, education, or continuity of labor-force experience. Female-headed families are more likely to be poor than are male-headed families. Essentially, most women are still economically dependent upon men.

The final topic dealt with in this chapter was barriers to women's occupational achievement. Women are discriminated against as a result of their socialization experiences as well as by a variety of public policies at both the federal and local levels. In addition, the work situation of token women was described in order to show that sex-role ideology has less to do with women's lack of achievement than does simple discrimination.

NOTES

1. A couple of exceptions are Hacker (1951) and Rossi (1964). This chapter is relatively ahistorical. For some background see Chafe (1972; 1977), Baxandall et al. (1976), and Huber (1976).
2. This analysis loosely follows Bernard (1971:65–102).

3. It should be noted that the emphasis on women's place in the home has always served as an ideal for white, middle-class, married women. Some females were either encouraged or had to work for pay such as young, unmarried whites along with blacks and immigrants.

4. The source for these figures is U.S. Bureau of the Census (1977a:tables 570 and 574). It is often assumed that all men are in the labor force. However, in 1975, "only" 77 percent of all men were working or looking for work. This is a fairly stable figure.

5. Among men, 30 percent disapproved of women earning money if their husbands could support them. These unpublished data were supplied under the auspices of the Inter-University Consortium for Political and Social Research. Madeline Haug made the computer run.

6. The source for this assertion is U.S. Bureau of the Census (1977a:table 573).

7. On all this material, see Whitehurst (1977) and her citations.

8. See Gove (1972a), Gove and Tudor (1973), Gove and Herb (1974). For a qualifying note to Gove's findings, see Warheit et al. (1975). A good summary of the literature which has an excellent bibliography is in Bachrach (1975). Chesler's (1972) outstanding *Women and Madness* describes in vivid terms why some women seek help, what they experience, and how they are or (often) are not helped.

9. It should be noted that female admissions to the various professional schools, especially law and medicine, have risen appreciably in recent years, so the proportion of women in the professions will increase, albeit slowly, over the next few years.

10. These data are from U.S. Bureau of the Census (1977a:table 670).

11. The source for these data is U.S. Bureau of the Census (1976g:table 10–5). Note that the income levels given are for 1974, not 1975.

12. These data on educational attainment by sex are from U.S. Bureau of the Census (1977a:tables 231, 244, and 245).

13. Data of the sort reported by Suter and Miller (1973) in Table 7 are, by the way, extraordinarily difficult to obtain.

14. The source for this assertion is U.S. Bureau of the Census (1977a:table 663).

15. The source for these data is U.S. Bureau of the Census (1976a:table 19). See Chapter 8 for an analysis of the way in which governmental measures of poverty are manipulated.

16. As an aside, Griffiths (1976) also observes that women receive less pension benefits generally. They are less likely to have access to a private pension fund because they are often in occupations that do not have such plans. Even when women do have access to private pension funds they receive relatively low benefits because they had low wages.

14
STATUS ATTAINMENT
AND
SOCIAL MOBILITY

Chapters 7 through 13 of this book dealt with the extent and dimensions of inequality in the United States. Relatively little attention has been given to what Blau and Duncan (1967) call "the process of stratification"; that is, how people get into or out of positions. That process is the topic of this concluding chapter.

In order to deal adequately with it, four issues are discussed. First, the key factors in the process of status attainment in the United States are outlined. Status attainment refers to the way in which people acquire positions in the occupational, educational, and other social hierarchies. Understanding the process of status attainment is a necessary prelude to the analysis of social mobility. Second, some key issues in the study of social mobility are briefly noted. Third, overall patterns of social mobility are analyzed. And, fourth, the consequences of social mobility are identified.

The literature on status attainment and social mobility is quite long and represents some of the best work that sociologists do. Those who wish to claim that sociology is a scientific discipline often point to this literature because it represents the use of the most sophisticated and elegant methodological techniques in sociology (path analysis, regression, stochastic processes, and the like). One benefit of the use of these techniques is that they force clear conceptual thinking. Researchers are required to state propositions precisely and to test exactly what they hypothesize. As a result, recent findings in the area of status attainment and social mobility are more cumulative than is normally the case in sociological research.[1]

STATUS ATTAINMENT

Most of the literature on status attainment focuses upon either educational or occupational achievements. These are presumed to be the most important "success values" a person might have in American society (see Williams, 1970). This section is organized into four parts. (1) Blau and Duncan's ground-breaking study, *The American Occupational Structure*, is briefly summarized (as it pertains to the issue of status attainment among males). (2) The most recent additions to the status-attainment literature are sketched. (3) The relevance of these findings to blacks and women is shown. (4) The major problems and criticisms of this literature are briefly noted.

The American Occupational Structure

In this monumental study, Blau and Duncan (1967) initiated the current theoretical and methodological bases for the study of both status attainment and mobility. Here the exposition focuses on their analysis of status attainment. Like many other observers, they emphasize that all stratification systems can be viewed as being a mixture of ascribed and achieved factors. It will be recalled that, as noted in Chapter 6, ascription refers to the process of assigning individuals to positions on non-performance-related grounds, based upon their membership in certain categories or their inherited characteristics.[2] These categories or characteristics can be such things as age, sex, race, religion, family background, region of birth, and many more. Achievement refers to the process of obtaining positions based upon one's own efforts. However, Blau and Duncan (1967:163) go beyond this commonplace distinction by suggesting that sociologists should study the causal sequence by which people attain positions.

We think of the individual's life-cycle as a sequence in time that can be described, however partially and crudely, by a set of classificatory or quantitative measurements taken at successive stages. . . . Given this scheme, the questions we are continually raising in one form or another are: How and to what degree do the circumstances of birth condition subsequent status? And how does status attained (whether by ascription or achievement) at one stage of the life-cycle affect the prospects for a subsequent stage?

With the help of the U.S. Bureau of the Census, Blau and Duncan provide an initial answer to these two questions by analyzing a sample of 20,700 American men, aged 20 to 65, in 1962. This sample is representative of the 45 million civilian noninstitutionalized male population in the United States at that time. No claims are made to represent the process of status attainment for any other aggregate, such as women. Other researchers have subsequently expanded the model to deal with the female status-attainment process (see below).

As noted in the quotation, Blau and Duncan wish to know not only what factors in an individual's life-cycle influence the status-attainment process, but also how much each factor affects subsequent ones. They construct a path model of the process by which people obtain positions that includes measures of the influence of five variables: father's education, father's occupation, son's education, son's first job, and son's occupation at the time of the survey. Moreover, they assert that a causal chain exists in which father's educational and occupational attainment precedes son's education, son's educational attainment precedes his first job, and son's first job precedes his subsequent jobs (see Lauman et al., 1970:302–307; Blau and Duncan, 1967:165–68).[3]

Blau and Duncan's findings can be summarized in the following way.[4] (1) Father's education and his occupation are very strongly correlated with each other. (2) Father's education and occupation each moderately influence son's educational attainment. (3) Son's level of education strongly determines both his first job and his subsequent occupation. Thus, a man's background (as indicated by his father's socioeconomic status) indirectly influences his occupational status attainment because of its strong relationship to his educational accomplishments. (4) A son's first job directly influences his subsequent occupation. (5) At the same time, however, father's occupation has a moderate but direct influence on a son's first job. (6) Finally, father's occupation also has a direct but weak relationship to son's subsequent occupation.

In sum, the status-attainment process for males between the ages of 20 and 65 in 1962 can be sketched by means of a path model as an interrelated chain of ascribed and achieved factors. While the importance of ascribed factors is greatest when a boy is young, what he "brings with him" in the form of family background (father's characteristics) continues to influence his accomplishments throughout life. Further, in terms of the two questions Blau and Duncan pose above, it can be said that in American society a boy's circumstances at birth decisively influence his chance for educational or occupational success. However, as Blau and Duncan surmise, status attained at each stage of the life-cycle decisively affects the prospects at each subsequent stage such that achieved factors (over which the individual has more control) assume greater importance with age. The most significant of the achieved factors is clearly education. As Blau and Duncan observe, "education operates primarily to induce variation in occupational status that is independent of initial status."

A brief methodological note is necessary at this point. The construction of path models involves the assignation of mathematical weights, called path coefficients, to particular relationships among variables. For example, Blau and Duncan found that the relationship between son's education and his first job is .44. This is a relatively strong relationship. Blau and Duncan also found that the relationship between father's occupation and son's current job is .12. This is a relatively weak relationship. However, in every path model there are residual values—that is, mathematical weights assigned to all the unmeasured variables—that could possibly affect the factors included in the model, as will be shown below. In sociology, it is generally the case that residual values are quite high—higher, in fact, than the coefficients included in the model. For example, the values of the residual factors in Blau and Duncan's model of status attainment range from .75 to .86. The unmeasured variables taken into account by the residual values include the effects of random variation as well as more specific variables such as physical handicaps, toilet training, religion, and all the other thousands of things that are not included.

Critics commonly assert that large residual values indicate that not much variation has been "explained" and that the important goal is to reduce their size (see Coser, 1976). However, Blau and Duncan (1967:175) argue that the size of the residuals "is no guide whatever to the validity of a causal interpretation. . . . The relevant question about the residual is not really its size at all, but whether the unobserved factors it stands for are properly represented as being uncorrelated with the measured antecedent variables." It is conceivable that all the factors that have a systematic causal effect could be included in a path model and that the residual values would still be quite large. The researchers' goal is to discover each of the factors the influence of which is nonrandom. It is always an empirical question whether all the important variables are included in a path model. A great deal of research has been devoted to finding the intervening variables that enhance the basic model developed by Blau and Duncan. However, while this work has contributed a great deal of additional knowledge about the status-attainment process, the residual values in all subsequent models remain high.[5]

Recent Findings About Status Attainment
Subsequent research on the process of status attainment has filled in the basic Blau and Duncan model considerably. Whereas Blau and Duncan focus exclusively on structural variables, much of the subsequent literature has taken its cue from the symbolic-interactionist tradition in sociology and focused upon a variety of social-psychological factors that might intervene in the status-attainment process. The major variables in the process of status attainment as it

Figure 1. The Process of Status Attainment in the United States

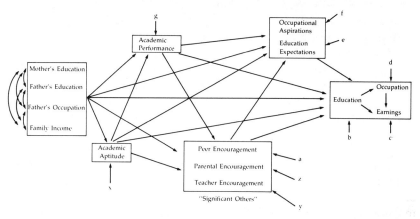

Source: Adapted from K. L. Alexander, B. K. Eckland, and L. S. Griffin, "The Wisconsin Model of Socioeconomic Achievement: A Replication." *American Journal of Sociology* 81 (September 1975): 325.

is currently conceptualized are shown in Figure 1. In order to simplify the figure, some factors have been grouped together for presentation here. Since the figure is intended as a summary of many studies, specific path coefficients are omitted. The residual values are denoted by letters.

As can be seen in the figure, the literature shows the following six specific findings. First, in addition to father's education and occupation, mother's education and family income have been shown to influence the status-attainment process at all stages of a child's life. All these variables are intercorrelated with each other. As one might guess, the socioeconomic status of a child's family decisively and directly affects the early stages of status attainment: academic aptitude, academic performance, significant others' evaluations, aspirations, and educational attainment.

Because the variables have been grouped together here, the direct effect of family socioeconomic status on a child's eventual occupation is not shown in Figure 1. However, as in the original findings by Blau and Duncan, a direct but lessened relationship exists between the two.

Second, it has also been shown that academic aptitude or ability affects the status-attainment process (Duncan, 1968). Aptitude or ability is measured by either an achievement or intelligence test. As might be expected, aptitude most strongly affects academic performance (for example, grade-point average) and educational attainment. As Duncan (1968:8) observes, "progress through the grades of the school system is influenced at least as much by how bright you are as by 'who' you are."[7] However, aptitude also influences two social-psychological variables that intervene in the status-attainment process: one's aspirations, and the kind of encouragement from others that one receives as a child.

A word of explanation about the nature of these factors is necessary here. Two kinds of aspirations have been shown to be important in the status attainment literature: educational expectations and occupational aspirations. They generally refer to children's plans or expectations about obtaining higher levels of education and the kind of jobs they expect (or would like) to have. Significant others are those people who influence the development of a child's self-concept and who affect one's thinking about educational, occupational, and other life goals. They are important here because, as Wilson and Portes (1975:345) note, "significant others adjust their expectations according to their assessments of the individual's potential."

③ Third, although children's level of academic performance has been shown to be strongly dependent upon their family background and ability, performance itself directly influences subsequent elements in the status-attainment process—mainly, the level and kind of encouragement received from others, the level of aspirations that children develop, and their ultimate educational attainment. In effect, significant others also adjust their expectations—and hence the level and kind of encouragement they provide—according to how well the child has done in school. However, the relationship between performance in school (and a host of other academic factors) and eventual occupational attainment is more problematic and quite controversial (see Jencks, 1972; Levine and Bane, 1975). While nearly all researchers agree that level of education affects occupational attainment, whether academic performance while in school also directly influences occupation is doubtful, except to the extent that performance qualifies one for further education.

④ Fourth, there are three sorts of significant others identified in Figure 1. Both parents and teachers affect children's aspirations and their ultimate educational attainment (Sewell and Shah, 1968a; 1968b). As noted above, this influence occurs in combination with the effect of academic performance. Essentially, "a person develops and adjusts his aspirations in accordance with both the evaluation he receives from others and his own self-assessment of abilities on the basis of . . . academic performance" (Wilson and Portes, 1975: 345). Further, peers have also been shown to influence the development of both aspirations and educational attainment (Spady, 1970; Wegner and Sewell, 1970; Hout and Morgan, 1975). As a qualifying note, Duncan et al. (1972) found the relationship between significant others and educational attainment to be weak.

⑤ Fifth, educational and occupational aspirations also have an independent influence on educational attainment (Hout and Morgan, 1975).

Sixth, educational attainment directly and strongly influences occupational attainment. This finding has been replicated in many studies. Further, both occupation and education are related to earnings. As a demurrer, Jencks (1972) did not find this last relationship.

In summary, Blau and Duncan, along with others in this research tradition, have shown in a relatively precise way how the circumstances of birth influence the status-attainment process among men. They have also identified the most important factors that intervene at each stage of men's life-cycle and affect prospects for each subsequent stage. Status attainment can be viewed as a chain of interrelated ascribed and achieved factors. The initial variables affecting status attainment, which continue to influence it at each stage, are ascribed: family background and academic ability. Then come a series of variables influencing educational attainment: academic performance, various significant others, and aspirations. Finally, the most significant factor affecting occupational attainment among men is educational attainment.

Status Attainment Among Blacks and Women

The literature on status attainment among blacks and women is meager in length and the findings are contradictory. Only a few conclusions are possible. Although the model presented in Figure 1 above best fits white males, it appears as though essentially the same factors also influence status attainment among black males, white females, and black females (Hout and Morgan, 1975). Further, among these three categories of people, it is also the case that education is the major influence on occupational attainment. However, as noted in chapters 12 and 13, the payoff in income based on education is not as great for these other categories of people as it is for white males (Duncan, 1968).

Unfortunately, there is little agreement on the strength of the other variables in the model (that is, the value of the path coefficients). For example, Treiman and Terrell (1975) report that father's occupation and education have greater effect on sons, while mother's attributes are more influential on daughters. But McClendon (1976) failed to find such a relationship. McClendon also reports that the process of educational attainment is similar for both males and females. But Hout and Morgan (1976) found significant differences in this process among white males, black males, white females, and black females. Their research suggests that while the variables affecting each group are essentially the same, the strength of individual factors varies greatly according to sex and race.

Thus, although it is a safe bet that higher educational attainment will increase the occupational attainment of all categories of people, white males are still better off than others. Further, while it is clearly the case that higher socioeconomic status on the part of parents influences both the educational and occupational achievements of children, white males are again better off than others. What is unclear, however, is the way in which the social-psychological variables shown in Figure 1 influence black males and females and white females.

The process of female status attainment presents special conceptual and methodological problems. For example, Featherman and Hauser (1976) measure occupational attainment by prestige scores. On this basis, they argue that females' educational and occupational achievements kept pace with those of males between the years 1962 and 1973.[8] However, this finding is somewhat misleading. Although McClendon (1976) reports a similarity in occupational prestige scores by sex, he also notes that the status hierarchies measured by prestige scores are built on quite dissimilar occupational structures. As shown in Chapter 13, most working women are employed in low-level white-collar jobs, while less than half of all men are in nonmanual occupations. It is this difference that produces female prestige parity with males. It does not, of course, produce income parity. Nor does it change the fact that within both the blue- and white-collar categories females tend to occupy the lower-status jobs.

The major source of confusion regarding female status attainment lies in the fact that women are often allocated roles outside the paid labor force. As a result, women have two channels of status attainment and mobility available to them. The first is by means of their educational and occupational accomplishments. The second is by marriage. Men generally do not have this second mobility track as an option. Further, status attainment by marriage depends upon the family background and educational accomplishments of women, but a variety of additional factors—physical attractiveness, personal skills, and unique needs and desires—are also important (see Taylor and Glenn, 1976). Tentative findings suggest that patterns of female marital mobility (from father's social status to husband's) are similar to patterns of male occupational mobility (Havens and Tully, 1972; Tyree and Treas, 1974; Chase, 1975). Patterns of female occupational mobility are much different, due to the effects of discrimination and marital mobility.

Some Criticisms of the Status-Attainment Literature

Although research into the process of status attainment represents important methodological and conceptual advances in sociology, there are several significant criticisms that can be made of this literature. Surprisingly, however, few critical analyses have appeared in print (exceptions are Crowder, 1974; Coser, 1976).

The first major weakness in the status-attainment literature is that two important social strata are ignored: the poor and the rich. The longitudinal data used by Sewell and his associates (only some of which was cited above) deals exclusively with high school graduates in the state of Wisconsin. Hout and Morgan's (1976) recent study used only 12th-grade students in Louisville, Kentucky. However, one of the most important characteristics of the poor is their lack of education (see Chapter 8). Important questions can be asked about the status-attainment process, or lack of it, among those who dropped out of school. Further, it would be most interesting to see the way in which the status-attainment models would be altered if the poor were included in analyses.

The rich are virtually never included in sample surveys and their children generally do not attend public schools. As a result, they are simply not a part of studies of status attainment. This exclusion is important because, despite the small proportion of the population that is rich, such persons exercise disproportionate amounts of power in the United States. Hence, it is possible that they are able to influence not only their own but others' educational and occupational achievements. Essentially, the status-attainment literature deals with the way two social strata, blue-collar and white-collar people, acquire positions. As a result, the conclusions in the literature must be misleading.

The second major criticism is even more significant. Research into the process of status attainment fails to take into account the importance of power as a constraining force in American society. Stemming from Blau and Duncan's concern, nearly all the literature has addressed the relationship between achieved and ascribed factors in American social life. As noted, ascription has been taken as referring to the effects of family background. Further, many researchers seem to have assumed that the United States is heading toward a more meritocratic (that is, achievement-oriented) society. For example, Blau and Duncan (1967:163–64) describe the stratification system in America in the following terms.

In a liberal democratic society we think of the more basic principle as being that of achievement. Some ascriptive features of the system may be regarded as vestiges of an earlier epoch, to be extirpated as rapidly as possible. Public policy may emphasize measures designed to enhance or to equalize opportunity—hopefully, to overcome ascriptive obstacles to the full exercise of the achievement principle.

Thus, American society is seen as being composed of positions that people acquire based upon their family background and their achievements, with increasing emphasis on the latter. As a result, it is argued that "superior status cannot any more be directly inherited but must be legitimated by actual achievements" (Blau and Duncan, 1976:430).

By emphasizing the importance of achievement, Blau and Duncan (along with others in this research tradition) imply that the most significant factors in obtaining positions are individual initiative and what Duncan has called "blind luck." Surely both of these factors are important. But some of the phenomena categorized by "blind luck" are neither random nor irrelevant to the process of status attainment. For instance, the literature on this process ignores the enduring importance of sponsorship. Some sponsorship into powerful positions is, of course, based upon family background, but even apart from that, it can be argued that age, sex, race, and personality criteria are also applied. The pervasive influence of sponsorship on the status attainment process can be suggested by one of Duncan's own analogies. He argues again that American society emphasizes achievement. In this context, Duncan (1968: 685) believes that the sociologist's task is analogous to that of a person betting on a horse race. In such a race the trick is to figure out which horse has the most ability while taking into account its handicap (how much weight it carries). Like horses, some people "begin the race with heavy packs upon their backs and many obstacles in their course, while others enjoy freedom from such impediments." Clearly, informed bettors could improve their chances by properly evaluating the weight each person carries in the race for occupational success and the way this weight is sometimes changed over time (with education).

However, as Crowder (1974) observes, the informed bettor could also benefit from some information that Duncan does not concern himself with, or at least does not share. Who organizes and benefits from the race? Like casinos, race tracks rarely lose money. Who decides how much prize money the winners will get? Who do the race organizers favor and why? What are the chances of either the bettors or the runners ever getting a chance to organize the race itself and thereby realize the excess profit (Marx would call this "surplus value")? These questions, which neither Duncan nor the status attainment literature address, point toward the importance of power. There are major constraints on the acquisition of positions in American society. These constraints operate on blacks and whites, males and females. The status-attainment literature simply does not confront these issues.

Two remaining problems in the status attainment literature can be briefly noted. First, the literature seems to have an ideological bias in that it generally fails to recognize the structural sources of poverty (Crowder, 1974). If people have a generally equal opportunity for participation in American society, even allowing for the fact that some begin the "race" for status attainment with more disadvantages than do others, then it can be argued that those who fail clearly deserve the consequences. They were not ambitious enough or smart enough or had "bad luck." What has happened, of course, is that popular stereotypes of poor people have made their appearance in sociological analyses (see Chapter 8). Secondly, many writers in this tradition seem to have a fundamental incapacity to make themselves clear. This task is especially vital when the research is dominated by mathematical formulae, which appear mysterious to many readers, including professionals in the field.

ISSUES IN THE STUDY OF SOCIAL MOBILITY

Types of Social Mobility

Although the two topics are closely related, studies of social mobility are generally less concerned with the causal process by which individuals attain positions and more concerned with simply assessing the extent of movement from one occupation to another. There are two types of mobility: horizontal and vertical.

Horizontal mobility refers to changes of occupational position that do not involve corresponding changes in social strata. For example, a coal miner may migrate to the city and become a dockworker or a lawyer may be elected a judge. This form of mobility is pervasive in American society, but it is of relatively little concern to sociologists.[9] Vertical mobility refers to changes in occupational status that are accompanied by upward or downward changes in strata. For example, the son of a physician may decide to become a truck driver or a janitor may go to school during the day and eventually become an accountant. Upward or downward changes in occupational category are usually taken as being indicators of vertical mobility because one's job is the best single manifestation of one's position in the stratification hierarchy (see Gordon, 1973; Vanneman, 1977).

Because sociologists are interested in whether American society is becoming more "open" in the sense of providing equal opportunity for all, the most important studies of mobility deal with vertical movement. In the remainder of this chapter, mobility or social mobility refers only to upward or downward changes in social strata as indicated by people's occupations.

Rate and Range of Social Mobility

In studying social mobility, three questions are of overriding importance. (1) What is the pattern of intergenerational mobility in the United States? This question is answered by comparing children's occupations with those of their parents. As is usual in the stratification literature, most studies deal with men, by comparing fathers' and sons' occupations. (2) What is the rate of intragenerational mobility in the United States? This question is answered by comparing a person's first full-time occupation with his final or main occupation. Again, the literature deals almost exclusively with males. (3) What is the range of social mobility? This question is concerned with

how far people move upward or downward. That is, do people typically move across several social strata, either upward or downward,
or do they typically move only to adjacent social strata? The first sort
of move is illustrated by the mythical heroes of Horatio Alger, who
moved from poverty to great wealth in their own lifetimes. The second type of move is illustrated by the son of a construction worker
who becomes a public school teacher.

It has been found that the best way to assess the rate and range of
movement, inter- and intragenerationally, is to compare systematically three types of occupational origins and destinations: (1) father's
main job with son's main job; (2) father's main job with son's first
full-time job; and (3) son's first job with son's subsequent main job.
The first two comparisons are intergenerational; the last is intragenerational. By making these comparisons, a relatively complete picture of both the rate and range of mobility among males can be obtained.

As in the study of status attainment, the inclusion of females in
analyses of social mobility presents significant, and exciting,
methodological problems.[10] One reason for comparing mobility rates
between generations is to assess whether the stratification system is
becoming more open in the sense of emphasizing achievement. But
if the openness of the stratification system is based only upon the
study of male mobility rates, then the results are likely to "over-
state" the case because of the twin effects of female status attainment through marriage and sexual discrimination. Conversely,
evaluating the openness of the stratification system based upon the
study of female occupational mobility rates is likely to "understate"
the case for the same reasons. As a result, the "true" rate of social
mobility is simply not known as of yet. Unless otherwise specified,
all the data reported below deal with patterns of male occupational
mobility, its causes and consequences.

PATTERNS OF SOCIAL MOBILITY IN THE UNITED STATES
The most complete and authoritative source on patterns of mobility
in the United States is Blau and Duncan's *The American Occupational
Structure* (1967). In addition to their analysis of the process of status
attainment, Blau and Duncan describe the dynamic aspects of the
American system of social stratification in terms of the flow of manpower from one occupational category to another, both inter- and
intragenerationally. The seventeen categories they used are listed in
Table 1. This section first summarizes their major findings and then
notes some recent trends in occupational mobility. As an aside, it
should be noted that no secondary source can present more than a
superficial summary of Blau and Duncan's work.[11]

Blau and Duncan's eight major findings are as follows. First, there
is a great deal of occupational inheritance in American society. That

Table 1 Occupational Categories Used in Peter M. Blau and O. D. Duncan,
The American Occupational Structure (New York: John Wiley, 1967).

1. Professionals (self-employed)
2. Professionals (salaried)
3. Managers
4. Sales (nonretail)
5. Proprietors
6. Clerical
7. Sales (retail)
8. Crafts (manufacturing)
9. Crafts (other)
10. Crafts (construction)
11. Operatives (manufacturing)
12. Operatives (other)
13. Service
14. Laborers (manufacturing)
15. Laborers (other)
16. Farmers
17. Farm Laborers

is, in the most general terms, the dominant intergenerational tendency is that fathers in white-collar occupations tend to have sons who work in white-collar occupations and fathers in blue-collar jobs tend to have sons in blue-collar jobs. However, the sons of farmers are an anomaly. On the one hand, they display high levels of occupational inheritance. On the other hand, because of the impact of high fertility rates and technological changes, the dominant tendency is for farmers' sons to move into blue-collar occupations where farm-related skills often can be used.

Phrased differently, Blau and Duncan's first finding is that there are three great classes in the United States: white-collar workers, blue-collar workers, and farm workers. These classes form semipermeable barriers to social mobility, both upward and downward. When the sons of white-collar workers are downwardly mobile, they generally move into other white-collar jobs, even though such occupations may bring less remuneration or satisfaction than some blue-collar jobs. Blau and Duncan suggest that the need for the prestige of being "white collar," together with the lack of salable manual skills, prevents a great deal of downward mobility. Similarly, when the sons of blue-collar workers are downwardly mobile, they generally move to other blue-collar jobs. The combination of lack of skills and job opportunities prevents movement into farming occupations. Conversely, a great deal of upward mobility from blue-collar to white-collar occupations is prevented by lack of necessary skills and, often, lack of respect for white-collar work. As Sennett and Cobb (1973) have shown, many blue-collar workers do not believe that "pencil pushers" really work. After all, they do not sweat or get dirty.

Blau and Duncan's ②second major finding is that, despite the assertion above, social mobility is pervasive in American society. Overall, upward mobility is more prevalent in the United States than is downward mobility. This is true intergenerationally, when father's occupation is compared to son's main job. However, the tendency for upward mobility is not revealed when father's occupation and son's first job are compared. In this case, there is a great deal of downward mobility. Evidently, temporary downward mobility occurs for many sons while they acquire needed skills. Finally, the tendency for relatively large numbers of men to be upwardly mobile also occurs intragenerationally, when son's first job is compared to son's main job.

The ③third finding Blau and Duncan report is that "short-distance movements exceed long-distance ones," both intra- and intergenerationally. The "closer two occupations are to one another in the status hierarchy, the greater is the flow of manpower between them" (pp. 36–37). There are discrepancies, of course. Some of them are apparently due to barriers erected by the skills required in different industries. For example, there is an "excessive" amount of downward intergenerational mobility from fathers who were operatives in manufacturing (category no. 11 in Table 1) "to" sons who are laborers in similar industries (category no. 15). As another example, the sons of craft workers (category no. 8) often move into managerial and salaried professional occupations (categories no. 2 and 3). This tendency may reflect the entrepreneurial socialization that many such children receive (Turner, 1970), as well as a reluctance to accept the lower levels of income which often characterize blue-collar jobs.

Blau and Duncan place the second and third findings into perspective by observing that the two most important causes of occupational mobility in the United States have been differences in fertility rates and the impact of technological changes. Historically, technological changes acted as a "pull" factor, stimulating upward movement by reducing the need for people to till the soil and perform menial labor. This reduction freed individuals to move into the expanding number of white-collar jobs. As they note, the two occupational categories that have expanded most between 1940 and 1960 are salaried professionals and managers, while the three that contracted most are farm laborers, farmers, and laborers in manufacturing. The fact that families in these last three occupations also have high fertility rates has acted as a "push" factor, moving people upward in the job hierarchy. Essentially, the number of jobs contracted in just those areas where there were a large number of people. Many of these individuals were, in effect, forced to move. However, as shown above, most moves are short-distance ones. Few sons of farmers end up in professional occupations.

What seems to happen is rather that the pressure of displaced manpower at the bottom and the vacuum created by new opportunities at the top start a chain reaction of short-distance movements throughout the occupational structure. This push of supply at the bottom and pull of demand at the top create opportunities for upward mobility from most origins, as the vacancies left by sons moving up can be filled by sons from lower strata (p. 66).

Blau and Duncan's fourth finding is that mobility rates among blacks are substantially lower than those among whites, even when family background and educational attainment of fathers are controlled statistically. As one might expect, the effect of racial discrimination is greatest in the South. In a later analysis of the 1962 data, Duncan (1968d:11) concluded that the relationship between mobility rates among black and white men can be described in the following way.[12]

Negro men who originated at the lower levels were likely to remain there; white men were likely to move up. Negro men who originated at the higher levels were likely to move down; white men were likely to stay there. Although Negro social origins are not as favorable as those of whites, this is the lesser part of the explanation of racial differences in occupational achievement. The greater part of the explanation lies in inequalities within the process of mobility itself.

The fifth finding is that there are regional differences in the chance for social mobility. Both black and white southerners, including those who migrate north, have inferior chances for upward mobility compared to the chances of those from other regions (pp. 213–19).

Still, the sixth finding is that foreign born immigrants and their children are not handicapped by their origins. Although their overall occupational attainment is less than that of native-born Americans, when they are matched with natives of equal level of education and similar family backgrounds there are no differences in patterns of mobility.

The seventh finding is that geographical mobility and vertical mobility are related to one another (pp. 250–75). Those who move are more likely to be upwardly mobile than are those who do not move. Nonmigrants are more likely to be downwardly mobile. However, the relationship between migration and mobility is not uniform. The most successful migrants are those who move from and to large cities, or those who move from large cities to small cities. Migrants to large cities from rural areas tend to be less successful. Nonetheless, the reason that migration is often associated with upward mobility is that people move to places where jobs are available.

The eighth finding that will be reported here is that size of family and birth order are related to mobility (pp. 307–16). Because they are likely to get a better education, children from smaller families are more likely to be upwardly mobile, especially the first child in small families. In large families, on the other hand, the last child often has the best chance for upward mobility. Again, this relationship appears to be due to the likelihood of the younger child's getting a better education.

Trends in Patterns of Mobility

The patterns of mobility portrayed above have not changed much over time.[13] Although studies of social mobility during the nineteenth century are hampered by unsystematic data, it appears that Blau and Duncan's findings of great intergenerational stability coupled with relatively high rates of upward mobility are appropriate to earlier times as well (see Pessen, 1974; Thernstrom and Sennett, 1969; and Hazelrigg, 1974).

In a series of articles, Hauser and his associates have applied new methodological techniques to a number of studies of mobility during this century as well as to some data available since 1962. They show conclusively that, once changes in the occupational structure are held constant, there have been no changes in patterns of occupational mobility during this century. In effect, most of the opportunity for upward mobility among American men has been caused by the changing occupational structure. This finding has important implications, for there is no particular reason to expect the occupational structure to continue to change in the direction of increasing numbers of white-collar jobs.

In summary, the stratification system in the United States is very stable, in part because there is a great deal of intergenerational occupational inheritance. At least among males, the dominant tendency can be expressed by the simple phrases, "from blue collar to blue collar" and "from white collar to white collar." Although many sons of farmers also become farmers, disproportionate numbers move off the farms and into blue-collar jobs. The major reason for this movement is high rates of fertility coupled with technological advances, which have created opportunities at the top of the occupational hierarchy. These two factors also account for a great deal of the mobility that has occurred in the United States. However, most moves are short distance. Some other important findings are that mobility rates are lower among blacks than whites, southerners have inferior chances for upward mobility, mobility rates among immigrants are no different than those among native Americans, migrants are more likely to experience upward mobility, and children from smaller families have better chances of upward mobility than do those from larger families.

THE CONSEQUENCES OF SOCIAL MOBILITY

Seeman (1977:757) has recently observed that "many sociologists are convinced that both downward and upward occupational mobility have important personal and social consequences." These consequences are presumed to center around the social and psychological disruption that the experience of mobility engenders for the individual. It has been argued that such disruption can involve withdrawal from familial relations (Litwak, 1960), suicide (Breed, 1963), decreased rates of social participation (Kessin, 1971), and a variety of maladaptive psychological symptoms (Kessin, 1971). Further, mobility has been associated with both political apathy and extremism (Wilensky and Edwards, 1959; Lipset and Bendix, 1959; Lopreato, 1967).

The reasoning behind these assertions is that the mobile person, in either direction, finds that the values, beliefs, and behaviors that were appropriate in the former environment are inappropriate in the new one. As Jackman (1973:464) puts it, "he can no longer identify with his old friends from his origin status and yet he does not fit in with his new status group either." This problem is compounded if new acquaintances in the destination stratum are snobbish, if the move is of extreme range, if mobility is viewed as a unique event, or if the fact of a person's origin is visible to all.

However, this interpretation of the effects of social mobility now appears to be incorrect. More recent data suggest that an acculturation hypothesis may more nearly describe the consequences of mobility of individuals. This argument was first developed by Blau (1956) but generally ignored until recently. It is based upon theories of reference-group behavior and anticipatory socialization (Merton and Rossi, 1968). Essentially, it is argued that mobile individuals make a series of attitudinal and behavioral adjustments as a result of steadily increasing identification with persons at their status of destination. These adjustments are not presumed to be either difficult or disruptive. And the result is neither immediate nor total, since people's origins continue to influence them. Hence, as Bean et al. (1973) argue, "the acculturation hypothesis predicts that attitudinal and behavioral responses for mobile individuals will fall between those of nonmobile peers at status of origin and destination."

There is now a great deal of literature supporting this argument. In studies of various forms of alienation (Seeman, 1977; Bean et al., 1973; Jackson and Curtis, 1972), voluntary association membership (Vorwaller, 1970), job satisfaction (Laslett, 1971), and racial prejudice (Hodge and Treiman, 1966), it has been shown that mobile individuals are influenced by both their origins and destinations. In these areas, the existence of independent and disruptive mobility effects is doubtful.

This same finding occurs when the political characteristics of mobile persons are examined. Jackman (1973) found that when mobile and nonmobile individuals are compared, the acculturation hypothesis best describes mobile individuals' feelings of personal and political efficacy. Studies of voting behavior reveal similar results. For example, Knoke (1973) found that the political party preferences of mobile American men show the effect of both their occupational origin and their destination. His finding is reflected in Table 2, which compares the party preferences of mobile and stable individuals of both sexes in 1975.[14] In examining the table, it should be recalled that party affiliation is associated with socioeconomic status such that higher-status persons tend to be Republicans and lower-status persons tend to be Democrats.

Just as the acculturation hypothesis predicts, mobile individuals stand between those who are stable. Those who have been mobile, in either direction, are more likely to identify themselves as independents than are stable blue- or white-collar people. Mobile persons are more likely to identify themselves as Democrats than are white-collar stables, but less likely than are blue-collar stables. Similarly, mobile persons are less likely to identify themselves as Republicans than are stable white-collar people, but more likely than blue-collar stables. In sum, then, the disruptive consequences of social mobility are not very great. People who experience mobility are influenced by both their origins and their destinations.

SUMMARY

Status attainment refers to the process by which people acquire occupational positions. The most important factors affecting status attainment are parental background and educational accomplishment, along with a variety of intervening social-psychological variables: aspirations and encouragement from significant others. The status-attainment process is most clear for white males (Figure 1). Although the same factors affect blacks and women, their relative strength is not clear. The major weaknesses of the status-attainment literature are that it focuses only on two social strata—blue- and white-collar people—and it fails to take into account the important structural factors that influence occupational achievement.

The study of mobility is generally not carried out in causal terms. Rather, the literature focuses on three origin and destination comparisons: father's job to son's main job, father's job to son's first job, and son's first job to son's main job. There are two major findings. (1) There is a great deal of occupational inheritance in the United States. (2) At the same time, mobility is pervasive in the United States both inter- and intragenerationally, with upward mobility being more prevalent than downward. These two trends appear to

Table 2 Intergenerational Social Mobility and Political Party Preference Among Employed Persons, 1975

Political Party Preference	Stable White Collar[a] (N = 134)	Blue-Collar Father, White-Collar Son (N = 240)	White-Collar Father, Blue-Collar Son (N = 54)	Stable Blue Collar[a] (N = 274)
Democrat	27%	35%	35%	50%
Independent	43	44	46	36
Republican	31	21	19	15
	101%	100%	100%	101%

Source: Unpublished data made available under the auspices of the Inter-University Consortium for Political and Social Research.

[a]Does not add to 100% because of rounding.

have been stable over time because of the effect of strata-related differences in fertility rates and the impact of technological change. Finally, despite sociological stereotypes, the disruptive consequences of mobility are few. Most changes that occur to individuals can be best explained by the effects of origin and destination statuses, not the effects of mobility.

NOTES

1. Nonetheless, this research tradition is marred by a great deal of trash—poor writing, trivial topics, and a certain arcane nature. When he described path analysis as little more than a "method in search of a substance," Coser (1975) was voicing the disaffection of many sociologists.

2. Sociologists have long been interested in the problem of ascription. For some recent analyses, see Marwell (1976) and Mayhew (1968). The classic study is by Linton (1936).

3. Of course, this sequence of events does not always occur. Occasionally, "older" people return to finish high school or attend college after their children's education has ended. Sometimes a person will enter the full-time labor force for a few years before going back to school. However, such persons are still fairly uncommon.

4. Unfortunately, it is not possible to reprint either the path model or mobility tables from *The American Occupational Structure*. With considerable lack of grace, O. D. Duncan refused permission for me to quote from this work. His refusal is quite curious for three reasons. First, Peter Blau kindly gave his permission. Second, the same material has been reprinted in many other places, including introductory textbooks (for example, Leslie et al., 1976) and stratification texts (for example, Abrahamson et al., 1976). Third, and most important, these data were originally gathered by the Census Bureau and their analysis was financed by a federal grant. When I inquired as to why he refused permission, Duncan wrote the following to me: "I declined to sign the permission form you sent earlier for my own reasons, and I am not obliged to detail them for you or anyone else."

5. Crowder (1974) rejects this entire line of reasoning, this article is the most important criticism of Duncan's work specifically and the status attainment literature generally.

6. Overviews of the status attainment process as it is currently conceptualized are in Sewell et al. (1969); Sewell et al. (1970), Sewell and Hauser (1972; 1975), and Duncan et al. (1972). Two more recent replications of the model are in Alexander et al. (1975) and Wilson and Portes (1975). Some of the research on more specific aspects of the model, and there is a great deal of it, is cited in the text.

7. Those interested in discrimination in the public schools can simply turn Duncan's assertion around: progress through the school system is influenced at least as much by who you are as by how bright you are.

8. The referent here is to Duncan's (1961) Socioeconomic Index (SEI) scores, not to the measures of occupational prestige reported in Chapter 7.

9. Horizontal mobility is also called situs mobility (see Morris and Murphy, 1959). It is a far greater concern to economists and others interested in the relationship between economic fluctuations and labor force movement. For a good review of recent data on horizontal mobility, see Sommers and Eck (1977).

10. The literature on female occupational mobility is short and contradictory. For example see Chase (1975), Tyree and Treas (1974), and Havens and Tully (1972).

11. This assertion would be true even if it were possible to present the outflow matrices from *The American Occupational Structure*. It should be noted that this chapter

originally contained an extended explication of Blau and Duncan's procedures. However, it is not possible to meaningfully explain their procedures without reference to actual data. As indicated in note 4, Duncan refused permission to reprint these figures.

12. Hauser and Featherman (1974) have recently shown that Blau and Duncan's conclusions are still appropriate as of 1972.

13. See Hauser and Featherman, (1973), Hauser et al. (1975a; 1976b). They review Rogoff (1953), Jackson and Crockett (1964), Blau and Duncan (1967), Tully et al. (1970).

14. These data are from a nationwide random sample of adult Americans. Ellen Van Velsor made the computer run to obtain the table.

REFERENCES

Abels, J.

1965   The Rockefeller Billions. New York: Macmillan.

Abrahamson, M.

1973   "Functionalism and the Functional Theory of Stratification: An Empirical Assessment." American Journal of Sociology 78 (March): 1236–45.

1974   "In Defense of the Assessment." American Journal of Sociology 80 (November): 732–38.

Abrahamson, M., E. H. Mizruchi, and C. Hornung

1976   Stratification and Mobility. New York: Macmillan.

Acker, J.

1973   "Women and Social Stratification: A Case of Intellectual Sexism." American Journal of Sociology 78 (January): 936–46.

Ackerman, F., H. Birnbaum, J. Wetzler, and A. Zimbalist

1971   "Income Distribution in the United States." Review of Radical Political Economics 3 (Summer): 20–43.

Adams, A. V., and G. Nestel

1976   "Interregional Migration, Education, and Poverty in the Urban Ghetto: Another Look at Black-White Earning Differentials." Review of Economics and Statistics 58 (May): 156–66.

Aldrich, H. E.

1973   "Employment Opportunities for Blacks in the Black Ghetto: The Role of White-Owned Businesses." American Journal of Sociology 78 (May): 1403–25.

Alexander, K. L., B. K. Eckland, and L. J. Griffin

1975   "The Wisconsin Model of Socioeconomic Achievement: A Replication." American Journal of Sociology 81 (September): 324–42.

Alford, R. R.

1967   "Class Voting in the Anglo-American Political Systems." In S. M. Lipset and S. Rokkan (eds.), Party Systems and Voter Alignments: Cross-National Perspectives. New York: Free Press.

Allardt, E.
  1968   "Theories About Social Stratification." Pp. 14–24 in J. A. Jackson (ed.), Social Stratification. London: Cambridge University Press.
Allston, J. P., and K. I. Dean
  1972   "Socioeconomic Factors Associated with Attitudes Toward Welfare Recipients and the Causes of Poverty." Social Service Review 46 (March): 13–23.
Althauser, R. P., S. S. Spivack, and B. M. Amsel
  1975   The Unequal Elites. New York: John Wiley.
Althusser, L.
  1970   For Marx. New York: Vintage.
Anderson, B.
  1970   The Negro in the Public Utility Industries. Philadelphia: University of Pennsylvania Press.
Armer, J. M.
  1968   "Intersociety and Intrasociety Correlations of Occupational Prestige." American Journal of Sociology 74 (July): 28–36.
Aron, R.
  1966   "Social Class, Political Class, and Ruling Class." Pp. 201–10 in R. Bendix and S. M. Lipset (eds.), Class, Status, and Power. New York: Free Press.
  1968   Main Currents in Sociological Thought, vol. I. Garden City, N.Y.: Doubleday Anchor.
  1970   Main Currents in Sociological Thought, vol. II. Garden City, N.Y.: Doubleday Anchor.
Atkinson, D.
  1972   Orthodox Consensus and Radical Alternatives. New York: Basic Books.
Bach, G. L., and J. B. Stephenson
  1974   "Inflation and the Redistribution of Wealth." The Review of Economics and Statistics 56 (February): 1–13.
Bachrach, L. L.
  1975   Marital Status and Mental Disorder: An Analytical Review, Washington, D.C.: National Institute of Mental Health.
Bacon, L.
  1971   "Poverty Among Interregional Rural-to-Urban Migrants." Rural Sociology 36 (June): 125–40.
Baker, S. H., and B. Levenson
  1975   "Job Opportunities of Black and White Working Class Women." Social Problems 22 (April): 510–32.
Baltzell, E. D.
  1958   Philadelphia Gentlemen. New York: Free Press.
  1964   The Protestant Establishment. New York: Random House.
Banfield, E. C.
  1968   The Unheavenly City. Boston: Little, Brown.
  1975   The Unheavenly City Revisited. Boston: Little, Brown.
Barber, B.
  1957   Social Stratification. New York: Harcourt, Brace, and World.
  1968   "Social Stratification." Pp. 288–96 in D. P. Sills (ed.), Encyclopedia of the Social Sciences, vol. 7. New York: Macmillan.
Bardolph, R.
  1970   The Civil Rights Record: Black Americans and the Law, 1849–1970. New York: Crowell.
Barth, E., and W. Watson
  1964   "Questionable Assumptions in the Theory of Social Stratification." Pacific Sociological Review 7 (Spring): 10–16.

Bateman, W., and J. Allen
1971   "Income Maintenance: Who Gains and Who Pays." Pp. 286–317 in S. A. Levitan (ed.), Blue Collar Workers. New York: McGraw-Hill.
Baxandall, R., L. Gordon, and S. Reverby
1976   America's Working Women: A Documentary History. New York: Vintage Books.
Bean, F. D., C. M. Bonjean, and M. G. Burton
1973   "Intergenerational Occupational Mobility and Alienation." Social Forces 52 (September): 62–73.
Beeghley, L., and E. W. Butler
1974   "The Consequences of Intelligence Testing in the Public Schools Before and After Desegregation." Social Problems 21 (June): 740–54.
Bell, C. S.
1976   "Working Wives and Family Income." Pp. 239–62 in J. R. Chapman (ed.), Economic Independence for Women. Beverly Hills, Calif.: Sage.
Bendix, R.
1962   Max Weber: An Intellectual Portrait. Garden City, N.Y.: Doubleday Anchor.
1969   Nation Building and Citizenship. Garden City, N.Y.: Doubleday Anchor.
1974   "Inequality and Social Structure: A Comparison of Marx and Weber." American Sociological Review 39 (April): 149–61.
Bendix, R., and S. M. Lipset
1966   "Karl Marx's Theory of Social Classes." Pp. 6–11 in R. Bendix and S. M. Lipset (eds.), Class, Status, and Power. New York: Free Press.
Benoit-Smullyan, E.
1944   "Status, Status Types, and Status Interrelations." American Sociological Review 9 (April): 151–61.
Berg, I.
1970   Education and Jobs: The Great Training Robbery. New York: Praeger.
Berger, A. S., and W. Simon
1974   "Black Families and the Moynihan Report: A Research Evaluation." Social Problems 22 (December): 145–61.
Berlin, I.
1963   Karl Marx: His Life and Environment. New York: Oxford University Press.
Bernard, J.
1971   Women and the Public Interest. Chicago: Aldine-Atherton.
Berreman, G. D.
1960   "Caste in India and the United States." American Journal of Sociology 66 (September): 120–27.
Biderman, A. D., and L. M. Sharp
1968   "The Convergence of Military and Civilian Occupational Structures: Evidence from Studies of Military Retired Employment." American Journal of Sociology 73 (January): 381–99.
Billingsley, A.
1968   Black Families in White America. Englewood Cliffs, N.J.: Prentice-Hall.
Binzin, P.
1970   Whitetown U.S.A. New York: Vintage.
Birnbaum, N.
1953   "Conflicting Interpretations of the Rise of Capitalism: Marx and Weber." British Journal of Sociology 4 (June): 125–41.
Black, D. J.
1970   "The Production of Crime Rates." American Sociological Review 35 (August): 733–47.

Blalock, H. M.
  1966   "Comment: Status Inconsistency and the Identification Problem." Public
          Opinion Quarterly 30 (Spring): 130–32.
  1967a   "Status Inconsistency and Interaction: Some Alternative Models." Ameri-
          can Journal of Sociology 73 (November): 305–15.
  1967b   "Status Inconsistency, Social Mobility, Status Integration, and Structural
          Effects." American Sociological Review 32 (October): 790–800.
Blau, P. M.
  1956   "Social Mobility and Interpersonal Relations." American Sociological Re-
          view 21 (June): 290–95.
Blau, P. M., and O. D. Duncan
  1967   The American Occupational Structure. New York: John Wiley.
Blauner, R.
  1964   Alienation and Freedom: The Factory Worker and His Industry. Chicago:
          University of Chicago Press.
Bluestone, B.
  1974   "Labor Markets, Defense Subsidies, and the Working Poor." Pp. 191–210
          in P. A. Roby (ed.), The Poverty Establishment. Englewood Cliffs, N.J.:
          Prentice-Hall.
Blum, Z. D., and P. H. Rossi
  1969   "Social Class Research and Images of the Poor: A Bibliographic Review."
          Pp. 343–97 in D. P. Moynihan (ed.), On Understanding Poverty. New
          York: Basic Books.
Bott, E.
  1972   "The Concept of Class as a Reference Group." Pp. 47–68 in G. W. Thiel-
          bar and S. D. Feldman (eds.), Issues in Social Inequality. Boston: Little,
          Brown.
Bowles, S.
  1972   "Getting Nowhere: Programmed Class Stagnation." Society 9 (June):
          42–49.
Box, S., and J. Ford
  1969   "Some Questionable Assumptions in the Theory of Status Inconsistency."
          Sociological Review 17 (July): 187–201.
Brandmeyer, G.
  1965   "Status Consistency and Political Behavior: A Replication and Extension of
          Research." Sociological Quarterly 6 (July): 241–56.
Breed, W.
  1963   "Occupational Mobility and Suicide Among White Males." American
          Sociological Review 28 (April): 179–88.
Brim, O. G.
  1966   "Socialization Through the Life-Cycle." In O. G. Brim and S. Wheeler
          (eds.), Socialization After Childhood. New York: John Wiley.
Bronfenbrenner, U.
  1958   "Socialization and Social Class Through Time and Space." Pp. 400–425 in
          E. C. Maccoby et al. (eds.), Readings in Social Psychology. New York:
          Holt, Rinehart, and Winston.
Broom, L., and F. L. Jones
  1977   "Problematics in Stratum Consistency and Stratum Formation: An Austra-
          lian Example." American Journal of Sociology 82 (January): 808–25.
Buckley, W.
  1958   "Social Stratification and the Functional Theory of Social Differentiation."
          American Sociological Review 23 (August): 369–75.
Bureau of Labor Statistics
  1976   Handbook of Labor Statistics, 1975. Washington, D.C.: U.S. Government
          Printing Office.

1977   Handbook of Labor Statistics, 1976. Washington, D.C.: U.S. Government
          Printing Office.
Byrne, J. J.
   1975   "Occupational Mobility of Workers." Monthly Labor Review 98 (February):
          53–59.
Cain, G. G., and H. W. Watts
   1970   "Problems in Making Policy Inferences from the Coleman Report." Ameri-
          can Sociological Review 35 (April): 228–41.
Campbell, R. R., D. M. Johnson, and G. Stangler
   1974   "Return Migration of Black People to the South." Rural Sociology 39
          (Winter): 514–28.
Carmichael, S., and C. V. Hamilton
   1967   Black Power: The Politics of Liberation in America. New York: Vintage.
Centers, R.
   1949   The Psychology of Social Classes: A Study of Class Consciousness. Prince-
          ton, N.J.: Princeton University Press.
Chafe, W. H.
   1972   The American Woman: Her Changing Social, Economic, and Political
          Roles, 1920–1970. New York: Oxford University Press.
   1977   Women and Equality. New York: Oxford University Press.
Chambliss, W. J.
   1969   Crime and the Legal Process. New York: McGraw-Hill.
Chapman, J. R.
   1976   Economic Independence for Women. Beverly Hills, Calif.: Sage.
Chase, I.
   1975   "A Comparison of Men's and Women's Intragenerational Mobility in the
          United States." American Sociological Review 40 (August): 483–505.
Chesler, P.
   1972   Women and Madness. New York: Avon.
Chinoy, E.
   1955   Automobile Workers and the American Dream. New York: Doubleday.
Chiricos, T. G., P. D. Jackson, and G. P. Waldo
   1972   "Inequality in the Imposition of a Criminal Label." Social Problems 19
          (Spring): 553–72.
Clark, K. B.
   1965   Dark Ghetto. New York: Harper Torchbooks.
Clark, R.
   1970   Crime in America. New York: Simon and Schuster.
Cohen, P. S.
   1968   Modern Social Theory. New York: Basic Books.
Coleman, J. S., et al.
   1966   Equality of Educational Opportunity. Washington, D.C.: U.S. Government
          Printing Office.
   1973   "Symposium on Jencks' 'Inequality.'" American Journal of Sociology. 78
          (May): 1523–44.
Congressional Budget Office
   1976   The Unemployment of Nonwhite Americans: The Effects of Alternative
          Policies. Background Paper No. 11 prepared for the Congress, July 19.
          Washington, D.C.: U.S. Government Printing Office.
Congressional Quarterly
   1975   "Open Committee Trend in House and Senate," Congressional Quarterly
          33 (July 11): 81–83.
Converse, P. E.
   1958   "The Shifting Role of Class in Political Attitudes and Behavior." Pp.

388–99 in E. Maccoby et al. (eds.), Readings in Social Psychology, 3rd ed. New York: Holt, Rinehart, and Winston.

Coombs, L. C., R. Freedman, J. Friedman, and W. F. Platt
1970   "Premarital Pregnancy Status Before and After Marriage." American Journal of Sociology 75 (March): 800–30.

Coser, L. A.
1956   The Functions of Social Conflict. New York: Free Press.
1965   "The Sociology of Poverty." Social Problems 13 (Fall): 140–48.
1967   "Karl Marx and Contemporary Sociology." Pp. 137–52 in L. A. Coser (ed.), Continuities in the Study of Social Conflict. New York: Free Press.
1967a   "Violence and the Social Structure." Pp. 53–72 in L. A. Coser (ed.), Continuities in the Study of Social Conflict. New York: Free Press.
1974   "Domestic Servants: The Obsolescence of an Occupational Role." Pp. 67–88 in L. A. Coser, (ed.), Greedy Institutions. New York: Free Press.
1975   "Two Methods in Search of a Substance." American Sociological Review 40 (December): 691–700.
1976   "Reply to My Critics." The American Sociologist 11 (February): 33–38.

Coser, L. A., and R. L. Coser
1974   "The Housewife and Her Greedy Family." Pp. 89–102 in L. A. Coser (ed.), Greedy Institutions. New York: Free Press.

Coser, R. L., and G. Rokoff
1971   "Women in the Occupational World: Social Disruption and Conflict." Social Problems 18 (Spring): 535–54.

Coward, B. E., J. A. Williams, Jr., and J. R. Feagin
1974   "The Culture of Poverty Debate: Some Additional Data." Social Problems 21 (June): 621–33.

Crowder, N. D.
1974   "A Critique of Duncan's Stratification Research." Sociology 8 (January): 19–45.

Cutler, S. J.
1976   "Age Differences in Voluntary Association Memberships." Social Forces 55 (September): 43–58.

Cutright, P.
1967a   "Inequality: A Cross-National Analysis." American Sociological Review 32 (August): 562–77.
1967b   "Income Redistribution: A Cross-National Analysis." Social Forces 46 (December): 180–90.
1971a   "Income and Family Events: Family Income, Family Size, and Consumption." Journal of Marriage and the Family 33 (February): 161–73.
1971b   "Income and Family Events: Marital Stability." Journal of Marriage and the Family 33 (May): 291–306.
1973   "Illegitimacy and Income Supplements." Pp. 90–138 in Joint Economic Committee of the Congress (subcommittee on Fiscal Policy), The Family, Poverty, and Welfare Programs: Factors Influencing Family Instability. Washington, D.C.: U.S. Government Printing Office.
1974   "Region, Migration and the Earnings of White and Black Men." Social Forces 53 (December): 297–305.

Dahrendorf, R.
1958a   "Out of Utopia: Toward a Reorientation of Sociological Analysis." American Journal of Sociology 64 (September): 115–27.
1958b   "Toward a Sociology of Social Conflict." Journal of Conflict Resolution 1 (June): 170–83.
1959   Class and Class Conflict in Industrial Society. Stanford, Calif.: Stanford University Press.

1967   Conflict After Class. New York: Humanities Press.

1968a   "Preface." Pp. v-x in Ralf Dahrendorf (ed.), Essays in the Theory of Society. Stanford, Calif.: Stanford University Press.

1968b   "In Praise of Thrasymachus." Pp. 129–50 in Ralf Dahrendorf (ed.), Essays in the Theory of Society. Stanford, Calif.: Stanford University Press.

1968c   "On the Origin of Inequality Among Men." Pp. 151–78 in Ralf Dahrendorf (ed.), Essays in the Theory of Society. Stanford, Calif.: Stanford University Press.

Dalia, J. T., and A. M. Guest

1975   "Embourgeoisement Among Blue Collar Workers." Sociological Quarterly 16 (Summer): 291–304.

Darian, J. C.

1976   "Factors Influencing the Rising Labor Force Participation Rates of Married Women with Pre-School Children." Social Science Quarterly 56 (March): 614–30.

Davidson, C.

1972   Biracial Politics. Baton Rouge, La.: Louisiana State University Press.

Davidson, C., and C. M. Gaitz

1974   "Are the Poor Different? A Comparison of Work Behavior and Attitudes Among the Urban Poor and Nonpoor." Social Problems 22 (December): 229–45.

Davis, K.

1948   Human Society. New York: Macmillan.

1953   "Reply to Tumin." American Sociological Review 18 (August): 386–91.

1959   "The Abominable Heresy: A Reply to Dr. Buckley." American Sociological Review 24 (February): 82–83.

Davis, K., and W. E. Moore

1945   "Some Principles of Stratification." American Sociological Review 7 (April): 242–49.

Della Fave, L. R.

1974   "The Culture of Poverty Revisited: A Strategy for Research." Social Problems 21 (June): 609–20.

Demerath, N. J., III

1965   Social Class in American Protestantism. Chicago: Rand McNally.

Diggins, J. P.

1972   "Thoreau, Marx, and the 'Riddle' of Alienation." Social Research 39 (Winter): 571–98.

Domhoff, G. W., and H. B. Ballard (eds.)

1968   C. Wright Mills and the Power Elite. Boston: Beacon Press.

Dubin, R.

1957   "Approaches to the Study of Social Conflict: A Colloquium." Journal of Conflict Resolution 1 (June): 1–10.

Duncan, O. D.

1961   "A Socioeconomic Index for All Occupations." Pp. 109–38 in A. J. Reiss (ed.), Occupations and Social Status. New York: Free Press.

1966   "Methodological Issues in the Analysis of Social Mobility." Pp. 51–97 in N. Smelser and R. M. Lipset (eds.), Social Structure and Mobility in Economic Development. Chicago: Aldine.

1968a   "Ability and Achievement." Eugenics Quarterly 15 (March): 1–11.

1968b   "Inheritance of Poverty or Inheritance of Race." Pp. 85–110 in D. P. Moynihan (ed.), On Understanding Poverty. New York: Basic Books.

1968c   "Social Stratification and Mobility: Problems in the Measurement of Trend." Pp. 675–719 in E. B. Sheldon and W. E. Moore (eds.), Indicators of Social Change. New York: Russell Sage.

    1968d   "Patterns of Occupational Mobility Among Negro Men." Demography 5
             (#1): 11–22.
Duncan, O. D., D. L. Featherman, and B. Duncan
    1972   Socioeconomic Background and Achievement. New York: Seminar Press.
Duncan, R. P., and C. C. Perrucci
    1976   "Dual Occupation Families and Migration." American Sociological Review
             41 (April): 252–61.
Dupre, L.
    1966   The Philosophical Foundations of Marxism. New York: Harcourt, Brace
             and World.
Edelhertz, H.
    1970   The Nature, Impact, and Prosecution of White Collar Crime. Washington,
             D.C.: National Institute of Law Enforcement and Criminal Justice.
Eisenstadt, S. N.
    1968   "Prestige, Participation, and Strata Formation." Pp. 62–103 in J. A.
             Jackson (ed.), Social Stratification. New York: Cambridge University Press.
Eitzen, D. S.
    1970   "Status Inconsistency and Wallace Supporters in a Midwestern City." So-
             cial Forces 48 (June): 493–98.
Elder, G. H.
    1965   "Family Structure and Educational Attainment." American Sociological
             Review 39 (February): 81–96.
Engels, F.
    1954   Anti-Duhring. Moscow: Foreign Languages Publishing House.
    1959   "Letters on Historical Materialism." Pp. 395–412 in Lewis Feuer (ed.), K.
             Marx and F. Engels, Basic Writings on Politics and Philosophy. Garden
             City, N.Y.: Doubleday Anchor.
Epstein, C. F.
    1970   "Encountering the Male Establishment: Sex-Status Limits on Women's
             Careers in the Professions." American Journal of Sociology 75 (May):
             965–82.
    1971   Woman's Place: Options and Limits in Professional Careers. Berkeley,
             Calif.: University of California Press.
Erlanger, H. S.
    1974   "Social Class and Corporal Punishment in Childrearing: A Reassessment."
             American Sociological Review 39 (February): 68–85.
Fallers, L. A.
    1966   "Review of Lenski, Power and Privilege." American Sociological Review
             31 (October): 718–19.
Farley, R.
    1977   "Trends in Racial Inequalities: Have the Gains of the 1960's Disappeared in
             the 1970's?" American Sociological Review 42 (April): 189–208.
Farley, R., and A. I. Hermalin
    1971   "Family Stability: A Comparison of Trends Between Blacks and Whites."
             American Sociological Review 36 (February): 1–17.
Farley, R., and A. F. Taeuber
    1974   "Racial Segregation in the Public Schools." American Journal of Sociology
             79 (January): 888–905.
Feagin, J. R.
    1975   Subordinating the Poor: Welfare and American Beliefs. Englewood Cliffs,
             N.J.: Prentice-Hall.
Featherman, D. L., and R. M. Hauser
    1976   "Changes in the Socioeconomic Stratification of the Races, 1962–73." So-
             cial Forces 82 (November): 621–51.

1976a   "Sexual Inequalities and Socioeconomic Achievement in the U.S., 1962–73." American Sociological Review 41 (June): 462–83.

Feldman, S. D.
1973   "Impediment or Stimulus? Marital Status and Graduate Education." American Journal of Sociology 78 (January): 982–94.

Felson, M., and D. Knoke
1974   "Social Status and the Married Woman." Journal of Marraige and the Family 36 (August): 516–21.

Ferber, M. A., and J. A. Huber
1975   "Sex of Student and Instructor: A Study of Student Bias." American Journal of Sociology 80 (January): 949–63.

Fernandez, J. P.
1975   Black Managers in White Corporations. New York: John Wiley.

Fernbach, D.
1974a   "Introduction." Pp. 1–64 in K. Marx, The Revolutions of 1848. New York: Vintage.
1974b   "Introduction." Pp. 7–34 in K. Marx, Surveys from Exile. New York: Vintage.
1974c   "Introduction." Pp. 9–72 in K. Marx, The First International and After. New York: Vintage.

Ferree, M. M.
1976   "Working Class Jobs: Housework and Paid Work as Sources of Satisfaction." Social Problems 23 (April): 431–41.

Finn, P., and A. R. Hoffman
1976   Exemplary Projects: The Prosecution of Economic Crime. Washington, D.C.: Law Enforcement Assistance Administration.

Flaim, P. O., T. F. Bradshaw, and C. L. Gilroy
1975   "Employment and Unemployment in 1974." Monthly Labor Review 98 (February): 3–14.

Form, W. F.
1973   "Auto Workers and Their Machines: A Study of Work, Factory, and Job Satisfaction in Four Countries." Social Forces 52 (September): 1–15.

Form, W. H., and J. A. Geschwender
1962   "Social Reference Basis of Job Satisfaction: The Case of Manual Workers." American Sociological Review 27 (April): 228–37.

Fremon, C.
1970   Central City and Suburban Employment Growth, 1965–67. Washington, D.C.: The Urban Institute.

Friedan, B.
1963   The Feminine Mystique. New York: Norton.

Friedland, W. F.
1973   Revolutionary Thought. Unpublished Manuscript.

Friedlander, S. L.
1972   Unemployment in the Urban Core. New York: Praeger.

Friedrichs, R.
1970   A Sociology of Sociology. New York: Free Press.

Fullerton, H. N., and P. O. Flaim
1976   "New Labor Force Projections to 1990." Monthly Labor Review 99 (December): 3–13.

Furstenberg, G. M. von, B. Harrison, and A. R. Harowitz
1974   Patterns of Racial Discrimination. Lexington, Mass.: Heath.

Gabennesch, H.,
1972   "Authoritarianism as a World View." American Journal of Sociology 77 (March): 857–75.

Galbraith, J. K.
1967   The New Industrial State. New York: New American Library.
Gallman, R. E.
1969   "Trends in the Size Distribution of Wealth in the Nineteenth Century."
        Pp. 1–31 in L. Soltow (ed.), Six Papers on the Size Distribution of Wealth.
        New York: National Bureau of Economic Research.
Gans, H. J.
1972   "The Positive Functions of Poverty." American Journal of Sociology 78
        (September): 275–89.
Garfinkle, S. H.
1975   "Occupations of Women and Black Workers, 1962–74." Monthly Labor
        Review 98 (November): 25–35.
Gaulden, J. C.
1971   The Money-Givers: An Examination of the Myths and Realities of Founda-
        tion Philanthropy in America. New York: Random House.
Geschwender, J. A.
1968   "Status Inconsistency, Social Isolation, and Individual Unrest." Social
        Forces 46 (June): 477–83.
Gibbs, J. C., and W. T. Martin
1962   "Urbanization, Technology, and the Division of Labor: International Pat-
        terns." American Sociological Review 27 (October): 667–77.
Gibbs, J. P., and D. L. Poston, Jr.
1975   "The Division of Labor: Conceptualization and Related Measures." Social
        Forces 53 (March): 468–75.
Giddens, A.
1971   Capitalism and Modern Social Theory: An Analysis of the Writings of
        Marx, Durkheim, and Max Weber. New York: Cambridge University
        Press.
1973   The Class Structure of the Advanced Societies. New York: Harper & Row.
Glenn, N. D., and E. Gotard
1977   "The Religion of Blacks in the United States: Some Recent Trends and
        Current Characteristics." American Journal of Sociology 83 (September):
        443–51.
Glenn, N. D., J. P. Alston, and D. Weiner
1970   Social Stratification: A Research Bibliography. Berkeley, Calif.: Glendes-
        sary Press.
Glenn, N. D., S. K. Hoppe, and D. Weinter
1974   "Social Class Heterogamy and Marital Success: A Study of the Empirical
        Adequacy of a Textbook Generalization." Social Problems 24 (April): 539–
        50.
Glock, C. Y., and R. Stark
1965   Religion and Society in Tension. Chicago: Rand McNally.
Gockel, G. L.
1969   "Income and Religious Affiliation: A Regression Analysis." American
        Journal of Sociology 74 (May): 632–47.
Goldstein, S.,
1969   "Socioeconomic Differentials Among Religious Groups in the U.S." Amer-
        ican Journal of Sociology 74 (May): 612–31.
Goldthorpe, J. H., and K. Hope
1972   "Occupational Grading and Occupational Prestige." Pp. 19–80 in K. Hope
        (ed.), The Analysis of Social Mobility: Methods and Approaches. New
        York: Oxford University Press.
1974   The Social Grading of Occupations: A New Approach and Scale. New
        York: Oxford University Press.

Goldthorpe, J. H., D. Lockwood, F. Bechhofer, and J. Platt
  1969   The Affluent Worker in the Class Structure. New York: Cambridge University Press.
Goode, E.
  1966   "Social Class and Church Participation." American Journal of Sociology 72 (July): 102–11.
Goode, W. J.
  1973   "Functionalism: The Empty Castle." Pp. 64–96 in W. J. Goode (ed.), Explorations in Social Theory. New York: Oxford University Press.
Goodwin, L.
  1972a   Do the Poor Want to Work? Washington, D.C. The Brookings Institution.
  1972b   "How Suburban Families View the Work Orientations of the Welfare Poor: Problems in Social Stratification and Public Policy." Social Problems 19 (Winter): 337–48.
Gordon, D. M.
  1971   "Class and the Economics of Crime." The Review of Radical Economics 3 (Summer).
Gordon, M. M.
  1963   Social Class in American Sociology. New York: McGraw-Hill.
Gould, W. B.
  1977   Black Workers in White Unions. Ithaca, N.Y.: Cornell University Press.
Gove, W. R.
  1972a   "The Relationship Between Sex Roles, Marital Status, and Mental Illness." Social Forces 51 (September): 34–44.
  1972b   "Sex, Marital Status, and Suicide." Journal of Health and Social Behavior 13 (June): 204–13.
  1973   "Sex, Marital Status, and Mortality." American Journal of Sociology 79 (July): 45–67.
Gove, W. R., and T. R. Herb
  1974   "Stress and Mental Illness Among the Young: A Comparison of the Sexes." Social Forces 53 (December): 256–65.
Gove, W. R., and J. F. Tudor
  1973   "Adult Sex Roles and Mental Illness." American Journal of Sociology 78 (January): 812–35.
Grad, S.
  1973   "Relative Importance of Income Sources for the Aged." Social Security Bulletin 36 (August): 37–45.
Grandjean, B.
  1975   "An Economic Analysis of the Davis-Moore Theory of Stratification." Social Forces 53 (June): 543–52.
Grandjean, B., and F. Bean
  1975   "The Davis-Moore Theory and Perceptions of Stratification: Some Relevant Evidence." Social Forces 54 (September): 166–80.
Greeley, A. M.
  1974   "Political Participation Among Ethnic Groups in the United States: A Preliminary Reconnaissance." American Journal of Sociology 80 (July): 170–204.
Green, E.
  1970   "Race, Social Status, and Criminal Arrest." American Sociological Review 35 (June): 476–90.
Green, M. J., J. M. Fallows, and D. R. Zwick
  1972   Who Runs Congress? New York: Bantam.
Green, R. W. (ed.)
  1959   Protestantism and Capitalism: The Weber Thesis and Its Critics. Lexington, Mass.: Heath.

Griffiths, M. W.
1976   "How Much Is a Woman Worth? The American Public Policy." Pp. 23–38
        in J. R. Chapman (ed.), Economic Independence for Women. Beverly
        Hills, Calif.: Sage.
Grimm, J. W., and R. N. Stern
1974   "Sex Roles and Internal Labor Market Structures: The 'Female' Semi-
        Professions." Social Problems 21 (June): 690–705.
Gross, E.
1968   "Plus ca Change. . . ? The Sexual Structure of Occupations Over Time."
        Social Problems 16 (Fall): 198–208.
Grossman, A.
1975   Multiple Job Holders in May, 1974. Special Labor Force Report 177.
        Washington, D.C.: Bureau of Labor Statistics, U.S. Department of Labor.
Grunker, W. J., D. D. Cooke, and A. W. Kirsch
1970   Climbing the Job Ladder: A Study of Employee Advancement in Eleven
        Industries. New York: Shelley.
Guest, A. M.
1974   "Class Consciousness and American Political Attitudes." Social Forces 52
        (June): 496–510.
Gurin, G. and P. Gurin
1970   "Expectancy Theory in the Study of Poverty." Journal of Social Issues 26
        (#2): 83–103.
Gusfield, J. R., and M. Schwartz
1963   "The Meanings of Occupational Prestige." American Sociological Review
        28 (April): 265–71.
Hacker, H. M.
1951   "Women as a Minority Group." Social Forces 30 (October): 60–69.
Hahn, H. H.
1968   "Northern Referenda on Fair Housing: The Response of White Voters."
        Western Political Quarterly 21 (September): 483–95.
Hall, R. H.
1975   Occupations and the Social Structure, 2d ed. Englewood Cliffs, N.J.:
        Prentice-Hall.
Haller, A. O., and D. M. Lewis
1966   "The Hypothesis of Intersocietal Similarity in Occupational Prestige
        Hierarchies." American Journal of Sociology 72 (September): 210–18.
Halsey, A. H.
1973   "The Sociology of Education." Pp. 247–302 in N. J. Smelser (ed.), Sociol-
        ogy: An Introduction, 2d ed. New York: John Wiley.
Hamilton, H. D.
1970   "Voting Behavior in Open Housing Referenda." Social Science Quarterly
        51 (December): 715–29.
Hamilton, R. F.
1972a   Class and Politics in the United States. New York: John Wiley.
1972b   "Black Demands, White Reactions, and Liberal Alarms." Pp. 130–53 in
        Levitan (ed.), Blue Collar Workers. New York: McGraw-Hill.
1972c   "Liberal Intelligentsia and White Backlash." Pp. 227–38 in I. Howe (ed.),
        The World of the Blue Collar Worker. New York: Quadrangle.
Hammerman, H.
1973   "Minorities in Construction Referral Unions." Monthly Labor Review 5
        (May).
Hammerman, H., and M. Rogoff
1975   "The Union Role in Title VII Enforcement." Civil Rights Digest 7 (Spring):
        22–34.

Harbeson, G. E.
1971   Choice and Challenge for the American Woman, rev. ed. Cambridge, Mass.: Schenkman.
Harrington, M.
1971   The Other America. Baltimore, Md.: Penguin.
Harrison, B.
1974   Urban Economic Development: Suburbanization, Minority Opportunity, and the Condition of the Central City. Washington, D.C.: The Urban Institute.
Hartman, M.
1974   "On the Definition of Status Inconsistency." American Journal of Sociology 80 (November): 706–21.
Hauser, R. M., and D. L. Featherman
1973   "Trends in the Occupational Mobility of U.S. Men, 1962–1970." American Sociological Review 38 (June): 302–10.
1974   "White-Nonwhite Differentials in Occupational Mobility Among Men in the United States, 1962–1972." Demography 11 (May): 247–65.
Hauser, R. M., J. N. Koffel, H. P. Travis, and P. J. Dickinson
1975a   "Temporal Change in Occupational Mobility: Evidence for Men in the United States." American Sociological Review 40 (June): 279–97.
1975b   "Structural Changes in Occupational Mobility Among Men in the United States." American Sociological Review 40 (October) 585–98.
Havens, E. M.
1973   "Women, Work, and Wedlock: A Note on Female Marital Patterns in the U.S." American Journal of Sociology 78 (January): 975–81.
Havens, E. M., and J. C. Tully
1972   "Female Intergenerational Occupational Mobility: Comparisons of Patterns?" American Sociological Review 37 (December): 774–77.
Hawkes, R.
1972   "Some Methodological Problems in Explaining Social Mobility." American Sociological Review 37 (June): 294–300.
Hazelrigg, L. E.
1974   "Occupational Mobility in Nineteenth Century U.S. Cities: A Review of Some Evidence." Social Forces 53 (September): 21–32.
Heatherington, E. M., and R. D. Parke
1975   Child Psychology: A Contemporary View. New York: McGraw-Hill
Hechter, M.
1974   "The Political Economy of Ethnic Change." American Journal of Sociology 79 (March): 1151–78.
1976   "Response to Cohen: Max Weber on Ethnicity and Ethnic Change." American Journal of Sociology 81 (March): 1162–69.
Hedges, J. N.
1975   "How Many Days Make a Workweek?" Monthly Labor Review 98 (April): 29–36.
Herriot, R. A., and H. P. Miller
1971   "The Taxes We Pay." Conference Board Record 8 (May): 31–40.
Hindelang, M. J.
1975   Public Opinion Regarding Crime, Criminal Justice, and Related Topics. Washington, D.C.: Law Enforcement Assistance Administration.
Hiltz, S. R.
1971   "Black and White in the Consumer Financial System." American Journal of Sociology 76 (May): 987–98.
Hirschi, T.
1972   "Social Class and Crime." Pp. 503–20 in G. W. Thielbar and S. D. Feldman (eds.), Issues in Social Inequality. Boston: Little, Brown.

Hodge, R. W.
1973   "Toward a Theory of Racial Differences in Employment." Social Forces 52 (September): 16–30.

Hodge, R. W., and D. J. Treiman
1966   "Occupational Mobility and Attitudes Towards Negroes." American Sociological Review 31 (February): 93–102.
1968   "Class Identification in the United States." American Journal of Sociology 73 (March): 535–47.

Hodge, R. W., D. J. Treiman, and P. H. Rossi
1966a   "A Comparative Study of Occupational Prestige." Pp. 309–21 in R. Bendix and S. M. Lipset (eds.), Class, Status, and Power, 2d ed. New York: Free Press.

Hodge, R. W., P. M. Siegel, and P. H. Rossi
1966b   "Occupational Prestige in the United States: 1925–63." Pp. 322–34 in R. Bendix and S. M. Lipset (eds.), Class, Status, and Power, 2d ed. New York: Free Press.

Hodgson, G.
1975   "Do Schools Make a Difference?" Pp. 22–44 in D. M. Levine and M. J. Bane (eds.), The "Inequality" Controversy. New York: Basic Books.

Hook, S.
1962   From Hegel to Marx. Ann Arbor, Mich.: University of Michigan Press.

Hope, K.
1975   "Models of Status Inconsistency and Social Mobility Effects." American Sociological Review 40 (June): 322–43.

Hopple, G.
1974   "Protest Attitudes and Social Class: Working Class Authoritarianism Revisited." Sociology and Social Research 60 (#3): 229–46.

Horan, P. M., and P. L. Austin
1974   "The Social Bases of Welfare Stigma." Social Problems 21 (June): 648–57.

House, J. S., and E. B. Harkins
1975   "Why and When Is Status Inconsistency Stressful?" American Journal of Sociology 81 (September): 395–412.

Hout, M., and W. R. Morgan
1975   "Race and Sex Variations in the Causes of the Expected Attainments of High School Seniors." American Journal of Sociology 81 (September): 364–94.

Huaco, G. A.
1973   "The Functionalist Theory of Stratification: Two Decades of Controversy." Pp. 411–27 in M. Tumin (ed.), Readings in Social Stratification. Englewood Cliffs, N.J.: Prentice-Hall.

Huber, J.
1976   "Towards a Socio-Technological Theory of the Women's Movement." Social Problems 23 (April): 371–88.

Huber, J., and W. H. Form
1973   Income and Ideology. New York: Free Press.

Hunt, L. L., and J. G. Hunt
1975   "Race and the Father-Son Connection: The Conditional Relevance of Father Absence for the Orientations and Identities of Adolescent Boys." Social Problems 23 (October): 35–52.

Hyman, H. H., and C. R. Wright
1971   "Trends in Voluntary Association Memberships of American Adults: A Replication Based on Secondary Analysis of National Sample Surveys." American Sociological Review 36 (April): 191–206.

Inkeles, A.
1969   "Social Stratification in the Modernization of Russia." Pp. 150–53 in P.

Hollander (ed.), American and Soviet Society, Englewood Cliffs, N.J.: Prentice-Hall.

Inkeles, A., and P. H. Rossi
1956 "National Comparisons of Occupational Prestige." American Journal of Sociology 61 (January): 329–39.

Jackman, M. R.
1972 "Social Mobility and Attitude Toward the Political System." Social Forces 50 (June): 462–72.

Jackman, M.R., and R. W. Jackman
1973 "An Interpretation of the Relation Between Objective and Subjective Social Status." American Sociological Review 38 (October): 569–82.

Jackman, R. W.
1974 "Political Democracy and Social Inequality: A Comparative Analysis." American Sociological Review 39 (February): 29–45.
1975 Politics and Social Equality. New York: John Wiley.

Jackson, E. F.
1962 "Status Consistency and Symptoms of Stress." American Sociological Review 27 (August): 469–80.

Jackson, E. F., and P. J. Burke
1965 "Status and Symptoms of Stress: Additive and Interaction Effects." American Sociological Review 30 (August): 556–64.

Jackson, E. F., and H. J. Crockett, Jr.
1964 "Occupational Mobility in the United States: A Point Estimate and Trend Comparison." American Sociological Review 29 (February): 5–15.

Jackson, E. F., and R. R. Curtis
1972 "Effects of Vertical Mobility and Status Inconsistency: A Body of Negative Evidence." American Sociological Review 37 (December): 701–13.

Jackson, E. F., W. S. Fox, H. J. Crockett, Jr.
1970 "Religion and Occupational Achievement." American Sociological Review 35 (February): 48–62.

Jacobson, B., and W. Jacobson
1975 "Only Eight Percent: A Look at Women in Medicine." Civil Rights Digest 7 (Summer): 20–28.

Janowitz, M.
1975 "Sociological Theory and Social Action." American Journal of Sociology 81 (July): 82–108.

Jencks, C. S.
1972 Inequality: A Reassessment of the Effect of Family and Schooling in America. New York: Basic Books.

Johnson, M. P., and R. R. Sell
1976 "The Cost of Being Black." American Journal of Sociology 82 (July): 183–90.

Johnson, T. A.
1976 "Urban League Finds 25.4% of Blacks Are Still Jobless." New York Times, August 3.

Kahl, J. A., and J. A. Davis
1955 "A Comparison of Indexes of Socio-economic Status." American Sociological Review 20 (June): 317–25.

Kahn, R. L.
1972 "The Meaning of Work: Interpretations and Proposals for Measurement." In A. Campbell and P. E. Converse (eds.), The Human Meaning of Social Change. New York: Russell Sage.

Kain, J. F.
1968 "Housing Segregation, Negro Employment, and Metropolitan Decentralization." Quarterly Journal of Economics 82 (May).

1974   "Housing Segregation, Black Employment, and Metropolitan Decentralization: A Retrospective View." Pp. 5–20 in Furstenberg, Harrison, and Horowitz (eds.), Patterns of Racial Discrimination. Lexington, Mass.: Heath.

Kain, J. F., and J. J. Pesky
1969   "Alternatives to the Gilded Ghetto." The Public Interest 14 (Winter): 74–83.

Kallen, D. J., and D. Miller
1971   "Public Attitudes Toward Welfare." Social Work 16: 83–90.

Kanter, R. M.
1976   "The Impact of Hierarchical Structures on the Work Behavior of Women and Men." Social Problems 23 (April): 415–30.
1977   "Some Effects of Proportions on Group Life: Skewed Sex Ratios and Responses to Token Women." American Journal of Sociology 82 (March): 965–90.

Kaplan, H. R., and C. Tausky
1972   "Work and the Welfare Cadillac: The Function of and Commitment to Work Among the Hard-Core Unemployed." Social Problems 19 (Spring): 469–83.

Keech, W. R.
1968   "The Impact of Negro Voting: The Role of the Vote in the Quest for Equality. Chicago: Rand McNally.

Keller, S., and M. Zavalloni
1964   "Ambition and Social Class: A Respecification." Social Forces 43 (October): 58–70.

Kelly, K. D., and W. J. Chambliss
1966   "Status Consistency and Political Attitudes." American Sociological Review 31 (June): 375–82.

Kenkel, W. F.
1956   "The Relationship Between Consistency and Politico-Economic Attitudes." American Sociological Review 21 (June): 365–68.

Kerckhoff, A. C.
1972   Socialization and Social Class. Englewood Cliffs. N. J.: Prentice-Hall.

Kessin, K.
1971   "Social and Psychological Consequences of Intergenerational Mobility." American Journal of Sociology 77 (July): 1–18.

Kirsch, B. A., and J. L. Lengermann
1972   "An Empirical Test of Robert Blauner's Ideas on Alienation in Work as Applied to Different Type Jobs in a White Collar Setting." Sociology and Social Research 56 (#2): 180–94.

Knoke, D.
1973   "Intergenerational Occupational Mobility and the Political Party Preferences of American Men." American Journal of Sociology 78 (March): 1448–68.
1976   Change and Continuity in American Politics: The Social Bases of Political Parties. Baltimore, Md.: Johns Hopkins University Press.

Kohn, M. L.
1976   "Occupational Structure and Alienation." American Journal of Sociology 82 (July): 111–30.

Kohn, M. L., and C. Schooler
1973   "Occupational Experience and Psychological Functioning: An Assessment of Reciprocal Effects." American Sociological Review 38 (February): 97–118.

Kolko, G.
1962   Wealth and Power in America. New York: Praeger.
Komarovsky, M.
1967   Blue Collar Marriage. New York: Vintage Books.
Kravis, I. B.
1968   "Income Distribution: Functional Share." Pp. 132–45, vol. 7 in D. P. Sills (ed.), International Encyclopedia of the Social Sciences. New York: Macmillan.
Lampman, R. J.
1962   The Share of Top Wealthholders in National Wealth, 1922–1956. New York: National Bureau of Economic Research.
Land, K. C.
1970   "Path Models of Functional Theories of Stratification as Representations of Cultural Beliefs on Stratification." Sociological Quarterly 11 (Fall): 474–84.
Landecker, W. S.
1960   "Class Boundaries." American Sociological Review 25 (December): 868–76.
Langer, E.
1970   "Inside the New York Telephone Company." In W. L. O'Neil (ed.), Women at Work. New York: Quadrangle.
Lasch, C.
1975   "Inequality and Education." Pp. 45–62 in D. M. Levine and M. J. Bane (eds.), The "Inequality" Controversy. New York: Basic Books.
Laslett, B.
1971   "Mobility and Work Satisfaction." American Journal of Sociology 77 (July): 19–35.
Lauer, R. H.
1971   "The Middle Class Looks at Poverty." Urban and Social Change Review 5 (Fall): 8–10.
Lauman, E. O.
1966   Prestige and Association in an Urban Community. Indianapolis: Bobbs-Merrill.
Lauman, E. O., P. M. Siegel, and R. W. Hodge
1970   The Logic of Social Hierarchies. Chicago: Markham.
Law Enforcement Assistance Administration
1972   Survey of Inmates of Local Jails, 1972. Washington, D.C.: U.S. Government Printing Office.
1976   Criminal Victimization in the United States. Washington, D.C.: U.S. Government Printing Office.
1976b   Survey of Inmates of State Correctional Facilities, 1974: Advance Report. Washington, D.C.: U.S. Government Printing Office.
Leavy, M. D.
1974   "Comment on Abrahamson's 'Functionalism and the Functional Theory of Stratification: An Empirical Assessment.'" American Journal of Sociology 80 (November): 724–27.
Lebowitz, B. D.
1974   "Concept Formation and Concept Rejection: The Case of Status Inconsistency." Paper presented at the meetings of the American Sociological Association in Montreal.
Leiberson, S.
1971   "An Empirical Study of Military-Industrial Linkages." American Journal of Sociology 76 (January): 562–85.
Leiberson, S., and G. V. Fuguitt
1967   "Negro-White Occupational Differences in the Absence of Discrimination." American Journal of Sociology 73 (September): 188–200.

Leggett, J. C.
1969   "Economic Insecurity and Working Class Consciousness." Pp. 372–83 in
        J. L. Roach et al. (eds.), Social Stratification in the United States. En-
        glewood Cliffs, N.J.: Prentice-Hall.
LeMasters, E. E.
1975   Blue Collar Aristocrats. Madison, Wis.: University of Wisconsin Press.
Lenski, G.
1952   "American Social Classes: Statistical Strata or Social Groups?" American
        Journal of Sociology 58 (September): 139–54.
1954   "Status Crystallization: A Non-Vertical Dimension of Social Status."
        American Sociological Review 19 (August): 405–13.
1963   The Religious Factor. Garden City, N.Y.: Doubleday Anchor.
1966   Power and Privilege: A Theory of Social Stratification. New York:
        McGraw-Hill.
1967   "Status Inconsistency and the Vote: A Four Nation Test." American
        Sociological Review 32 (April): 288–301.
1975   "Social Structure in Evolutionary Perspective." Pp. 135–53 in P. M. Blau
        (ed.), Approaches to the Study of Social Structure. New York: Free Press.
Leslie, G. R., Larson, R., and Gorman, B. J.
1976   Introductory Sociology, 2d ed. New York: Oxford University Press.
Levine, A., and J. Crumrine
1975   "Women and the Fear of Success: A Problem in Replication." American
        Journal of Sociology 80 (January): 964–74.
Levine, D. M., and M. J. Bane
1975   The "Inequality" Controversy: Schooling and Distributive Justice. New
        York: Basic Books.
Levine, D. U., and J. K. Meyer
1977   "Level and Rate of Desegregation and White Enrollment Decline in a Big
        City School System." Social Problems 24 (April): 451–63.
Levinson, R. M.
1975   "Sex Discrimination and Employment Practices: An Experiment with Un-
        conventional Job Inquiries." Social Problems 22 (April): 533–42.
Levison, A.
1975   The Working Class Majority. Baltimore, Md.: Penguin.
Lewis, O.
1965   La Vida. New York: Random House.
1969   "The Culture of Poverty." Pp. 187–200 in D. P. Moynihan (ed.), On Un-
        derstanding Poverty. New York: Basic Books.
Liebow, E.
1967   Tally's Corner: A Study of Negro Streetcorner Men. Boston: Little, Brown.
Linton, R.
1936   The Study of Man. New York: Appleton-Century-Crofts.
Lipset, S. M.
1959   "Democracy and Working Class Authoritarianism." American Sociological
        Review 24 (August): 482–502.
1961   "Working Class Authoritarianism: A Reply to Miller and Riessman."
        British Journal of Sociology 12 (Fall): 277–81.
1963   Political Man. Garden City, N.Y.: Doubleday Anchor.
Lipset, S. M., and R. Bendix
1959   Social Mobility in Industrial Society. Berkeley, Calif.: University of Califor-
        nia Press.
Lipset, S. M., and E. Raub
1970   The Politics of Unreason: Right Wing Extremism in America, 1790–1970.
        New York: Harper & Row.

Lipset, S. M., and H. L. Zetterberg
1966   "A Theory of Social Mobility." Pp. 561–74 in R. Bendix and S. M. Lipset (eds.), Class, Status, and Power. New York: Free Press.
Lipsitz, L.
1965   "Working Class Authoritarianism: A Reevaluation." American Sociological • Review 30 (February): 103–109.
Litwak, E.
1960   "Occupational Mobility and Extended Family Cohesion." American Sociological Review 25 (February): 9–21.
Long, L. H.
1974   "Poverty Status and Receipt of Welfare Among Migrants and Nonmigrants in Large Cities." American Sociological Review 39 (February): 46–56.
1974a   "Women's Labor Force Participation and the Residential Mobility of Families." Social Forces 52 (March): 342–48.
Long, L., and L. R. Heltman
1975   "Migration and Income Differences Between Black and White Men in the North." American Journal of Sociology 80 (May): 1391–1409.
Lopreato, J.
1967   "Upward Social Mobility and Political Orientation." American Sociological Review 32 (August): 586–92.
1968   "Authority Relations and Class Conflict," Social Forces 49 (January): 70–79.
1970   The Italian Americans. New York: Random House.
Lopreato, J., and L. Alston
1970   "Ideal Types and the Idealization Strategy." American Sociological Review 35 (February): 88–96.
Lopreato, J., and L. Lewis
1963   "An Analysis of Variables in the Functional Theory of Stratification." Sociological Quarterly 4 (August): 301–10.
Lundberg, F.
1968   The Rich and the Super-Rich. New York: Bantam Books.
1975   The Rockefeller Syndrome. New York: Kensington.
Lynd, R. S., and H. M. Lynd
1929   Middletown. New York: Harcourt, Brace.
1937   Middletown in Transition. New York: Harcourt, Brace.
Mack, R. W., and R. C. Snyder
1957   "The Analysis of Social Conflict—Toward Overview and Synthesis." Journal of Conflict Resolution 1 (June): 212–48.
Mackenzie, G.
1967   "The Economic Dimension of Embourgeoisement." British Journal of Sociology 18 (March): 29–44.
Magee, B.
1973   Karl Popper. New York: Viking Press.
Marsh, R. M.
1971   "The Explanation of Occupational Prestige Hierarchies." Social Forces 50 (December): 214–22.
Marwell, G.
1975   "Why Ascription? Parts of a More or Less Formal Theory of the Functions and Dysfunctions of Sex Roles." American Sociological Review 40 (August): 445–55.
Marx, G.
1967   "Religion: Opiate or Inspiration of Civil Rights Militancy Among Negroes?" American Sociological Review 32 (February): 64–72.

Marx, K.
1934   The Class Struggles in France (1848–50). New York: International Publishers.
1963   The Eighteenth Brumaire of Louis Bonaparte. New York: International Publishers.
1964   Economic and Philosophic Manuscripts of 1844. New York: International Publishers.
1967   Capital. New York: International Publishers.
1970a   "Preface" Pp. 19–23 in K. Marx, A Contribution to the Critique of Political Economy. New York: International Publishers.
1970b   "Introduction." Pp. 188–217 in K. Marx, A Contribution to the Critique of Political Economy. New York: International Publishers.
1974a   The Revolutions of 1848. Political Writings, vol. I. D. Fernbach (ed.). New York: Vintage.
1974b   Surveys from Exile. Political Writings, vol. II. D. Fernbach (ed.). New York: Vintage.
1974c   The First International and After. Political Writings, vol. III. D. Fernbach (ed.). New York: Vintage.
Marx, K., and F. Engels
1947   The German Ideology. New York: International Publishers.
1959   Basic Writings on Politics and Philosophy. L. Feuer (ed.) Garden City, N.Y.: Doubleday Anchor.
Mason, K. O., J. L. Czajka, and S. Arber
1976   "Change in Women's Sex-Role Attitudes, 1964–1974." American Sociological Review 41 (August): 573–96.
Masters, S. H.
1975   Black-White Income Differentials: Empirical Studies and Policy Implications. New York: Academic Press.
Mathews, D. R., and J. W. Prothro
1966   Negroes and the New Southern Politics. New York: Harcourt Brace Jovanovich.
Mayhew, L.
1968   "Ascription in Modern Societies." Sociological Inquiry 38 (Spring).
McClelland, D. C.
1961   The Achieving Society. New York: Van Nostrand.
McClelland, D.C., et. al.
1958   "A Scoring Manual for the Achievement Motive," Pp. 179–204 in J. W. Atkinson (ed.), Motives in Fantasy, Action, and Society. Princeton, N.J.: Van Nostrand.
McClendon, M. J.
1976   "The Occupational Status Attainment Processes of Males and Females." American Sociological Review 41 (February): 52–64.
1977   "Structural and Exchange Components of Vertical Mobility." American Sociological Review 42 (February): 56–73.
McEaddy, B. J.
1975   Educational Attainment of Workers, March 1974. Special Labor Report 175. Washington, D.C.: U.S. Department of Labor.
McKinley, D.
1964   Social Class and Family Life. Glencoe, Ill.: Free Press.
Merton, R. K., and A. K. Rossi
1968   "Contributions to the Theory of Reference Group Behavior." Pp. 279–334 in R. K. Merton (ed.), Social Theory and Social Structure. New York: Free Press.

Metropolitan Life
1975   "Work Disability by Occupation." Statistical Bulletin 56 (November): 9–11.
        New York: Metropolitan Life Insurance.
Meyer, J. W., and P. E. Hammond
1971   "Forms of Status Inconsistency." Social Forces 50 (September): 91–101.
Milbrath, L.
1965   Political Participation. Chicago: Rand McNally.
Miller, H. M.
1971   "A Profile of the Blue Collar Worker—A View Through the Census Data."
        Pp. 47–75 in S. Levitan (ed.), Blue Collar Workers: A Symposium on Mid-
        dle America. New York: McGraw-Hill.
1971a   Rich Man, Poor Man. New York: Crowell.
Miller, S. M., and F. Riessman
1961   "Working Class Authoritarianism: A Critique of Lipset." British Journal of
        Sociology 12 (Fall): 263–76.
Miller, S. M., and P. Roby
1970   "The Future of Inequality. New York: Basic Books.
Mills, C. W.
1951   White Collar. New York: Oxford University Press.
1956   The Power Elite. New York: Oxford University Press.
1959   The Sociological Imagination. New York: Oxford University Press.
1972   "Review of Warner and Lunt, 'The Social Life of a Modern Community.'"
        Pp. 179–92 in G. W. Thielbar and S. D. Feldman (eds.), Issues in Social
        Inequality. Boston: Little, Brown.
Mintz, M., and J. S. Cohen
1971   America, Inc.: Who Owns and Operates the United States? New York:
        Dell.
Mitchell, R. E.
1964   "Methodological Notes on a Theory of Status Crystallization." Public
        Opinion Quarterly 28 (Spring): 315–25.
Mondale, W. F.
1975   "Treasury Study Shows 'Tax Expenditures' Benefit Wealthy Most." Con-
        gressional Record—Senate 121 (June 2).
Moore, W. E.
1963   Social Change. Englewood Cliffs. N.J.: Prentice-Hall.
1963a   "But Some Are More Equal Than Others." American Sociological Review
        28 (February): 13–18.
Morris, R. T., and R. J. Murphy
1959   "The Situs Dimension in Occupational Mobility." American Sociological
        Review 24 (April): 231–39.
1969   "A Paradigm for the Study of Class Consciousness." Pp. 345–58 in J. L.
        Roach, L. Gross, and O. D. Gursslin (eds.), Social Stratification in the
        United States. Englewood Cliffs, N.J.: Prentice-Hall.
Mosteller, F., and D. P. Moynihan (eds.)
1972   On Equality of Educational Opportunity. New York: Vintage.
Moynihan, D. P.
1965   The Negro Family: The Case for National Action. Washington, D.C.: U.S.
        Department of Labor.
Mueller, C. W., and B. G. Campbell
1977   "Female Occupational Achievement and Marital Status: A Research Note."
        Journal of Marriage and the Family 39 (August): 587–94.
Mueller, C. W., and W. T. Johnson
1975   "Socioeconomic Status and Religious Participation." American Sociological
        Review 40 (December): 785–800.

Muraskin, W. A.
1975   "Review of 'Regulating the Poor.'" Contemporary Sociology 4 (November): 607–13.
Myrdal, G.
1944   An American Dilemma: The Negro Problem and Modern Democracy. New York: Harper.
National Advisory Commission on Civil Disorders
1968   Report of the National Advisory Commission on Civil Disorders. New York: Bantam
National Opinion Research Center
1947   "Jobs and Occupations: A Popular Evaluation." Opinion News 9 (September 1): 3–13.
Nelson, H. M., T. W. Madron, and R. L. Yokley
1975   "Black Religion's Promethean Motif: Orthodoxy and Militancy." American Journal of Sociology 81 (July): 139–46.
Newman, D. J.
1958   "White Collar Crime." Law and Contemporary Problems 23 (Autumn).
Nie, N. H., S. Verba, and J. R. Petrocik
1976   The Changing American Voter. Cambridge, Mass.: Harvard University Press.
Nisbet, R. A.
1969   Social Change and History. New York: Oxford University Press.
Nye, F. I., and F. M. Berardo
1975   The Family: Its Structure and Interaction. New York: Macmillan.
Office of Management and Budget
1973   Social Indicators, 1973. Washington, D.C.: U.S. Government Printing Office.
Ogren, E. H.
1973   "Public Opinions About Public Welfare." Social Work 18 (January): 101–8.
Ollman, B.
1968   "Marx's Use of 'Class.'" American Journal of Sociology 73 (March): 573–80.
1971   Alienation: Marx's Conception of Man in Capitalist Society. New York: Oxford University Press.
Olsen, M. E., and N. C. Tully
1972   "Socioeconomic-Status Inconsistency and Preference for Political Change." American Sociological Review 37 (October): 560–74.
Oppenheimer, V. K.
1970   The Female Labor Force in the United States. Berkeley, Calif.: Population Monograph Series, University of California.
1973   "Demographic Influence on Female Employment and the Status of Women." American Journal of Sociology 78 (January): 946–61.
O'Rand, A., and R. A. Ellis
1974   "Social Class and Time Perspective." Social Forces 53 (September): 53–61.
Orden, S. R., and N. M. Bradburn
1969   "Working Wives and Marriage Happiness." American Journal of Sociology 24 (January): 392–407.
Orshansky, M.
1965   "Counting the Poor: Another Look at the Poverty Profile." Social Security Bulletin 28 (July): 3–29.
1969   "How Poverty Is Measured." Social Security Bulletin 32 (February): 37–41.
Orum, A. M.
1966   "A Reappraisal of the Social and Political Participation of Negroes." American Journal of Sociology 72 (July): 32–46.

Ossowsky, S.
1963   Class Structure in the Social Consciousness. London: Routledge & Kegan Paul.
Pachter, H.
1974   "The Idea of Progress in Marxism." Social Research 41 (Spring): 136–62.
Padfield, H., and R. Williams
1973   Stay Where You Were: A Study of Unemployables in Industry. Philadelphia: J. B. Lippincott.
Papanek, H.
1973   "Men, Women, and Work: Reflections on the Two Person Career." American Journal of Sociology 78 (January): 852–72.
Parsons, T.
1937   The Structure of Social Action. New York: McGraw-Hill.
1942   "Max Weber and the Contemporary Political Crisis." The Review of Politics 4 (January): 61–76; (April): 155–72.
1951   The Social System. New York: Free Press.
1954a   "An Analytical Approach to the Theory of Social Stratification." Pp. 69–88 in T. Parsons, Essays in Sociological Theory, rev. ed. New York: Free Press.
1954b   "A Revised Analytical Approach to the Theory of Social Stratification." Pp. 386–439 in T. Parsons, Essays in Sociological Theory, rev. ed. New York: Free Press.
1954c   "Age and Sex in the Social Structure of the United States." Pp. 89–103 in T. Parsons, Essays in Sociological Theory, rev. ed. New York: Free Press.
1954d   "The Kinship System of the Contemporary United States." Pp. 177–96 in T. Parsons, Essays in Sociological Theory, rev. ed. New York: Free Press.
1967   "Introduction to Max Weber's The Sociology of Religion." Pp. 35–78 in T. Parsons, Sociological Theory and Modern Society. New York: Free Press.
Paukert, F.
1973   "Income Distribution at Different Levels of Development: A Survey of the Evidence." International Labour Review 108 (August–September): 97–125.
Pearlin, L. I.
1975   "Status Inequality and Stress in Marriage." American Sociological Review 40 (June): 344–57.
Pearlin, L. I., and M. L. Kohn
1966   "Social Class, Occupation, and Parental Values: A Cross National Study." American Sociological Review 31 (August): 466–79.
Pechman, J. A., and B. A. Okner
1972   "Individual Income Tax Erosion by Income Classes." Pp. 13–40 in Joint Economic Committee of the 92nd Congress, The Economics of Federal Subsidy Programs: A Compendium of Papers, Part I. Washington, D.C.: U.S. Government Printing Office.
Penn, R.
1975   "Occupational Prestige Hierarchies: A Great Empirical Invariant?" Social Forces 54 (December): 352–64.
Perkins, D., and G. G. Van Deusen
1968   The United States of America: A History, I. New York: Macmillan.
Pessen, E.
1971   "The Egalitarian Myth and the American Social Reality: Wealth, Mobility, and Equality in the 'Era of the Common Man.'" American Historical Review 76 (October): 989–1034.
Pessen, E. (ed.)
1974   Three Centuries of Social Mobility in America. Lexington, Mass.: D. C. Heath.

Peterson, W.
  1964   "Religious Statistics in the United States." Pp. 248–70 in W. Peterson (ed.), The Politics of Population. New York: Doubleday.
Piven, F. F., and W. C. Cloward
  1971   Regulating the Poor: The Forms and Functions of Public Welfare. New York: Vintage.
Placek, P. J., and G. E. Hendershot
  1974   "Public Welfare and Family Planning: An Empirical Assessment of the 'Brood Sow' Myth." Social Problems 21 (June): 658–73.
Pleck, J. H.
  1977   "The Work-Family Role System." Social Problems 24 (April): 417–27.
Popper, K.
  1963   Conjectures and Refutations: The Growth of Scientific Knowledge. New York: Harper Torch.
  1964   The Poverty of Historicism. New York: Harper Torch.
Portes, A.
  1971   "On the Interpretation of Class Consciousness." American Journal of Sociology 77 (September): 228–44.
  1972   "Status Inconsistency and Lower-Class Leftist Radicalism." Sociological Quarterly 13 (Summer): 361–82.
President's Commission on Income Maintenance Programs
  1969   Poverty Amid Plenty: The American Paradox. Washington, D.C.: U.S. Government Printing Office.
President's Commission on Law Enforcement and the Administration of Justice
  1967   The Challenge of Crime in a Free Society. Washington, D.C.: U.S. Government Printing Office.
Presser, H. B., and L. S. Salsberg
  1975   "Public Assistance and Early Family Formation: Is There a Pronatalist Effect?" Social Problems 23 (December): 226–41.
Projector, D. S.
  1964   "Survey of Financial Characteristics of Consumers." Federal Reserve Bulletin 50 (March): 285–93.
Projector, D. S., and G. S. Weiss
  1966   Survey of Financial Characteristics of Consumers. Washington, D.C.: Board of Governors of the Federal Reserve System.
Purcell, T. V.
  1960   Blue Collar Man: Patterns of Dual Allegiance in Industry. Cambridge, Mass.: Harvard University Press.
Quadagno, J.
  1976   "Occupational Sex-typing and Internal Labor Market Distributions: An Assessment of Medical Specialities." Social Problems 23 (April): 442–53.
Quinn, R. P., et al.
  1974   Job Satisfaction: Is There a Trend? Manpower Research Monograph No. 30, U.S. Department of Labor. Washington, D.C.: U.S. Government Printing Office.
Quinney, R.
  1964   "The Study of White Collar Crime: Toward a Reorientation of Theory and Research." Journal of Criminal Law, Criminology and Police Science 55 (June): 208–14.
Rainwater, L.
  1964   Family Design: Marital Sexuality, Family Size and Contraception. Chicago: Aldine.
  1974   What Money Buys: Inequality and the Social Meanings of Income. New York: Basic Books.

Rainwater, L., and W. L. Yancey
1967   The Moynihan Report and the Politics of Controversy. Cambridge, Mass.: MIT Press.
Reisman, D.
1952   "Review of 'White Collar.'" American Journal of Sociology 57 (March): 513–15.
Reiss, A. J. (ed.)
1961   Occupations and Social Status. New York: Free Press.
Rinehart, J. W.
1971   "Affluence and the Embourgeoisement of the Working Class: A New Look." Social Problems 19 (Fall): 148–62.
Ritter, K. V., and L. L. Hargens
1975   "Occupational Positions and Class Identifications of Married Working Women: A Test of the Asymmetry Hypothesis." American Journal of Sociology 80 (January): 934–48.
Roach, J. L., L. Gross, and O. D. Gursslin
1969   Social Stratification in the United States. Englewood Cliffs, N.J.: Prentice-Hall.
Robinson, J., T. Juster, and F. Stafford
1976   America's Use of Time. Ann Arbor, Mich.: Institute for Social Research.
Rodman, H.
1963   "The Lower Class Value Stretch." Social Forces 42 (December): 205–15.
Rodman, H., P. Voydanoff, and A. E. Lovejoy
1974   "The Range of Aspirations: A New Approach." Social Problems 22 (December): 184–98.
Rogoff, N.
1953   Recent Trends in Occupational Mobility. New York: Free Press.
Rose, A.
1967   The Power Structure. New York: Oxford University Press.
Rosen, B. C.
1956   "The Achievement Syndrome: A Psychosocial Dimension of Social Stratification." American Sociological Review 21 (April): 203–11.
1959   "Race, Ethnicity, and the Achievement Syndrome." American Sociological Review 24 (February): 47–60.
1961   "Family Structure and Achievement Motivation." American Sociological Review 26 (August): 574–85.
Rosen, B. C., H. J. Crockett, and C. Z. Nunn (eds.)
1969   Achievement in American Society. Cambridge: Mass.: Schenkman.
Rosenbaum, D. E.
1977   "A New Rights Drive Perplexes Nation." New York Times, July 3, pp. 1 and 28.
Rosenfeld, E.
1951   "Social Stratification in a Classless Society." American Sociological Review 16 (December): 766–74.
Rosenthal, R., and L. Jacobson
1968   Pygmalion in the Classroom: Teacher Expectation and Pupils' Intellectual Development. New York: Holt, Rinehart, and Winston.
Rossi, A. S.
1964   "Equality Between the Sexes: A Modest Proposal." Daedalus 93 (Spring): 607–52.
Roth, G.
1971a   "[Weber's] Historical Relationships to Marxism." Pp. 227–52 in R. Bendix and G. Roth, Scholarship and Partisanship: Essays on Max Weber. Berkeley, Calif.: University of California Press.

1971b   "The Genesis of the Typological Approach." Pp. 253–65 in R. Bendix and
         G. Roth, Scholarship and Partisanship: Essays on Max Weber. Berkeley,
         Calif.: University of California Press.
Ryder, N. B., and C. F. Westoff
1971   Reproduction in the United States, 1965. Princeton, N.J.: Princeton Uni-
         versity Press.
Schaffer, R.
1977   Mothering. Cambridge, Mass.: Harvard University Press.
Schiller, B. R.
1973   "Empirical Studies of Welfare Dependency: A Survey." The Journal of
         Human Resources 8 (Supplement).
Schreiber, E. M., and G. T. Nygreen
1970   "Subjective Social Class in America: 1945–68." Social Forces 48 (March):
         348–56.
Schulz, D. A.
1969   "Coming Up Black: Patterns of Ghetto Socialization. Englewood Cliffs,
         N.J.: Prentice-Hall.
Schuman, H.
1971   "The Religious Factor in Detroit: Review, Replication, and Reanalysis."
         American Sociological Review 36 (February): 30–47.
Schwartz, R.
1955   "Functional Alternatives to Inequality." American Sociological Review 20
         (August): 424–30.
Seeman, M.
1977   "Some Real and Imaginary Consequences of Social Mobility: A French-
         American Comparison." American Journal of Sociology 82 (January): 757–
         82.
Segal, D. R.
1969   "Status Inconsistency, Cross-Pressures, and American Political Behavior."
         American Sociological Review 34 (June): 352–58.
Sennett, R., and J. Cobb
1973   The Hidden Injuries of Class. New York: Vintage Books.
Sewell, W. H., and R. M. Hauser
1972   "Causes and Consequences of Higher Education: Models of the Status At-
         tainment Process." American Journal of Agricultural Economics 54 (De-
         cember): 851–61.
1975   Education, Occupation, and Earnings: Achievement in the Early Career.
         New York: Academic Press.
Sewell, W. H., and V. P. Shah
1968a   "Social Class, Parental Encouragement, and Educational Aspirations."
         American Journal of Sociology 73 (March): 559–72.
1968b   "Parent's Education and Children's Educational Aspirations and Achieve-
         ment." American Sociological Review 33 (April): 191–209.
Sewell, W. H., W. H. Haller, and G. W. Ohlendorf
1970   "The Educational and Early Occupational Attainment Process: Replication
         and Revision." American Sociological Review 35 (December): 1014–27.
Sewell, W. H., W. H. Haller, and A. Portes
1969   "The Educational and Early Occupational Attainment Process." American
         Sociological Review 34 (February): 82–91.
Sexton, P., and B. Sexton
1971   Blue Collars and Hard Hats. New York: Random House.
Shepard, J. M.
1971   Automation and Alienation: A Study of Office and Factory Workers. Cam-
         bridge, Mass.: MIT Press.

Shoemaker, D. J., D. R. Smith, and J. Lowe
1973   "Facial Stereotypes of Deviants and Judgments of Guilt or Innocence." Social Problems 51 (June): 427–33.
Shostak, A. B.
1969   Blue Collar Life. New York: Random House.
Siegel, P. M.
1965   "On the Cost of Being Negro." Sociological Inquiry 35 (Winter): 41–57.
Silver, A.
1967   "The Demand for Order in Civil Society: A Review of Some Themes in the History of Urban Crime, Police and Riot." Pp. 1–24 in D. J. Bordua (ed.), The Police: Six Sociological Essays. New York: John Wiley.
Simmel, G.
1955   Conflict and the Web of Group Affiliations. New York: Free Press.
1971   On Individuality and Social Forms. Chicago: University of Chicago Press.
Simpson, G. E., and J. M. Yinger
1972   Racial and Cultural Minorities, 4th ed. New York: Harper and Row.
Simpson, R.
1956   "A Modification of the Functional Theory of Social Stratification." Social Forces 35 (December): 1956.
Simpson, R. L., and I. H. Simpson
1960   "Correlates and Estimation of Occupational Prestige." American Journal of Sociology 66 (September): 134–40.
Skolnick, A. M., and S. R. Dales
1975   "Social Welfare Expenditures, Fiscal Years 1950–75." Research and Statistics Note, no. 21 (November 28). Washington, D.C.: Department of Health, Education, and Welfare.
Smelser, N. J.
1973   "Introduction." Pp. vii–xxxviii in K. Marx, On Society and Social Change. Chicago: University of Chicago Press.
Smelser, N. (ed.)
1973a   Sociology: An Introduction, 2nd ed. New York: John Wiley.
Smith, J. D.
1974   "The Concentration of Personal Wealth in America, 1969." Review of Income and Wealth 20 (June): 143–80.
Smith, J. D., and S. D. Franklin
1974   "The Concentration of Personal Wealth." American Economic Review 64 (May): 162–67.
Snyder, D., and P. M. Hudis
1976   "Occupational Income and the Effects of Minority Competition and Segregation: A Reanalysis and Some New Evidence." American Sociological Review 41 (April): 209–34.
Soltow, L.
1975   "The Wealth, Income, and Social Class of Men in Large Northern Cities of the United States in 1860." Pp. 233–76 in J. D. Smith (ed.), The Personal Distribution of Income and Wealth. New York: National Bureau of Economic Research.
Sommers, D., and A. Eck
1977   "Occupational Mobility in the American Labor Force." Monthly Labor Review 100 (January): 3–19.
Spady, W.
1970   "Lament for the Letterman: Effects of Peer Status and Extracurricular Activities on Goals and Achievements." American Journal of Sociology 75 (January): 680–702.
Special Task Force to the Secretary of Health, Education, and Welfare
1973   Work in America. Cambridge, Mass.: MIT Press.

Stark, R.
1972   "The Economics of Piety: Religious Commitment and Social Class." Pp. 483–503 in G. W. Thielbar and S. D. Feldman (eds.), Issues in Social Inequality. Boston: Little, Brown.

Stein, M.
1960   The Eclipse of Community. New York: Harper Torchbooks.

Stern, P. M.
1974   The Rape of the Taxpayer. New York: Vintage.

Stinchcombe, A.
1963   "Some Empirical Consequences of the Davis-Moore Theory of Stratification." American Sociological Review 28 (October): 805–8.

1968   Constructing Social Theories. New York: Harcourt, Brace, and World.

Stouffer, S. A.
1955   Communism, Conformity, and Civil Liberties. Garden City, N.Y.: Doubleday.

Streib, G. F.
1976   "Social Stratification and Aging." Ch. 7 in R. H. Binstock and E. Shanas (eds.), The Handbook of Aging and the Social Sciences. New York: Van Nostrand Reinhold.

Sullerot, E.
1971   Woman, Society, and Change. New York: McGraw-Hill.

Suter, L. E., and H. P. Miller
1973   "Income Differences Between Men and Career Women." American Journal of Sociology 78 (January): 962–74.

Sutherland, E. H.
1949   White Collar Crime. New York: Holt, Rinehart, and Winston.

Swigert, V. L., and R. A. Farrell
1976   Murder, Inequality, and the Law. Lexington, Mass.: D.C. Heath.
1977   "Normal Homicides and the Law." American Sociological Review 42 (February): 16–31.

Taueber, K. E., and A. F. Taueber
1965   Negroes in Cities: Residential Segregation and Neighborhood Change. Chicago: Aldine.

Tausky, C.
1965   "Parsons on Stratification: An Analysis and Critique." Sociological Quarterly 6 (Spring): 128–38.

Taylor, P. A., and N. D. Glenn
1976   "The Utility of Education and Attractiveness for Females' Status Attainment Through Marriage." American Sociological Review 41 (June): 484–97.

Terkel, S.
1972   Working. New York: Pantheon.

Thernstrom, S.
1964   Poverty and Progress. Cambridge, Mass.: Harvard University Press.

Thernstrom, S., and R. Sennett (eds.)
1969   Nineteenth Century Cities. New Haven, Conn.: Yale University Press.

Thompson, G. B.
1974   "Work Experience and Income of the Population Aged 60 and Older, 1971." Social Security Bulletin 37 (November): 3–20.

Thompson, K. H.
1971   "Upward Social Mobility and Political Orientation: A Re-evaluation." American Sociological Review 36 (April): 223–34.

Thurow, L. C.
1976   "The Economic Status of Minorities and Women." Civil Rights Digest 8 (Winter-Spring): 2–10.

Thurow, L. B., and R. E. B. Lucas
  1972   The American Distribution of Income: A Structural Problem. Washington, D.C.: Joint Economic Committee, 92nd Congress.
Tilly, C.
  1973   "Race and Migration to the American City." Pp. 38–39 in Feagin (ed.), The Urban Scene. New York: Random House.
Tocqueville, A. de
  1969   Democracy in America. Garden City, N.Y.: Anchor Books.
Treiman, D. J.
  1966   "Status Discrepancy and Prejudice." American Journal of Sociology 71 (May): 651–64.
  1970   "Industrialization and Social Stratification." Pp. 207–34 in E. O. Lauman (ed.), Social Stratification: Research and Theory for the 1970's. New York: Bobbs-Merrill.
Treiman, D. J., and K. Terrell
  1975   "Sex and the Process of Status Attainment: A Comparison of Working Men and Women." American Sociological Review 40 (April): 174–200.
Tully, J., E. F. Jackson, and R. F. Curtis
  1970   "Trends in Occupational Mobility in Indianapolis." Social Forces 49 (December): 186–99.
Tumin, M.
  1953   "Some Principles of Stratification: A Critical Analysis." American Sociological Review 18 (August): 378–86.
  1955   "Rewards and Task Orientations." American Sociological Review 20 (August): 419–23.
  1963   "On Inequality." American Sociological Review 28 (February): 19–26.
  1967   Social Stratification: The Forms and Functions of Inequality. Englewood Cliffs, N.J.: Prentice-Hall.
Turner, J. H.
  1970   "Entrepreneurial Environments and the Emergence of Achievement Motivation in Adolescent Males." Sociometry 33 (June): 147–66.
  1972   Patterns of Social Organization. New York: McGraw-Hill.
  1972a   American Society: Problems of Structure: New York: Harper & Row.
  1974   The Structure of Sociological Theory. Homewood, Ill.: Dorsey Press.
  1975   "Marx and Simmel Revisited: Reassessing the Foundations of Conflict Theory." Social Forces 53 (June): 618–26.
Turner, J. H., and Beeghley, L.
  1974   "Current Folklore in the Criticisms of Parsonian Action Theory." Sociological Inquiry 44 (1): 47–63.
Turner, J. H., and C. E. Starnes
  1976   Inequality: Privilege and Poverty in America. Santa Monica, Calif.: Goodyear.
Tyree, A., and J. Treas
  1974   "The Occupational and Marital Mobility of Women." American Sociological Review 39 (June): 293–302.
U.S. Bureau of the Census
  1973   "Voting and Registration in the Election of November, 1972." Current Population Reports, Series P-20, no. 253. Washington, D.C.: U.S. Government Printing Office.
  1975a   "The Social and Economic Status of the Black Population in the United States, 1974." Current Population Reports, Series P-23, no. 54. Washington, D.C.: U.S. Government Printing Office.
  1975b   "Money Income in 1973 of Families and Persons in the United States." Current Population Reports, Series P-60, no. 97. Washington, D.C.: U.S. Government Printing Office.

1975c   Statistical Abstract of the United States, 1976. Washington, D.C.: U.S. Government Printing Office.

1975d   Historical Statistics of the United States, Colonial Times to 1970, Bicentennial Edition, pt. 2. Washington, D.C.: U.S. Government Printing Office.

1975e   "School Enrollment—Social and Economic Characteristics of Students: October, 1974." Current Population Reports, Series P-20, no. 286. Washington, D.C.: U.S. Government Printing Office.

1976a   "Money Income and Poverty Status of Families and Persons in the United States: 1974 and 1975 Revisions." Current Population Reports, Series P-60, no. 103. Washington, D.C.: U.S. Government Printing Office.

1976b   Statistical Abstract of the United States, 1977. Washington, D.C.: U.S. Government Printing Office.

1976c   "Premarital Fertility." Current Population Reports, Series P-23, no. 63. Washington, D.C.: U.S. Government Printing Office.

1976d   "College Plans of High School Seniors: October, 1974." Current Population Reports, Series P-20, no. 284. Washington, D.C.: U.S. Government Printing Office.

1976e   "Voting and Registration in the Election of November, 1974." Current Population Reports, Series P-20, no. 293. Washington, D.C.: U.S. Government Printing Office.

1976f   "Education Attainment in the United States: March, 1975." Current Population Reports, Series P-20, no. 295. Washington, D.C.: U.S. Government Printing Office.

1976g   "A Statistical Portrait of Women." Current Population Reports, Series P-23, no. 58. Washington, D.C.: U.S. Government Printing Office.

1976h   "Major Field of Study of College Students: October, 1974." Current Population Reports, Series P-20, no. 289. Washington, D.C.: U.S. Government Printing Office.

1976i   "Money Income in 1974 of Families and Persons in the United Statates." Current Population Reports, Series P-60, no. 101. Washington, D.C.: U.S. Government Printing Office.

1977a   Statistical Abstract of the United States, 1977. Washington, D.C.: U.S. Government Printing Office.

1977b   "Marital Status and Living Arrangements: March, 1976." Current Population Reports, Series P-20, no. 306. Washington, D.C.: U.S. Government Printing Office.

U.S. Chamber of Commerce

1974   White Collar Crime. Washington, D.C.: U.S. Chamber of Commerce.

U.S. Civil Rights Commission

1974   Women and Poverty. Washington, D.C.: U.S. Government Printing Office.

U.S. Commission on Civil Rights

1967   Racial Isolation in the Public Schools. Washington, D.C.: U.S. Government Printing Office.

U.S. Department of Health, Education, and Welfare

1972   Welfare Myths vs. Facts, Washington, D.C.: U.S. Government Printing Office.

1974   Digest of Educational Statistics, 1973. Washington, D.C.: U.S. Government Printing Office.

1976   The Measure of Poverty. Washington, D.C.: U.S. Government Printing Office.

1976a   Digest of Educational Statistics, 1975. Washington, D.C.: U.S. Government Printing Office.

U.S. Internal Revenue Service
  1973   Statistics of Income—1969, Personal Wealth. Washington, D.C.: U.S. Government Printing Office.
  1976   Instructions for Form 1040. Washington, D.C.: U.S. Government Printing Office.
U.S. News and World Report
  1975   "Those Income Tax Rates Tell Only Half the Story." U.S. News and World Report (November 24): 90–92.
Valentine, C. A.
  1968   Culture and Poverty. Chicago: University of Chicago Press.
Van Til, S. B.
  1974   "Race, Poverty, and Labor Force Participation." Social Science Quarterly 55 (December): 657–69.
Van Valey, T. L., W. C. Roof, and J. E. Wilcox
  1977   "Trends in Residential Segregation, 1960–1970." American Journal of Sociology 82 (January): 826–45.
Van Velsor, E., and L. Beeghley
  1977   "Class Identification Among Employed Married Women." Unpublished Manuscript.
Vanfossen, B., and R. Rhodes
  1974   "A Critique of Abrahamson's Assessment." American Journal of Sociology 80 (November): 727–32.
Vanneman, R.
  1977   "The Occupational Composition of American Classes: Results from Cluster Analysis." American Journal of Sociology 82 (January): 783–807.
Vanneman, R., and F. C. Pampel
  1977   "The American Perception of Class and Status." American Sociological Review 42 (June): 422–37.
Verba, S., and N. H. Nie
  1972   Participation in America: Political Democracy and Social Equality. New York: Harper & Row.
Verba, S., N. H. Nie, and J. Kim
  1971   The Modes of Democratic Participation: A Cross-National Comparison. Beverly Hills, Calif.: Sage.
Villemez, W. J.
  1974   "Ability vs. Effort: Ideological Correlates of Occupational Grading." Social Forces 53 (September): 45–52.
Vorwaller, D. J.
  1970   "Social Mobility and Membership in Voluntary Associations." American Journal of Sociology 75 (January): 481–95.
Waite, L. J.
  1976   "Working Wives: 1940–60." American Sociological Review 41 (February): 65–79.
Walker, K. E.
  1969   "Time Spent in Household Work by Homemakers." Family Economics Review 3: 5–6.
  1970   "Time Spent by Husbands in Household Work." Family Economics Review 4: 8–11.
Wallick, F.
  1972   The American Worker: An Endangered Species. New York: Ballatine Books.
Warheit, G. J., C. Holzer, and S. Arey
  1976   "Sex, Marital Status, and Mental Health: A Reappraisal." Social Forces 55 (December): 459–70.

Warner, W. L.
  1949   Democracy in Jonesville. New York: Harper & Row.
  1963   Yankee City, abridged ed. New Haven, Conn.: Yale University Press.
Weber, M.
  1946   From Max Weber: Essays in Sociology. New York: Oxford University Press.
  1947   The Theory of Social and Economic Organization. New York: Free Press.
  1949   The Methodology of the Social Sciences. New York: Free Press.
  1950   General Economic History. New York: Free Press.
  1958   The Protestant Ethic and the Spirit of Capitalism. New York: Scribner's.
  1968   Economy and Society. New York: Buckminster Press.
Wegner, E., and W. H. Sewell
  1970   "Selection and Context as Factors Affecting the Probability of Graduation from College." American Journal of Sociology 75 (January): 665–79.
Weingart, P.
  1969   "Beyond Parsons? A Critique of Ralf Dahrendorf's Conflict Theory." Social Forces 48 (December): 151–65.
Weiss, L., and J. G. Williamson
  1972   "Black Education, Earnings, and Interregional Migration." Review of Economics and Statistics 52 (May): 150–59.
Weitzman, L.
  1975   "Socialization." Pp. 105–44 in J. Freeman (ed.), Women: A Feminist Perspective. Palo Alto, Calif.: Mayfield.
Wellman, D.
  1974   "Manpower Training for Low Wage Work." Pp. 128–38 in P. A. Roby (ed.), The Poverty Establishment. Englewood Cliffs, N.J.: Prentice-Hall.
Wells, J.
  1975   "Voting Rights in 1975: Why Minorities Still Need Protection." Civil Rights Digest 7 (Summer): 13–19.
Wesolowski, W.
  1966   "Some Notes on the Functionalist Theory of Stratification." Pp. 64–69 in R. Bendix and S. M. Lipset (eds.), Class, Status, and Power. New York: Free Press.
Westcott, D. N.
  1975   "Trends in Overtime Hours and Pay, 1969–74." Monthly Labor Review 98 (February): 45–52.
Whitehurst, C. A.
  1977   Women in America: The Oppressed Majority. Santa Monica, Calif.: Goodyear.
Wilensky, H. L., and H. Edwards
  1959   "The Skidder: Ideological Adjustments of Downwardly Mobile Workers." American Sociological Review 24 (April): 215–31.
Williams, G.
  1975   "A Research Note on Trends in Occupational Differentiation by Sex." Social Problems 22 (April): 543–48.
Williams, R. M.
  1970   American Society, 3d ed. New York: Alfred A. Knopf.
Williamson, J. B.
  1974a   "Beliefs About the Welfare Poor." Sociology and Social Research 58 (January): 163–75.
  1974b   "The Stigma of Public Dependency: A Comparison of Alternative Forms of Public Aid to the Poor." Social Problems 22 (December): 213–28.

Williamson, J. B., and K. M. Hyer
   1975   "The Measurement and Meaning of Poverty." Social Problems 22 (June): 652–62.
Williamson, J. G.
   1976   "The Sources of American Inequality, 1896–1948." Review of Economics and Statistics 58 (November): 387–97.
Willie, C. V.
   1969   "Intergenerational Poverty." Poverty and Human Resources Abstracts 4 (January–February).
Wilson, K. L., and A. Portes
   1975   "The Educational Attainment Process: Results from a National Sample." American Journal of Sociology 81 (September): 343–63.
Wright, J. D.
   1972   "The Working Class, Authoritarianism and the War in Vietnam." Social Problems 20 (Fall): 133–50.
Wright, S.
   1975   "Work Response to Income Maintenance: Economic, Sociological and Cultural Perspectives." Social Forces 53 (June): 553–62.
Wrong, D. H.
   1952   "Our Troubled Middle Classes." American Mercury, January, pp. 107–13.
   1959   "The Functionalist Theory of Stratification: Some Neglected Considerations." American Sociological Review 24 (December): 772–82.
Zeitlin, I. M.
   1973   Rethinking Sociology. New York: Appleton-Century-Crofts.

NAME
INDEX

A

Abels, J., 232
Abrahamson, M., 51, 53, 320
Acker, J., 271
Ackerman, F., 214
Adams, A. V., 245
Aldrich, H. E., 246
Alexander, K. L., 305, 320
Alford, R. R., 179
Alger, H., 312
Allardt, E., 86
Allen, J., 161
Alston, J. P., 137
Alston, L., 6, 57
Althauser, R. P., 247
Althusser, L., 25
Anderson, B., 239
Armer, J. M., 110, 120
Aron, R., 24, 25, 26, 27, 40, 41, 186, 224
Atkinson, D., 67
Austin, P. L., 140

B

Bach, G. L., 232
Bachrach, L. L., 300

Bacon, L., 245
Baker, S. H., 295
Ballard, H. B., 232
Baltzell, E. D., 231
Bane, M. J., 306
Banfield, E. C., 141, 142, 244, 245
Barber, B., 103, 115
Bardolph, R., 252, 264–65
Barth, E., 115
Bateman, W., 161
Baxandall, R., 299
Bean, F., 51, 317
Beeghley, L., 71, 115, 120, 149
Bell, C. S., 291
Bendix, R., 21, 22, 23, 24, 35–36, 38, 39, 40, 41, 93, 107, 109, 317
Benoit-Smullyan, E., 117
Berardo, F. M., 273
Berg, I., 149, 200
Berger, A. S., 263–64
Berlin, I., 1, 2, 24
Bernard, J., 171, 272, 273, 274, 276, 299
Berreman, G. D., 102
Biderman, A. D., 232
Billingsley, A., 263, 264
Binzin, P., 174
Birnbaum, N., 10, 41
Black, D. J., 180

Blalock, H. M., 118, 121
Blau, P. M., 101, 161, 301–5, 307, 309–10, 312–16, 320, 321
Blauner, R., 174, 175, 178
Bluestone, B., 133
Blum, Z. D., 140, 145, 151
Bott, E., 105
Bowles, S., 174
Box, S., 119
Bradburn, N. M., 274
Brandmeyer, G., 118
Breed, W., 317
Brim, O. G., 293
Bronfenbrenner, U., 172
Broom, L., 100
Buckley, W., 53
Bureau of Labor Statistics (BLS), 157, 158–59, 160, 162, 178, 179, 188–89, 201, 247, 270, 282
Burke, P. J., 118
Butler, E. W., 149
Byrne, J. J., 162, 179

C

Cain, G. G., 199, 202
Campbell, B. G., 277
Campbell, R. R., 270
Carmichael, S., 243
Centers, R., 111, 112, 113, 114
Chafe, W. H., 299
Chambliss, W. J., 118, 147
Chapman, J. R., 281, 292
Chase, I., 308, 320
Chesler, P., 300
Chinoy, E., 175, 296
Chiricos, T. G., 256
Clark, K. B., 264
Clark, R., 147, 194
Cloward, W. C., 139, 151
Cobb, J., 109, 313
Cohen, J. S., 201
Cohen, P. S., 68
Coleman, J. S., 200, 202, 265, 267
Congressional Budget Office, 241, 242–43, 270
Congressional Quarterly, 230
Converse, P. E., 114
Coombs, L. C., 148, 152
Coser, L. A., 21, 61, 64, 69–70, 139, 151, 281, 283, 304, 308, 320

Coser, R. L., 276, 281
Council of Economic Advisers, 151
Coward, B. E., 142
Crockett, H. J., Jr., 321
Crowder, N. D., 308, 310, 320
Crumrine, J., 297
Curtis, R. F., 317
Cutler, S. J., 201
Cutright, P., 87, 137, 149, 172, 245

D

Dahrendorf, R., 2, 55–71, 73, 96, 97. See also Subject Index
Dales, S. R., 151
Dalia, J. T., 178
Darian, J. C., 275
Davidson, C., 136, 179
Davis, J. A., 96
Davis, K., 43–53, 55, 90, 93, 95, 96. See also Subject Index
Dean, K. I., 137
Della Fave, L. R., 141
Demerath, N. J., 111, 118
Diggins, J. P., 3
Domhoff, G. W., 232
Duncan, O. D., 101, 161, 237, 270, 301, 302–5, 306, 307, 309–10, 312–16, 320, 321
Duncan, R. P., 277, 278
Dupre, L., 3
Durkheim, E., 24, 25, 40

E

Eck, A., 320
Ecland, B. K., 305
Edelhertz, H., 194
Edwards, H., 317
Eisenstadt, S. N., 49, 95
Eitzen, D. S., 118
Ellis, R. A., 142
Elder, G. H., 197
Engels, F., 6, 8, 12, 13, 24, 25
Epstein, C. F., 284, 288, 289, 298
Equality of Educational Opportunity, 265–66
Erlanger, H. S., 172, 180
Evers, C., 253

Heltman, L. R., 244–45
Hendershot, G. E., 137, 138
Herb, T. R., 300
Hermalin, A. I., 261, 270
Herriot, R. A., 225
Hiltz, S. R., 270
Hindelang, M. J., 170
Hirschi, T., 146, 169
Hodge, R. W., 106, 111, 113, 116, 120, 243, 317
Hodgson, G., 202
Hoffman, A. R., 194, 195
Hook, S., 12, 25
Hope, K., 109, 119, 120, 121
Hopple, G., 163
Horan, P. M., 140
House, J. S., 118
Hout, M., 306, 307, 309
Huaco, G. A., 53
Huber, J. A., 298
Huber, J., 139, 272–73, 293, 298, 299
Hudis, P. M., 240
Hume, D., 71
Hunt, J. G., 264
Hunt, L. L., 264
Hyer, K. M., 125, 141
Hyman, H. H., 192, 201

I

Inkeles, A., 91, 108
Internal Revenue Service, 210–11, 213, 219, 220, 232, 233
Inter-University Consortium for Political Research, 270, 300, 319

J

Jackman, M. R., 109, 113, 114, 317, 318
Jackman, R. W., 87, 88, 89, 91, 109, 113, 114, 317, 318
Jackson, E. F., 118, 193, 317, 321
Jacobson, B., 284
Jacobson, W., 284
Jacobson, L., 267
Janowitz, M., 66
Jencks, C. S., 200, 202, 306, 307
Johnson, L. B., 251
Johnson, M. P., 270
Johnson, T. A., 241
Johnson, W. T., 168
Jones, F. L., 100

K

Kahl, J. A., 96
Kahn, R. L., 175
Kain, J. F., 246
Kallen, D. J., 151
Kanter, R. M., 295, 296–97, 298
Kaplan, H. R., 136
Keech, W. R , 254
Keller, S., 198
Kelly, K. D., 118
Kenkel, W. F., 118
Kennedy, J. F., 251
Kerckhoff, A. C., 149,
Kessin, K., 317
Kim, J., 145, 190
Kirsch, B. A., 201
Knoke, D., 115, 251, 270, 318
Kohn, M. L., 174, 197
Kolko, G., 204, 232
Komarovsky, M., 171, 172
Kravis, I. B., 214

L

Lampman, R. J., 209, 210
Land, K. L., 51
Landecker, W. S., 96
Langer, E., 296
Lasch, C., 202
Laslett, B., 317
Lauer, R. H., 151
Lauman, E. O., 109, 303
Law Enforcement Assistance Administration, 147, 169, 180, 193
Leavy, M. D., 51
Lebowitz, B. D., 121
Leggett, J. C., 114
LeMasters, E. E., 171, 172–73, 175, 180
Lengermann, J. E., 201
Lenski, G., 73–91, 93, 97, 116, 117, 118, 119, 193
Leslie, G. R., 320
Levenson, B., 295
Levine, A., 297
Levine, D. M., 306
Levine, D. U., 268
Levinson, R. M., 293–94
Levison, A., 154, 160, 162, 163, 164, 166, 178, 239
Lewis, D. M., 120
Lewis, L., 51
Lewis, O., 141–42

Lieberson, S., 232
Liebow, E., 142–43, 270
Linton, R., 320
Lipset, S. M., 24, 107, 109, 162–63, 172, 179, 232, 317
Lipsitz, L., 179
Litwak, E., 317
Long, L., 244–45, 270
Long, L. H., 138, 244, 277, 278
Lopreato, J., 6, 51, 57, 201, 317
Lucas, R. E. B., 232
Lundberg, F., 201, 213, 223, 232
Lynd, H. M., 301
Lynd, R. S., 201

M

Mack, R. W., 64, 69
Mackenzie, G., 159
Magee, B., 21
Marsh, R. M., 106, 108, 109, 110, 111, 120
Martin, W. T., 22
Marwell, G., 320
Marx, G., 259
Marx, K., 1–26, 28–30, 41, 55, 69, 73, 84, 88, 89, 93, 94, 95, 97, 111–12, 310. *See also* Subject Index
Mason, K. O., 273, 286
Masters, S. H., 245, 246
Mathews, D. R., 251
Maynew, L., 320
McClelland, D. C., 201
McClendon, M. J., 307, 308
McEaddy, B. J., 173
McKinley, D., 197
Merton, R. K., 317
Metropolitan Life, 161
Meyer, J. K., 268
Meyer, J. W., 117
Milbrath, L., 190
Miller, D., 151
Miller, H. M., 127, 156
Miller, H. P., 225, 290, 300
Miller, S. M., 124, 127, 129, 163
Mills, C. W., 55, 56, 90, 181, 182, 185–86, 201, 224, 232
Mintz, M., 201
Mitchell, R. E., 121
Mondale, W. F., 227
Moore, W. E., 43–53, 55, 56, 68, 90, 93, 95, 96. *See also* Davis-Moore *in* Subject Index
Morgan, W. R., 306, 307, 309

Morris, R. T., 112, 320
Mosca, G., 73
Mosteller, F., 267
Moynihan, D. P., 260, 262–64, 267
Mueller, C. W., 168, 277
Muraskin, W. A., 151
Murphy, R. J., 112, 320
Myrdal, G., 257

N

National Advisory Commission on Civil Disorders, 235
National Council of Churches, 179
National Opinion Research Corp., 106, 110, 115, 120, 250
National Urban League, 241
Nelson, H. M., 260
Nestel, G., 245
Newman, D. J., 193
Nie, N. H., 145, 165–66, 190, 191, 192, 201, 249
Nisbet, R. A., 3, 13, 25, 68, 87, 110
NORC. *See* National Opinion Research Center
Nye, F. I., 273
Nygreen, G. T., 113, 114, 120

O

Office of Economic Opportunity, 150–51
Office of Management and Budget, 205
Ogren, E. H., 151
Okner, B. A., 226
Ollman, B., 7–8, 9, 12, 18–19, 24, 25
Olsen, M. E., 118, 119
Oppenheimer, V. K., 275, 280
O'Rand, A., 142
Orden, S. R., 274
Orshansky, M., 124, 125, 127, 150
Orum, A. M., 201
Ossowsky, S., 8

P

Pachter, H., 13
Padfield, H., 144, 151
Pampel, F. C., 113–14, 116
Papanek, H., 280, 281, 286
Parke, R. D., 273
Parsons, T., 23, 28, 40, 44, 52–53, 55–57, 65, 71, 73, 86, 96, 115, 120

Paukert, F., 87, 88, 89, 91
Pearlin, L. I., 180, 197
Pechman, J. A., 226
Penn, R., 111
Perkins, D., 232
Perrucci, C. C., 277, 278
Pesky, J. J., 246
Pessen, E., 206–8, 210, 222, 316
Peterson, W., 179
Pettigrew, T., 270
Piven, F. F., 139, 151
Placek, P. J., 137, 138
Pleck, J. H., 277
Popper, K., 21, 24
Portes, A., 111, 121, 306, 320
Poston, D. L., Jr., 8
*President's Commission on Income
    Maintenance Programs*, 133
*President's Commission on Law
    Enforcement and the
    Administration of Justice*, 146, 148
Presser, H. B., 137, 148
Projector, D. S., 205, 206, 210, 212,
    215, 216, 218, 219, 222, 232
Prothro, J. W., 251
Purcell, T. V., 296

Q

Quadagno, J., 284
Quinn, R. P., 176, 180
Quinney, R., 193

R

Raab, E., 179
Rainwater, L., 148, 149, 152, 171,
    172, 262, 263
Reisman, D., 201
Reiss, A. J., 110
Rhodes, R., 51
Riessman, F., 163
Rinehart, J. W., 178
Ritter, K. V., 115
Roach, J. L., 121
Robinson, J., 277
Roby, 124, 127, 129
Rockefeller, N., 213, 232
Rodman, H., 143
Rogoff, M., 269, 321
Rokoff, G., 276
Rose, A., 224, 232
Rosen, B. C., 197, 198

Rosenbaum, D. E., 270
Rosenfeld, E., 53
Rosenthal, R., 267
Rossi, A. K., 317
Rossi, A. S., 299
Rossi, P. H., 107, 108, 109, 140, 145,
    151
Roth, G., 30, 41
Ryder, N. B., 148

S

Salsberg, L. S., 137, 148
Schaffer, R., 273
Schiller, B. R., 135, 136
Schmidt, C., 25
Schooler, C., 174
Schreiber, E. M., 113, 114, 120
Schulz, D. A., 270
Schuman, H., 193
Schwartz, M., 110
Schwartz, R., 47, 53
Seeman, M., 317
Segal, D. R., 118
Sell, R. R., 270
Sennett, R., 109, 313, 316
Sewell, W. H., 306, 308–9, 320
Sexton, B., 179
Sexton, P., 179
Shah, V. P., 306
Sharp, L. M., 232
Shepard, J. M., 201
Shoemaker, D. J., 258
Shostak, A. B., 164
Siegel, P. M., 107, 109, 270
Silver, A., 254
Simmel, G., 24, 64, 69, 139, 151
Simon, W., 263–64
Simpson, G. E., 265, 270
Simpson, I. H., 108
Simpson, R., 48, 49, 53
Simpson, R. L., 108
Skolnik, A. M., 151
Smelser, N. J., 12, 24, 99
Smith, J. D., 209, 210, 211, 232
Snyder, D., 240
Snyder, R. F., 64, 69
Social Security Administration, 150
Soltow, L., 208, 209
Sommers, D., 320
Spady, W., 306
*Special Task Force to the Secretary of
    Health, Education, and Welfare*,
    175

SUBJECT
INDEX

Assumptions
   in Dahrendorf's work, 56–57,
      65–66, 67, 69–70
   in Marx's social theory, 2–6
   in science, 65
   in study of sexual inequality,
      271–72
   in theory building, 70
Authoritarianism. *See* Working-class
   authoritarianism
Authority, 36–37, 58–59, 66–67, 70,
   81
Auto industry, job satisfaction in,
   176
Automation, 155, 174

B

"Barely solvent" level of wealth,
   211, 222
Biculturality of poor people, 144
Birth control, 90, 137, 273. *See also*
   Family planning
Birth order, and social mobility, 316
Blacks
   and class identification, 114
   economic characteristics, 236–43
   and labor unions, 238–39
   occupational distribution trends
      of, 237–40
   and poverty, 130–32, 134
   social characteristics, 248
   and status inconsistency, 118
   white attitudes toward, 164, 165.
      See also Caste, Nonwhites,
      Race, Racial Discrimination,
      Segregation
Black economic subordination,
   causes of, 243–49
Black elected officials, 252, 253
Black family, 260–64
Black managers, 239–40
Black politics, 249–54
Black professionals, 240
Black religion, 258–60
Black social mobility, 315
Black status attainment, 307–8
"Blind luck" in status attainment,
   310
Blue-collar alienation, 174–77
Blue-collar education, 173–74
Blue-collar family life, 171–73
Blue-collar job satisfaction, 175–77

Blue-collar occupations, 154–56
   blacks in, 238–39
   prestige of, 107–8
   and sex, 282–83
Blue-collar politics, 162–67
Blue-collar religion, 167–68
Blue-collar wives, labor force
   participation of, 279–80
Blue-collar work force, 178
Blue-collar workers, 33, 100–101,
   153–80. *See also*
      Embourgeoisement, Poor,
      Poverty, Working class
   and class, 113, 116, 313
   economic characteristics, 156–62
   and legal system, 168–71
   numbers, 156
   in status attainment studies, 309
Bonds, government, tax-exempt, 227
Bourgeois mode of production, 14
Bourgeoisie, 11, 12, 15, 18. *See also*
   Embourgeoisement
Budget levels, Bureau of Labor
   Statistics, 158–59, 188, 189.
   See also Poverty level
Business, noncorporate, and the
   rich, 220
Business crime, 194, 195
Bureaucracy and capitalism, 29
Bureaucratization, 186

C

Calvinism, 28
Capital, 7, 26, 41
Capital gains, 227–28
Capital-producing property, 100–101
Capitalism, 11, 14–17, 21, 28, 29, 186
Capitalists, 7
Caste, 36, 102, 235
Causal models, 57
Causation, 30, 71
Central cities and poverty, 134
Change, 99
   in Marx's work, 12–14, 21
   in Dahrendorf's work, 57, 59, 69
Chicanos, 238
Child-rearing practices, 149, 172,
   197, 273
Children, and female labor force
   participation, 275, 276
China, 77
Church membership, 146, 167, 192

and job satisfaction, 175
Empirical analysis, Lenski's, 87–88
"Empirical invariants," 106
Empiricism, 3, 5–6, 52–53
Employed mothers and child rearing, 273
Employers, and sexual discrimination, 293–94
Employment and female mental health, 278–80
Employment tests, and racism, 242–43
Engels, collaboration with Marx, 24, 25
Entrepreneurial characteristics, and achievement motivation, 197–98
Entrepreneurs, 32–33
Environment, 75, 94
Equal Employment Opportunity Commission, 294
Equal Pay Act of 1963, 293
Equivalent evaluation, postulate of, 115
Estate, accumulation of, and wealth, 205–6
"Estate multiplier technique," 210–11
Ethnicity, 30, 36, 41, 79, 118
Evaluation of occupations, differential, 110
Evaluation of social positions, 95, 96
Evolution
    in Davis-Moore thesis, 46, 48
    in Lenski's work, 73–74, 77, 87, 88
    in Weber's work, 40

F

Fair housing referenda, 166
Families, richest, 220, 223
Families, single-parent, by race, 262
Families with children, by race and income, 262
Family, 9, 47, 100
    black, 260–64
    traditional, 281
    as unit of social analysis, 114, 116, 271
Family background, 30, 35–36, 303, 305
Family income, calculation of, 178
Family income and status attainment, 305
Family life, 148–49, 171–73, 196–99

Family planning, 137–38, 148
Family size, 124–25, 137–38, 148–49, 172, 315–16
Family stability, effect on black children, 263–64
Farmers and farm laborers, 155, 238, 313
Father's education and male status attainment, 303, 305
Father's occupation and male status attainment, 303, 305
"Fear of success," 297
Female-headed families, 125, 291, 292
Female roles, and two-person career, 281–82
Female social mobility, 312
Female status attainment, 303, 307–8
Females in selected detailed occupations, 285
Fertility rates, 261, 272–73, 314–15
Feudal mode of production, 14, 15
Food budget, and poverty index, 127
Force, 84
Force concentration, in Lenski's work, 76, 78, 79, 80, 83
Ford family, wealth of, 223
Free market, 38
Fringe benefits, 161, 188–89
From Hegel to Marx, 25
Functional importance of positions, 45–46, 48–49
Functional necessity of inequality, 45, 48–49, 50
Functional prerequisites, 48–49
Functionalist analysis of social stratification, 43–53, 115. See also Davis-Moore thesis
    and conflict theory, 73–74, 82, 84–86
    criticism of, 47–50, 55–56
Functionally unique positions, 49
Functions of inequality, 45–46

G

"German Ideologists," 5, 25
The German Ideology, 24, 25
Ghettos, 245, 246
Government, blacks in, 253–54
Government bonds, 220
Government intervention and concentration of wealth, 209

Group, organized, 62
Group formation, 4–5, 11, 34, 59, 61, 63

H

Health insurance, 161
Heuristic device, 48–49, 57, 68–69, 99
Heuristic model of social stratification, 93–103
Historical determinism, 29
Historical laws of development, 7, 28
"Historical materialism," 29–30
Historical stages of production, 6
Homemaking and sex roles, 273–74
Horizontal mobility, 161, 311, 320
Horticultural societies, advanced, 76, 77, 78–79, 83
Horticultural societies, simple, 76, 78, 83
House of Representatives, and tax law secrecy, 230
Housewives, 276, 279–81
Housework, 277, 278–79
Housing segregation, 246–47, 265
Human nature, 4, 23, 82, 85
Hunting and gathering societies, 76, 77–78, 83

I

Ideal type, 6, 30, 37, 186, 274
Ideological leaders, 17, 20
Ideology, 10, 17, 20, 23, 62
Illegitimacy, 137, 148, 171–72, 261
Immigrants, social mobility of, 315
Immigration and historical trends in wealth, 252
"Imperatively coordinated associations," 58
Incas, 77
Income
  blue-collar, 156–60
  and crime victimization, 169
  and female poverty, 290–92
  as measure of wealth, 160, 204–5
  and occupational prestige, 120
  and wealth, 205, 214–22
  white-collar, 187–89
Income deficiency, 124

Income differences
  by continuity of labor-force participation, 289–90
  by education and race, 247–48
  by education and sex, 288–89
  by occupation and sex, 287–88
  white- and blue-collar, 187–88
Income distribution, 90, 129, 187, 236–37
"Income revolution," 129
Income sources and levels of wealth, 214, 217–22
Income sources and tax rates, 227–28
Income tax, 225–29, 294
India, 77
Individual, role of in Weber's work, 28
Individualism, 31
Industrial deaths, 161, 179
Industrial societies, 39–40, 76, 80–82, 83
Industrial unions, 155, 239
Industrialization, 20, 40
  and class formation, 16, 17, 186
  and Communism, 21
  and division of labor, 22, 80
  and fertility rates, 272–73
  and inequality, 16–17, 22, 87–88, 89, 91
  and job satisfaction, 176, 177
Inequality, 20, 23, 44, 62, 84, 85
  and distributive systems, 75–76
  and division of labor, 9
  and fairness, 47–48
  and industrialization, 22, 87–88, 89, 91
  in Marx's work, 2–6, 9, 11, 18
  social functions of, 45–46
  and stratification systems, 94, 95–97, 98
  and type of society, 77, 78, 81, 83
Inevitability, historical, 14, 15, 16, 21, 28
Inheritance, occupational, 312–13
Inheritance of wealth, 208, 222–23
Institutionalized racism, 243
Instrumental rationality, 31–32, 39
Intensity of conflict, 62, 64
Interest, 10, 20, 58–59, 96–97
  and class, 17, 31–32
  and political parties, 37
Intergenerational mobility, 77, 78, 79, 80, 311–12

Internal Revenue Service (IRS), 210
Internalization, 62
Intragenerational mobility, 77, 78, 79, 80, 189, 311–12
Investments, and wealth, 217, 219

J

Job characteristics, importance of, 175, 176
Job discrimination, 246–47, 293–98
Job satisfaction, blue-collar, 175–77
Job security, 160–61, 188
Junkers, 32, 35

K

Key concepts in Dahrendorf's work: definitions, 62
Key variables in Marx's work: definitions, 8–10, 20

L

Labor force, 270
Labor-force participation
  continuity of, 289–90
  female, 275–80, 308
  male, 300
  of poor, 136–37
Labor markets, 241–42
Labor supply, and trends in wealth, 232
Labor unions, 155, 166, 238–39
Laborers, 155
Law and discretion, 257
"Law of transformation of quantity to quality," 13
Laws of distribution, 81, 86
Laws of historical development, 7
Leadership cadre, 62
Legal characteristics and socioeconomic status, 100
Legal system, 30–31, 100. *See also* Crime, Criminal justice, Police, Prisoners
  and blue-collar workers, 168–71
  and poverty, 146–48
  and race, 256–58
  and white-collar workers, 193–96
Legal system of authority, 36–37

Lenski, G., 73–91
  criticism of, 84–88
  theory of social stratification, 74–84, 86–87
Letters on Historical Materialism, 25
Liberalism, of blacks, 250
Lifestyle, and Bureau of Labor Statistics intermediate budget, 158–59
Lifestyle and status, 35
"Lower class value stretch," 143–44

M

Machines, intellectual bias against, 177
"Male head of household," 115–16, 271
Male-headed families and poverty, 125–26, 292
Male occupational mobility, 311–16
Male status attainment, 303–7
Managerial occupations, blacks in, 239
Managers and proprietors, 182, 183–84
Manual labor, 114, 154, 177
Marital stability, 149, 172–73, 197, 260–61
Marital status
  and female economic subordination, 291–92
  and mental disorders, 279
  and poverty line, 125
  and race, 260–61
  and religious participation, 168
Marital stress and working wives, 274
Maritime societies, 90
Marriage
  age of, 148, 171, 196
  blue-collar attitudes toward, 171
  and female status attainment, 308
  status inequality in, 180
Marx, K., 1–26
  collaboration with Engels, 24, 25
  terms defined, 20
  translations of, 24
  and Weber, 27, 28–30, 41
Marxism, 29
Material goods, 20
Mating behavior, 148, 171–72, 196–97, 231

Primary labor market, 241–42
Prison sentence length by race, 256
Prisoners, characteristics of, 147, 193
Privilege, 44, 74–75, 77, 78, 85, 86
Production, 11, 39
  stages of, 6
Productive capacity, 20
Productive forces, 13–14
Productivity, 75, 76
  and inequality, 81
  and type of society, 77, 78, 79, 80, 83
Professionals, 182, 183
  black, 240
  female, 283, 284
Progress, belief in, in Marx, 3, 12–13
Proletariat, 12, 15, 16, 18, 186
Promotion opportunities and work orientation, 296
Property, 32–34, 38. See also Income, Wealth
Property relations, 9–10, 13, 14
Propertyless classes, 33–34
The Protestant Ethic and the Spirit of Capitalism, 27, 41, 192
Protestantism, 28, 258
Public health, and white-collar crime, 195

Q

"Quasi-groups," 59, 66–67

R

Race
  and criminal justice, 254–58
  and education, 247–48, 264–68
  and female employment, 300
  and imprisonment, 147
  and occupational distribution trends, 237–40
  and poverty, 130–32, 134
  and status inconsistency, 118
  and unemployment, 241–43
Race, migration, and welfare, 138
Racial discrimination
  and black family structure, 263–64
  and blue-collar whites, 164
  in corporations, 239–40
  in employment, 131–32
  and income, 245, 248–49
  and sex, 248

and unemployment, 242–43
Racial inequality, 235–70
"Radicals," in Lenski's work, 73
Rank of position, 46, 56, 96
"Rational-legal system of domination," 31
"Rationalists," 57
Real estate ownership, and rich, 220
Regional differences in mobility, 315
Regulation of conflict, 62
Relations of production, 16
"Relative deprivation," 61
"Relative distance" of occupations, 198
Religion, 30, 45, 100. See also Church membership
  black, 258–60
  blue-collar, 167–68
  and poverty, 146
  and socioeconomic status, 100, 192–93
  white-collar, 167–68, 192–93
Religious preference by race, 258–59
Rentiers, 32–33, 34, 35
Reproduction and sex roles, 272–73
Republican Party, and blacks, 250
Residence and wealth in 19th century, 208
Residence and poverty, 130, 133–35
Residual values, 304
Responsibility, and occupational prestige, 108–9
Revolution, 11, 14, 20
  conditions of, 18, 22–23, 26
  and science, 29
  and theory, 1–2
Revolutionary epochs, 14
Revolutionary writings, 1–2
Rewards, 47, 53, 70, 108
  as resources, 40–41, 96
  unequal, 44–45, 95
Reward levels, 48
Rich, 100–101, 203–33. See also Superrich, Top wealthholders
  and education, 231
  and inheritance of wealth, 223
  numbers of, 206
  and politics, 224–31
  social characteristics, 231
  in status attainment literature, 308–9
"Rich" level of wealth, 211, 212–13
Richest families, 220, 223
Rights of positions, 44
Rockefeller family, 213, 223, 232

Role conflict, 276
Role segregation in marriage, 172, 180, 197
Roles, 58, 62
Rome, 77
Ruling class, 8, 40, 224, 229
Rural poor, 125, 130, 134–35

S

Sales occupations, 182, 184, 239
Scarcity of personnel, differential, 46
Schools and achievement, 199–200, 267
Schools and job discrimination against women, 294–95
School segregation, 264–65
Science, 41
  assumptions in, 65
  and revolution, 29
Science as a Vocation, 41
Scientific method, 74
Scientific order, 65–66, 71
Secondary labor market, 242
Segregation. *See* Housing segregation, School segregation
Self-esteem and labor force participation, 279–80
Self-interest, 74
Semiskilled workers, 155
Senate Finance Committee, and tax law secrecy, 230
Service occupations, 155, 286
SES. *See* Socioeconomic status
Sex. *See also* Female, Male, Wives, Women
  and income, 157, 287
  and mental disorders, 279
  and occupational distribution, 157
  and occupational prestige ranking, 108
  and poverty, 132
  and racial discrimination, 248
  and status inconsistency, 118
Sex, education, and occupation, 173
Sex-role ideology, 272–74
  and job discrimination, 293–98
Sex-role stereotyping, and female occupations, 286
Sexism, in achievement motivation research, 198
Sexual discrimination, 271–300
"Significant others," 267, 306
Single-parent families by race, 262

Siriono, 77
"Situational interpretation" of poverty, 142–43
Situs mobility, 320
Skills, 33, 155, 176, 244, 314
Slavery, and black family, 262
Social change, 38, 64, 68, 87
Social consensus, 10
Social facts, 3, 24
"Social honor," 23, 35
Social inequality, universality of, 47
Social institutions, 9, 39–40, 99, 100, 101, 102
Social mobility, 100, 102–3, 301, 311–20. *See also* Horizontal, Intergenerational, Intragenerational, Occupational, and Vertical mobility
  and class, 38
  consequences of, 317–18
  in Dahrendorf's work, 56, 62, 68
  and education, 200
  extent of, 314
  female, 312
  in Marx's work, 16, 17, 20
  and poverty, 142
  by race, 315
  range of, 311–12, 314
  trends in, 316
Social mobility rates, 101, 311–12
Social outsiders and poverty, 130, 133
Social Security, 225, 294
Social stability, and occupational prestige, 110
Social stratification
  in America, 99–103, 316
  functional necessity of, 44
  noneconomic elements in, 30, 33, 34–36
Social stratification process, 301–21
Social stratification process, models of
  Dahrendorf's, 57–59, 60, 66–68
  Marx's, 2, 7–17
Social stratification systems, 90, 94–99
Social stratification theory, 93
  Dahrendorf's, 56–64, 68
  Lenski's, 74–84, 86–87
  Marx's, 17–21
The Social System, 56
Social systems, 94
Socialism, and occupational prestige, 111

Socialization, 20, 293
Societal action, 34, 41
Society, 39–40, 85
  types of, 76–82
Socioeconomic index scores, 237, 238
Socioeconomic status (SES), 100, 105
  and academic achievement, 267–68
  and class identification, 113
  and criminal behavior, 168–69
  and job satisfaction, 176
  parental, and occupational attainment, 303, 305
  and religion, 192–93
Some Principles of Stratification, 43–44, 50
Spain, 77
Sponsorship, 310
Stages of history, 10–17, 21
Stages of production, historical, 6
Standard of living, and poverty index, 127–28
State, 39–40, 75–76, 84, 85. *See also* Polity
  and type of society, 78, 79, 80, 83
Status, 23, 30, 31, 34–36, 74–75, 105–6
  and the rich, 231
Status ascription, 47
Status attainment, 97, 100, 301–11
  female, 303, 307–8
  male, 303–7
Status attainment literature, 308–11
"Status borrowing," 115
"Status congruence," 121
"Status crystallization," 121
Status groups, 31, 35–40
Status inconsistency, 39, 96, 101, 105, 116–19
Status inequality, and marriage, 180
Status maintenance and education, 200
Stock ownership by rich, 220
Stress, psychological, and status inconsistency, 118
Stroking behavior, 274
"Structural change," in Dahrendorf's work, 62, 68, 71
Subordinates, 9, 17, 20, 62
  and occupational prestige, 108–10
Superordination, and occupational prestige, 109–10
"Superrich" level of wealth, 211–13, 223

Symbolic interactionist tradition, 304
Synthesis of functionalist and conflict perspectives in Lenski's work, 73–91
Systems theory, 12, 82, 84

T

Tax deductions, 228
"Tax expenditure," 226, 227–28
Tax laws, 224–31
  and sexual discrimination, 294
Tax loopholes, 226–27, 229–30
Tax rates, 225–27
"Tax welfare," 228–29
Taxes, progressive, 224–26
Taxes, regressive, 224–25
Technological causation, 30
Technological changes and social mobility, 314–15
Technological determinism, 89–90
"Technological efficiency," 77
Technology, 45, 75, 76, 87, 90
  and type of society, 77, 78, 79, 80, 81
Teleology, illegitimate, 50
Teleology and social systems, 94
Thematic Apperception Test (TAT), 197–98, 201
Theory and revolution in Marx, 1–2
Theory construction, Dahrendorf's, 71
"Thesis," in Lenski's work, 73–74
Token women, 296–98
Tolerance, blue-collar, 163–64
Top wealthholders, 213, 219–22. *See also* Rich, Superrich
Training, occupational, and rank, 46
Trust funds, 219, 220
Two-person career, 280–82

U

Unemployment, 160–61, 241–43. *See also* Job security
Urbanization, 17, 20, 22, 78, 79, 80
Utilitarianism, 86
"Utopians," 57

V

Values, 52, 86–87, 89, 96, 98
  and poverty, 141–44